Palgrave Studies in Economic History

Series Editor
Kent Deng
London School of Economics
London, UK

Palgrave Studies in Economic History is designed to illuminate and enrich our understanding of economies and economic phenomena of the past. The series covers a vast range of topics including financial history, labour history, development economics, commercialisation, urbanisation, industrialisation, modernisation, globalisation, and changes in world economic orders.

More information about this series at
http://www.palgrave.com/gp/series/14632

Alexandr Akimov · Gennadi Kazakevitch
Editors

30 Years since the Fall of the Berlin Wall

Turns and Twists in Economies, Politics, and Societies in the Post-Communist Countries

Editors
Alexandr Akimov
Department of Accounting, Finance
and Economics
Griffith University
Southport, QLD, Australia

Gennadi Kazakevitch
Department of Economics
Monash University
Clayton, VIC, Australia

ISSN 2662-6497   ISSN 2662-6500 (electronic)
Palgrave Studies in Economic History
ISBN 978-981-15-0319-1   ISBN 978-981-15-0317-7 (eBook)
https://doi.org/10.1007/978-981-15-0317-7

© The Editor(s) (if applicable) and The Author(s), under exclusive license to Springer Nature Singapore Pte Ltd. 2020
This work is subject to copyright. All rights are solely and exclusively licensed by the Publisher, whether the whole or part of the material is concerned, specifically the rights of translation, reprinting, reuse of illustrations, recitation, broadcasting, reproduction on microfilms or in any other physical way, and transmission or information storage and retrieval, electronic adaptation, computer software, or by similar or dissimilar methodology now known or hereafter developed.
The use of general descriptive names, registered names, trademarks, service marks, etc. in this publication does not imply, even in the absence of a specific statement, that such names are exempt from the relevant protective laws and regulations and therefore free for general use.
The publisher, the authors and the editors are safe to assume that the advice and information in this book are believed to be true and accurate at the date of publication. Neither the publisher nor the authors or the editors give a warranty, expressed or implied, with respect to the material contained herein or for any errors or omissions that may have been made. The publisher remains neutral with regard to jurisdictional claims in published maps and institutional affiliations.

Cover illustration: © Heiko Küverling/Alamy Stock Photo

This Palgrave Macmillan imprint is published by the registered company Springer Nature Singapore Pte Ltd.
The registered company address is: 152 Beach Road, #21-01/04 Gateway East, Singapore 189721, Singapore

Foreword

The consequences of the fall of communism in 1989/1991 are still with us today. The reworking of the international order that had been based on the Cold War bifurcation is continuing as the US is struggling to manage the shift from superpower to hegemonic power, and perhaps with the rise of China back to being only one of a number of superpowers. Russia struggles to find its Post-Soviet identity while many of the former members of what was called the Eastern bloc struggle with their membership of the EU and what that means domestically. For many of the countries that overthrew their communist governments, the task of establishing a political and socio-economic system that serves all of the people remains a challenge. Economic reform, ethnic division and an unresponsive polity remain issues in some of these countries.

Within this context, the idea of evaluating the records of former members of the USSR and the Soviet bloc after three decades is timely. The essays in this volume, first presented at the Fourteenth Conference of the Australasian Association for Communist and Post-Communist Studies in early 2019, survey the progress made following the collapse of the communist system in Europe. Written by both established and emergent scholars, these essays cast light on major dimensions of the fate of the post-communist states, from economic reform through foreign policy, domestic dissent, citizenship, crime, the law and other areas of life. Although there is a strong focus on Central Asia and on Russia, attention is also given to some of the countries of Central Europe. These papers will make an important contribution to our understanding of the post-communist trajectories of many of the countries that formerly made up the communist world.

Graeme Gill
The University of Sydney
Sydney, Australia

Contents

1   30 Years After the Fall of the Berlin Wall: Trends and the Current State of Communism and Post-communism in Europe and Asia   1
Gennadi Kazakevitch and Alexandr Akimov

Part I   How Communism and Post-Communism are Tracking

2   A Taxonomy of Post-communist Economies After 30 Years of Reforms   13
Gennadi Kazakevitch

3   The Central Asian Countries' Economies in the Twenty-First Century   31
Richard Pomfret

4	The Post-communist Transition of the Western Balkans: EUropeanisation with a Small Enlargement Carrot *Milenko Petrovic*	57
5	Organised Crime in—and from—Communist and Post-communist States *Leslie Holmes*	83

Part II   Values, Security and Foreign Policy in Russia

6	U.S.–Russia Relations in the Last 30 Years: From a Rapprochement to a Meltdown *Victoria V. Orlova*	117
7	Russia's Growing Relationship with Iran: Strategic or Tactical? *Ian Parmeter*	139
8	Energy Integration in Eurasian Economic Union: Preliminary Study on Progress and Policy Implications *Elena Shadrina*	151
9	Mediating Populist Discourse in Russia via YouTube: The Case of Alexey Navalny *Sofya Glazunova*	191

Part III   Economy and Society in Central Asia

10	Why Uzbekistan and Kazakhstan Are Not Singapore: Comparing the First 25 Years of Reforms *Alexandr Akimov*	217
11	Money Can't Buy Me Love, but It Can Buy Apples: An Analysis of Fruit and Vegetable Demand in Uzbekistan *Alisher Ergashev*	243

12 Squandering Remittances Income in Conspicuous
    Consumption? 271
    Jakhongir Kakhkharov and Muzaffar Ahunov

13 Equal Citizenship, Language, and Ethnicity Dilemmas
    in the Context of the Post-socialist Legal Reforms in
    Central Asia 289
    Aziz Ismatov

Part IV East and West: History, Liberalism, Culture and Political Change

14 The Horrors of Exclusion: Zygmunt Bauman's
    Sociological Journey 311
    Raymond Taras

15 Failures and Successes: Soviet and Chinese
    State-Socialist Reforms in the Face of Global Capitalism 327
    Roger D. Markwick

16 Legal Continuity and Change: Two Russian Revolutions
    and Perestroika Through the Prism of Kelsen's
    Grundnorm and Hart's Secondary Rules 353
    Anna Taitslin

17 'Fleeing Communism': Yugoslav and Vietnamese
    Post-war Migration to Australia and Changes to
    Immigration Policy 405
    Nina Markovic Khaze and Adam Khaze

Index 427

List of Figures

Fig. 2.1 The relationship between economic freedom and GDP per capita: correlation, linear regression, and scatter plot for post-communist countries in 2018 (*Source* Statistical estimation by the author based on *Index of Economic Freedom*, https://www.heritage.org/index/explore?view=by-region-country-year&u=636916527549820517. *Notes* 27 observations; correlation coefficient: 0.6430) 16

Fig. 2.2 The relationship between economic freedom and GDP per capita: correlation, linear regression, and scatter plot for all countries in 2018 (*Source* Statistical estimation by the author based on *Index of Economic Freedom*, https://www.heritage.org/index/explore?view=by-region-country-year&u=636916527549820517. *Notes* 132 observations; correlation coefficient: 0.6731) 17

Fig. 3.1 GDP change in FSU economies, 1989 = 100 (*Source* This figure is reproduced here with full permission of the copyright holder UNU-WIDER. The figure originally featured in Popov, Vladimir [2001] 'Where do we stand a decade after the collapse of the USSR?' *WIDER Angle*, 2 (2001). Launching Cornia, G.A., and V. Popov [Eds.], *Transition*

	and Institutions: The Experience of Gradual and Late Reformers, UNU-WIDER Studies in Development Economics, Oxford University Press)	38
Fig. 3.2	World price of oil, US dollars per barrel, 1991–2016 (*Source* Author's creation based on http://pubdocs.worldbank.org/en/561011486076393416/CMO-Historical-Data-Monthly.xlsx)	40
Fig. 3.3	Projected Kashgar–Osh–Uzbekistan railway (*Source* Author's creation based on https://www.un.org/Depts/Cartographic/map/profile/kyrgysta.pdf)	54
Fig. 8.1	Institutions for energy integration in the EAEU (*Source* Shadrina [2018, p. 119])	161
Fig. 8.2	Principal legal provisions for energy integration in the EAEU (*Source* Author)	162
Fig. 8.3	Share of Russia's oil and gas and Kazakhstan's oil in EU-28 imports, % (*Source* Author, based on ITC Trade Map data retrieved from https://www.trademap.org. *Note* calculated based on value in US$)	173
Fig. 8.4	Route of the Nord Stream 2 (*Source* https://www.nord-stream2.com/en/pdf/document/125/)	175
Fig. 9.1	Concept map in Leximancer of 52 English transcripts of YouTube videos of Alexey Navalny (*Source* Image by the author based on the information transcribed from the YouTube videos by Alexey Navalny. *Note* The configuration of the map in Leximancer: theme size—57%; visible concepts—100%)	201
Fig. 9.2	Concept cloud in Leximancer of 52 English transcripts of YouTube videos of Alexey Navalny (*Source* Image by the author based on the information transcribed from the YouTube videos by Alexey Navalny. *Note* The configuration of the map in Leximancer: Visible Concepts: 100%; Theme Size: 57%)	206
Fig. 10.1	Corruption in Singapore, Kazakhstan and Uzbekistan (*Source* Author's creation based on Transparency International [2019])	232
Fig. 11.1	Conceptual framework (*Source* Adapted from Bouis, Raney, and McDermott [2013], Gillespie, Harris, and Kadiyala [2012], Masset, Haddad, Cornelius, and Isaza-Castro [2011], Ruel [2002]. *Note* Interactions	

	between the shadowed boxes are analysed explicitly while outlining the white box linkages in the Supply-Demand-Diet-Nutrition-Health nexus)	245
Fig. 11.2	Research area: food consumption survey, Tashkent province, Uzbekistan (*Source* Author's compilation)	247
Fig. 11.3	Research area: fruit & vegetable market survey, Tashkent province, Uzbekistan (*Source* Author's compilation)	249
Fig. 11.4	Procedure of calculation of fruit and vegetable intake (Adapted from Martin-Prevel et al. [2015], Herrador et al. [2015], WHO [2008])	251
Fig. 11.5	Dynamics of fruit and vegetable retail price index in 2013–2014, UZS per kilo (*Source* Author's representation based on the Fruit and vegetable market survey)	254
Fig. 11.6	Actual and recommended intakes of fruit and vegetables, grams/day/person (*Source* Author's illustration based on the food consumption survey and the recommendations from WHO [2003])	258

List of Tables

Table 2.1	The dynamics of post-communist systems from 1998 to 2018, in association with countries characterised by similar levels of economic freedom	18
Table 2.2	Clusters including post-communist and communist countries, and examples of other countries with comparable economic mechanisms	25
Table 3.1	Initial conditions: republics of the USSR 1989/1990	32
Table 3.2	EBRD transition indicators, 1999 and 2009	36
Table 3.3	Growth in real GDP, 1989–1999 (%)	37
Table 3.4	Economic and social indicators, 2002	41
Table 3.5	Economic performance 2000–2014	42
Table 3.6	Economic performance 2015–2017	45
Table 3.7	Economic and social indicators, 2015/2016	51
Table 4.1	Indicators of post-communist democratisation and marketisation	63
Table 4.2	Progress in EU accession	69
Table 5.1	Perceived impact of OC on domestic businesses	100
Table 8.1	Connectivity to gas pipeline network in EAEU member-states, share of population with access to pipeline gas, 2016, %	156
Table 8.2	Share of energy trade in intra-EAEU trade, 2017, %	159

Table 8.3	The EU's targets for energy and climate, %	171
Table 8.4	Share of Russia in national extra-EU imports of oil and gas, share of trade in value, 2018, %	174
Table 8.5	Two paths for energy integration	177
Table 9.1	Main themes and concepts of 52 English transcripts of YouTube videos of Alexey Navalny	202
Table 9.2	Main frames and concepts from 52 English transcripts of Navalny's videos	209
Table 10.1	Comparative post-independence economic performance of Singapore and Kazakhstan and Uzbekistan	237
Table 11.1	Per capita supply and intake of fruit and vegetables in Uzbekistan, grams per day	244
Table 11.2	Calculation of threshold values for household income groups	253
Table 11.3	Structure of the food knowledge index	256
Table 11.4	Summary statistics of the model variables	259
Table 11.5	Parameter estimates of the fruit and vegetable intake regression model	261
Table 12.1	Descriptive statistics	279
Table 12.2	Households with and without migrants	280
Table 12.3	Mean differences in household spending for certain items (in logs of Uzbek soums)	282

1

30 Years After the Fall of the Berlin Wall: Trends and the Current State of Communism and Post-communism in Europe and Asia

Gennadi Kazakevitch and Alexandr Akimov

The fall of the Berlin Wall in 1989 was a historic milestone, which catalysed the transformation of communist regimes across the world. In the past three decades, we have seen significant reforms take hold in several former communist states, particularly in Eastern Europe and the post-Soviet countries, where socioeconomic and political ideals have gradually gravitated towards different forms of democracy and market economy. Meanwhile, in Asia, we have seen astonishing economic growth and a movement from central planning to the market, but few democratic reforms (e.g. in China and Vietnam), and some very specific hybrid regimes (e.g. in the former Soviet republics of Central Asia

---

G. Kazakevitch (✉)
Department of Economics, Monash University, Clayton, VIC, Australia
e-mail: gennadi.kazakevitch@monash.edu

A. Akimov
Department of Accounting, Finance and Economics, Griffith University, Mount Gravatt, QLD, Australia
e-mail: a.akimov@griffith.edu.au

© The Author(s) 2020
A. Akimov and G. Kazakevitch (eds.), *30 Years since the Fall of the Berlin Wall*, Palgrave Studies in Economic History, https://doi.org/10.1007/978-981-15-0317-7_1

such as Azerbaijan), while the unpredictable, isolationist North Korea remains a source of instability for the broader region.

The unfulfilled expectation that the post-Berlin-Wall transformation would lead to the best Western standards of liberal democracy and market economy has stimulated a considerable compendium of research into the history, politics, economics and sociology of transition, which it is impossible to acknowledge in its entirety in the format of a book introduction. Nonetheless, let us start with a review of the most significant recent publications, all of which address the key question: whether and why not all the post-communist countries have been equally successful in their transition.

Five years ago, marking the 25th anniversary of the collapse of the Berlin Wall, Berend and Bugaric (2015) argued that, contrary to the view expressed by some researchers and commentators, the post-communist region of Europe has not become 'normal' and is no nearer to its Western neighbours than before. In reality, 'The region still belongs to the periphery of Europe with a mostly dual economy and low level of income' (p. 219). Where some sectors, such as banking, have modernized, they have been subsidiaries of Western multinationals, while the political systems are often authoritarian, and democratic 'form' gives cover to non-democratic content.

Furthermore, Bugaric (2015) claims that Central and Eastern European countries are facing a very serious crisis of constitutional democracy, because the rule-of-law institutions in these countries are less robust than in Western ones. Western democracies have many checks and balances that cope more successfully with attacks on their liberal institutions: Their courts, media, human rights organizations, and ombudsmen have longer and better-developed traditions of independence and professionalism. In contrast, the examples of Hungary and Slovenia (and now Poland too) show that even the most advanced post-communist democracies are not immune to backsliding and reverting, in a relatively short period of time, from consolidated democracies into distinct forms of semi-authoritarian and diminished democratic regimes.

While agreeing with others that no former communist country has been completely successful in catching up with the technologically advanced Western nations, Norkus (2015) distinguishes two groups: those that have decreased the GDP gap with advanced market economies since 1989–1990, and those that haven't. Rather than comparing general historic and cultural differences, Norkus emphasizes specific causal conditions for their progress or failure in convergence, such as implementation of 'consensus-style' market reforms, neighbourhood with advanced affluent countries, peaceful transition, accession to the European Union (EU), endowment with natural resources, and state sovereignty before post-communism. Bohle (2016) also links the relative success of the post-communist countries in transition to their membership of the EU.

Meanwhile, there is a substantial difference between the evolution of post-communist Central and Eastern Europe and that of China (Roland, 2018). In Central and Eastern Europe, the driver for transition has been the collapse of communist state structures, while in China there has been a determined will to prevent such an outcome: 'This reconceptualization helps to better understand the emergence of bad institutions and corruption in Eastern Europe under the market economy as well as the absence of political liberalization in China and the strengthening of the power of the Communist Party in recent years' (p. 589).

Roland (2012) explains and predicts the success or otherwise of the post-communist transformation by reference to long-term history. He distinguishes between Russia, which during the most recent 100 years was modernizing economically but remained politically very autocratic, Central Europe, which was economically very prosperous and well-integrated into Western Europe but was experiencing nationalistic tensions, and China, which was opening up to the outside world, searching for modern institutions capable of unifying it, but under military command. Even though all these countries have experienced several decades of post-communist regimes, long-running trends in their characters have not changed.

Cooley (2019) suggests that, since 2005, many of the post-communist governments increasingly view Western pillars of liberalism as threatening their domestic authority and regime survival. This has been why they have actively supported Russian-led initiatives to curtail Western influence: 'As a result, the ecology of the post-Communist space has transformed from one where the liberal order was briefly dominant to one where new illiberal regional organizations, practices, and counter-norms have flourished and now regularly interact with liberal counterparts' (p. 588). Ágh (2016) claims that all of the East-Central European countries have been diverging from the EU mainstream in recent years, especially Hungary, because of the socioeconomic crises these countries have faced. Such backlashes have also been observed in Slovenia (Bugaric & Kuhelj, 2015) and the Czech Republic (Hanley & Vachudova, 2018).

Similar processes of reforms going backwards have been observed in Russia. Among other authors, Becker and Vasileva (2017) trace the history of Russia's political-economic development since the early 1990s as one of initial liberalization and, a decade later, subsequent re-statization. They argue that endemic Russian patrimonialism hindered the rise of economically facilitated state capacity, increasing the proportion of government involvement in the economy and giving rise to excessive regulation. We would, perhaps, include Belarus, as well as the former Soviet republics of Central Asia, Azerbaijan and Armenia, in such an analysis.

Graney (2019) introduces a new approach to 'Europeanization' in the post-Soviet world since 1989, which includes political, security and cultural-civilizational aspects. She accepts the failure of the political science premise of the superiority of Europe over other places and spaces in the mentality of most of the political elites and populations of the former Soviet Union space. This gives her a tool for innovative case studies of all the post-Soviet countries.

Aslund (2018) argues that the absence of real property rights, lack of social reforms and institutional development in post-communist judicial systems have been the biggest problems in those post-communist countries not belonging to the EU, even if there has been an initial understanding of the need for comprehensive economic reform programmes.

There is a considerable body of literature looking at corruption as an endemic impediment to successful transition. Skąpska (2009) refers to the famous argument of Max Weber, that there is a strong and direct connection between the rule of law and economic success, and the establishment of the rule of law facilitates the functioning of an efficient economy. These principles are long-lasting and deeply embedded in

Western European and North American legal cultures and mentalities. By contrast, in recent developments in Eastern and Central Europe, especially the privatization of state-owned property, one observes growing corruption, nepotism and clientelism as important mechanisms of law-making. These contribute to the pathologies of post-communist economic transformation following the fall of the Berlin Wall.

The historic pretext to corruption was not similar in every communist regime, according to Kostadinova (2012), and this might explain why the levels of corruption among post-communist democracies are different. Thus, Pavroz (2017) discusses a specifically Russian paradox: the combination of high levels of corruption with a strong and relatively effective government. Based upon the concept of corruption as a political and administrative rent, the author considers the formation of the corruption-oriented model of governance in Russia and concludes that it does not have a future, making the point that effective anti-corruption measures in Russia can be carried out only through change of the current regime and the consequent realization of democratic, market and administrative reforms. In a similar vein, Lankina (2012), Libman and Obydenkova (2013) and Ivlevs and Hinks (2018) all report statistical links between the prevalence of corruption and membership of the Communist Party before transition.

To mark the occasion of 30 years since the fall of the Berlin Wall, this volume examines and compares transition outcomes in the countries directly affected by this momentous event. It also looks back at the history of the region and introduces some unique themes as yet unfamiliar to a wider audience. Finally, it brings to the reader's attention contemporary topics affecting individual post-communist countries, such as political discourse in Russia, economic development in Central Asia, and problems of accession to the EU in South-Eastern Europe.

The book consists of four related parts and seventeen chapters. Part I consists of four chapters that focus on broad cross-country analysis of transition economies. Thus, Chapter 2 uses cluster analysis and the Index of Economic Freedom to link economic performance over the last 20 years with the level of development of market institutions. It covers a broad selection of the ex-USSR countries of Eastern and South-Eastern Europe, as well as some communist countries of Asia and

Central America. Chapter 3 provides an overview of the economic transition of some relatively slow reformers, the Central Asian republics of the former Soviet Union. The chapter argues that recent developments in relation to China's 'Belt and Road Initiative' provide a unique window of opportunity to reset their development policies towards greater integration into the global economy. In contrast, Chapter 4 focuses on the South-Eastern European region. The aspirations of Western Balkan states to join the EU seem to have been met with hesitancy on the part of the major players in the Union to accept new members. The chapter argues that the resulting uncertainty around the prospects of EU accession has led to slower democratization and market reform in the region. Chapter 5 provides a cross-country examination of the problem of organized crime in a selected number of communist and post-communist economies, including the regional giants Russia and China. The chapter finds that the problem is equally challenging for both post-communist and communist countries; it argues that with technological transformation and globalization, and the consequent transnationalization of organized crime, the problem might be too difficult to overcome for individual countries, requiring collective efforts and international organizations, such as Interpol, if it is to be resolved.

In Part II, the focus of the book narrows to deal with a range of contemporary policy issues faced by the largest country of the former Eastern bloc—Russia. The section starts in Chapter 6 with a discussion of the relationship between the two military superpowers, Russia and the US. The chapter argues that the traditional approach of confrontation inherited from the Cold War era is outdated and illogical. Modern challenges, such as terrorism, cybersecurity, and space exploration in search of scientific breakthroughs require a concerted effort from these two global players. In contrast, Chapter 7 looks at Russian relationships with a regional player and ally in the Middle East—Iran. The chapter argues that this relationship is tactical rather than strategic and is driven by specific goals such as counteracting American (and other) influences in Syria. With an ever-expanding world population, the growing need for energy resources is often at the forefront of international geopolitical and economic relationships. Chapter 8 examines the energy integration of Russia's neighbours and allies in the Eurasian Economic Union

(EAEU) and concludes that in the absence of an effective energy integration mechanism within the latter, Russia and other regional members have to use existing institutional frameworks, such as the World Trade Organization and the Energy Charter Treaty, to build and diversify their energy cooperation in the areas of renewable energy and energy research and development. Finally, in this part of the volume, Chapter 9 deals with the use of contemporary media tools in Russian political discourse. It focuses, in particular, on the opposition leader Alexei Navalny, and his skilful use of digital instruments to promote his populist agenda based on frames of 'anti-corruption' and 'free and fair elections'.

The 2016 death of the authoritarian leader of Uzbekistan has led to renewed dynamism and cooperation in the Central Asian region. Moreover, it helped to renew interest in the analysis of contemporary problems faced by the country. Part III of this book aims to fill some of the large gaps in the literature in relation to the economic and political developments of Uzbekistan and its neighbours. It starts in Chapter 10 with an assessment of the legacy of the authoritarian leaders of Uzbekistan and Kazakhstan—Islam Karimov and Nursultan Nazarbayev, respectively—25 years after independence. The political and economic outcomes are benchmarked against those of the authoritarian leader of postcolonial Singapore, Lee Kuan Yew, to whose success both leaders have either openly or implicitly aspired. By way of contrast, Chapter 11 examines the problem of poor fruit and vegetable consumption in Uzbekistan and the resultant micronutrient deficiencies. It finds that despite overall production of fruit and vegetables in Uzbekistan being more than sufficient to cover the nutritional needs of the population, consumption remains inadequate, possibly because of inadequate nutritional education. Chapter 12 focuses on the issue of large-scale migration of Uzbek citizenry in pursuit of seasonal work in Russia and other countries. In particular, it looks at the issue of how the remittances of such seasonal labour workers are used by their families, finding that most of the capital thus generated is used not for productive purposes but rather is lost to conspicuous consumption. Finally, Chapter 13 deals with the sensitive issue of language, ethnicity and citizenship in Central Asia. It finds that although lack of knowledge of the native language in Central Asian republics has not served as an obstacle to ethnic minorities in obtaining citizenship, it constrained their ability to pursue successful careers in the public sector.

The final section of the book, Part IV, takes us back into history before the last 30 years of transition, providing us with four unique historical themes. Chapter 14 tells the story of the life and research of Zygmunt Bauman, a Polish Jew who had to migrate from Poland to Israel and, eventually, to England as a result of an anti-Semitic purge in 1968. The chapter tracks the trajectory of his views on the politics of migration, in light of changing migration flows into Europe from the 1960s to recent times. Chapter 15 provides a comparative analysis of the 1980s reforms adopted by the Soviet Union and the People's Republic of China in the light of domestic and international challenges. The chapter seeks to establish why reforms in one have led to collapse while reforms in the other brought economic resurgence. Chapter 16 builds a case for comparison of the legal changes that occurred in post-revolutionary Russia, and those modern Russia has experienced following the dissolution of the Soviet Union. It finds that the October 1917 revolution completely dismantled the secondary rules of recognition and adjudication, whereas the post-Soviet transformation brought more gradual replacement of the Soviet secondary rules. In the final theme of the section, Chapter 17 focuses on communist and post-communist migration to Australia, examining the case of post-World War II migration from the former Yugoslavia and comparing it with the post-Vietnam War migration from Vietnam. The chapter finds a significant impact on the latter migration in terms of the dismantling of the White Australia policy.

References

Ágh, A. (2016). The decline of democracy in east-central Europe: Hungary as the worst-case scenario. *Problems of Post-communism, 63*(5–6), 277–287.
Aslund, A. (2018). Ten lessons from a quarter of a century of post-communist economic transformation. *Economics of Transition and Institutional Change, 26*(4), 851–862.

Becker, U., & Vasileva, A. (2017). Russia's political economy re-conceptualized: A changing hybrid of liberalism, statism and patrimonialism. *Journal of Eurasian Studies, 8*(1), 83–96.

Berend, I. T., & Bugaric, B. (2015). Unfinished Europe: Transition from communism to democracy in central and eastern Europe. *Journal of Contemporary History, 50*(4), 768–785.

Bohle, D. (2016). East central Europe in the European Union. In A. Cafruny, L. S. Talani, & G. Pozo Martin (Eds.), *The Palgrave Handbook of Critical International Political Economy*. London: Palgrave Macmillan.

Bugaric, B. (2015). A crisis of constitutional democracy in post-communist Europe: "Lands in-between" democracy and authoritarianism. *International Journal of Constitutional Law, 13*(1), 219–245.

Bugaric, B., & Kuhelj, A. (2015). Slovenia in crisis: A tale of unfinished democratization in east-central Europe. *Communist and Post-communist Studies, 48*(4), 273–279.

Cooley, A. (2019). Ordering Eurasia: The rise and decline of liberal internationalism in the post-communist space. *Security Studies, 28*(3), 588–613.

Graney, K. (2019). *Russia, the former Soviet Republics, and Europe since 1989: Transformation and tragedy*. Oxford: Oxford University Press.

Hanley, S., & Vachudova, M. A. (2018). Understanding the illiberal turn: Democratic backsliding in the Czech Republic. *East European Politics, 34*(3), 276–296.

Ivlevs, A., & Hinks, T. (2018). Former Communist Party membership and bribery in the post-socialist countries. *Journal of Comparative Economics, 46*(4), 1411–1424.

Kostadinova, T. (2012). *Political corruption in Eastern Europe: Politics after communism*. Boulder, CO: Lynne Rienner Publishers.

Lankina, T. (2012). Unbroken links? From imperial human capital to post-communist modernisation. *Europe-Asia Studies, 64*(4), 623–643.

Libman, A., & Obydenkova, A. (2013). Communism or communists? Soviet legacies and corruption in transition economies. *Economics Letters, 119*(1), 101–103.

Norkus, Z. (2015). Catching up and falling behind: Four puzzles after two decades of post-communist transformation. *Comparative Economic Research, 18*(4), 63–79.

Pavroz, A. (2017). Corruption-oriented model of governance in contemporary Russia. *Communist and Post-communist Studies, 50*(2), 145–155.

Roland, G. (2012). The long-run weight of communism or the weight of long-run history? In G. Roland (Ed.), *Economies in transition: The long-run view*. London: Palgrave Macmillan.

Roland, G. (2018). The evolution of postcommunist systems. *Economics of Transition, 26*(4), 589–614.

Skąpska, G. (2009). The rule of law, economic transformation and corruption after the fall of the Berlin Wall. *Hague Journal on the Rule of Law, 1*(2), 284–306.

Part I

How Communism and Post-Communism are Tracking

2

A Taxonomy of Post-communist Economies After 30 Years of Reforms

Gennadi Kazakevitch

Introduction

The concept of transition from one economic system to another implies an identification of a starting point as well as a destination. In the case of economic transition from the countries under communist rule with mostly centrally planned economies, the starting point can be found within the Soviet Union model as well as each country's own history. Meanwhile, understanding the destination can be only based on the knowledge about the existing market systems, in general, rather than on (inexistent) previous historic experience of such a transition. By default, both reform strategists within the post-communist countries, and foreign analysts tend to think of destination as being a "perfect" democracy with an economic system similar to the best performing industrialised market economies of Western Europe, Northern America, Japan and, perhaps, Australia, and New Zealand.

G. Kazakevitch (✉)
Department of Economics, Monash University,
Clayton, VIC, Australia
e-mail: gennadi.kazakevitch@monash.edu

© The Author(s) 2020
A. Akimov and G. Kazakevitch (eds.), *30 Years since the Fall of the Berlin Wall*,
Palgrave Studies in Economic History, https://doi.org/10.1007/978-981-15-0317-7_2

In the euphoria of dramatic historic changes of late 1980s–early 1990s it was easy not to recognise that the destination of post-communist transition could be different. The family of the existing market (or mostly market) economies includes various kinds of systems. Democratic countries with liberal market economies have different levels of productivity and living standards, different proportions of the public sector, different safety net provisions, and different regulatory mechanisms. On the other hand, successful market economies are not always democracies, at least in the Western meaning of this word. For example, Singapore is a well-performing free-market economy with an authoritarian political regime.

The countries, which do not fall into the category of mostly liberal market systems are also characterised by different proportion of public and private ownership, different principles of economy-governing legislation and government regulation, different levels of performance, stability, prosperity, and social welfare. In countries, such as Latin American ones, economic and political instability, considerable, but not always reasonable government involvement in economic life, and endemic corruption have remained important and pressing features for decades and centuries. There have been examples, such as Argentina, of rapid economic growth followed by drastic decline. From time to time, some of these economies were engaged in comprehensive and largely successful economic reforms, which were supposed to improve their predominantly market systems. Meanwhile, rapid and intensive reforms were followed by periods of slow and gradual change.

By the late 1990s, post-communist countries in transition had demonstrated substantial differences in the speed, sequence, and success of their economic reforms towards a "perfect" market system situation. The question was then, and is now—after 3 decades of reforms,

- whether the transition has been ongoing, and whether the transitional economies (or some of them) have been on their further way to a desirable "perfect" market economic system;
- or whether the transition was already over by the end of the first decade of reform;

* or is it over by now, with each of the former communist countries transformed to a particular type of a market economy, analogous to one of the existing forms, although at some distance from the "perfect" one?

In the letter case, further transformation to a perfect system can take substantial time.

This chapter is a considerable extension of a project attempted at answering this question based on the experience and data available more than 20 years ago (Kazakevitch, 1998). Then, only one Economic Freedom data set was available—for the year 1998; and the data on post-communist countries was incomplete. This project is based on the Economic Freedom data sets for 21 years.

Why Economic Freedom Data?

First, this data comprehensively ranks economic systems based on various qualitative indicators. Then, there is a visible correlation between the level of economic freedom and the welfare of the nation, measured as GDP per capita. This is true for all countries and, separately, post-communist countries (see Figs. 2.1 and 2.2). Therefore, improving economic freedom is a desirable goal.

The available data allows for tracing the progress of reforms from 1998 to 2018. In addition, compared to (Kazakevitch, 1998), the range of post-communist countries is extended from the former Soviet Bloc countries, including Former Soviet republics and post-communist countries of Eastern and Central Europe. China and other countries still ruled by communist countries were not considered in 1998, for the reason that those countries did not declare that they were in the process of post-communist transformation. Today it is clear that some aspects of their reforms towards market economies and economic freedom have been more successful than in some "officially" post-communist economies. In addition, some countries that used to be parts of former Yugoslavia are also included because, unlike in 1998, consistent data for most of them is now available. The only post-communist country that is and should not

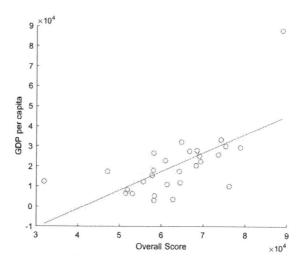

Fig. 2.1 The relationship between economic freedom and GDP per capita: correlation, linear regression, and scatter plot for post-communist countries in 2018 (*Source* Statistical estimation by the author based on *Index of Economic Freedom*, https://www.heritage.org/index/explore?view=by-region-country-year&u=636916527549820517. Notes 27 observations; correlation coefficient: 0.6430)

be included is East Germany because the data for East Germany is not collected separately from the whole Germany. Even though the former communist part of Germany has experienced enormous economic and social problems, in terms of economic mechanism, this part of the now united country has expediently achieved the West German and European Union Standards due to considerable financial assistance and implementation of West German federal laws and regulations.

After removing missing variables or for some countries, the total number of countries included in the database is 132. This covers more than 90% of the world's population and 99% of the world's GDP.

The simplest way to interpret the Economic Freedom data is comparing countries based on the integrated scalar economic freedom indicator or on its categories reflecting different aspects of economic freedom. After excluding incomplete data, the following categories are taken into consideration: property rights; corruption; government spending; business

2 A Taxonomy of Post-communist Economies After 30 Years ...

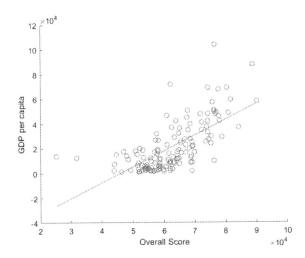

Fig. 2.2 The relationship between economic freedom and GDP per capita: correlation, linear regression, and scatter plot for all countries in 2018 (*Source* Statistical estimation by the author based on *Index of Economic Freedom*, https://www.heritage.org/index/explore?view=by-region-country-year&u=636916527549820517. *Notes* 132 observations; correlation coefficient: 0.6731)

freedom; monetary freedom; trade freedom; investment freedom; and financial freedom. Based on the comprehensive qualitative analysis of the survey data, the authors of the survey assign a quantitative rating (0–100) for each category for each country. Using these ratings an integrated rating (0–100) is produced for each country, where 100 is the maximum level of economic freedom. Based on those ratings, 4 groups of countries are also identified: "free", "partly free", "mostly not free", and "not free".

This data is already rich enough for comparing the dynamics of post-communist systems from 1998 to 2018, in association with selected countries characterised by similar levels of economic freedom. To make this comparison, the countries are ranked from 1 to 132—from the highest to the lowest rating for 1998, and separately—for 2018. Then, the countries are sorted from 1 to 132 with respect to the year 2018. As a result, we can see how the rank has changed from 1998 to 2018 (Table 2.1).

Table 2.1 The dynamics of post-communist systems from 1998 to 2018, in association with countries characterised by similar levels of economic freedom

Country	Rank 1998	Rank 2018
Hong Kong	1	1
Singapore	65	2
New Zealand	93	3
Switzerland	4	4
Australia	6	5
Ireland	10	6
Estonia	**14**	**7**
United Kingdom	5	8
Canada	24	9
United Arab Emirates	15	10
Iceland	17	11
Denmark	31	12
Luxembourg	104	13
Sweden	49	14
Georgia	**112**	**15**
Netherlands	3	16
United States	8	17
Lithuania	**12**	**18**
Chile	9	19
Malaysia	81	20
Norway	44	21
Czech Republic	**25**	**22**
Germany	47	23
Finland	51	24
Korea, South	35	25
Latvia	**75**	**26**
Japan	20	27
Israel	28	28
Austria	40	29
Botswana	54	30
Romania	**98**	**31**
Uruguay	23	32
Jamaica	33	33
Kazakhstan	**121**	**34**
Rwanda	68	35
Colombia	39	36
Armenia	**108**	**37**
Peru	56	38
Malta	118	39
Poland	**43**	**40**
Bulgaria	**114**	**41**

(continued)

2 A Taxonomy of Post-communist Economies After 30 Years ...

Table 2.1 (continued)

Country	Rank 1998	Rank 2018
Cyprus	26	42
Bahrain	7	43
Belgium	45	44
Thailand	32	45
Panama	41	46
Hungary	**84**	**47**
Costa Rica	38	48
Turkey	64	49
Spain	58	50
Philippines	72	51
Jordan	34	52
Mexico	94	53
Slovenia	**48**	**54**
Albania	92	55
Azerbaijan	**119**	**56**
Indonesia	52	57
France	76	58
Guatemala	37	59
Portugal	89	60
El Salvador	19	61
South Africa	11	62
Kyrgyz Republic	**53**	**63**
Italy	74	64
Kuwait	103	65
Paraguay	42	66
Côte d'Ivoire	106	67
Fiji	78	68
Uganda	46	69
Morocco	120	70
Dominican Republic	79	71
Bosnia and Herzegovina	**131**	**72**
Croatia	**105**	**73**
Oman	96	74
Honduras	85	75
Burkina Faso	88	76
Tanzania	69	77
Nicaragua	101	78
Tunisia	50	79
Cambodia	67	80
Guyana	99	81
Namibia	95	82
Nigeria	29	83

(continued)

Table 2.1 (continued)

Country	Rank 1998	Rank 2018
Moldova	**82**	**84**
Tajikistan	**122**	**85**
Russia	**126**	**86**
Belarus	**127**	**87**
Gabon	71	88
China	**97**	**89**
Trinidad and Tobago	16	90
Mali	61	91
Greece	66	92
Belize	73	93
Barbados	30	94
Madagascar	90	95
Benin	60	96
Ghana	83	97
Swaziland	59	98
Haiti	116	99
Mongolia	**62**	**100**
Senegal	2	101
Bangladesh	102	102
Kenya	77	103
India	107	104
Pakistan	13	105
Zambia	57	106
Nepal	21	107
Mauritania	80	108
Burma	115	109
Lesotho	70	110
Egypt	87	111
Lebanon	110	112
Vietnam	**124**	**113**
Ethiopia	109	114
Argentina	18	115
Guinea	63	116
Malawi	27	117
Cameroon	111	118
Ukraine	**123**	**119**
Uzbekistan	**130**	**120**
Brazil	100	121
Iran	128	122
Chad	113	123
Ecuador	55	124
Suriname	125	125

(continued)

Table 2.1 (continued)

Country	Rank 1998	Rank 2018
Turkmenistan	129	126
Mozambique	36	127
Algeria	86	128
Bolivia	22	129
Zimbabwe	117	130
Cuba	132	131
Venezuela	91	132

Source Ranking by the author based on *Index of Economic Freedom*, https://www.heritage.org/index/explore?view=by-region-country-year&u=636916527549820517
Post-communist and communist countries are highlighted in Bold fonts

One can notice a few visible shifts. Estonia had achieved the highest rank out of the post-communist economics already in 1998. By 2018 it has moved to the group of top 10 in the world. Georgia has moved from the rank 112 (mostly unfree) to 15 (mostly free). This is due to swift reforms undertaken by President Saakashvili, including cutting red tape that made running business difficult; inviting foreign investments; simplifying the tax code, but tackling tax evasion; and starting a privatisation campaign. Latvia, Romania, Kazakhstan, Albania, and Azerbaijan have considerably improved their ratings, joining mostly free economics. Bosnia and Herzegovina and Croatia have also improved their ranks, while Mongolia dropped it from 62 to 100. Finally, Bulgaria, due to swift adoption of the EU regulation and practices has moved from 114 to 41.

Meanwhile, for most of the countries their shift is insignificant. This means that they had achieved a particular, high or low standing in terms of economic freedom, but their standing has not radically changed since 1998. These are Lithuania, Czech Republic, Poland, Slovenia, Kyrgyz Republic, Moldova, Tajikistan, Russia, Belarus, Vietnam, Ukraine, Uzbekistan, Turkmenistan, and Cuba.

Why Cluster Analysis?

The cluster analysis gives further insight into the economic freedom standing of the post-communist countries, compared to the dynamics of the integrated index. The qualitative data associated with each of the economic freedom categories allows for much more than its original use. It gives an opportunity to undertake a structured comparative analysis of economic systems included in the survey, and classify them as a multidimensional vector criterion rather than a scalar rank. Then, falling of a particular country into a particular group (cluster) can be interpreted as closeness of that country, in terms of its socio-economic system, to other members of the corresponding group.

For the purpose of such an analysis, the Economic Freedom survey data is associated with the following characteristics of economic mechanism.

Property rights. This includes legislated, and protected by law, private ownership. In the case of perfect market system all types of transactions and activities with private property can be permitted by the default. An owner has a right protected by law, to decide how a particular property will be used, to receive income generated by its use, transfer property rights by sale, gift, or will, and keep the income in the case of sale. If a system is different from a perfect one, certain kinds of restrictions on property use and transfers may be imposed beyond reasonable regulation justified by national security, safety and health standards, and environment conservation. Furthermore, some types of property and business activities (such as land, mineral resources, infrastructure utilities, defence industries, education, and health care) can be excluded from private ownership. Consequently, transactions of the corresponding assets can be restricted or forbidden. In some countries, property rights legislation can exist, but not indorsed, or can be distorted by corruption. Finally, property rights can be inexistent, or monopolised by the government.

Government integrity and corruption. Corruption is an obstacle to economic freedom by inducing a shift from competitive business decisions to the ones of vested interest to corrupted officials at different levels of government. The more corruption and the less government integrity, the less is trust in public institutions, the higher are costs of running business, the less efficient are economic decisions, and in the worst situations, parts or the whole economy are paralysed. The lack of government integrity caused by such practices reduces public trust in economic activities, and increases the costs of running business.

Government spending. The government spending component in GDP includes government procurement of goods and services as well as welfare entitlement transfers. The greater proportion of GDP government spends, the lesser proportion is left for competitive and efficient market.

Business freedom. It is defined by entrepreneurial rights and corporate legislation. In liberal market economics rules for establishing and running business are simple and easily observable.

However, regulations can be restrictive, include unreasonably complex rules and bureaucratic procedures making establishing new businesses difficult. Other forms of restriction include price control, administrative barriers to entry, non-competitive government recruitment, and in worst cases excluding considerable parts of the economy from private business entrepreneurship.

Due to incomplete information for some countries, we also include, in this characteristic, the freedom of workers to sell their labour force and to join independent unions.

Monetary freedom. Monetary freedom combines a measure of price stability with an assessment of price controls. Both uncontrolled inflation and price controls distort market activity. Price stability without microeconomic intervention is the ideal state of a free market according to *Index of Economic Freedom*. These are defined by the existence of an independent central bank or a comparable institution setting an interest rate base, and controlling inflation; free entrepreneurship in the banking sector; and supply-demand determination of market interest rates.

International trade freedom. This characteristic concerns restrictive tariffs and quotas, export taxes and other barriers to import and export. Alternatively, non-market control can prevail in the determination of the directions and volumes of trade and exchange rate.

Investment freedom. Domestic and foreign investors are concerned with investment climate in a particular country. In addition to monetary freedom, this includes if there is an established securities market; if return on investments are determined by the market and not by the government; if there are non-discriminatory opportunities to invest on a competitive basis; if international in and out transactions or holdings are unreasonably restricted by the government; and if the government bodies are involved in credit allocation. Alternatively, non-market control can prevail in the determination of direction and volume of investments.

Financial freedom. This indicator measures the development of capital market; to what extent the government intervenes and regulates banks and financial services; and to what extent the government influences allocation of credit.

For each country and each year of observation, the above-mentioned characteristics together form vectors of values between 0 and 100. These vectors are used for a taxonomy of countries according to their predominant economic mechanisms. The method of Hierarchical Cluster Analysis (Kaufman & Rousseeuw, 1990) is used to classify the countries included in the survey (excluding missing values). The method attempts to identify relatively homogenous groups of cases (countries) based on the included characteristics. A statistical algorithm is used that starts each case (country) in a separate cluster, and then combines clusters until only the specified number of clusters is left, and each of the cases (countries) belongs to one or another cluster. The ranking of courtiers according to the integrated Countries' Economic Freedom indexes can be in a different order, compared to countries' appearance in clusters. This is essentially because clusters are based on the relative magnitude of distance of different variables from each other, not just on the value of the integrated index.

Attempts were made to obtain interpretable classifications based on 5 to 10 cluster brackets. For the purpose of this study, the eight-cluster classification, out of which 5 clusters contain post-communist and communist countries, appear to be the most interpretable. Meanwhile, the following comments preceding the discussion of the obtained classification may help to not misinterpret the results.

Generally speaking, belonging to a particular cluster reflects the relative closeness of the countries included in this cluster to each other in terms of economic freedom. However, it cannot be so with regard to two neighbouring clusters. The neighbouring clusters can be different in a limited number of characteristics, and each of the characteristics can deviate from a "perfect" market system not always in the same direction.

Table 2.2 Clusters including post-communist and communist countries, and examples of other countries with comparable economic mechanisms

Cluster 1	Cluster 2	Cluster 3	Cluster 4	Cluster 5
Estonia	**Albania**	**Azerbaijan**	**Turkmenistan**	**Cuba**
Australia	**Armenia**	**Belarus**	**Uzbekistan**	Venezuela
Austria	**Bosnia and Herzegovina**	**China**	Uruguay	
Belgium	**Bulgaria**	**Mongolia**	Iran	
Canada	**Poland**	**Belarus**	Nicaragua	
Denmark	**Croatia**	**Romania**	Zimbabwe	
Finland	**Czech Republic**	**Russia**	Ethiopia	
France	**Georgia**	**Kyrgyz Republic**		
Germany	**Hungary**	**Moldova**		
Iceland	**Lithuania**	**Tajikistan**		
Ireland	**Latvia**	Argentina		
Japan	**Kazakhstan**	Ecuador		
New Zealand	**Romania**	El Salvador		
Netherlands	**Slovenia**	India		
Norway	Israel	Indonesia		
Sweden	Italy	Kenya		
Switzerland	Costa Rica	Malaysia		
United Kingdom	Luxembourg	Malta		
United States	Mauritania	Mexico		
	Paraguay	Peru		
	Portugal	Argentina		
	South Africa	Bolivia		
	Spain			
	Chile			
	Colombia			
	Cyprus			
	Greece			

Source Cluster analysis by the author based on *Index of Economic Freedom*, https://www.heritage.org/index/explore?view=by-region-country-year&u=6369
16527549820517
Post-communist and communist countries are highlighted in Bold fonts

Closeness between countries, in terms of the proposed taxonomy based on the Economics Freedom measurements, does not always mean their closeness in terms of the level of economic and technological development, GDP per capita, or other indicators of living standards.

(See below as Estonia appears in the range of the most developed market economies in terms of economic freedom, while being quite behind them in terms of living standards). The only reason the countries are associated with each other is the comparability of their economic mechanisms at the times of the survey, in terms of the above-mentioned Economic Freedom characteristics. The positioning of a post-communist country in a particular cluster can be also interpreted as a momentum (existent or not) towards further development (or otherwise).

The ratings of the elements of Economic Freedom are based on a comprehensive qualitative analysis of countries included in the survey. They also depend on structured criteria and in most cases seem to be pretty well justified. Nevertheless, some of the ratings can be attributed to rather subjective opinions of researchers with regard to specific information on a particular country. As a result, some countries are in clusters they, intuitively, should not be. In addition, the reforms continue on, and what was true even at the time of the most recent survey is sometimes no longer the case.

All those deficiencies, however, do not distort the overall picture significantly, nor do they undermine the methodology or conclusions suggested in this chapter. Keeping in mind all the above considerations let us consider the former and currently communist countries within the suggested taxonomy of economic systems. The 5 relevant clusters are presented in Table 2.2.

Cluster 1 includes the countries with developed market mechanisms. Belonging to this cluster could be considered as a desirable destination for post-communist countries in their transformation into market economy. **Estonia** is the only post-communist country, which so far has joined this family of "perfect market systems". Estonia has been praised, in the academic literature and media, as the most successful post-communist economy (see, for example Rahn, 2015). Soon abandoning its communist regime and gaining independence from the Soviet rule, this small nation has adopted the basic constitutional right to hold property. There are no significant restrictions on selling or exchanging property, and the individuals can structure the property holdings that they choose. At the same time the country adopted legislation on privatisation and implemented it swiftly and successfully.

Country's labour market and labour rights have been established according to liberal market economy standards. Workers have the right to form and join independent labour unions, and the regulation of wages in the private sector has been eliminated. Entrepreneurial rights are observed through reasonable procedures such as registration of companies. Price control has been almost completely eliminated. Meanwhile prices for some essential commodities and utilities are regulated, including electricity, energy inputs, and passenger transport.

Financial markets and investors' rights have been established and observed. There is no regulatory control on return on investments. The EU standards of the monetary system have been established and implemented, including the central bank with reserve functions. There are no restrictive barriers of capital inflow or outflow except taxation on repatriated profit.

Cluster 2 includes the largest number of post-communist countries: Albania, Armenia, Bosnia and Herzegovina, Bulgaria, Poland, Romania, Croatia, Czech Republic, Georgia, Hungary, Kazakhstan, Lithuania, Latvia, and Slovenia. These countries have more or less successfully built market economies, but with some limitations.

One of the most considerable limitations is the unfordable level of social security outlays, particularly analysed in (Aidukaite, 2011). This is mainly due to the atavisms of the Soviet/Communist type welfare state, which implies that the voting population expect welfare guarantees from the political power they support. Another limitation—the duality of economies analysed in (Berend & Bugaric, 2015; Bugaric, 2015). The proportion of black and grey economies as well as the level of corruption, and tax evasion in those countries considerably exceed those of Western democracies. These features are endemic to transitional economies belonging to Cluster 2, and cannot be overcome during the lifetime of one generation, and in the meantime restrict business freedom and economic growth.

Cluster 3 includes Azerbaijan, Belarus, China, Mongolia, Belarus, Russia, Kyrgyz Republic, and Moldova. Politically they all demonstrate features of authoritarianism, as in China; authoritarianism with simulated elements of democracy, as in Russia, Kazakhstan, and Belarus; or "imperfect" democracy, as in Romania. The economic systems formed in those countries are characterised in the literature as state capitalism. Those countries have managed to develop quasi-market economies, but with high proportion of state ownership, including state-owned corporations in the key industries (Ahrens & Hoen, 2019; Becker & Vasileva, 2017). Particularly, In China, the very notion of private ownership is not accepted, and different forms of quasi-private ownership have been legislated instead, including cooperatives, joint ventures, and land use rights. In the area of international trade, governments control the export of major commodities, and impose arbitrary constraints on export and import. Different levels of restriction on labour mobility are exercised; and the formation and practice of independent labour unions are constrained. Foreign investments are heavily regulated, and the monetary systems, including foreign exchange are controlled by governments rather than independent reserve banks and foreign exchange markets.

Cluster 4 includes Turkmenistan and Uzbekistan. These two former soviet republics are further away from democracies and market economies. They have retained the state ownership over major enterprises and banking systems, allowing small business activities. Prices for basic food items are controlled. International trade and foreign exchange are in the hands of the governments. There is no workers' right for unionism. Overall, there is almost no economic freedom in either of these countries.

Cluster 5 consists of only two countries, Cuba and Venezuela. In the absence of data on North Korea, Cuba is the only communist country with a one-party system where market economic reforms are in a rudimental state. Meanwhile Venezuela under Chavez and Madura has been moving in the opposite direction—from a middle-income market economy to a centrally controlled and failing system.

Looking at the clusters, the post-communist economies are associated with, a conclusion follows that they have joined one of two broader families of countries. One of them includes countries with long economic histories of established market economic systems or successful developing nations (Clusters 1 and 2). In terms of economic freedom classification, they are either mostly free (Cluster 1); or free, but with restrictions regarding some economic freedom characteristics. (Cluster 2). Another family of countries mostly consists of less successful developing nations and South American regimes (Clusters 3 and 4). They are market economies, but with substantial constraints and institutional failures (Cluster 3), or mostly unfree (Cluster 4).

Both families of countries have experienced considerable periods of structural, institutional, and regulatory adjustments, which have lead to ether successful or quite less successful outcomes.

In conclusion, looking at the dynamics of post-communist countries in the recent 20 years, one can see that, from the current positioning in terms of economic freedom, a long journey should be expected towards further improvements.

References

Ahrens, J., & Hoen, H. W. (2019). The emergence of state capitalism in Central Asia: The absence of normative power Europe. In M. Neuman (Ed.), *Democracy promotion and the normative power Europe framework*. Cham: Springer.

Aidukaite, J. (2011). Welfare reforms and socio-economic trends in the 10 new EU member states of Central and Eastern Europe. *Communist and Post-Communist Studies, 44*(3), 211–219.

Becker, U., & Vasileva, A. (2017). Russia's political economy re-conceptualized: A changing hybrid of liberalism, statism and patrimonialism. *Journal of Eurasian Studies, 8*(1), 83–96.

Berend, I. T., & Bugaric, B. (2015). Unfinished Europe: Transition from communism to democracy in Central and Eastern Europe. *Journal of Contemporary History, 50*(4), 768–785.

Bugaric, B. B. (2015). A crisis of constitutional democracy in post-Communist Europe: "Lands in-between" democracy and authoritarianism. *International Journal of Constitutional Law, 13*(1), 219–245.

Index of Economic Freedom. https://www.heritage.org/index/explore?view=by-region-country-year&u=636916527549820517.

Kaufman, L., & Rousseeuw, P. J. (1990). *Finding groups in data: An introduction to cluster analysis* (1st ed.). New York: Wiley.

Kazakevitch, G. (1998). Is the transition already over in the Former Soviet Block countries? An attempt at a taxonomy of post-communist economies. *Russian and Euro-Asian Bulletin, 7*(7), 1–7.

Rahn, R. (2015, September 22). Why Estonia is a country for the future. *The Washington Times*.

3

The Central Asian Countries' Economies in the Twenty-First Century

Richard Pomfret

Introduction

The Central Asian republics were among the poorest and most culturally distinct in the Union of Soviet Socialist Republics (USSR), although for their income levels they had high social indicators (Table 3.1).[1] Nevertheless, there was little pressure to leave the USSR in the 1980s and early 1990s, in contrast to the Baltic, Caucasus and Ukrainian republics. The disintegration of the USSR in the second half of 1991 was unanticipated and not particularly welcome in Central Asia, although the First Secretaries appointed by Mikhail Gorbachev quickly transformed themselves into national presidents.

---

[1] In this paper Central Asia refers to Kazakhstan, the Kyrgyz Republic, Tajikistan, Turkmenistan and Uzbekistan. In the final Soviet census in 1989, the last four and Azerbaijan were the poorest republics with the highest proportion of under-provisioned households (Pomfret, 1995).

R. Pomfret (✉)
University of Adelaide, Adelaide, SA, Australia
e-mail: richard.pomfret@adelaide.edu.au

© The Author(s) 2020
A. Akimov and G. Kazakevitch (eds.), *30 Years since the Fall of the Berlin Wall*,
Palgrave Studies in Economic History, https://doi.org/10.1007/978-981-15-0317-7_3

Table 3.1 Initial conditions: republics of the USSR 1989/1990

	Population (million) mid-1990	Per capita GNP[a] (1990)	Gini coefficient (1989)	Poverty (% of population)[b] (1989)	Terms of trade[c]	Life expectancy (years)	Adult literacy (percentage)
USSR	289.3	2870	0.289	11.1			
Kazakh	16.8	2600	0.289	15.5	+19	69	98
Kyrgyz	4.4	1570	0.287	32.9	+1	66	97
Tajik	5.3	1130	0.308	51.2	−7	69	97
Turkmen	3.7	1690	0.307	35.0	+50	66	98
Uzbek	20.5	1340	0.304	43.6	−3	69	99
Armenia	3.3	2380	0.259	14.3	−24	72	99
Azerbaijan	7.2	1640	0.328	33.6	−7	71	96
Georgia	5.5	2120	0.292	14.3	−21	73	95
Belarus	10.3	3110	0.238	3.3	−20	71	98
Moldova	4.4	2390	0.258	11.8	−38	69	99
Russia	148.3	3430	0.278	5.0	+79	69	99
Ukraine	51.9	2500	0.235	6.0	−18	70	99
Estonia	1.6	4170	0.299	1.9	−32	70	99
Latvia	2.7	3590	0.274	2.4	−24	69	99
Lithuania	3.7	3110	0.278	2.3	−31	71	98

Source Pomfret (2006, p. 4)
[a]GNP per capita in US dollars computed by the World Bank's synthetic *Atlas* method; [b]poverty = individuals in households with gross per capita monthly income less than 75 rubles; [c]impact on terms of trade of moving to world prices, calculated at 105-sector level of aggregation using 1990 weights

When the Russian Federation adopted rapid price liberalization in January 1992, the Central Asian republics had no option other than to follow, at least with respect to traded goods. Through 1992 and much of 1993, while the ruble remained the common currency, the new independent states had little room for macroeconomic policy manoeuvre. The early 1990s were characterized by hyperinflation and the whole decade by a difficult transition from central planning to market-based economies.

None of the Central Asian countries had previous history as independent states. A common perception in the 1990s was that their prospects for long-term survival were poor. Nevertheless, they have survived for over a quarter of a century, which is a better record than that of the new states created from the break-up of the Habsburg, Hohenzollern and Romanoff empires in 1919, all of which had lost their independence two decades later.[2] Moreover, Central Asia has seen no interstate wars and has no frozen conflicts comparable to those in Azerbaijan, Moldova, Georgia and Ukraine.[3]

This paper focusses on the economic record of the independent Central Asian states, although politics and the external environment cannot be ignored. Three periods are identified. The 1990s were dominated by nation-building and the transition from central planning to market-based economies. From the turn of the century until 2014 the global resource boom brought large windfall gains to oil and gas exporters, as well as some mineral producers, and the poorer countries received substantial remittances from migrant workers in energy-rich countries, notably Russia. Finally, the years since 2014 have seen improved intra-regional relations and cooperation as the five countries seek to diversify their economies away from resource or remittance dependence.

Creating New Nations and Market-Based Economies

The Communist first secretaries of the five Soviet republics quickly transformed themselves into national presidents and, apart from in Tajikistan, created political systems in which power was concentrated in the president. The five countries joined the United Nations in June 1992. In Tajikistan the president was quickly displaced and a bitter civil war involving religious parties and regional warlords lasted until 1997, after which President Rakhmon created a super-presidential regime.

---

[2]The post-1919 new independent states mostly came under German control after 1939 and became Soviet satellites for four decades after 1945. Estonia, Latvia and Lithuania were absorbed by the USSR. Yugoslavia was conquered by Axis forces in 1941.

[3]There have been tensions and some border violence, particularly associated with enclaves in the patchwork borders of the densely populated Ferghana Valley, but the only full-scale war has been the 1992–1997 Tajik civil war.

There were occasional expressions of discontent, but the five presidents consolidated their power and domestic political stability was established by the end of the 1990s. The external environment was stable, largely because no other countries showed much interest in the region.[4]

The newly independent countries faced three major economic shocks. Central planning had been weakening in the late Soviet era, but there had been no experiments with market mechanisms in Central Asia. When the Union collapsed suddenly and Russia liberalized prices, the countries were forced into transition into market-based economies with very few officials experienced in foreign trade, macroeconomic policy or even understanding of how markets worked. The second shock was the descent into hyperinflation as countries had neither adequate domestic tax systems nor access to capital markets in order to fund public expenditures.[5] Thirdly, Central Asian republics had been highly integrated into Soviet supply chains, often for processing their raw materials, and these chains quickly broke down amidst monetary confusion and the introduction of transport costs.[6]

The five countries adopted diverse transition strategies. Kyrgyzstan was first to adopt a national currency and first to bring annual inflation below 50%, as a prerequisite for an effective market economy. Kazakhstan also started along the path of rapid reform but became mired in rent-seeking as valuable enterprises were privatized and foreign

---

[4]Russian influence was greatest, but President Yeltsin had little political interest beyond Russia's border—matters would have been different if Almaty-born Zhirinovsky had won the 1996 Russian election with his programme of extending Russia's reach to the Indian Ocean. China was mainly concerned with delimiting its western border and limiting support for Uighur separatism. The USA established embassies; US companies invested, notably Chevron and ExxonMobil in the Tengiz oilfield, but they did not need government support. The EU provided technical assistance, but amounts were small and the flagship TRACECA project was ineffective.

[5]The problem was exacerbated in 1992 and 1993 by the use of common currency. Each republic could issue ruble credits to pay for public spending, but no institution had control over the money supply, which created a free-rider problem as the credit-issuer gained all the benefits from money creation but only contributed marginally to national inflation (Pomfret, 2016).

[6]The issue of whether Central Asian republics as primary product suppliers to the rest of the Soviet Union had been subsidized or taxed is impossible to answer, e.g. due to many transactions taking place within All-Union enterprises. A striking example of disruption was a sugar refinery, the largest industrial enterprise in the Kyrgyz republic accounting for 3% of GDP, that processed Cuban cane sugar and was immediately unprofitable once transport costs had to be paid.

investors sought oil contracts. At the other extreme, Turkmenistan's President introduced minimal economic reform. Uzbekistan was also a gradual reformer but more proactive in introducing market mechanisms in the mid-1990s. Tajikistan was a special case insofar as the collapse of the central government led to rapid transition to a market economy but without the public institutions required to support an efficient economy.

Given their shared historical, geographical and cultural background and diverse approaches to establishing market economies, the Central Asian economies were often viewed as a natural experiment in resolving debates over the speed of transition and sequencing of reform.[7] By the EBRD Transition Indicators there was by 1999 a clear ranking from most reformed to least reformed: Kyrgyz Republic, Kazakhstan, Tajikistan, Uzbekistan, Turkmenistan. The types of market-based economies had been established; for all five countries the Indicators changed little after the turn of the century (Table 3.2).

An issue in evaluating the natural experiment is the huge measurement problems, especially in the early 1990s, when the output and consumption mix changed dramatically and creation of effective statistics agencies was not high on the nation-building agenda. The widespread informal economy was poorly captured in the data, and some practices were non-transparent (e.g. Uzbekistan did not report output of gold, its second-largest export) or misleading (e.g. when Turkmenistan was not paid for its gas exports it still recorded the sales as exports and the IOUs were treated as foreign assets, although they would eventually only be paid at deep discounts).

Nevertheless, all data and casual observation point to a steep transitional recession with 1989 living standards only achieved after the turn of the century (Table 3.3). Falling GDP per capita plus increasing inequality led to massive increases in poverty in the two poorest countries,

---

[7]The region is geographically well defined to the east, west and south and the five countries share cultural characteristics. They are all Muslim-majority societies and four of the national languages are Turkic (Tajik is Farsi-related). In the USSR a distinction was made between Kazakhstan and Central Asia; the former had a more mixed population, more Europeanized culture and higher human capital and living standards. On debates over transition strategies, see Pomfret (2002).

Table 3.2 EBRD transition indicators, 1999 and 2009

		Large scale privati-zation	Small scale privati-zation	Enterprise restructur-ing	Price liberali-zation	Trade and forex system	Competition policy	Banking and interest rates	Securities markets and NBFIs	Overall infra-structure reform
Kazakhstan	1999	3.00	4.00	2.00	4.00	3.33	2.00	2.33	2.00	2.00
	2009	3.00	4.00	2.00	4.00	3.67	2.00	2.67	2.67	2.67
Kyrgyz Republic	1999	3.00	4.00	2.00	4.33	4.33	2.00	2.00	2.00	1.33
	2009	3.67	4.00	2.00	4.33	4.33	2.00	2.33	2.00	1.67
Tajikistan	1999	2.33	3.00	1.67	3.67	2.67	2.00	1.00	1.00	1.00
	2008	2.33	4.00	1.67	3.67	3.33	1.67	2.33	1.00	1.33
Turkmenistan	1999	1.67	2.00	1.67	2.67	1.00	1.00	1.00	1.00	1.00
	2009	1.00	2.33	1.00	2.67	2.00	1.00	1.00	1.00	1.00
Uzbekistan	1999	2.67	3.00	2.00	2.67	1.00	2.00	1.67	2.00	1.33
	2009	2.67	3.33	1.67	2.67	2.00	1.67	1.67	2.00	1.67

Source European Bank for Reconstruction and Development *Transition Report* 2000 and 2010

Table 3.3 Growth in real GDP, 1989–1999 (%)

	1989	1990	1991	1992	1993	1994	1995	1996	1997	1998	1999	1999; 1989=100
Kazakhstan	0	0	−13	−3	−9	−13	−8	1	2	−2	2	**63**
Kyrgyz Republic	8	3	−5	−19	−16	−20	−5	7	10	2	4	**63**
Tajikistan	−3	−2	−7	−29	−11	−19	−13	−4	2	5	4	**44**
Turkmenistan	−7	2	−5	−5	−10	−17	−7	−7	−11	5	16	**64**
Uzbekistan	4	2	−1	−11	−2	−4	−1	2	3	4	4	**94**

Source European Bank for Reconstruction and Development *Transition Report Update*, April 2001, 15

Note Pomfret (2006, pp. 107–122) discusses the conceptual problems associated with measuring GDP during the transition from central planning to a market-based economy

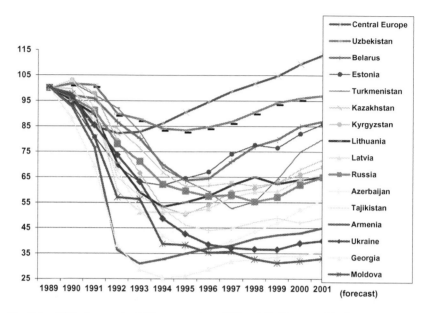

Fig. 3.1 GDP change in FSU economies, 1989 = 100 (*Source* This figure is reproduced here with full permission of the copyright holder UNU-WIDER. The figure originally featured in Popov, Vladimir [2001] 'Where do we stand a decade after the collapse of the USSR?' *WIDER Angle*, 2 (2001). Launching Cornia, G.A., and V. Popov [Eds.], *Transition and Institutions: The Experience of Gradual and Late Reformers*, UNU-WIDER Studies in Development Economics, Oxford University Press)

the Kyrgyz Republic and Tajikistan (Anderson & Pomfret, 2003). Higher initial incomes and valuable oil and gas exports helped to alleviate the situation in Kazakhstan and Turkmenistan, although evidence for the latter is opaque. Uzbekistan, by contrast, had the shallowest transitional recession of any former Soviet republic (Fig. 3.1).

Before we can judge the relative merits of the transition strategies, however, we must consider the extent to which they laid the foundations for sustainable long-term growth. The Kyrgyz Republic's experience showed that rapid reform alone was insufficient without the institutional structure to support an efficient market economy (e.g. rule of law and lack of impunity for corrupt practices); to maintain public expenditures, the government ran up external debts that exceeded 100% of GDP by the turn of the century, leading to a debt crisis. Uzbekistan, the regional success story of the 1990s, introduced draconian foreign exchange controls in 1996 and the negative consequences were becoming apparent by the end of the decade. The twenty-first century might have shed light on relative long-term success, but before we could judge the outcomes the resource boom dominated. Oil and gas exporters Kazakhstan and Turkmenistan had huge windfall gains, while resource-poor Kyrgyz Republic and Tajikistan became labour exporters dependent on remittances from Russia. Uzbekistan, more or less self-sufficient in gas and with valuable minerals such as gold and copper, lay somewhere in between. These outcomes had little to do with transition strategies.

The Resource Boom

In the twenty-first century, the Central Asian countries have had fairly well-performing economies. In part, this is because the impacts of transition were asynchronous with uncompetitive former state enterprises going out of business fairly rapidly and new activities slow to start. Recovery from a deep transitional trough inevitably involved faster economic growth, and the deepest trough, in Tajikistan gave greatest scope for higher-percentage-change recovery. Differences in economic performance after 2000 were surely influenced by the type of market economy that each country had created in the 1990s, but that effect was outweighed by other determinants of growth, especially the resource boom.

The resource boom favoured several important Central Asian resource exports, including gold, copper and other minerals, but oil and gas saw the most dramatic boom. Oil prices soared from under $20 a barrel in 1999 to over $130 in 2008; after a sharp but brief dip in 2008, oil prices recovered to over $100 until 2014, when a more sustained decline to lower prices signalled the end of the boom (Fig. 3.2). Already by the early 2000s, despite sluggish growth in real output during the 1990s, the energy exporters had substantially higher per capita incomes (Table 3.4).

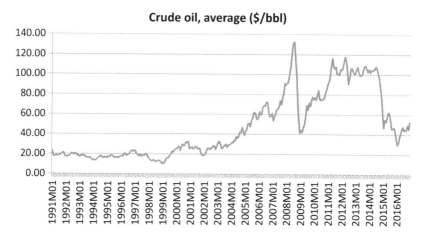

Fig. 3.2 World price of oil, US dollars per barrel, 1991–2016 (*Source* Author's creation based on http://pubdocs.worldbank.org/en/561011486076393416/CMO-Historical-Data-Monthly.xlsx)

For Kazakhstan the boom created a perfect storm. The Tengiz oilfield was just coming into full production, so that oil exports soared in quantity just as their price was increasing. Discovery in 2000 of the Kashagan offshore oilfield, the largest new discovery in the world for several decades, was followed by an investment boom. Construction of new pipelines reduced previous dependence on the Russian oil pipeline monopoly and as world prices rose it became feasible to build longer more expensive pipelines to the Mediterranean in 2003 and to China, increasing choice of routes and reducing transport costs. Kazakhstan clearly pulled ahead of its southern neighbours.

As a natural gas exporter Turkmenistan also benefited from the resource boom, but the impact was delayed by dependence on Russian pipelines. Turkmenistan no longer had problems receiving payment from customers, but the opaque arrangements often involved barter and prices far below what Russia was receiving for its gas exports to Europe. Eventually, in 2006 President Niyazov, who rarely travelled, went to Beijing to negotiate an agreement with China and a gas pipeline built between 2006 and 2009 ended dependence on Russia.

Table 3.4 Economic and social indicators, 2002

	Population	Population aged under 15	Urban population	Life expectancy at birth	GDP	GDP per capita	GDP per cap @ PPP	ODA	ODA per capita	Armed forces
	Millions	Percentage of total	Percentage of total	Years	$ billion	$	International dollars	$ million	$	Thousands
Kazakhstan	15.5	26	56	66	24.6	1656	5870	188.3	12.2	60
Kyrgyz Republic	5.1	33	34	68	1.6	320	1620	186.0	36.7	11
Tajikistan	6.2	37	25	69	1.2	193	980	168.4	27.2	6
Turkmenistan	4.8	35	45	67	7.7	1601	4300	40.5	8.5	18
Uzbekistan	25.7	35	37	70	7.9	314	1670	189.4	7.4	52

Source Pomfret (2006, p. 19), based on UNDP *Human Development Report 2004*

Table 3.5 Economic performance 2000–2014

	Real GDP growth	Consumer price inflation	Overall fiscal balance	Current account balance
	Annual change (%)	Year average (%)	Percent of GDP	Percent of GDP
Kazakhstan	7.7	8.4	3.1	−0.6
Kyrgyz Republic	4.5	8.6	−3.9	−2.3
Tajikistan	7.8	13.4	−2.5	−4.3
Turkmenistan	11.1	5.6	3.8	−7.4
Uzbekistan	7.0	14.5	−1.1	5.2

Source International Monetary Fund *Regional Economic Outlook: Middle East and Central Asia*, October 2018, 37

Note "Real" GDP is difficult to define when prices change rapidly. Turkmenistan data must be treated with caution as misreporting was widely suspected

The main energy resource of the Kyrgyz Republic and Tajikistan, hydroelectricity, was difficult to develop due to conflicts with downstream countries dependent on water for irrigation.[8] For these countries, the main impact of the resource boom was through demand for manual labour in Russia; by 2013 the remittances to GDP ratio in Tajikistan was the highest in the world and in the Kyrgyz Republic third-highest. Even more migrant workers went from Uzbekistan, although as a proportion of the population, and remittances as a share of GDP, the percentages were lower than for the smaller Kyrgyz and Tajik economies. Uzbekistan also became self-sufficient in gas and benefited from increased mineral prices (Table 3.5).

The positive economic performance was not matched by political change. Turkmenistan's President Niyazov died in 2006 and, after brief hopes of a new order, his successor maintained the same political and economic model. The presidents of Kazakhstan, Tajikistan and Uzbekistan tightened their grip. The Kyrgyz president tried to do the same, but President Akayev was overthrown by a popular uprising in

---

[8]Even when hydroelectricity is generated there is need for investment in transmission lines before the electricity can be traded, unlike oil which can be shipped by rail or barge before pipelines are built.

2005 and his successor shared the same fate in 2010. Central Asia's first, and so far only, female president then guided the Kyrgyz Republic to a more balanced relationship between parliament and president before stepping down.

Foreign interest in Central Asia became more pronounced with the energy boom and following the US invasion of Afghanistan in 2001. The USA used Central Asia as a transit route for supplies shipped through Baltic ports, especially after the Pakistan route became less reliable, and used airbases first in Uzbekistan and then in the Kyrgyz Republic to transport troops to and from Afghanistan.[9] President Putin was more interested in Russia's Near Abroad than Yeltsin had been, and he gradually started to differentiate between friends and enemies, culminating in creation of the Eurasian Economic Union (EAEU) between Russia, Belarus and Kazakhstan, which the Kyrgyz Republic joined in 2015 and Tajikistan considered joining. China's economic presence became stronger with the bazaars full of Chinese manufactures, with major infrastructure projects like the pipeline from Turkmenistan and many smaller projects such as road-building in Tajikistan and the Kyrgyz Republic, and with increasing investments in natural resource projects. Despite popular worries about being swamped by China, the Central Asian governments were generally successful in maintaining balance between external powers, often claiming to be successfully pursuing multi-vector diplomacy.

The governments were less successful in promoting intra-regional cooperation. Attempts at regional cooperation and integration floundered and by 2005 the main regional bodies were all based outside Central Asia.[10] The 2006–2009 Turkmenistan–Uzbekistan–Kazakhstan–China gas

---

[9]The Manas Transit Center in Bishkek airport faced domestic opposition and Russian pressure to close it, but it remained open and a source of revenue for the Kyrgyz Republic until US demand dropped in 2014. Fuel contracts to the Center were a major source of corruption, as sons of presidents monopolized the contracts from the early 2000s until 2010, stoking the popular discontent that led to the overturn of presidents in 2005 and 2010.

[10]The secretariat of the Commonwealth of Independent States and that of the Union of Five (predecessor of the EAEU) were in Moscow, the Shanghai Cooperation Organization in Beijing, the Economic Cooperation Organization in Tehran, the Special Program for the Economies of Central Asia (SPECA) in the UN regional offices in Geneva and Bangkok, and Central Asian Regional Economic Cooperation (CAREC) at the Asian Development Bank in Manila.

pipeline was a rare example of regional cooperation and was a win-win outcome as Turkmenistan exported gas and the other two countries received transit fees (and the option to export gas through the pipeline in future). The fact that the five countries had competing rather than complementary economies partially explained the non-cooperation, but the prevalence of autocratic rulers also mattered as personal relations, especially between the presidents of Uzbekistan and Tajikistan and of Uzbekistan and Turkmenistan, were often dire.

Overall, the resource boom underpinned a period of rising incomes. Apart from in the Kyrgyz Republic, the autocratic leaders were able to stay in power while making little change to their economic or political strategies. Increased external interest in the region turned out to be non-threatening, largely because Central Asia was far from central to the major powers' foreign policies and Central Asian leaders were not desperate for any power's favours.

Seeking Diversification

The end of the oil boom in 2014 was the signal for change in economic policy thinking in Central Asia. The break was highlighted by the sudden and large depreciation of the Russian ruble which overnight reduced the value of remittances to the Kyrgyz Republic, Tajikistan and Uzbekistan. Kazakhstan saw its oil revenues fall and Turkmenistan saw orders for its natural gas cut by Russia and by Iran. All five governments appeared to recognize the need for economic diversification away from a handful of primary products or from dependence on remittances. Given the small size of domestic markets, diversification implied a fresh look at opening up to the global economy (Table 3.6).

A striking feature of the transition in Central Asia was the creation of different varieties of market-based economies by 2000. Fifteen years later there was an added layer of differentiation resulting from the resource boom. Nevertheless, the shift to more outward-oriented polices was clear in what had been the more closed economies. Turkmenistan agreed to the construction of a new rail line from Kazakhstan to Iran, and the Turkmen, Kazakh and Iranian presidents celebrated completion

Table 3.6 Economic performance 2015–2017

	Real GDP growth Annual change (%)			Consumer price inflation Year average (%)			Overall fiscal balance Percent of GDP			Current account balance Percent of GDP		
	2015	2016	2017	2015	2016	2017	2015	2016	2017	2015	2016	2017
Kazakhstan	1.2	1.1	4.0	6.7	14.6	7.4	−6.3	−5.4	−6.5	−2.8	−6.5	−3.4
Kyrgyz Republic	3.9	4.3	4.6	6.5	0.4	3.2	−2.3	−5.9	−4.4	−16.0	−11.6	−4.0
Tajikistan	6.0	6.9	7.1	5.8	5.9	7.3	−1.9	−9.8	−6.8	−6.0	−5.2	−0.5
Turkmenistan	6.5	6.2	6.5	7.4	3.6	8.0	−0.7	−2.4	−2.8	−15.6	−19.9	−11.5
Uzbekistan	7.9	7.8	5.3	8.5	8.0	12.5	−1.6	−0.5	−3.7	0.7	0.6	3.5

Source International Monetary Fund *Regional Economic Outlook: Middle East and Central Asia*, October 2018, 37

Note Turkmenistan data must be treated with caution

with a highly publicized ceremony to hammer in the final spike in December 2014. After the September 2016 death of Uzbekistan's President Karimov, his successor removed the exchange controls that hampered international transactions and quickly began bridge-building with neighbours. This paved the way for Uzbekistan, which is the most populous Central Asian country and has common borders with all four other Central Asian countries and Afghanistan, to resume its position as the cross-roads of Asia. In 2019, Uzbekistan followed the Kyrgyz Republic and Kazakhstan in removing visa requirements for many countries' citizens visiting the country.

The challenges of diversification are internal and external. Domestic economies must become sufficiently efficient that producers can increase output or develop new goods and services that are competitive in export markets. At the same time, the hard and soft infrastructure of international trade must also be improved. For traditional exports (e.g. cotton, gold, minerals, oil and gas) comparative advantage was sufficiently strong that high trade costs did not prevent trade, but export competitiveness of other goods depends on reducing the costs of international trade.

Since 2016 Central Asia has faced a window of opportunity for non-traditional exports. A rail "Landbridge" of regular freight train services now links Europe and China via Central Asia, and in recent years freight volumes have been doubling annually.[11] The Eurasian Landbridge began by connecting regional value chains in East Asia and Europe, primarily transporting car components from Germany to factories in China and electronics goods from China to Europe, but more services have gradually been offered and the composition of freight diversified (Pomfret, 2019b). The Landbridge passes through Central Asia, bringing abundant transit revenues to Kazakhstan, but the trains do not stop.

---

[11]In 2015 traffic on the China–Kazakhstan–Russia–EU route amounted to 46,000 TEUs. In 2016 it grew to 104,500 TEUs and in 2017 to 175,000 TEUs, which is on target for the goal of a million TEUs in 2020 announced by United Transport and Logistics Company—Eurasian Rail Alliance (UTLC ERA). See "Eurasian rail traffic in 2018 heading to a million TEUs," *Railfreight.com*, 24 December 2018—at https://www.railfreight.com/specials/2018/12/24/eurasian-rail-traffic-in-2018-heading-to-a-million-teus/.

China has embraced the Landbridge as part of the One Belt One Road project announced in Kazakhstan in September 2013, and formally launched in Beijing in May 2017 as the Belt and Road Initiative (BRI). Interestingly, official Chinese maps show the Belt passing south of the Caspian Sea through Iran and Turkey to Europe rather than the main current Landbridge route through Kazakhstan and Russia, north of the Caspian.[12] China may be seeking to avoid dependence on a single route on which there could be hold-up possibilities for transit countries to raise rates, or China may be seeking access to markets in Iran, the Middle East and North Africa. Irrespective of Chinese motives a second Central Asian route clearly offers potential benefits to the southern Central Asian countries.

Improved infrastructure of a modern rail network offers a window of opportunity, especially if China follows up on proposals to upgrade to high-speed lines. Whether Central Asian producers can take advantage of the window will depend on their governments improving domestic conditions for doing business and on facilitating trade through better soft infrastructure, e.g. removing bureaucratic and border regulations that inhibit firms and delay transport.

Challenges and Conclusions

Trade facilitation should be a win-win. The experience of the Turkmenistan–Uzbekistan–Kazakhstan–China pipeline built between 2006 and 2009 illustrated the benefits of cooperation. The prospects for regional cooperation to reduce regional trade costs are more positive than in earlier decades when leaders were focussed on nation-building or accumulating revenues from resource exports. Moreover, within the government and the wider population, Central

---

[12]A fortnight after UN sanctions on Iran were eased in January 2016, President Xi visited Tehran and the first train to Tehran left China before the end of the month. By the end of 2017, regular freight service between Ningxia, a Muslim-majority Autonomous Region of China, had been established.

Asian countries (with the possible exception of Turkmenistan) have far greater global-awareness than in 1991 (Box).[13]

Low-hanging fruit include, literally, fruit and vegetable exports from Central Asia to Russia, China and Iran and the Middle East. Centuries ago melons from Bukhara were prized in Damascus, and more recently until the 1990s Uzbekistan and Kyrgyzstan had flourishing fruit and vegetable sales in Russia; the trade collapsed because of the high trade costs of transiting Kazakhstan and entering Russia, but in 2019 trucks are much less likely to face ad hoc stops and fees. The Kyrgyz Republic has already shown that new exports can be developed in agriculture (beans), manufacturing (garments) and services (entrepôt bazaars).[14] With more cordial upstream–downstream relations the Kyrgyz Republic and Tajikistan should be able to develop their hydroelectric resources without risking armed conflict with Uzbekistan, and Afghanistan and South Asia offer huge potential markets. Of course, the infrastructure of transmission lines needs to be built, and that in turn depends on security in Afghanistan and Pakistan.

An important constraint on benefitting from Chinese rail links and potential infrastructure financing under the BRI is widespread suspicion of China in Central Asia which has a counterpart in China's concerns about Central Asian (especially Kazakh and Kyrgyz) support for Uighurs. Hurley, Morris, and Portelance (2018) have highlighted the non-transparency of Chinese aid and possibility of debt dependence, with Sri Lanka as the principal evidence and the Kyrgyz Republic included in their list of eight countries most at risk. The risk arises from China's eagerness to build a rail connection between Kashi and Andijan that would offer a shorter route from China to Iran and reduce dependence on transiting through Kazakhstan. Uzbekistan is also keen on the

---

[13]At the presidential level there has been a generational shift. In December 1991 the presidents were Nabiyev (Tajikistan, b.1930), Karimov (Uzbekistan, b.1938), Niyazov (Turkmenistan, b.1940), Nazarbayev (Kazakhstan, b.1940) and Akayev (Kyrgyzstan, b.1944). In 2019, the presidents—Rakhmon (Tajikistan, b.1952), Tokayev (Kazakhstan, b.1953), Berdimukhamedov (Turkmenistan, b.1957), Mirziyoyev (Uzbekistan, b.1957) and Jeenbekov (Kyrgyz Republic, b.1958)—were in their thirties when the USSR and central planning ended.

[14]On beans, see Tilekeyev (2013) and Tilekeyev, Mogilevsky, Abdrazakova, and Dzhumaeva (2018); on garments, see Birkman, Kaloshnika, Khan, Shavurov, and Smallhouse (2012), Jenish (2014) and Spector (2018); and on bazaars, see Kaminski and Mitra (2012).

project. However, if the Kyrgyz Republic were to finance construction of the line it would incur a debt roughly equal to GDP and with limited prospects of benefits beyond transit fees, which may be insufficient to service loans (see Appendix for more discussion).[15]

> **A Snapshot of Central Asia Today**
>
> Central Asia has changed greatly since 1992. In Almaty, a wannabe hamburger joint called *Shaggies* was the hot eating place; the young waitresses were heavily made up with short skirts, sending an image in contrast to Soviet drabness for those who could afford it and also the impression that they were working in top new jobs. By 2017, *Shaggies* was long-gone. Hamburgers were on offer at *McDonalds* or *Burger King* at prices affordable for the majority and of consistent quality (and clean toilets), but self-service. Further along Kunaev Street *Starbucks* and *KFC* are also doing good business. The advent of multinational fast food chains reflects not just higher disposable incomes, but also greater ease of doing business and reduced concern among franchisees that any profits would be a magnet for legal or illegal bandits.
>
> All of this is in huge contrast to the winter of 1996–1997. In the depth of the transitional recession, poverty was highly visible even in the city centre, and few locals had cash to spend in cafes. Now the cafe culture is ubiquitous in Almaty city centre, and people worry about middle-income problems such as the traffic jams due to rapid increase in car ownership. Inequality appears to have increased, and is certainly visible in the number of Mercedes, Bentleys and other luxury cars. Yet even in rural areas of Kazakhstan or the Kyrgyz Republic signs of improved living standards are common.
>
> In May 2017, I drove from Almaty to Bishkek, the Kyrgyz capital, and then from Bishkek to Naryn. Bishkek-Naryn is a four-hour drive through sparsely populated areas where cattle- and sheep-herders still ride on horseback (although the scattered houses mostly had parked cars). Naryn, a market town of 30,000 people, is less prosperous than Bishkek, but the bazaar was full of food, including citrus from Turkey and bananas from Ecuador, and of clothing and household goods from China. People looked healthy, and younger people wore styles that would not be out of place in

---

[15]The debt dependence hypothesis has several links for which data are imprecise. Chinese assistance is invariably as loans rather than grants and, although interest rates are claimed to be low, there is little evidence of their size. The costs of the rail link are uncertain, depending in part on the route; the shortest route passes through very sparsely populated countryside and the Kyrgyz government would prefer a longer more northerly route that would cost more.

> western Europe, North America or East Asia. Mobile phones were ubiquitous; my car driver had two, one for messaging and the other for phone calls, because rates varied among the major service suppliers.
> It is not the same across all of Central Asia. Tashkent is bustling but less affluent than Almaty or Astana, and Kyrgyz friends said that the cost of living was higher than in Bishkek. Turkmenistan, the least reformed and most closed of the five countries, has many remnants of the authoritarian Soviet regime, with a grandiose capital and, by the sparse evidence, ongoing lack of access to many modern goods and services, especially in rural areas. However, even in Turkmenistan, mobile phone penetration (subscriptions per inhabitant) is over 100%.

Conclusion

The five Central Asian countries faced unanticipated challenges and major shocks after December 1991. During the difficult transition decade of the 1990s, the governments established nations with different market-based economies and similar super-presidential regimes. During the 1999–2014 resource boom, the five countries' experiences diverged in a different dimension, with Kazakhstan and Turkmenistan benefiting from large oil and gas windfall gains, Uzbekistan benefitting to a lesser extent from mineral exports, and the Kyrgyz Republic, Tajikistan and, to a lesser extent, Uzbekistan becoming sources of migrant labour to the booming Russian economy (Table 3.7). During these two periods, the five countries made little attempt to integrate into the global economy beyond exporting raw materials and unskilled labour.

Since 2014 there has been a general recognition in the region that the resource boom is over and economic diversification is necessary. Fortuitously, this new perspective coincides with changes that create a potential window of opportunity as overland transport links across Eurasia are becoming more important and efficient. Whether individual countries can seize the opportunity to trade to the east and the west will depend on domestic conditions and on regional cooperation, given the importance of transit arrangements for most Central Asian trade. There are positive harbingers in the late 2010s, especially in Uzbekistan which

Table 3.7 Economic and social indicators, 2015/2016

	Population	Life expectancy at birth	GDP	GDP per capita	GNI per cap @ PPP	GNI per cap @ PPP	External debt	Internet users	Armed forces
	2015	2015	2016[a]	2016[a]	2015[a]	2016	2015	2016	2015
	HDR	HDR	WDI	WDI	HDR	WDI	WDI	WDI	WDI
	Millions	Years	$ billion	$	International 2011 dollars		$ million	Per 100 people	Thousands
Kazakhstan	17.6	69.6	133.7 (217.9)	8710 (12,602)	22,093 (20,867)	22,910	13,624	54.9	71
Kyrgyz Republic	5.9	70.8	6.6 (7.4)	1100 (1269)	3097 (3044)	5920	2368	28.3	20
Tajikistan	8.5	69.6	7.0 (9.2)	1110 (1114)	2601 (2517)	3500	1700	17.5	16
Turkmenistan	5.4	65.7	36.2 (47.9)	6670 (9032)	14,026 (13,066)	16,060	247	12.2	37
Uzbekistan	29.9	69.4	67.2 (62.6)	2220 (2037)	5748 (5567)	6240	3795	43.6	68

Source Pomfret (2019a), based on UNDP *Human Development Report 2016*; World Bank *World Development Indicators*
[a]2014 in parentheses

is the largest and most centrally located country in Central Asia, but whether they will be followed by positive economic developments will only be seen in the 2020s.

Appendix: The Kashgar–Osh–Uzbekistan Railway

The Urumqi-Kashi (Kashgar) railway was completed in 2000. In the early 2000s, China proposed extending the railway with a Kashi-Andijon line, linking to Uzbekistan's rail network, and was supported by Uzbekistan.[16] The China–Kyrgyzstan–Uzbekistan railway would traverse and tunnel from China's far western rail terminus at Kashi to the Kyrgyz–Uzbek border at Kara-Su, 20 kilometres north of Osh. The new line would then connect with Fergana Valley's existing rail network, which links the region's major cities and the GM Uzbekistan plant in Andijon.[17] However, the project was dormant between 2005 and 2010 due to political instability in the Kyrgyz Republic and poor relations between presidents Bakiyev and Karimov.

After visiting China in April 2011, Kyrgyz Deputy Prime Minister (and later Prime Minister) Babanov suggested that the deal would be signed in a matter of months, with only the site of the transfer station and the source of funding left to be resolved. Kyrgyz railways are set at Russian wide gauge (1520 millimetres), while China's are standard gauge (1435 millimetres).[18] In late 2011, Babanov floated the idea that mineral concessions would be offered in exchange for Chinese

---

[16]For example, at the UNECE-ESCAP Third Expert Group Meeting on Developing Euro-Asian Transport Linkages held in Istanbul on 27–29 June 2005. https://www.unece.org/fileadmin/DAM/trans/main/eatl/docs/3rd_EGM_Doc3_e.pdf.

[17]Uzbekistan often refers to the project as an upgraded rail link Tashkent–Angren–Pap-Andijon–Osh–Irkeshtam–Kashi–Lianyungang. Lianyungang–Andijon is the route for Korean car components going to the GM Uzbekistan assembly plant.

[18]China may prefer to lay standard gauge track all the way to Andijon. However, if there is to be a south–north link to Bishkek creating a domestic rail network, then Kyrgyzstan would prefer the transfer to be at the China–Kyrgyz border (Smith, 2012). In February 2015, Kyrgyz President Atambayev was reported to have decided to build a change of gauge station at Tuz-Bel, 47 kilometres east of Kara-Su. https://24.kg/archive/en/bigtiraj/174417-news24.html/.

funding of the railway. Similar suggestions had been made by presidents Akayev and Bakiyev, both of whose regimes were discredited by public perceptions that the authorities were selling off the country to foreign interests, and Babanov's proposal was denounced by rival politicians, nationalists, and activists. By early 2012, President Atambayev was claiming the government had no intention of dealing minerals for infrastructure, and in any case China, not Kyrgyzstan would profit from operating the railway to recoup its investment (Smith, 2012).[19] Nevertheless, on his first official visit to Tashkent in June 2012, President Atambayev discussed the project in detail, and President Karimov confirmed Uzbekistan's interest. In June 2013, the new Chinese Ambassador in Bishkek in his first press conference underlined Beijing's desire to see the rail link completed.

In June 2016, Xi Jinping and Islam Karimov opened the Angren-Pap railway. The 19.2-kilometre Qamchiq Tunnel eliminates the need for Uzbek trains to transit Tajikistan to reach the Ferghana Valley from Tashkent and provides an all-weather alternative to the road over the 2267-metre Angren Pass.[20] By improving the onward connection to Tashkent and the main trunk lines of Central Asia, the Angren-Pap link increases the attractiveness of a railway from Kashgar to the Ferghana Valley. The China–Kyrgyzstan–Uzbekistan railway network could be integrated into China's Belt and Road Initiative via connections to ports in Pakistan, Iran and Turkey.

During the visit of Kyrgyz President Sooronbai Jeenbekov to Uzbekistan on 13 December 2017, the China–Kyrgyzstan–Uzbekistan railway came to the forefront as the most important infrastructure project. "In terms of the railway construction project, the working groups of the two countries will meet on December 25 this year. Already today we see the beginning of the practical implementation of the agreements

---

[19]Smith also speculated that "Russia and Kazakhstan may be quietly stifling the entire project, as it would weaken their control over Central Asia's trade with China. Kazakhstan is already improving its own rail connections with China to absorb excess demand, and Russia does not want Kyrgyzstan to become a transit country for Chinese goods yet again."

[20]The inaugural train from Angren to Pap passed through the tunnel in 16 minutes. The rail line, built by China Railway Tunnel Group, also includes 25 bridges and 6 viaducts (Maitra, 2017).

Fig. 3.3 Projected Kashgar–Osh–Uzbekistan railway (*Source* Author's creation based on https://www.un.org/Depts/Cartographic/map/profile/kyrgysta.pdf)

on the establishment of joint ventures and production lines," Jeenbekov said. Also, there were plans for the development of road transport and regular passenger routes.[21]

Although the Kyrgyz Republic is projected to earn up to $200 million per year in transit fees, as well as improving transport links

---

[21] A truck convoy pioneered the Andijon–Osh–Irkeshtam–Kashi road route in November 2017 with the intention of setting up regular freight services in 2018; "Andijan-Osh-Irkeshtam-Kashgar transport corridor to start operating as of Feb 25", *Tashkent Times* 19 February 2018.

within and beyond the country, there is domestic opposition to the Kashi to Kara-Su rail project. Some opposition is anti-Chinese, including concerns that the construction workers will be Chinese not Kyrgyz. The main critique is that an east-west line across southern Kyrgyzstan will further accentuate the country's north–south divisions, linking Osh more closely to Uzbekistan, and even China, than to Bishkek (Pale, 2015; Smith, 2012) (Fig. 3.3).[22]

References

Anderson, K., & Pomfret, R. (2003). *Consequences of creating a market economy: Evidence from household surveys in Central Asia*. Cheltenham: Edward Elgar.
Birkman, L., Kaloshnika, M., Khan, M., Shavurov, U., & Smallhouse, S. (2012). *Textile and apparel cluster in Kyrgyzstan*. Cambridge, MA: Harvard University Kennedy School and Harvard Business School.
Hurley, J., Morris, S., & Portelance, G. (2018). *Examining the debt implications of the Belt and Road Initiative from a policy perspective* (CGD Policy Paper No. 121). Washington, DC: Center for Global Development.
Jenish, N. (2014). *Export-driven SME development in Kyrgyzstan: The garment manufacturing sector* (Institute of Public Policy and Administration Working Paper No. 26). Bishkek: University of Central Asia.
Kaminski, B., & Mitra, S. (2012). *Borderless bazaars and regional integration in Central Asia: Emerging patterns of trade and cross-border cooperation*. Washington, DC: World Bank.
Maitra, R. (2017). *The multiple dimensions of China's 'One Belt One Road' in Uzbekistan*. Washington, DC: The Schiller Institute. Retrieved from http://www.schillerinstitute.org/economy/phys_econ/2016/1227-obor-uzbek/ou.html.
Pale, S. (2015). Kyrgyzstan and the Chinese 'New Silk Road'. *New Eastern Outlook*. Retrieved September 3, 2015, from http://journal-neo.org/2015/09/03/kyrgyzstan-and-the-chinese-new-silk-road/.

---

[22]Chinese governments favour the more direct and cheaper Irkeshtam route via Sary-Tash but this is a lightly populated part of the Kyrgyz Republic. Kyrgyz governments have favoured a route via Torugart, but rather than the direct route west to Kara-Su and Andijon would prefer a longer route but going north through At-Bashy and Kazarman.

Pomfret, R. (1995). *The economies of Central Asia*. Princeton, NJ: Princeton University Press.
Pomfret, R. (2002). *Constructing a market economy: Diverse paths from central planning in Asia and Europe*. Cheltenham, UK: Edward Elgar.
Pomfret, R. (2006). *The Central Asian economies since independence*. Princeton, NJ: Princeton University Press.
Pomfret, R. (2016). Currency union and disunion in Europe and the former Soviet Union. *CESifo Forum, 17*(4), 43–47.
Pomfret, R. (2019a). *The Central Asian economies in the twenty-first century: Paving a New Silk Road*. Princeton, NJ: Princeton University Press.
Pomfret, R. (2019b). The Eurasian Landbridge and China's Belt and Road Initiative: Demand, supply of services, and public policy. *The World Economy, 42*(6), 1642–1653.
Popov, V. (2001). Where do we stand a decade after the collapse of the USSR? *WIDER Angle, 2*, 6–8. Launching G. A. Cornia & V. Popov (Eds.), *Transition and institutions: The experience of gradual and late reformers*. Oxford, UK: UNU/WIDER Studies in Development Economics, Oxford University Press.
Smith, M. (2012). China–Kyrgyzstan–Uzbekistan railway project brings political risks. *Central Asia Caucasus Analyst*. Retrieved March 7, 2012, from https://www.cacianalyst.org/publications/analytical-articles/item/12459-analytical-articles-caci-analyst-2012-3-7-art-12459.html.
Spector, R. (2018). A regional production network in a predatory state: Export-oriented manufacturing at the margins of the law. *Review of International Political Economy, 25*(2), 169–189.
Tilekeyev, K. (2013). *Productivity implications of participation in export activities: The case of farmers in Talas Oblast of Kyrgyzstan* (Institute of Public Policy and Administration Working Paper No. 17). Bishkek: University of Central Asia.
Tilekeyev, K., Mogilevsky, R., Abdrazakova, N., & Dzhumaeva, S. (2018). *Production and exporting of kidney beans in the Kyrgyz Republic: Value chain analysis* (Institute of Public Policy and Administration Working Paper No. 43). Bishkek: University of Central Asia.

4

The Post-communist Transition of the Western Balkans: EUropeanisation with a Small Enlargement Carrot

Milenko Petrovic

Introduction

Following the collapse of communism in the late 1980s and the opening of the European Union's enlargement process to the east, only three post-communist states from the Balkans—Bulgaria, Romania and Croatia—were able to meet the required conditions and become members of the European Union alongside their Balkan neighbour Greece and the other 24 members of this organisation. The other Balkan states, which were labelled (together with Croatia) the 'Western Balkans' by the EU in the late 1990s are still waiting to be 'further EUropeanised' and meet the EU's accession conditions. While EU officials and a number of scholars (e.g. Cirtautas & Schimmelfennig, 2010; Huntington, 1993, 1996; Janos, 2000; Seroka, 2008) argue that the main cause of the 'Europeanisation delay' of the Western Balkans lies primarily in the inability of the states' sociopolitical structures to adopt core EU norms

M. Petrovic (✉)
University of Canterbury, Christchurch, New Zealand
e-mail: milenko.petrovic@canterbury.ac.nz

and values—particularly those related to the functioning of institutions of democracy and respect of the rule of law—the reality appears to be less clear cut. A closer look at the empirical facts reveals that the agent-driven actions from both sides—the EU and the political leadership of its leading member states on the one side, and the political elites of the Western Balkan states on the other—have played a much stronger role in the (non) Europeanisation of the latter group of states, than have structural factors.

While Balkan countries were socio-economically less developed than the countries of East Central Europe (ECE) and the Baltics, political developments and conditions of multiparty authoritarianism in all these countries (with the exception of Czechoslovakia) were very similar before they fell under communist rule after the Second World War (Crampton, 1997; Petrovic, 2013; Rotshield, 1974). Forty years of communist institutional and ideological rebuilding have further equalised political and socio-economic conditions throughout the communist world. If there was an impact of past legacies on political and socio-economic developments and the different pace of post-communist transition after the collapse of communism, it was primarily related to the existence of differences in the character and strength of communist rule in particular groups of communist states and the impact that these differences have had on the formation (or non-formation) of pro-reformist and pro-EU political elites. As defined and argued by this author in his 2013 monograph (Petrovic, 2013), the key role in the creation of important anti-communist national(ist) and/or liberal democratic political alternatives in the ECE communist states played some weaknesses in rule of domestic communist elites, combined with a history of violent Soviet (or Soviet-driven) suppression of major protests and incentives for change or reform (Ekiert, 1996, 2003) and the existence of strong anti-Russian and anti-Soviet sentiment in the Baltic states, Poland and Hungary (but not in Czechoslovakia). The virtual non-existence of such political alternatives and, consequently, their pro-reformist post-communist successors in four Balkan communist states[1] was primarily the result of the firm rule of domestic communist leaders who were able (in contrast to their counterparts in ECE) to secure some legitimacy for their rule. Some specific socio-economic structures established in these states throughout the period of communist rule, particularly those related to extensive industrialization and to (the related) significant increase in people's living standards during the period from the early 1950s to the mid-1970s were only of secondary importance in this regard. It was a corrective factor which helped the Balkan communists to (partially) legitimise their dictatorial rule (Petrovic, 2013, Chapter 3). Hence, the slow progress of all the Balkan states in post-communist reform and EUropeanisation (i.e. adoption of the core EU values and norms through the EU association and accession process—see section "EUropeanisation with an Ever-Increasing Number and Toughness of Conditions") during the 1990s, was a direct result of the lack of liberal democratic political forces and the establishment of the political system of so-called illiberal democracy[2] in these states after the collapse of communist rule.

However, if the Balkan peoples and their political leaders (most of whom were the members of the former communist *nomenklatura*) bear unto themselves the largest share of responsibility for the non-reformist pathways of their countries and the consequent establishment of much weaker links with the EU during the 1990s, they can hardly be (solely) blamed for the continuation of the slow pace of Europeanisation of their countries after the early 2000s, when all the Balkan states had elected pro-reformist and pro-EU governments. While the EU was fairly generous in providing accession assistance to the ECE and Baltic

---

[1]Albania, Bulgaria, Romania and Yugoslavia. After the violent dissolution of communist Yugoslavia in the early 1990s and separation of Montenegro and Kosovo from Serbia in 2006 and 2008, respectively, the present 'country account' of post-Yugoslav states in addition to these three also includes Slovenia, Croatia, Bosnia and Herzegovina and North Macedonia (whose official name was FYR Macedonia until February 2019—see Footnote 12).

[2]which pretended rather than introduced necessary political democratisation and economic transformation/marketisation (Petrovic, 2013, pp. 108–113; Vachudova, 2005, pp. 37–59; Zakaria, 1977).

states during the 1990s and early 2000s, the accession offer given to the Western Balkan states in the Thessaloniki Agenda of 2003[3] was more conditional from the very beginning. Not only did the EU already in 2006 tighten the 1993 Copenhagen conditions for the Western Balkan membership candidates, but it has (in order to 'avoid repeating mistakes' from the 2004/07 enlargement round) continued to make these conditions even tougher and to introduce additional accession conditions for these states ever since.

The following section of the paper explains how the ever-increasing number and toughness of the accession conditions has become the main cause of the very slow progress of the Western Balkan states in their bid towards EU membership. The third, final section of the paper critically addresses the prospects for completing the accession process and (consequently) the further Europeanisation of these states through the prism of the current (tightened) accession conditions.

EUropeanisation with an Ever-Increasing Number and Toughness of Conditions

Although it is generally used in a much broader sense and related to the transfer of political, socio-economic and cultural values, norms and attitudes developed in (predominantly Western) European countries and societies to non-European countries (Featherstone, 2003; Flockhart, 2010), the meaning of the term 'Europeanisation' in the modern political science literature dominantly corresponds to the process of European integration, and is in fact EU-centric (Flockhart, 2010, p. 789). It is primarily used to define the process of transfer (and adoption) of norms, procedures and regulations which exist at the EU level to the political, legal and social structures of the member states (Radealli, 2003) or to the countries which wish to become EU

---

[3] *The Thessaloniki agenda for the Western Balkans: Moving towards European Integration*, adopted by the conclusions of the EU General Affairs and External Relations Council of 16 June 2003 and endorsed in the conclusions (Art. 41) of the European Thessaloniki Council of 19–20 June 2003.

members (Grabbe, 2003, 2006). The term will be used in this chapter as given in its title—'EUropeanisation', i.e. in the context of the ability of candidate countries for EU membership to meet the EU's accession conditions and thereby comply with and adopt the core EU values and norms[4] which are incorporated in the accession conditions (Manners, 2002). While Ian Manners in his seminal paper identifies five core norms which comprise the EU's normative power or 'normative power Europe',[5] this chapter focuses on those core accession conditions (i.e. values and norms) for which the measurement tools have been developed and extensively utilised by undisputed international research centres and organisations. The Freedom House's democracy score, Transparency International's Corruption Perception Index (TICPI) and indicators of economic transition from the European Bank for Reconstruction and Development (EBRD) will be used as the basic denominators of successful compliance with the accession conditions and thereby the successful adoption of EU values and norms by individual countries.

As discussed in the introduction, slow progress in post-communist transition and EUropeanisation of all the Balkan countries in the years following the collapse of communist rule was a direct consequence of the political conditions in which regime change occurred in these countries. Political elites in ECE and the Baltic states, mainly recruited from the former anti-communist (and pro-Western) liberal democratic opposition, rushed to pull their countries out of the deep economic and social crisis of the early 1990s (Lavigne, 1999, Chapters 4–7; Petrovic, 2013, Chapter 1) by anchoring their post-communist reforms and economic transformation to the establishment

---

[4]However, at places where the discussion considers the adoption of (Western) European values and norms in a broader sense, not directly related to the adoption of EU regulations and norms through the accession process, the term will be referred to without a capital 'U'—'Europeanisation'.

[5]*Peace, liberty democracy*, the *rule of law*, and respect for *human rights*, 'all of which are expressed in the preamble and founding principles of the TEU, the development co-operation policy of the Community (TEC art. 177), the common foreign and security provisions of the Union (TEC art. 11), and the membership criteria adopted at the Copenhagen European Council in 1993' (Manners, 2002, p. 242).

of closer ties and (after 1993) the process of accession to the EU. However, the post-communist political elites in the Balkan states were dominated by members of the former communist nomenklatura who preferred an 'illiberal concept' of democracy (see Footnote 2) and were therefore not genuinely interested in substantial reforms and even less so in obtaining the EU's conditional assistance for reforms. Moreover, the successor states of former Yugoslavia sank into wars and ethnic conflicts. Under such conditions one certainly could not have expected the Balkan post-communist states to be able to meet any of the basic accession conditions defined at the European Council meeting in June 1993: '[s]tability of institutions guaranteeing democracy, the rule of law, human rights and respect for and protection of minorities, the existence of a functioning market economy…' (European Council, 1993, 7.A. iii). Nevertheless, as soon as governmental power was taken by 'real reformers' and pro-European political actors in Romania and Bulgaria in 1996 and 1997, respectively, relations between these two and the EU improved, and they opened accession negotiations in February 2000, together with three 'late reformers' from ECE and the Baltics: Slovakia, Latvia and Lithuania (see indicators in Table 4.1). Soon after, significant acceleration in the post-communist political and economic transition of these two countries[6] was rewarded by membership of the EU, on 1 January 2007 (only two and a half years after the ECE and the Baltic states had joined on 1 May 2004).

While foreign financial and economic assistance was enormously important for all of the countries that, after 40 years of communist economic underachievement, had fallen in the deep transitional socio-economic crisis, the EU's conditional offer of membership and the opening of accession negotiations (which also included significant financial assistance), was the most valuable assistance by far in conducting and consolidating economic reforms and democratic institutions in post-communist states. By being required to fulfil the above-defined accession conditions through successful negotiation of the 31 (35 after

---

[6]However, the level of corruption in them remained very high throughout a long period after their accession (Table 2).

Table 4.1 Indicators of post-communist democratisation and marketisation

	Democracy score*			TICPI***				Economic transition**		
	1999	2006	2014	2017	1999	2006	2014	2017	1999	2006	2014[a]
Hungary	*1.88*	*2.14*	*2.96*	*3.71*	*52*	*52*	*54*	*45*	*3.7*	*3.9*	*3.9*
Poland	*1.58*	*2.36*	*2.18*	*2.89*	*42*	*37*	*61*	*60*	*3.5*	*3.7*	*4.1*
Slovakia	*2.71*	*2.14*	*2.61*	*2.61*	*37*	*47*	*51*	*50*	*3.3*	*3.7*	*4.0*
Latvia	*2.29*	*2.07*	*2.07*	*2.07*	*34*	*47*	*55*	*58*	*3.1*	*3.6*	*3.9*
Lithuania	*2.29*	*2.29*	*2.36*	*2.36*	*38*	*48*	*58*	*59*	*3.1*	*3.7*	*3.9*
Romania	3.54	3.29	3.46	3.46	33	31	43	48	2.8	3.3	3.7
Bulgaria	3.58	2.89	3.29	3.39	33	40	43	43	2.8	3.5	3.7
Croatia	4.46	3.75	3.68	3.75	27	34	48	49	3.0	3.5	3.8
N. Macedonia	3.83	3.82	4.07	4.36	33	27	45	35	2.7	3.1	3.6
Albania	4.75	3.82	4.14	4.11	23	26	33	38	2.6	2.9	3.5
Bosnia-Hrz	5.42	4.04	4.46	4.64	N/A	29	39	38	2.0	2.6	3.1
Montenegro	5.50	3.93	3.89	3.93	N/A	N/A	42	46	1.6	2.5	3.3
Serbia	5.50	3.68	3.68	3.96	24	27	41	41	1.4	2.7	3.2
Kosovo	N/A	N/A	5.14	4.93	N/A	N/A	33	39	N/A	N/A	2.9

Source Freedom House, Nations in Transit (various years); EBRD, Transition Report (various years); Transparency International, Corruption Perception Index (various years)

[a]The EBRD significantly changed its methodology for calculating indicators of economic transition after 2014 so that the data for more recent years are incomparable to those of previous years and could not be included in the table

*Freedom House, Nations in Transit (NIT) 'democracy score' (1 being the highest: full democracy; 7 being the lowest). As the NIT publication (issued annually in June) shows the state of play during the previous year, the scores given in the above table for particular years (e.g. 2017) are actually published in the NIT publication for the following year (2018 in this case)

**EBRD economic transition indicators (4.33 = standards of advanced industrial [market]economies; 1 = standards of a centrally planned economy)

***Transparency International's Corruption Perception Index (100 being very clean; 0 being highly corrupt)

2005—see below) negotiation ('acquis') chapters, which represent the body of EU laws and regulations and cover the complete legal and institutional framework for the functioning of a country's economic and sociopolitical system, the candidate countries have in the same time received a design, content and instructions for how to introduce necessary post-communist reforms. The opening of the accession negotiations process with the EU has therefore significantly sped up and contributed to the successful building of democratic and market economy institutions in the candidate countries from former communist Europe, as none of them had any previous experience or resources for constructing and setting these up on their own.[7]

However, Albania and the ever-increasing number of successor states of former Yugoslavia (excluding Slovenia) had to wait much longer to receive the EU's invitation for accession and, with it, necessary support and assistance for their post-communist political and economic transformation. The first comprehensive EU incentive for closer cooperation with this group of post-communist states, which have been labelled the 'Western Balkans' was launched after the conclusion of the wars in Croatia and Bosnia and Herzegovina (B-H) in the mid-1990s, and its main objective was to restore peace and stability in the region together with boosting post-communist reforms. It was initially named the 'coherent strategy' and quickly evolved into the 'Stabilisation and Association Process' (SAP).[8] The SAP gained importance after the death of the Croatian authoritarian president Tudjman in December 1999 and the overthrow of the Serbian post-communist dictator Milošević in October the following year, when the two largest Western Balkan states finally obtained pro-reformist and pro-EUropean governments. The prospects for full EUropeanisation of the Balkans appeared to be highly promising by the adoption of the 'Thessaloniki Agenda' in June 2003, which clearly stated:

---

[7] The importance of the opening of the accession negotiation process, as the most important form of external assistance for the successful post-communist economic and sociopolitical transition of a former communist state, is discussed in greater detail in Petrovic (2017) (see also Lavigne, 1999; Petrovic, 2013; Pridham, 2005; Vachudova, 2005).

[8] For more details on this see EU General Affairs Council (1997) and EU General Affairs Council (1999).

The Western Balkans and support for preparation for future integration into European structures and ultimate membership into the Union is a high priority for the EU. The Balkans will be an integral part of a united Europe. (paragraph 2)

These political changes in the Western Balkan states and their improved relations and intensified cooperation with the EU were quickly effectuated through a very rapid improvement of democratic conditions, and the strong economic transformation of these states throughout the first half of the 2010s (Table 4.1). However, enlargement enthusiasm and hopes for the relatively quick accession of the Western Balkan states to the EU did not last long. Even before its mega-enlargement was completed with the accession of Bulgaria and Romania in 2007, the EU decided to 'renew [the] consensus on enlargement' (European Council, 2006, point 4). Adopted under the pressure of emerging *enlargement fatigue* and fears for the EU's 'absorption/enlargement capacity' (Petrovic, 2009; Petrovic & Smith, 2013; Phinnemore, 2006), the 'renewed consensus on enlargement' did not have any other purpose but to tighten accession conditions for new applicants. From that moment on, the basic objective of EU 'enlargement policy' towards the Western Balkan states was not to further speed up the accession of these states, but rather to try to avoid 'mistakes' from the previous enlargement rounds, particularly those related to the 'premature' accession of Romania and Bulgaria (Grabbe, 2014; Vachudova, 2014).

Instead of receiving further assistance and encouragement to complete the remaining necessary reforms that could enable them to more quickly and easily meet the existing accession conditions, the Western Balkan states have been given the tightened (second layer of) Copenhagen accession conditions (European Commission, 2006; European Council, 2006) and (rightfully deserved) SAP conditions regarding post-war reconciliation and peace-building in the region—both groups of conditions from which countries of the 2004/07 enlargement round were spared. Moreover, on top of these conditions, the Western Balkan candidates and potential candidates for EU membership also received the fourth layer of 'Copenhagen plus -plus -plus conditions' (Petrovic, 2017; Petrovic & Smith, 2013) in the form of requests for compliance with the EU's state-building incentives and proposals for solving intraregional disputes related to the contested statehood status of most Western Balkan states.[9] While the EU's request for the fulfilment of the Copenhagen accession conditions has, as discussed above, been of great assistance to the ECE and the Baltic post-communist states, through providing them with advice and guidelines for building democratic institutions and a market economy, the EU's request for compliance with its proposals for solving intraregional and intra-national statehood disputes was often a 'pure burden' on the Western Balkan states, which could not have much assisted, but only postponed, their EUropeanisation. As argued in Petrovic 2013, Chapter 5 (see also Bieber, 2011; Noutcheva 2009, 2012; Petrovic, 2017) most of these proposals and incentives, especially those regarding the centralisation of Bosnia and Herzegovina, the recognition of Kosovo's independence and the resolution of the Greek—North Macedonian dispute regarding the 'naming issue' did not only put 'high political costs of compliance on the targeted governments' (Schimmelfennig, 2008) but were also inappropriately formulated (or not formulated at all, with regards to the Greek-Macedonian dispute), with very little respect for the countries' specifics and realistic chances of meeting them. Despite some successes in initiating and managing the Belgrade-Pristina dialogue and maintaining peace and stability in B-H and Kosovo (foremost by the use of EU civil and military/police missions) these EU incentives were obvious examples of external demands which did not consider 'the strategic behaviour of domestic actors and constrains they face…[and therefore] neglect[ed] the rational interests of domestic actors and the dynamics of two-level game negotiations' (Börzel & Grimm, 2018, p. 124).

However, the list of hurdles which the Western Balkan states have had to face on their way to eventual EU membership did not end here. After the 'enlargement enthusiasm' in the core EU member states sank further with the emergence of the global financial and economic crisis

---

[9]Of all the Western Balkan states only Croatia, Montenegro and Albania were spared of this 'fourth layer' of accession conditions that related to the disputed statehood status of B-H, Kosovo (and Serbia) and North Macedonia.

of 2008/09, with the outbreak of the Eurozone crisis in 2010 and when it became certain that Croatia would join in 2013, the EU decided to further tighten the accession process for the new candidates, i.e. for the Western Balkan states.[10] This time the accession conditions were not officially changed, but the Commission decided to 'put particular emphasis on the three pillars of the rule of law, economic governance and public administration reform' (European Commission, 2014, p. 1). In other words, it was decided that the accession negotiations chapters which cover these three pillars should be opened among the first, and thoroughly negotiated to ensure 'a stronger focus on addressing fundamental reforms [in the candidate countries] early in the enlargement process' (ibid., p. 1). It was expected that the candidate countries would in this way be better prepared for accession (than was the case in the previous enlargement rounds) and therewith also ensure that 'enlargement is not at the expense of the effectiveness of the Union' (ibid., p. 1).

In this way the Western Balkan states have been, unlike the ECE and the Baltic post-communist states and even their Balkan neighbours Bulgaria and Romania, exposed to an ever-increasing number of conditions that they needed to meet on their way to EU accession. While such an EU approach can partially be grounded in a genuine need to assure the successful building of state and government institutions in the largely dysfunctional Bosnia and Herzegovina and Kosovo (and to some extent also in Albania which suffered from an enormously high level of corruption and weak governance—see e.g. Bogdani, 2015), it was largely counterproductive in the cases of Serbia, Montenegro and North Macedonia. By 2006, these three Western Balkan states were more or less on the same level of consolidation of their democratic institutions with that of Bulgaria, Romania and Croatia at the time when they opened accession negotiations with the EU in 2000 and 2005, respectively (compare indicators in Table 4.1, see also Petrovic & Smith, 2013).

---

[10]By that time Turkey's accession had effectively fallen from the enlargement agenda due to both increased opposition to it in the leading EU member states and internal developments in Turkey, particularly President Erdogan's increased authoritarianism and his lack of desire to comply with EU demands and meet accession conditions.

All in all, neither the tightened accession conditions of 2006 nor the 'three pillar' approach after 2012/2014 have contributed to significant improvements in the democratisation of any of the Western Balkan states (Table 4.1), but they definitely increased the burden (and time) to these states in acceding to the EU. If the success of the process of Europeanisation through enlargement conditionality is strongly determined by the credible membership perspective and the clarity and consistency of the accession conditions (Schimmelfennig, 2008; Zhelyazkova, Damjanovski, Nechev, & Schimmelfenning, 2018), and these two have not only been largely ignored but also accompanied with requirements for solving complex intraregional statehood disputes that did not have many chances to be positively responded by the domestic political elites—then it is obvious that the ability and/or capacity of the candidate countries to comply with the given accession conditions has become an insignificant criterion of successful accession/EUropeanisation. A state cannot be blamed for not meeting certain accession criteria if the criteria has not been clearly and realistically set, nor if the state is uncertain of the consequences of compliance and non-compliance.[11]

Can They Ever Be EUropeanised?

The ever-increasing toughness, number and vague character of some of the accession conditions had, as discussed in the previous section, significantly increased difficulties for the candidate states in meeting these conditions and resulted in the more or less completely stalled process of accession of the Western Balkan states to the EU during the

---

[11] In the thus far most comprehensively conceptualised theoretical explanation of Europeanisation through EU enlargement conditionality, Schimmelfenig (2008), following his and Sedelmeier's conceptualisation of 'the external incentives model of conditionality and Europeanization' (2005), identifies the following three crucial requirements for successful (external) Europeanisation: (i) the [credible] conditional offer of EU membership to the target government; (ii) the normative consistency of the EU's enlargement decisions; and (iii) low political compliance costs of the target government (p. 921). The third requirement also includes the 'capacity of candidate countries [to adopt and implement the suggested conditions/norms]' (Zhelyazkova et al., 2018, p. 19).

Table 4.2 Progress in EU accession

	Signed associa- tion/SA agreement	Entered into force	Membership application	Accession negoti- ations opened	Accession negoti- ations closed
Poland	16.12.1991	1.02.1994	1.04.1994	31.03.1998	12.12.2002
Hungary	16.12.1991	1.02.1994	8.04.1994	31.03.1998	12.12.2002
Slovakia	4.10.1993[a]	1.02.1995	27.06.1995	15.02.2000	12.12.2002
Latvia	12.06.1995	1.02.1998	27.10.1995	15.02.2000	12.12.2002
Lithuania	12.06.1995	1.02.1998	8.12.1995	15.02.2000	12.12.2002
Bulgaria	8.03.1993	1.02.1995	14.12.1995	15.02.2000	16.12.2004
Romania	1.02.1993	1.02.1995	22.06.1995	15.02.2000	16.12.2004
Albania	12.06.2006	1.04.2009	28.04.2009	No	No
Bosnia-Herzeg	16.06.2008	1.06.2015	15.02.2016	No	No
Croatia	9.04.2001	1.02.2005	20.02.2003	5.10.2005	30.06.2012
N. Macedonia	9.04.2001	1.04.2004	22.03.2004	No	No
Montenegro	15.10.2007	1.05.2010	15.12.2008	16.06.2012	No
Serbia	29.04.2008	1.09.2013	22.12.2009	14.01.2014 provis.[b]	No
Kosovo	27.10.2015	1.04.2016	No	No	No

Source European Commission Archive on Past Enlargements and other documents
[a]Czechoslovakia—16.12.1991
[b]The first chapters (35 and 32) were opened on 14 December 2015

first half of this decade (see Table 4.2). The only two exceptions were Montenegro and (since 2012 and particularly 2014) Serbia. The moderate progress in accession of these two, had however very little to do with their EUropeanisation through the adoption of the EU's norms and values incorporated in the (tightened) Copenhagen accession conditions, particularly not those related to the democracy standards and the rule of law (the first and the most import pillar in the post-2012 EU 'three pillars approach'). In accordance to its general approach to relations with neighbouring countries that the EU adopted after the emergence of enlargement fatigue in the mid-2000s and strengthened during the multiple crises that it faced after 2009/2010, the EU has almost exclusively insisted on compliance with its stability and security priorities in its relations with the Western Balkan candidates

(Bieber, 2018; Juncos & Whitman, 2015; Pomorska & Noutcheva, 2017). As these goals were mainly incorporated in the above discussed ill-prepared and often controversial EU incentives and proposals for solving intraregional (and intra-national) statehood disputes, such an approach could only have produced mixed, if not controversial outcomes. This explains why Montenegro, the country with a not very convincing democratic record, became the regional frontrunner in the accession process.

Although Serbia and North Macedonia have reached a similar (and in some respects higher) level of EUropeanisation than Montenegro (measured by the indicators shown in Table 4.1) and have not been led by a 'strong man', uninterruptedly for nearly three decades,[12] the progress in EU accession of these two countries was significantly slower than in the case of Montenegrin. The only reason for this was the EU's assessment of their (mainly unsatisfactory) record in contributing to the [re]solution of the statehood disputes in the region. As discussed in greater detail in Petrovic (2017), the cornerstone in Serbia's accession had become its 'commitment and achieved further progress... in the Belgrade-Pristina dialogue' (EU General Affairs Council, 2012, p. 1), whereas North Macedonia had to solve its dispute with Greece about its very name. Hence, while Montenegro, which has not had to comply with additional political demands related to regional statehood disputes, was allowed to open the accession negotiations earlier and has, as of June 2019, opened 32 (and closed 3) of 35 negotiating chapters, Serbia has (only) opened 17 chapters (two of them closed) in the same time (European Commission, 2019). North Macedonia, which until

---

[12]Montenegro is the only post-communist state in Europe which has never experienced an electoral change of ruling party or leader. The Democratic Party of Montenegrin Socialists (formerly the League of Montenegrin Communists) and its leader, Milo Djukanović have been in power throughout the whole period of post-communist (and even the last few years of communist) history of the country. Djukanović himself has served six terms as prime minister and two as president of the country during this period. He is current President of the country, elected in the election held on 18 May 2018 (for more details see e.g. Hopkins, 2012; Tomovic, 2016; Vachudova, 2014).

very recently was not able to make any progress in talks with Greece[13] is however still waiting to open accession negotiations (Table 4.2).

This approach by the EU to the Western Balkan states' accession, which prioritised regional and national political stability (as it was understood and defined in the respective EU policy incentives), rather than meeting democracy standards and progressing with other necessary socio-economic reforms, has not only further slowed down the accession (and therefore Europeanisation) of these states, but it also had certain backslide effects on the sociopolitical stability and successful implementation of earlier introduced reforms in these states. These were especially strong in North Macedonia and Bosnia and Herzegovina, although respect for democratic standards and the rule of law in Serbia has also deteriorated in recent years (Table 4.1).[14] While Serbia and Kosovo were able to make some progress (not without the considerable assistance of the European Commission and High Representative Mogherini—see European Commission, 2018a, pp. 51–52) in the 'Belgrade- Pristina dialogue' and for it were awarded with some headway in the accession process, the accession of both North Macedonia and B-H completely stalled after the late 2000s (Table 4.2).

The EU's inaction in 'the naming issue' and its waiting for the Macedonian and Greek political leaderships to solve it more or less by themselves (which they were unable to do for almost three decades)[15] and the consequent continuous postponement of the opening accession negotiations, have started to significantly cool off enlargement expectations (let alone enthusiasm) in North Macedonia. This has further contributed to an increase of political animosities and social unrest

---

[13]Due to its potential expansionistic connotation regarding the northern Greek province with the same name, Greece strongly opposed the use of the domestically preferred term 'Macedonia' as this country's name. As a result, the country was admitted to the UN in 1992 under the 'provisional' name 'Former Yugoslav Republic of Macedonia (FYRM)' which was in official use until February 2019. In accordance to the Prespes agreement signed by the Greek and (then) FYRM governments in June 2018 (Klapsis, 2018; Tzallas, 2018) the latter's name changed to North Macedonia which is now its internationally recognised name.

[14]See also Vachudova (2018) and Freedom House (2019).

[15]The two countries had agreed already in 1995, when they formalised bilateral relations to negotiate this problem under the auspices of the United Nations; however, these negotiations have been very occasional and informal and (until very recently) without any resolute political incentive which could have moved them forward.

that in 2015 and 2016 brought the country to the brink of civil war (see Bechev, 2015; Petrovic, 2017). Similarly, in B-H the EU in the late 2000s defined the necessity of the country's constitutional change towards greater centralisation and strengthening of the role of federal institutions as the *sine qua non* for its progress in the SA and accession process.[16] However, this 'necessity' was strongly opposed by the Bosnian Serb politicians and population (and to a large extent by the Bosnian Croats as well) and had zero chance of being consensually adopted at the national level (as required by the country's constitution—see e.g. Balkaninside, 2014; Inserbia.info, 2015). As such, this EU's requirement not only stopped the country's progress in the SAP process, but became an additional source of ethnic animosities and political conflicts which resulted in destabilisation rather than consolidation of democratic institutions in the country as a whole. Therefore, speaking in terms of EUropeanisation, it could be said that the EU with the above policy of inappropriate incentives or a lack of incentives for the resolution of intraregional and intra-national political disputes related to the statehood status, obstructed rather than supported the EUropeanisation of these two Western Balkan states during the first half of this decade.

By the mid-2010s, it seemed that the EU itself began to be aware of the backsliding effects of its state-building and conflict resolution policies in the Western Balkans and of its (too) restrained approach towards Western Balkan accession. It therefore launched the so-called Berlin Process in 2014, aimed to deliver certain policy measures that could speed up EU accession of the Western Balkan states through regular high-level meetings between the six Western Balkan governments and several EU Member States (Juncos & Whitman, 2015; Vurmo, 2018). Following this line, the European Commission stated in its 2015 report on (then FYR) Macedonia (European Commission, 2015a) that 'the last decade's reforms are being undermined...' and the EU council initiated in December 2014

---

[16]See European Commission, *Annual Progress Reports on Bosnia-Herzego-vina* for all years in the period 2007–2015 available from the Commission's website as well as Bieber (2010), Noutcheva (2012), and Tzifakis (2012).

(EU Foreign Affairs Council, 2014) a change to its approach towards developments in Bosnia and Herzegovina. It placed a focus on the solution of the 'outstanding socio-economic challenges [B-H] faces' (European Commission, 2015b, p. 4), rather than on changes to its constitutional order. This resulted in the quick adoption of the so-called 'Reform Agenda for Bosnia and Herzegovina 2015–2018' by all three levels of the government of Bosnia and Herzegovina (including those of the two entities) in July 2015 (Delegation of the European Union…, 2015). The Reform Agenda initiated common reform actions which were supported by the leaderships of all three major Bosnian and Herzegovinian ethnic groups and led to the adoption of legislative changes for the organisation of the local elections in October 2016, alongside some progress in the fight against corruption and organised crime (European Commission, 2016, pp. 5–6). These positive steps in the implementation of the Agenda were relatively quickly rewarded with the EU's decision to allow the Bosnian and Herzegovinian leadership to formally submit its application for EU membership in February 2016 (Table 4.2).

Following the launch of the Berlin Process, during 2015 and 2016 the EU and the Commission in particular were also busy trying to handle explosive developments in (then) FYR Macedonia (Bechev, 2015; Petrovic, 2017) which were brought back to 'normal' only after negotiations led by EU Commissioner Hahn brokered an agreement between the four Macedonian major parties on a 'tender truce' and the early elections in April 2016 (European Commission, 2015b). The elections, which were eventually held in November 2016, were won by the centre-right VMRO party of the incumbent semi-authoritarian Prime Minister Gruevski, but with a very slim majority which did not enable him to form a new government. After several months of negotiations there was formed the current coalition government led by Prime Minister Zaev (see e.g. Testorides, 2017) the leader of the Social Democratic Union of Macedonia (SDSM). As earlier stated 'less nationalist' and more open to compromise Zaev was able to finally solve the 'naming issue' with Greece in early June 2018 and in that way pave the way for his country to open the accession negotiations with the EU. These however, are still on hold (due to some 'new' internal EU dilemmas about its further enlargement—see below) despite the EU's earlier promises and high expectations in North Macedonia.

Optimism and expectations among the Western Balkan political elites particularly raised after the European Commission President Junker's announcement in his 2017 State of the Union speech (European Commission, 2017) that the EU can expect to enlarge its membership by 2025. However, the European Commission's Western Balkan Enlargement Strategy issued in February 2018, French President Macron's repeated statements that the 'recent enlargement[s] have weakened Europe' (Gray 2018) and even some of Junker's own later 'clarifications'[17] have considerably cooled this optimism and once again sent mixed signals to the Western Balkan states. Although the basic message of the strategy and the later-issued Commission's progress reports on the Western Balkan candidates and potential candidates for membership have tried to sound 'in line' with Junker's optimistic announcement, the outlined 'circumstances' under which this could happen can hardly be considered particularly encouraging for the Western Balkan aspirants to EU membership. In addition to the Commission's repeated insistence on further democratisation and the tightened criteria for closing Chapters 23 and 24 (on the rule of law, fundamental rights, freedom and security) the 2018 February Strategy also defined another 'hidden' accession condition for all the Western Balkan membership candidates—a requirement that they need to solve all their 'bilateral disputes…as a matter of urgency' (European Commission, 2018b, p. 7). This seems to be particularly demanding and challenging for the regional political elites. While Montenegro hopes to solve its only remaining (though nearly thirty-year-old) dispute with Croatia over the sea border relatively soon, the second regional frontrunner for EU membership, Serbia, and most of the remaining Western Balkan states have, as shown above, many more (and more serious) problems to resolve with their neighbours. Serbia also has to meet a particularly

---

[17]'The date we are indicating, 2025 is an indication not a promise. We have to know that in the old Europe, the western part of Europe but not only there, there is a kind of enlargement fatigue and this is obviously the case as far as Serbia and Montenegro are concerned' (Juncker, 2018).

challenging additional accession criterion (incorporated in negotiations of Chapter 35), which none of the previous candidates for EU membership have ever had to meet: to 'normalise' relations with its former province of Kosovo, which unilaterally declared its independence in 2008.[18] In accordance with the above-mentioned condition on the 'urgent' resolution of bilateral regional disputes in the Commission's 2018 strategy, Serbia is expected to sign a 'legally binding agreement' which will guarantee 'the full normalisation of [Serbia's] relations with Kosovo' (European Commission, 2018a, p. 4).

Although moderate progress has been achieved in relations between Kosovo and Serbia over the years that followed the launch of the EU facilitated 'Belgrade-Pristina dialogue' in Brussels in 2011, and the two parties had come quite close to a 'compromise solution' by late August 2018, inner divisions and views among EU officials and member states have effectively torpedoed the finalisation of the deal that could lead towards the signing of a 'legally binding agreement'. While the main EU officials—the High Representative Mogherini (who personally chaired the Brussels talks between the two presidents) and the Commissioner Hahn—and some EU member states (foremost Austria, Italy and Greece), together with the current US administration have supported the possible 'compromise solution' informally suggested by Serbia's and Kosovo's presidents Vucic and Thachi,[19] the leaders of other EU member states, particularly the UK and Germany, have resolutely rejected it. Claiming that any deal between the two parties that would include a 'redraw of borders' could be taken as precedent for other states with similar issues (foremost Bosnia and Herzegovina) and destabilise the region (Rettman, 2018), the latter have not only

---

[18]Kosovo's independence is still not officially recognised by Serbia, the UN and many other states (including 5 EU member states), but it is recognised by over 100 members of the UN and many important international organisations, such as the IMF, World Bank and (de facto) the EU itself.

[19]The main points of which are Serbia's recognition of Kosovo's independence in exchange for the alteration of current borders between the two (so that four Serb municipalities in north Kosovo will be swapped for one Albanian dominantly populated municipality in southern Serbia—see Gotev [2017]; *Politico*, August 2018) and securement of an exterritorial status for the Serbian monasteries in Kosovo (and perhaps some limited, mainly cultural autonomy for a few Serbian enclaves which will remain in Kosovo).

obstructed the 'done deal' which could have strongly boosted the EU accession bids of both Serbia and Kosovo, but have also encouraged nationalist and anti-EU stances in both governments. After the Kosovo Prime Minister Haradinaj (who also is a staunch opponent of any deal with Serbia which would include the border changes) increased the taxes on all good imports from Serbia for 100% in November 2018 (RadioFreeEurope RadioLiberty, 2019b) and Serbia's President Vucic repeatedly stated that Serbia will never recognise Kosovo if it does not get 'something in return' (RadioFreeEurope RadioLiberty, 2019a), Serbia and Kosovo seem to be further from finding a common stance and signing the 'legally binding agreement' than they have ever been since the beginning of their Brussels talks.

Conclusion

The slower EUropeanisation of the Western Balkan states in comparison with their post-communist counterparts that joined the EU in the previous enlargement rounds is not caused by their inadequate structural capacity to complete post-communist democratisation and socio-economic transition and adopt core EU values and norms. Rather, it is the result of decisions made by political elites in the Western Balkan states and in the EU. While all the Western Balkan states as well as Bulgaria and Romania were ruled by illiberal political leaders during the 1990s, who were not interested in post-communist reform and the EUropeanisation of their countries, the reasons for the postponed EUropeanisation of these states in the 2010s should be primarily sought in the lack of genuine interest of political elites in core EU member states in EU enlargement into the Western Balkans. Instead of providing more generous technical and financial assistance for reform which could have enabled the Western Balkan candidates and potential candidates for accession to meet the accession conditions easier, the EU after 2006 tightened the Copenhagen conditions for them and started to subject their accession to the fulfilment of additional political conditions which have little to do with post-communist democratisation and socio-economic transition but much more with regional stability and security. While Montenegro and Albania (and earlier Croatia) were spared requirements to comply with the additional EU conditions related to intraregional and intra-national disputes about statehood status, progress in the accession process of other candidates for EU membership from the Western Balkans in recent years has almost exclusively been determined by the EU's assessments of their compliance with this group of conditions. These additional accession conditions (or EU incentives) were often inappropriately formulated, with very little respect for a country's specifics and realistic chances of meeting them. Hence, it could be said that since 2006 the EU has adopted an obstructive, rather than supportive, stance towards the accession of the Western Balkan states which has not sufficiently assisted either the post-communist transition or EUropeanisation of these states.

Time will tell whether current members of the European Union will be able and willing to genuinely open the door of their organisation for a very small group of the Western Balkan states and herby support and assist the faster EUropeanisation of these states. Faster or slower, completion of post-communist transition and EUropeanisation of the Western Balkans is foremost a matter of political will, not of structural (in)capacity.

References

Balkaninside. (2014). *Milorad Dodik: Lack of consensus—Obstacle to EU accession*. Balkaninside. Retrieved April 15, 2014, from http://www.balkaninside.com/milorad-dodik-lack-of-consensus-obstacle-to-eu-accession.
Bechev, D. (2015). Breaking Macedonia's vicious circle. *EU Observer*. Retrieved May 8, 2015, from https://euobserver.com/opinion/128635; de Launey, G. (2015, May 6). *Power stragle in Macedonia*. BBC News. Available at: http://www.bbc.com/news/world-europe-32612508.
Bieber, F. (2010). *Constitutional reform in Bosnia and Herzegovina: Preparing for EU accession* (Policy Brief). Brussels: European Policy Centre.
Bieber, F. (2011). Building impossible states? State-building strategies and EU membership in the Western Balkans. *Europe-Asia Studies, 63*(10), 1783–1802.

Bieber, F. (2018). *It is time to ditch the Berlin process*. European Western Balkans. Retrieved July 10, 2018, from https://europeanwesternbalkans.com/2018/07/10/time-ditch-berlin-process/.

Bogdani, A. (2015). *Albanian justice system slammed as totally corrupt*. BalkanInsight. Retrieved June 9, 2015, from http://www.balkaninsight.com/en/article/judges-in-albania-pays-up-to-300-000-for-their-positions-report-says.

Börzel, T. A., & Grimm, S. (2018). Building good (enough) governance in postconflict societies & areas of limited statehood: The European Union & the Western Balkans. *Daedalus, 147*(1), 116–127.

Cirtautas, A. M., & Schimmelfennig, F. (2010). Europeanisation before and after accession: Conditionality, legacies and compliance. *Europe-Asia Studies, 62*(3), 421–441.

Crampton, R. J. (1997). *Eastern Europe in the twentieth century and after*. London and New York: Routledge.

Delegation of the European Union to Bosnia and Herzegovina. (2015). *Reform agenda for Bosnia and Herzegovina 2015–2018*. Retrieved from http://europa.ba/wp-content/uploads/2015/09/Reform-Agenda-BiH.pdf.

Ekiert, G. (1996). *The state against society: Political crises and their aftermath in East Central Europe*. Princeton, NJ: Princeton University Press.

Ekiert, G. (2003). Patterns of postcommunist transformation in Central and Eastern Europe. In E. Grzegorz & S. E. Hanson (Eds.), *Capitalism and democracy in Central and Eastern Europe. Assessing the legacy of communist rule* (pp. 89–119). Cambridge: Cambridge University Press.

EU Foreign Affairs Council. (2014, April 14). *Council conclusions on Bosnia and Herzegovina*. Luxembourg.

EU General Affairs Council. (1997, April 29/30). *Council conclusions on the application of conditionality with a view to developing a coherent EU-strategy for the relations with the countries in the region*, Annex III.

EU General Affairs Council. (1999, June 21–22). *Conclusions on the development of a comprehensive policy based on the commission communication on 'the stabilisation and association process for countries of south-eastern Europe*. Luxembourg.

EU General Affairs and External Relations Council. (2003, June 16). *The Thessaloniki agenda for the Western Balkans: Moving towards European integration*, council conclusions. Luxembourg, Annex A.

EU General Affairs Council. (2012, February 28). *Council conclusions on enlargement and the stabilisation and association process*. Brussels.

European Commission. (2006, November 8). *Enlargement strategy and main challenges 2006–2007: Including annexed special report on the EU's capacity to integrate new members*. COM (2006) 649 final, Brussels.

European Commission. (2014, October 8). *Enlargement strategy and main challenges 2014–15*. COM (2014) 700 final, Brussels.
European Commission. (2015a, November 10). *The former Yugoslav Republic of Macedonia report*. Commission Staff Working Document. SWD (2015) 214 Final, Brussels.
European Commission. (2015b, November 10). *Bosnia and Herzegovina report*. Commission Staff Working Document. SWD (2015) 214 Final, Brussels.
European Commission. (2016, November 9). *Bosnia and Herzegovina Report*. Commission Staff Working Document. SWD (2016) 365 Final, Brussels.
European Commission. (2017, September 13). *President Jean-Claude Juncker's State of the Union Address 2017*. Brussels. Retrieved from http://europa.eu/rapid/press-release_SPEECH-17-3165_en.htm.
European Commission. (2018a, April 17). *Serbia, 2018 report*. COM (2018) 450 final, Strasbourg.
European Commission. (2018b, February 6). *A credible enlargement perspective for and enhanced EU engagement with the Western Balkans*. COM (2018) 65 final, Strasbourg.
European Commission. (2019). *European neighbourhood policy and enlargement negotiations*. https://ec.europa.eu/neighbourhood-enlargement/countries/detailed-country-information/serbia_en.
European Commission. (Various years). *Annual reports on [each of] the Western Balkan states*. Brussels.
European Council. (1993, June 21–22). *Presidency conclusions*. Copenhagen.
European Council. (2006, December 14–15). *Presidency conclusions*. Brussels.
Featherstone, K. (2003). Introduction: In the name of 'Europe'. In K. Featherstone & C. M. Radaelli (Eds.), *The politics of Europeanization*. Oxford Scholarship Online.
Flockhart, T. (2010). Europeanization or EU-ization? The transfer of European norms across time and space. *Journal of Common Market Studies, 48*(4), 787–810.
Freedom House. (2019). *Democracy in retreat*. Freedom in the world 2019—Country reports. Retrieved from https://freedomhouse.org/report/freedom-world/freedom-world-2019/democracy-in-retreat.
Freedom House. (various years). *Nations in transit*. Retrieved from http://www.freedomhouse.org.
Gotev, G. (2017, August 15). *Belgrade seeks 'delimitation' for Serbs in Kosovo*. Euractive/Reuter. Available at: https://www.euractiv.com/section/global-europe/news/belgrade-seeks-delimitation-for-serbs-in-kosovo/.

Grabbe, H. (2003). Europeanization goes east: Power and uncertainty in the EU accession process. In K. Featherstone & C. M. Radaelli (Eds.), *The politics of Europeanization*. Oxford Scholarship Online.

Grabbe, H. (2006). *The EU's transformative power: Europeanization through conditionality in central and eastern Europe*. Houndmills, Basingstoke, Hampshire, and New York: Palgrave Macmillan.

Grabbe, H. (2014). Six lessons of enlargement ten years on: The EU's transformative power in retrospect and prospect. *Journal of Common Market Studies, 52*, 40–56.

Gray, A. (2018). *Macron pours cold water on Balkan EU membership hopes*. Politico. Retrieved May 17, 2018, from https://www.politico.eu/article/emmanuel-macron-pours-cold-water-balkans-eu-membership-enlargement.

Hopkins, V. (2012). *Montenegro: Mafia state in the EU neighbourhood*. Open Democracy. Retrieved July 5, 2012, from http://www.opendemocracy.net/valerie-hopkins/montenegro-mafia-state-in-euneighbourhood.

Huntington, S. P. (1993). The clash of civilizations. *Foreign Affairs, 72*(3), 22– 49.

Huntington, S. P. (1996). *The clash of civilizations and the remaking of world order*. New York: Simon & Schuster.

Inserbia.info. (2015). *Dodik: EU membership might not be the best path for BiH*. Inserbia.info. Retrieved November 19, 2015, from http://inserbia.info/today/2015/11/dodik-eu-membership-might-not-be-the-best-path-for-bih/.

Janos, A. C. (2000). *East central Europe in the modern world: The politics of the borderlands from Pre- to Postcommunism*. Stanford: Stanford University Press.

Juncker, J.-C. (2018). *Interview to Euronews: Jean-Claude juncker and EU 'enlargement fatigue'*. Euronews. Retrieved March 02, 2018, from https://www.euronews.com/2018/03/02/jean-claude-juncker-and-eu-enlargement-fatigue.

Klapsis, A. (2018). The Prespes agreement: A critical (re)evaluation. *Ekathimerini*. Retrieved September 30, 2019, from http://www.ekathimerini.com/233095/opinion/ekathimerini/comment/the-prespes-agreement-a-critical-reevaluation.

Juncos, A., & Whitman, R. (2015). Europe as a regional actor: Neighbourhood lost. *Journal of Common Market Studies, 53*(S1), 200–215.

Lavigne, M. (1999). *The economics of transition: From socialist economy to market economy* (2nd ed.). Houndmills, Basingstoke and New York: Palgrave. First edition 1995.

Manners, I. (2002). Normative power Europe: A contradiction in terms. *Journal of Common Market Studies, 52*, 122–138.

Noutcheva, G. (2009). Fake, partial and imposed compliance: The limits of the EU's normative power in the Western Balkans. *Journal of European Public Policy, 16*(7), 1065–1084.

Noutcheva, G. (2012). *European foreign policy and the challenges of Balkan accession: Conditionality, legitimacy and compliance.* London: Routledge.

Petrovic, M. (2009). (What about) the further enlargement of the EU? In between European enlargement fatigue and Balkan instability challenges. *Australian and New Zealand Journal of European Studies, 1*(2), 39–58.

Petrovic, M. (2013). *The democratic transition of post-communist Europe—In the shadow of communist differences and uneven Europeanisation.* Houndmills, Basingstoke: Palgrave Macmillan.

Petrovic, M., & Smith, N. (2013). In Croatia's slipstream or on an alternative road? Assessing the objective case for the remaining Western Balkan states acceding into the EU. *Southeast European and Black Sea Studies, 13*(4), 553–573.

Petrovic, M. (2017). Post-communist transition under the umbrella of uneven Europeanisation: East central Europe, the Baltic states and the Balkans. In M. Steven Fish, G. Gill, & M. Petrovic (Eds.), *A Quarter Century of Post-Communism Assessed* (pp. 41–74). Cham: Palgrave Macmillan.

Phinnemore, D. (2006). Beyond 25—The changing face of EU enlargement: Commitment, conditionality and the constitutional treaty. *Journal of Southern Europe and the Balkans, 8*(1), 7–26.

Pomorska, K., & Noutcheva, G. (2017). Europe as a regional actor: Waning influence in an unstable and authoritarian neighbourhood. *Journal of Common Market Studies, 55,* 165–176.

Pridham, G. (2005). *Designing democracy: EU enlargement and regime change in post-communist Europe.* New York: Palgrave Macmillan.

Radaelli, C. M. (2003). The Europeanization of public policy. In K. Featherstone, & C. M. Radaelli (Eds.), *The politics of Europeanization.* Oxford Scholarship Online.

RadioFreeEurope RadioLiberty. (2019a). *Serbia's Vucic says no recognition of Kosovo unless Belgrade gets something too.* Retrieved from https://www.rferl.org/a/serbia-s-vucic-says-no-recognition-of-kosovo-unless-belgrade-gets-something-too/29803920.html.

RadioFreeEurope RadioLiberty. (2019b). *Haradinaj says tax on Serbian goods, relations with Belgrade should not be linked.* Retrieved March 5, 2019, from https://www.rferl.org/a/kosovo-haradinaj-tax-serbian-goods-belgrade-relations-bosnia/29744510.html.

Rettman, A. (2018). EU eyes Kosovo and Serbia enlargement deal. *Euobserver.* Retrieved September 1, 2018, from https://euobserver.com/enlargement/142709.

Rothschield, J. (1974). *East central Europe between the two World Wars*. Seattle and London: University of Washington Press.

Schimmelfennig, F. (2008). EU political accession conditionality after enlargement: Consistency and effectiveness. *Journal of European Public Policy*, *15*(6), 918–937.

Schimmelfennig, F., & Sedelmeier, U. (Eds.). (2005). *The Europeanization of central and eastern Europe*. Ithaca, NY: Cornell University Press.

Seroka, J. (2008). Issues with regional reintegration of the Western Balkans. *Journal of Southern Europe and the Balkans*, *10*(1), 15–29.

Testorides, K. (2017). *Macedonia's Zaev wins confidence vote to form new government*. The Associated Press. Retrieved May 31, 2017, from http://www.pjstar.com/news/20170531/macedonias-zaev-wins-confidence-vote-to-form-new-government.

Tomovic, D. (2016). *Old Doubts Cling to Montenegro's new cabinet*. BalkanInsight. Retrieved December 1, 2016, from http://www.balkaninsight.com/en/article/montenegro-s-new-government-same-old-politics-11-30-2016.

Tzallas, T. (2018). *Macedonia name dispute: Problem solved?* EUROPP, LSE, London. Retrieved from https://blogs.lse.ac.uk/europpblog/2018/06/20/macedonia-name-dispute-problem-solved/.

Tzifakis, N. (2012). Bosnia's slow Europeanisation. *Perspectives on European Politics and Society*, *13*(2), 131–148.

Vachudova, M. A. (2005). *Europe undivided: Democracy, leverage and integration after communism*. Oxford and New York: Oxford University Press.

Vachudova, M. A. (2014). EU leverage and national interests in the Balkans: The puzzles of enlargement ten years on. *Journal of Common Market Studies*, *52*, 122–38.

Vachudova, M. A. (2018). EU enlargement and state capture in the Western Balkans. In J. Dzankic & M. Kmezic (Eds.), *Europeanisation of the Western Balkans: A failure of EU conditionality?* (pp. 63–85). Cham: Palgrave Macmillan.

Vurmo, G. (2018). The Western Balkans' EU Dream: Ambition calls for a new process. *CEPS Papers, 2018* (3), 1–12. Available at: https://www.ceps.eu/system/files/Vurmo%20on%20the%20Western%20Balkans.pdf.

Zakaria, F. (1997, November/December). The rise of illiberal democracy. *Foreign Affairs*, *76*(6), 22–43.

Zhelyazkova, A., Damjanovski, I., Nechev, Z., & Schimmelfenning F. (2018). European Union conditionality in the Western Balkans: External incentives and Europeanisation. In J. Dzankic & M. Kmezic (Eds.), *Europeanisation of the Western Balkans: A failure of EU conditionality?* (pp. 63–85). Cham: Palgrave Macmillan.

5

Organised Crime in—and from—Communist and Post-communist States

Leslie Holmes

Introduction

One of the less researched comparisons between Communist[1] and post-communist states since the early 1990s is organised crime (hereafter OC). Yet OC is now widely recognised—at least by Western governments—not merely as a serious crime issue, but also as a security threat. One major reason for this is that organised criminal groups (OCGs) often interact with terrorist groups (Shelley, 2014). Another is that they often corrupt officers of the state, subverting the latter's proper functioning. It is therefore important to analyse and compare the changing nature of OC in both the Communist and post-communist worlds.

---

[1] In line with an increasingly common convention, Communist refers here to actual political systems (practice), communist to the ideal of communism (theory).

L. Holmes (✉)
University of Melbourne, Melbourne, VIC, Australia
e-mail: leslieth@unimelb.edu.au

© The Author(s) 2020
A. Akimov and G. Kazakevitch (eds.), *30 Years since the Fall of the Berlin Wall*, Palgrave Studies in Economic History, https://doi.org/10.1007/978-981-15-0317-7_5

Although OC has become a major issue globally, both Communist and post-communist states are often identified as major sources of this problem. For example, in a 2018 article based on an interview with the Director-General of the UK's National Crime Agency (NCA), Lynne Owens, the following challenges to British law enforcement were noted -

There was *Russia's* attempt to kill Sergei Skripal. A *North Korean* cyber-attack. *Eastern European* slave traffickers. *Albanian* cocaine smugglers. (Sensitive to singling out nationalities, Owens used the term "western Balkans") ... In the cities, ex-military *eastern European* and *Baltic* state gangs are behind a spate of thefts of prestige cars stolen at night, driven to the ports and dispatched overseas before the owners wake up ... Other kinds of cybercrime include Wannacry, a piece of *North Korean* ransomware that paralysed much of the health system for four days in May 2017. (Perry, 2018: emphasis added—LTH)

- while a few days later, the *New York Times* (Wee, 2018) referred to the problem of illegal exports of the opioid drug fentanyl into the United States from *China*, which US authorities allege is the main illicit source of a drug that is now killing hundreds of Americans each week (NIDA, 2019). What these two newspaper articles highlighted is that a major and growing problem for developed Western states is OC from both Communist and post-communist states. This chapter explores the growth of such OC, with a particular focus on three Communist and four post-communist states.

Before proceeding with the analysis, however, four introductory caveats need to be noted. One is that the case-selection is skewed, in that the post-communist states chosen (Albania, Bulgaria, Russia and Serbia) are among the worst—though it will be demonstrated that OCGs from Communist states (those considered here are China, North Korea and Vietnam) have also become a significant problem transnationally.[2]

---

[2]While post-communist states such as Estonia, Poland and Slovenia appear to have far less of a problem of OC (and the related corruption) than the four selected for analysis here, many other states—including Lithuania, Romania and Ukraine—do have serious OC issues. Siegel-Rozenblit (2011, p. 5) claims that Asian OC is a 'relatively new phenomenon in the EU'.

The second is that the often-clandestine nature of OC, plus the fact that researching it can be dangerous, means that many non-academic sources have to be used here. However, such sources are mostly either well-regarded international organisations and NGOs, or else mass media with an established reputation for serious investigative journalism. Third, terms such as 'the Triads' or 'Russian OC' are blanket ones, needed for generalisation: In reality, the OC from any country comprises numerous groups that are often in competition with each other.

Fourth, the meaning of the term organised crime is contested: Rather than engage with this debate here (though see Holmes, 2016, pp. 1–14), we adopt a marginally modified version of the definition produced by the UK's NCA (2014, p. 7), viz. 'serious crime planned, coordinated and conducted by people working together on a continuing basis. Their motivation is mostly financial gain'.

The basic argument in this analysis is that OC has been expanding in *both* Communist and post-communist states, suggesting that the type of politico-economic system is less relevant to its fate than the amount of political will and administrative capacity. But even with strong political will, the transnationalisation of OC makes it difficult for individual states to cope with it. Unfortunately, different definitions and systems, plus mutual suspicion—a lack of trust—between many law enforcement agencies, renders the task of countering transnational OC (TOC) particularly problematic.

Albanian OC

Albania has been described as the 'new Colombia of Europe' (Daragahi, 2019), while the UK's NCA has identified Albanian OC as the biggest player both in Britain's illicit drug trade (Townsend, 2019) and in human trafficking into Britain's sex industry in recent times (OCCRP, 2018). A January 2019 article in the *Economist* (2019a) referred to Albanian OC as 'Piranhas from Tirana'. Michaletos (2012) claims that Albanian OC constitutes 'the largest enterprise in terms of sales and profits in South Eastern Europe'. Moreover, Albanian OC has a reputation for particularly nasty violence and misogyny—'Albanian speaking criminals are notorious for their use of extreme violence' (Europol, 2011, p. 39; see more generally on Albanian OCGs' culture Arsovska, 2015).[3]

Furthermore, there is evidence of Albanian OC's involvement in politics, especially relating to Kosovo's armed struggle for independence: Albanian OC has been cited as a major source of weapons for the KLA during the 1990s in a drugs-for-arms agreement. Given the often close ties between politicians and OC in so many countries, it is also worth noting here the (ultimately unproven) public allegations made in 2002 that the Prime Minister of Albania in 1991, Fatos Nano, was involved in the arms smuggling (Cameron, 2004).

One important source of members for Albanian OCGs is former security people from the Communist era, who were dismissed during President Sali Berisha's government downsizing in the early 1990s. According to Europol, 'Many group members have a secret service, police or paramilitary background' (Europol, 2011, p. 39).

While Albanian OC's presence internationally is a relatively new phenomenon, essentially dating from the 1990s, its history can be traced back to the sixteenth century, and many OCGs allegedly continue to be clan-based, as they were back then. According to Zhilla and Lamallari (2015), the growth and transnationalisation began in 1990, following alliance-building with Italian OC. But there appears to have been a major expansion following the 1997 Albanian economic crisis (the collapse of a pyramid scheme), and then again post-1999 in connection with the war in Kosovo. Since then, Albanian OCGs have spread as far as China and the Middle East, and have become a major presence in both Europe—especially Belgium, France, Italy (though less so there since a major clampdown in 2002) and the UK—and North America: in 2004, the FBI claimed that Albanian OC might even replace the ethnically Italian La Cosa Nostra as the dominant OC formation in many US cities (Frieden, 2004). Following this warning, however, US authorities clamped down hard on Albanian OC from 2005: This resulted in

---

[3]Europol and several other law enforcement agencies typically use the term 'Albanian speaking', rather than Albanian, since ethnically Albanian Kosovars are often involved in the criminal activity they are countering. Note that Athanassopoulou (2005, p. 4), inter alia, maintains that Kosovo is 'the notorious criminal capital' of South Eastern Europe.

somewhat less violence emanating from Albanian OCGs, though it has not been completely eliminated (US Attorneys, 2013).

In the past, Albanian OC was structured along traditional OC lines, with codes of honour (*besë*), a strict hierarchy, etc. However, the research conducted by Fabian Zhilla and Besfort Lamallari (2015, 2016) reveals that new forms began to emerge at about the same time the FBI began seriously targeting Albanian OC. Since then, there has been some trend towards more networked structures and less overt hierarchy (on criminal networks generally see Morselli, 2009, 2014).

Although Albanian OC is polycriminal (i.e. engaged in several types of criminal activity), it is particularly well-known for heroin trafficking; human trafficking and prostitution, esp. since the late 1990s; arms dealing (there were massive losses of weapons in Albania in 1997); and car trafficking (ramming expensive cars, such as in Italy, forcibly ejecting the driver, then 'exporting' the stolen car).

Bulgarian OC

OC has been a serious problem for Bulgaria since the mid-1990s. While other post-communist states were being admitted to the EU in 2004, Bulgaria's (and Romania's) entry was delayed to 2007, largely because of their problems with OC and corruption. Once admitted, these two South-East European states were under strict supervision: The EU introduced a new instrument—the Cooperation and Verification Mechanism (CVM)—specifically to monitor judicial reform, anti-corruption measures and, in the case of just Bulgaria, anti-OC measures. The CVM is enacted every six months, and has been identified by Eli Gateva (2013) as the first example of *post*-accession EU conditionality. In 2008, the EU warned Bulgaria that it would be financially punished if it did not seriously address corruption and OC, and, to press the point home, temporarily froze some of the funds earmarked for the country.

But this was not the only penalty Bulgaria has suffered on account of its OC problem. Like Romania, it had hoped to be admitted to the passport-free Schengen Area in 2011 (JHA, 2011); but it still had not been admitted as of June 2019—and the OC–corruption nexus is often cited by France and the Netherlands in particular as reasons why Bulgaria remains an unsuitable candidate for admission.

The EU and members of the Schengen Area are not the only critics of the OC situation in Bulgaria. In a confidential July 2005 cable sent from the US Embassy in Sofia, it was suggested that 'The strength and immunity from the law of organized crime (OC) groups is arguably the most serious problem in Bulgaria today' (Wikileaks, 2005).

On one level, this problem with OC is unusual, in that Bulgaria is the only state analysed in this chapter that essentially had no significant OC before the 1990s. According to Jovo Nikolov (1997, p. 80), Bulgarian OC was '… created by the "transitional state"', and does not predate the 1990s. Similarly, the well-regarded Sofia-based Center for the Study of Democracy maintains that '… the basic structures of organized crime in this country' emerged in 1995 (Bezlov & Tzenkov, 2007, p. 20).

Nikolov's (1997) analysis identifies three main components of Bulgarian OC in the 1990s—ex-wrestlers and other former athletes; ex-police officers (up to 17,000 law enforcement officers were dismissed in the early 1990s); and former members of the *nomenklatura* (an essentially similar but more complex breakdown is in Bezlov and Tzenkov, 2007, p. 12). The wrestlers are a particularly interesting group. They initially operated protection rackets, but some of these groups mutated into legitimate insurance companies and security firms after the change of government in 1997: the new government encouraged these OCGs to convert themselves into legal companies, and some did (Bezlov & Tzenkov, 2007, p. 21). However, many OCGs continued to act in a purely criminal way, and the 2000s have witnessed a large number of contract killings carried out by members of such gangs.

A major stimulus to Bulgarian OC in the early–mid-1990s was the UN sanctions imposed on neighbouring Yugoslavia because of the war in Bosnia. Bulgarian OC played a major role in sanctions-busting in smuggling items such as cigarettes (it is alleged that Romania was the main source of oil during the period of the sanctions).

Bulgarian OC is flexible and polycriminal, but is particularly well-known for counterfeiting, human trafficking and prostitution, cigarette smuggling, contract killing (e.g. mayors, investigative journalists), car trafficking and protection rackets. While it has become more transnational since the 1990s, it is still focused mainly on Europe.

Russian OC

In 1994, then head of the CIA James Woolsey testified to the US Congress that OC threatened democratic reform in Russia (cited in Boylan, 1996, p. 2006). In May 1996, the then heads of the CIA (John Deutch) and the FBI (Louis Freeh) took this a step further, both warning Congress that Russian OC and corruption were undermining the Russian system and could even pose a threat to the United States (cited in Webster, 1997, p. 3). For those who might see this as simply Western propaganda and scare-mongering, note that the Russian president himself, Boris Yeltsin, claimed in February 1993 that, 'Organised crime has become a direct threat to Russia's strategic interests and national security' (Talalayev, 1993).

The OC situation in Russia has changed significantly since the 1990s. The 2000s have been generally calmer (despite some claims OC would increase in the aftermath of the 2008 Global Financial Crisis), and there has been a marked decline in the role of the traditional OCGs, the *vory v zakone* (see below). At the same time, there has been a move by other OCGs into the more legal economy.

Joseph Serio's (2008, pp. 71–94) thorough analysis of numerous sources on Russian OC highlights the confusion and contradictions that arise from using differing methods for calculating its scale, yet concludes that there is widespread agreement that both the number of OCGs and the number of people involved in OC almost certainly *declined* in the 2000s. Vadim Volkov takes this one step further, arguing that the changes in Russian OC in the 2000s are such that the Russian 'mafia' has become extinct—'The "golden age" of the Russian mafia is clearly passed; the mafia turned out to be a one generation phenomenon' (Volkov, 2014, p. 159).

This is potentially misleading, and perhaps wishful thinking. For instance, Russian (and post-Soviet more generally) OC is still considered by Interpol to be a major concern that warrants one of only three dedicated Interpol anti-OC projects ('Millennium'), the working group of which continues to meet regularly (e.g. in Moscow in June 2017 and in L'viv, Ukraine in May 2018). In late 2017, Europol announced that it had recently played a role working with Spanish authorities to bring down two Russian OCGs heavily involved in money laundering (Europol, 2017a). Furthermore, many specialists have long perceived Russian OC to be major players in cybercrime (Holmes, 2015; Thomas, 2005). Thus Gragido, Molina, Pirc, and Selby (2013, p. 75) maintain that, 'Russia and Eurasian nations carved out of the former USSR have long been (and remain today) the arguable leaders [globally—LTH] of malicious cyber activity and cybercrime'. Europol's 2018 assessment of threat assessments on the internet makes several references to Russian OC's involvement in various kinds of cybercrime. Finally, *Fortune* magazine's most recent assessment of the wealth of the world's leading transnational OCGs rated Russia's Solntsevskaya Bratva the world's wealthiest (Matthews, 2014; Alux [2018] ranks Russian OC the world's 4th wealthiest OCG, behind the Japanese Yakuza, the Mexican Sinaloa Cartel and—richest of all—the Italian Camorra).

Russian OC is not new, although in a format that would normally be considered OC (as distinct from, for example, highway banditry), it dates only from the Soviet period. During the latter, the best-known OCGs were the so-called 'thieves-in-law' or 'thieves living by the code' (*vory v zakone*—see e.g. Galeotti, 2018; Siegel, 2012). Unlike many OCGs, ethnicity was not a relevant factor in rendering someone eligible to join the *vory*; rather, the prerequisite for joining was having served a prison sentence.

However, as the USSR began to liberalise in the late 1980s under Mikhail Gorbachev, so new OCGs began to emerge. This process intensified following the collapse of the Soviet Union in December 1991. During the 1990s, there were frequent violent conflicts between both the traditional *vory* and the much newer, less structured OCGs, as well as between the latter. As in so many other post-communist states, a major source of OCGs' new recruits was former members of the secret police (KGB) and other law enforcement officers.

The activities of Russian OC are diverse, but are said to have included in the 1990s the smuggling of nuclear materials (Lee, 1998), though this claim is now dismissed by most analysts. More recently, two of the principal foci are cybercrime and human trafficking. Russian OC can be found in many countries outside Russia, but is a particular problem in the United States and Israel.

Serbian OC

OC in Serbia is often called 'Naša Stvar', which is a direct translation of the Sicilian or American Mafia's alternative name, La Cosa Nostra (lit. 'Our Thing'). While its reputation for extreme violence is not as pronounced as that of Albanian OC, a 2009 report that gang members in Madrid had killed one of their own members with a hammer for alleged betrayal, put his body through a mincer and then eaten him, reveals that Serbian OC is by no means squeamish when it deems violence appropriate (Altozano, 2012; Worden, 2012).

Unlike Albanian OC, Serbian OC appears to have emerged relatively recently, in the early twentieth century; the 'Gang of Mountain Birds' under its leader Jovan 'Jovo' Čaruga is often cited as an early example. However, this was more like a gang of bandits than a modern form of OC, and in many ways the more appropriate starting point is the 1970s and 1980s, when gangs under leaders such as Ljubomir Magaš (better known as Ljuba Zemunac) and Željko Ražnatović (better known internationally as Arkan) became a significant problem for authorities. At that time, however, these OCGs operated mainly outside Serbia—in Magaš' case, first in Italy and then in Germany, while there were arrest warrants for Arkan in no fewer than seven West European states during the 1970s and 1980s, mostly for bank robberies, murders, and prison escapes. There is considerable circumstantial evidence that Arkan worked closely with the Yugoslav secret police (UDBA and its successor the SDB) during the 1970s and 1980s (CSD, 2004, p. 42).

It is ironic that what was widely perceived to be the most liberal Communist state experienced the most violent collapse and disintegration. Given its violent intervention in Bosnia-Herzegovina during the first half of the 1990s, Yugoslavia—by 1992 comprising only Serbia and Montenegro—was subject to UN sanctions 1992–1995. In order to circumvent these sanctions, the Yugoslav government collaborated with OC in smuggling oil, cigarettes, weapons and other items into the country (OSCE, 2011)—a fact explicitly acknowledged by the Yugoslav Prosecutor-General in January 1996 (OMRI, 1996). One analyst has gone so far as to argue that 'economic sanctions led to the over-criminalisation of Serbian population in 1990s' (Nikolić-Ristanović, 2004, p. 689).

The 2000s have seen continued activity by Serbian OC, and further evidence of collusion between OC and corrupt officials, especially law enforcement officers and politicians (IRBC, 2014; Mladenovic, 2012; OSCE, 2011). In 2012, the Centre for Investigative Reporting of Serbia published documented allegations of OC links to a Deputy Prime Minister—who subsequently became the Prime Minister and then President of Serbia (see too Rujevic, 2018).

In October 2016, the Serbian authorities acknowledged that the organised crime situation was worsening, and declared a 'war' on OC. Yet law enforcement was unable to prevent violent clashes between OCGs in Belgrade and Novi Sad in 2017, while a number of OC-related murders were reported in 2018 (Rujevic, 2018). The situation is still not under control.

Serbian OC is both flexible and polycriminal. There is evidence of its engagement in arms smuggling, cigarette smuggling—and threatening senior politicians, including the Minister of the Interior. Serbian authorities initially blamed Prime Minister Zoran Djindjić's 2003 assassination on the Zemun OCG, and eventually convicted a number of OC figures, including a leading member of the Zemun clan who had previously been a senior officer in the Special Operations Unit of the secret police and a close friend of Arkan. Serbian OC operates in several countries in Europe, the USA and Australia—but apparently not in Asia.

Chinese OC

OC in China is usually described by the generic term 'black societies' (*hei shehui*),[4] but the focus here is on the best-known of such groupings, the Triads. Chinese OC is now considered by some analysts to be the largest OC grouping globally; given the sheer size of the Chinese population (over 1.4 billion in 2019), this is not surprising. Moreover, Emil Plywaczewski (2002) has stated that several Western law enforcement agencies considered it one of the seven most serious international OC threats during the 1990s.

The origins and history of the Triads are disputed. They are traced back to the seventeenth century by some scholars (e.g. Wing Lo & Kwok, 2012), based on claims by Chinese revolutionary Sun Yat-sen—though Murray (1994), Chu (2000, pp. 12–13) and others maintain that they first emerged in the 1760s. Whether in the seventeenth or eighteenth century, China was ruled by the Qing dynasty (from 1644)—also known as the Manchu Dynasty, since the Emperors were Manchurian, not Han Chinese. According to several scholars (e.g. Lintner, 2002, pp. 41–42; Wing Lo & Kwok, 2012), the Triads were originally a political group whose goal it was to overthrow the Manchus and instal a Han Chinese emperor. But this political grouping mutated into an OCG in the nineteenth century that was increasingly attracted to the opium trade. For this reason, it focused primarily on Shanghai and Hong Kong, especially once the latter was separated from China and became a British colony.

Following the takeover of China by Mao and the Communists in 1949, there was a severe clampdown on all forms of 'black society', and the Triads became even more focused on Hong Kong. But as China began to open up to outside trade from the late 1970s, so the Triads and other OCGs began to move back into mainland China. Already in 1982–1983, the closest Chinese city

---

[4]There are two main forms of *hei shehui*—one of which (usually translated as dark societies—*hei* can mean both black and dark in Chinese) is more loosely organised than the other (black societies) and does not enjoy protection provided by corrupt state officials.

to Hong Kong—Shenzhen—launched a campaign ('Notice on Abolishing Black Society Activities') against OC. This was the first 'strike black' (*dahei*) anti-OC campaign in China, and resulted in the execution of more than 80 OCG members.[5]

The Triads and other OCGs are now found in many parts of China. But their style has changed. Having once been a classic 'traditional' type of OCG—with a strict hierarchy, a code, initiation ceremonies, and overt symbols of membership such as tattoos—there has in recent years been what Broadhurst and Lee (2009, p. 2) describe as a 'gentrification' of the Triads, as they have moved increasingly into the licit economy, become less code-adherent and opted for business suits rather than tattoos.

The Communist authorities have continued to pursue OCGs, having introduced several 'strike hard' campaigns in the twenty-first century. One recent development is the increasing use of public executions of OCG members involved in drug manufacturing and trafficking, as in Lufeng in 2018; Lufeng, in Southern Guangdong Province, is sometimes called 'the city of ice', being a major source of methamphetamine (including into Australia).

In January 2018, President and General Secretary Xi Jinping announced another major 3-year crackdown on OC, even claiming that OC was threatening Communist rule. By December 2018, this campaign had resulted in the removal of more than 1000 OCGs (Xinhua, 2018). Of particular concern to Xi is the so-called 'red–black nexus'—i.e. the frequent collusion between OCGs and corrupt Communist officials: the latter often provide a 'protective umbrella' (*baohusan*) to the former in return for bribes or a share of criminal profits (see e.g. Chin & Godson, 2006, p. 6). Xi has been clamping down on corruption almost since he took power in 2012, but appears to have become increasingly aware of—and concerned about—the linkages that frequently exist between OCGs and officials.

---

[5]China has two types of anti-OC campaigns—'strike black' (*dahei*), which are launched by local authorities, and 'strike hard' (*yanda*), which are national campaigns—See Broadhurst (2013, p. 100), Wang (2013, pp. 50–51).

The best-known case of the red–black nexus emanates from the city of Chongqing (Sichuan Province), and relates to the former party leader of that city (from 2007), Bo Xilai. In 2009, Bo initiated a major crackdown on OC, especially the Triads, which resulted in almost 5000 arrests between October 2009 and 2011. But not all of those arrested were OCG members; a considerable number were allegedly corrupt officials, including several senior police officers. Bo's campaign was one of the factors that made him extremely popular in Chongqing. But in 2012, he himself was first removed as party secretary of Chongqing (March), then expelled from the Chinese Communist Party (September). Finally, in mid-2013, Bo was charged, tried and found guilty of corruption, and was sentenced to life imprisonment.

The Bo case is significant not only because of the apparent hypocrisy between his campaign against the red–black nexus when he himself was later found guilty of the kinds of crimes he had so strongly criticised, but also because of the claims by many observers that a major reason for his trial and sentence was that he could have been a challenger to Xi, who was keen to promote many of the same 'leftist' (Maoist) ideas espoused by Bo (Dominguez, 2013; Zhao, 2016). Bo was a so-called princeling, meaning that he was the son of one of the Eight Elders of Chinese Communism, and had advocated a return to some of the more 'red' (i.e. Maoist Communist) policies that had been largely sidelined in recent years: Deng Xiaoping's economic policies had resulted not only in impressive growth and development, but also rising and extreme economic inequality, as well as corruption, in the country. It should be noted that Xi's anti-OC policy since January 2018 has also been seen as designed to counter *political* threats to his and the CCP's rule (*Economist*, 2019b).

Chinese OC is polycriminal: among its major activities are drug manufacturing and trafficking (the number of drug-related convictions in the PRC increased approximately fivefold 1991–2003, while the reader is reminded of the point above about trafficking of fentanyl into the United States); gambling (including in soccer); counterfeiting; people smuggling and human trafficking; money laundering; extortion; kidnapping and contract killing; protection (Wang, 2017); licit enterprise; and corruption.

Vietnamese OC

Vietnamese OCGs have a reputation for being among the most violent of the Asian OCGs, both at home and abroad. This was noted in late 1991 by a US Senate subcommittee: While acknowledging that Chinese OCGs (and street gangs) were often violent, Vietnamese ones were even worse (US Senate Sub-Committee, 1992, esp. 68, 218 and 268).

According to Schloenhardt (2010, p. 249), Vietnamese OCGs are primarily involved in the trafficking of drugs and humans. Vietnam's proximity to the so-called Golden Triangle (Laos—another Communist state—Myanmar and Thailand) helps to explain both foci: the area is known as one of the world's most prolific producers of opium (for heroin), while both Thailand itself and some of its neighbours are major sources of trafficked persons, in the international movement of whom Vietnamese OC is an important player. Given its role in both smuggling and international trafficking, it is not surprising that Vietnamese OC within Vietnam has since the 1990s been concentrated mostly in port areas such as Saigon (Ho Chi Minh City) and Haiphong.

While Vietnamese OC does not have as high a profile internationally as Russian or Chinese OC, it is certainly considered a serious problem by many law enforcement agencies outside Vietnam, not least in Europe (Siegel-Rozenblit, 2011, pp. 9–10). The spread of Vietnamese OC to other countries is linked to the mass emigration from unified Vietnam after 1975. Nevertheless, the problem has intensified since the 1990s. For instance, an Australian Parliamentary Committee referred in a February 1995 report to the growing threat from Vietnamese OCGs in comparison with the previous decade (Parliament of the Commonwealth of Australia, 1995). In 2013, Europol issued a warning against the re-emergence of Vietnamese OCGs in Europe (Europol, 2013): Schoenmakers, Bremmers, & Kleemans (2013) provide a detailed scholarly analysis of the role of Vietnamese OC in illicit cannabis production in the Netherlands, while Silverstone and Savage (2010) provide evidence of this—and of money laundering and child trafficking—from the UK. Much of the human trafficking of women for sex work is to Cambodia and China (Schloenhardt, 2010, p. 249).

The history of Vietnamese OC can be traced back at least to the 1920s, with the emergence of the paramilitary organisation Bình Xuyên that engaged in OC to fund its activities. While both North and South Vietnamese authorities clamped down on OC during the 1940s and 1950s, OC began to expand again in the 1960s and early 1970s; this was particularly so in (anti-Communist) South Vietnam, where the so-called Four Great Kings of Saigon's underworld became a significant force. Following the reunification of Vietnam under the Communists in 1975, the authorities initially clamped down hard on OC once again. But by the 1990s, control had slackened, and two major OCGs—one led by Truong Văn Cam (better known as Năm Cam), the other by one of the few major female OC leaders globally, Dung Hà—emerged as significant criminal forces. But this phase of domestic OC activity came to an end around the turn of the century. In 2000, Dung Hà was murdered by members of Năm Cam's gang (Cohen, 2002), while Năm Cam himself was executed in 2004 for a number of offences, including having ordered the killing of Dung Hà. He had been tried along with 154 other people, including a number of corrupt Communist officials who were found guilty of collusion with OC. Once again, the close ties between OC and corrupt officers of the state are evident.

Vietnamese OCGs engage in smuggling (including of wildlife products—Ngoc & Wyatt, 2013); gambling; prostitution; drug trafficking; cannabis cultivation; child trafficking; home invasions; extortion and fraud. Within Europe, they can mainly be found in Central and Eastern Europe, especially Czechia (Il Fatto Quotidiano, 2017).

North Korean OC

The Democratic People's Republic of Korea (DPRK) is renowned for being one of the world's most secretive states, so that much of the information cited here from scholars has to be based on Western intelligence reports, reports from defectors, etc. But there are also critical reports from China, a fellow Communist state and North Korea's closest ally.

One of the most striking aspects of OC in North Korea is that the state itself often appears to act like an OCG (Blancke, 2014), with numerous

North Korean officials having been accused in more than twenty countries of involvement in drug trafficking (Perl, 2004). The state's criminal activities are allegedly coordinated through the Communist (Korean Workers') Party's Central Committee Bureau 39, which was established in the mid-1970s (Gollom, 2017; Kan, Bechtol, & Collins, 2010). These allegations of state-sponsored OC activity have earned the DPRK the label of a 'mafia state' (Kelly, 2016; Wang & Blanke, 2014).

It seems that the state encouraged drug production and trafficking from the early 1990s until about 2005—initially of heroin, subsequently of methamphetamine—but at that time enjoyed a near-monopoly over this (Yun & Kim, 2010). However, a growing drug addiction problem at home then led to a state clampdown on production and trafficking (Hastings, 2014). One outcome of this change of government policy appears to have been a growth in citizen-initiated (i.e. private) drug-related OC from around 2005.

While a number of Western analysts have focused more on this non-state OC in recent years, several Chinese sources claim the state is still heavily involved. Thus, Peng Wang and Stephan Blancke (2014, p. 57) point out that:

> Chinese-language primary sources… show that while official DPRK state involvement in the large-scale production, trafficking and sale of illegal drugs may have lessened, it has not stopped, and the narcotics trade is still regarded by Kim Jong-un as an important means of earning hard currency… Published materials from China and South Korea suggest that, since the early 2000s, the North Korean government has managed to conceal its criminal activities by exporting the major part of its illegal drugs, especially methamphetamine, to northeast China… Moreover, the North Korean government has failed to control the increasing private participation in drug production and trafficking.

While the explanations for the North Korean state's involvement in OC activity are complex, one major factor—especially in the 2000s—is the authorities' reactions to international sanctions. North Korea has long been subject to US sanctions, which were first imposed in the 1950s, tightened in the 1980s (especially after the downing of Korean Airlines flight KAL 858 in 1987), temporarily eased in the 1990s, and have been further tightened again as the nuclear programme has developed in the twenty-first century. UN sanctions have also become progressively harsher since 2006, as the Pyongyang regime has pursued an increasingly active nuclear weapons testing policy.

In addition to drug production and trafficking, North Korea is alleged by some to be heavily involved in counterfeiting Western currencies, though this is disputed by others (Nanto, 2009). There is persuasive evidence on its involvement in wildlife smuggling. For example, some North Korean diplomats allegedly purchase rhinoceros horn in Africa and then smuggle it via diplomatic bags to China and Vietnam, where it is sold for a significant profit (Rademeyer, 2016, pp. 22–24). The state is also reputed to be involved in international trafficking of its own citizens, as a way of securing forced remittances from abroad: key destinations include Russia, China, and many countries in the Middle East and Africa (US Department of State, 2018, pp. 255–256). In addition to human trafficking, people smuggling—mainly to South Korea (often via Communist China, Laos and Vietnam, as well as via Thailand) and China (Davy, 2018, pp. 70, 97, 101)—is another profitable business for North Korean (and foreign) OC. Recently, the state itself is believed by some to have been involved in the hacking of a Bangladeshi bank in 2016 (Corkery & Goldstein, 2017). Finally, the DPRK is also alleged to be involved in the manufacture of fraudulent medicines (Lale-Demoz & Lewis, 2013, p. 135).

Like so many aspects of OC in and from North Korea, evidence on the composition of private OCGs is blurry. However, there is some proof that they include North Koreans, Korean Chinese, South Koreans and Japanese (Wang & Blancke, 2014, pp. 55–56).

Comparative Impact of OC on Business

One of the few comparative and over time sources on the impact of OC on licit businesses is the World Economic Forum's annual *Global Competitiveness Report*. Since this has only been produced in its current format since 2004 (with assessments for 2003), it cannot provide data for the 1990s. Nevertheless, in the absence of alternatives, the perceived

Table 5.1 Perceived impact of OC on domestic businesses

	2003	2006	2010	2014	2017
Albania	n.d.	3.8	5.2	4.3	4.3
Bulgaria	2.9	2.9	3.9	4.0	3.7
China	4.3	3.8	5.2	4.7	4.6
North Korea	n.d.	n.d.	n.d.	n.d.	n.d.
Russia	3.3	3.8	4.3	4.2	4.5
Serbia	3.6	4.3[a]	4.3	4.1	4.1
Vietnam	4.3	4.3	4.7	4.6	4.9

Source 2003—Sala-i-Martin (2004, p. 486); 2006—Schwab and Porter (2006, p. 414); 2010—Schwab (2010, p. 380); 2014—Schwab (2014, p. 420); 2017—Schwab (2017, pp. 43, 75, 91, 249, 257, 309)
[a]Includes Montenegro
The actual question asked was, in some variant, 'To what extent does organized crime (mafia-oriented racketeering, extortion) impose costs on businesses in your country?'. Scaling is 1–7, where 1 = to a great extent and 7 = not at all
n.d.—no data

impact of OC on our seven countries since 2003 can be compared by citing their scores for selected years.

It emerges from Table 5.1 that, as of 2017, Bulgarian businesses considered themselves to be more impacted by OC than businesses in any of the other countries focused on here, while Vietnamese businesses were apparently the least impacted.

Drivers of OC

There are numerous drivers of OC, including psycho-social and cultural ones. Moreover, many structural factors are specific to individual countries (e.g. the impact of the food crisis from 1994 and of the heavy rain-induced collapse of the poppy harvest in 1996 in North Korea; the effects of Deng Xiaoping's 'cat' metaphor on both Communist and popular morality[6]). Here, we briefly consider just three of the most significant structural (systemic) ones relevant to all or most of the cases analysed.

---

[6]In 1962, Deng argued that 'it doesn't matter whether a cat is black or white—if it catches mice, it is a good cat', which has often been interpreted as meaning that the authorities will turn a blind

Collapse of Communism

In the aftermath of the collapse of Communist systems in the USSR, Eastern Europe and some Asian states between 1989 and 1991, all of the formerly Communist states experienced serious economic and social problems (the DPRK's economy was also negatively impacted). The problems of inflation, negative economic growth and rising unemployment in post-communist states during the 1990s were compounded by the fact that new welfare systems and new laws were only slowly introduced: Given the widespread insecurity and the lack of legal clarity, it is not surprising that some were attracted to the potential gains offered by OC.

It has been noted that Russian (and Ukrainian) OCGs have been increasingly involved in cybercrime. While the USSR did not encourage critical creative thinking, its record on teaching physics, mathematics and computing skills was world-class, which helps to explain why Russian and Ukrainian OC figure so prominently in computer-based crime. While North Korean hackers are also a problem for many states and foreign citizens, a recent analysis suggests that Russians are considerably more adept at this than even the North Koreans or the Chinese, being some seven times faster than the former and more than 13 times faster than the latter at gaining access to others' networks, according to US cybersecurity company CrowdStrike (*Economist*, 2019c). While these figures refer to the speed of intelligence services—with civilian OC being much slower—it has been argued here that the distinction between the state and OC is sometimes very blurred.

One apparent difference between OCGs in Communist and post-communist states is that the latter include a large number of members who were once officers in either the security police, the conventional police, or sometimes the military.[7] In their endeavours to distance

---

eye to questionable practices as long as they achieve the ultimate objective of substantial economic growth. This is seen by some as having triggered widespread corruption in China once Deng came to power (1978), which in turn can stimulate OC.

[7]Some members of Vietnamese OCGs in the United States have been former Vietnamese military officers (US Senate Sub-Committee, 1992, pp. 170, 296), but from (non-Communist) South Vietnam.

themselves from their Communist pasts, many post-communist governments significantly downsized and restructured the security police. This not only resulted in many former officers feeling that their years of loyal service to the state had now been essentially dismissed or even implicitly criticised, but also widespread unemployment among such officers. This combination of alienation and unemployment was ripe for exploitation by OCGs, for whom former officers had considerable appeal as gang members. Among these attractions were the facts that they had mostly been weapons-trained; sometimes still had their weapons; had often been desensitised to killing; often knew and could explain how the state's intelligence system worked for investigating OC; and could in many cases identify potentially corruptible officers still employed by the state. While such people have often been recruited into OCGs from post-communist states, it appears that they are not typically members of Chinese OCGs (Wang, 2017, pp. 102–103).

Globalisation

While the notion of a 'borderless world' (Ohmae, 1990) is often exaggerated—it is far more borderless for capital than for people—there is no question that globalisation has been a major stimulus to the transnationalisation of OC. Within Europe, the introduction of the passport-free Schengen Area in 1995 has meant that once goods or people are smuggled into that zone, it has been easy to move them around. This is a major reason why Bulgaria and Romania have still not been admitted to Schengen.

The ideology of globalisation is neo-liberalism. With its emphasis on ends being more important than means (due process), downsizing the state, and not valuing the loyalty of long-term officers as functions that were once the exclusive responsibility of the state are either privatised or outsourced, neo-liberalism can be seen as a stimulus to both corruption and organised crime. Of course, this is not peculiar to the kinds of states considered in this chapter, but it is a factor that must be included in any attempt at explaining the rise of OC in Communist and post-communist states—none of which has been immune to the impact of globalisation.

Technological Revolution

In 2019, the world noted—if not necessarily celebrated—the 30th anniversary of Tim Berners-Lee's invention of the World Wide Web. The dramatic rise in access to the internet since the 1990s, and the development of the Darknet (Glenny, 2011; McCormick, 2013), has been a boon to OC, which has shown itself to be highly flexible and adept at using the web to its advantage. When it is borne in mind that even Interpol and the Pentagon have been hacked, it is clear that neither international nor domestic agencies are completely protected against ill-intentioned hackers, including OCGs.

Conclusion

OC is on the rise everywhere, and this chapter demonstrates that Communist states are just as prone to it as post-communist ones. In some cases, the particular focus of OC in post-communist states relates to the Communist legacy, which helps to explain some of the resonances between the two types of state.

One development since the 1990s that applies equally to Communist and post-communist states is the tendency for OC to become more transnational: This point applies to every one of the OCGs considered in this chapter. Furthermore, as demonstrated in the cases of both North Korea and Serbia/Yugoslavia (i.e. a Communist and a post-communist state), the application of international sanctions can have the unintended consequence of at least making states more reliant on OC and sometimes even encouraging states to act more like OCGs themselves.

According to a Europol report (2017b, p. 11), 'The most threatening OCGs are those which are able to invest their significant profits in the legitimate economy as well as into their own criminal enterprises'. This point resonates with the observation that there has been some 'gentrification' of OCGs in both post-communist (e.g. Russia) and Communist (China) states.

The approach to the law also appears to differ relatively little in practice between the Communist and many post-communist states. The four post-communist states considered here are far from perfect in terms of respect for the key tenets of the rule of law: according to the World Justice Project's *Rule of Law Index 2019* (2019, pp. 6–7), Albania scored 0.51 (on a 0–1 scale—the higher the figure, the greater the assessed adherence to the rule of law: see too Mavrikos-Adamou, 2014) and was ranked 71st out of 126 states and territories, while the respective figures for Bulgaria were 0.54 and 54th (see too Pavlovska-Hilaiel, 2015), for Russia were 0.47 and 88th (see too Smith, 2007), and for Serbia 0.50 and 78th (see too EWB, 2018). But the scores and ranks for China and Vietnam were not markedly different from the worst of these post-communist states, at 0.49/82nd and 0.49/81st, respectively (see too on China DiMatteo [2018], and on Vietnam Bui [2014]; North Korea has never been assessed in the Rule of Law Index, but it is assumed here that its score and rank would be the worst of the seven countries compared).

One of the most concerning findings when comparing OC in several Communist and post-communist states is that there are often close links between corrupt officers of the state and OCGs in both kinds of system: along with numerous sources, both concrete and strong circumstantial evidence has been cited in this chapter. There can be absolutely no question that such collusion means that the scale of OC in and from these countries is much greater than it would otherwise be.

Given the numerous similarities between OC in both Communist and post-communist states, are there any significant differences between the two types of system? One already noted is that former law enforcement officers are far more likely to be recruited into post-communist OCGs than into OCGs based in Communist states. Another is in the severity of the possible penalties for involvement in OC, especially drug-trafficking. Thus, all three Communist states considered here allow for the death penalty for murder, drug trafficking and human trafficking (the last of these in the cases of China and North Korea), whereas none of the post-communist states does. However, all of the post-communist states analysed here are members of the Council of Europe, which requires that member-states do not permit capital punishment,[8] whereas the death penalty is allowed in many non-Communist Asian states—again, especially for murder and drug trafficking. Hence, the difference here may relate less to the Communist/post-communist divide than to cultural differences.

Another difference relates to the role of civil society, including the mass and social media. While not as developed in some post-communist states as might be expected or wished for (Bernhard & Kaya, 2012; Howard, 2003; Petrova, 2007), civil society—including the mass and social media and NGOs—still enjoys greater freedom in most than in the Communist states (on China see Simon [2013], Spires [2018]: on North Korea, Szalontai & Choi [2014]: on Vietnam, Wischermann & Dang Thi Viet Phuong [2018]).

Consideration of the numerous ways in which states can seek to counter OC deserves at least a chapter in its own right. But briefly and arguably, the most important factor in addressing many sociopolitical problems, including OC, is political will—of political leaders, officials (especially in law enforcement), civil society, the business sector and ordinary citizens—and state capacity. Yet even this might not be enough in the case of OC. Its transnationalisation since the late 1980s poses significant problems for law enforcement agencies, most of which are domestic and often find it difficult to agree with other jurisdictions on definitions, data-sharing, extradition, etc. While some international agencies, such as the UNODC and Europol, are making concerted efforts to combat TOC, others (e.g. ASEANAPOL) are still doing far too little to address the problem. At present, TOC—including that from Communist and post-communist states—is usually at least one step ahead of the authorities.

---

[8]Russia does still in principle have the death penalty for murder and 'encroachment' on the lives of public officials, but there has been a moratorium on this since the mid-1990s.

References

Altozano, M. (2012, November 15). Who ate the Serbian gangster? *El Pais* (English edition). Retrieved from https://elpais.com/elpais/2012/11/15/inenglish/1352983479_984269.html.

Alux. (2018). *Top 10 richest criminal organizations* (Video). Retrieved from https://www.youtube.com/watch?v=MbRCGcVRz8I.

Arsovska, J. (2015). *Decoding Albanian organized crime: Culture, politics, and globalization*. Oakland, CA: University of California Press.

Athanassopoulou, E. (2005). Fighting organized crime in SEE. In E. Athanassopoulou (Ed.), *Fighting organized crime in southeast Europe* (pp. 1–6). Abingdon, England: Routledge.

Bernhard, M., & Kaya, R. (2012). Civil society and regime type in European post-communist countries: The perspective two decades after 1989–1991. *Taiwan Journal of Democracy, 8*(2), 113–125.

Bezlov, T., & Tzenkov, E. (2007). *Organized crime in Bulgaria: Markets and trends*. Sofia, Bulgaria: Center for the Study of Democracy.

Blancke, S. (2014, April). Criminal connections: State links to organised crime in North Korea. *Jane's Intelligence Review, 26*(4), 34–37.

Boylan, S. (1996). Organized crime and corruption in Russia: Implications for U.S. and international law. *Fordham International Law Journal, 19*(5), 1999–2027.

Broadhurst, R. (2013). The suppression of black societies in China. *Trends in Organized Crime, 16*(1), 95–113.

Broadhurst, R., & Lee, K.-W. (2009). The transformation of triad "dark societies" in Hong Kong: The impact of law enforcement, socio-economic and political change. *Security Challenges, 5*(4), 1–38.

Bui, T. (2014). Deconstructing the "socialist" rule of law in Vietnam: The changing discourse on human rights in Vietnam's constitutional reform process. *Contemporary Southeast Asia, 36*(1), 77–100.

Cameron, R. (2004, November 23). *Albanian PM escapes arms probe*. BBC News—Europe. Retrieved from http://news.bbc.co.uk/2/hi/europe/4031719.stm.

Chin, K., & Godson, R. (2006). Organized crime and the political-criminal nexus in China. *Trends in Organized Crime, 9*(3), 5–44.

Chu, Y.-K. (2000). *Triads as business*. London, England: Routledge.

Cohen, M. (2002). Murder and mystery. *Far Eastern Economic Review, 165*(27), 56–58.

Corkery, M., & Goldstein, M. (2017, March 22). North Korea said to be target of inquiry over $81 million cyberheist. *New York Times*. Retrieved from https://www.nytimes.com/2017/03/22/business/dealbook/north-korea-said-to-be-target-of-inquiry-over-81-million-cyberheist.html.

CSD. (2004). *Partners in crime: The risks of symbiosis between the security sector and organized crime in Southeast Europe*. Sofia, Bulgaria: Center for the Study of Democracy.

Daragahi, B. (2019, January 27). "Colombia of Europe": How tiny Albania became the continent's drug trafficking headquarters. *Independent*. Retrieved from https://www.independent.co.uk/news/world/europe/albania-drug-cannabis-trafficking-hub-europe-adriatic-sea-a8747036.html.

Davy, D. (2018). *Migrant smuggling in Asia and the Pacific: Current trends and challenges—Vol. 2*. Bangkok, Thailand: United Nations Office on Drugs and Crime.

DiMatteo, L. (2018). 'Rule of law' in China: The confrontation of formal law with cultural norms. *Cornell International Law Journal, 51*(2), 391–444.

Dominguez, G. (2013, August 20). Bo Xilai's trial—Last act of a major power play. DW (Deutsche Welle). Retrieved from https://www.dw.com/en/bo-xilais-trial-last-act-of-a-major-power-play/a-17031069.

Economist. (2019a). Piranhas from Tirana: The 'Albanian mafia' are not really a mafia. *Economist, 430*(9124), 40.

Economist. (2019b). Behind the mask; social control. *Economist, 430*(9132), 33.

Economist. (2019c). Do svidaniya secrecy; computer security. *Economist, 430*(9133), 73.

Europol. (2011). *OCTA 2011: EU organised crime threat assessment*. The Hague, the Netherlands: European Police Office.

Europol. (2013, November). *Early warning notification: Re-emergence of Vietnamese Organised Crime Groups (OCGs)*. Retrieved from https://www.europol.europa.eu/publications-documents/re-emergence-of-vietnamese-organised-crime-groups-ocgs.

Europol. (2017a, September 28). *Press release—Two main Russian mafia groups dismantled in Spain with Europol's support*. Retrieved from https://www.europol.europa.eu/newsroom/news/two-main-russian-mafia-groups-dismantled-in-spain-europol%E2%80%99s-support.

Europol. (2017b). *Serious and organised crime threat assessment: Crime in the age of technology*. The Hague, the Netherlands: European Police Office.

Europol. (2018). *Internet Organised Crime Threat Assessment (IOCTA) 2018*. The Hague, The Netherlands: European Union Agency for Law Enforcement Cooperation.

EWB. (2018, October 12). Rule of law in Serbia: Seven deadly sins of the judiciary system. *European Western Balkans*. Retrieved from https://europeanwesternbalkans.com/2018/10/12/rule-law-serbia-seven-deadly-sins-judiciary-system/.

Frieden, T. (2004, August 19). FBI: Albanian mobsters 'new mafia'. *CNN International*. Retrieved from http://edition.cnn.com/2004/LAW/08/18/albanians.mob/index.html.

Galeotti, M. (2018). *The Vory: Russia's super mafia*. New Haven, CT: Yale University Press.

Gateva, E. (2013). Post-accession conditionality—Translating benchmarks into political pressure? *East European Politics, 29*(4), 420–442.

Glenny, M. (2011). *DarkMarket: How hackers became the new mafia*. London, England: Bodley Head.

Gollom, M. (2017, December 8). Drugs, counterfeiting: How North Korea survives on proceeds of crime. *CBC World News*. Retrieved from https://www.cbc.ca/news/world/north-korea-criminal-empire-drugs-trafficking-1.4435265.

Gragido, W., Molina, D., Pirc, J., & Selby, N. (2013). *Blackhatonomics: An inside look at the economics of cybercrime*. Waltham, MA: Elsevier.

Hastings, J. (2014). The economic geography of North Korean drug trafficking networks. *Review of International Political Economy, 22*(1), 162–193.

Holmes, L. (2015). Cybercrime in Russia and CEE. In W. Schreiber & M. Kosienkowski (Eds.), *Digital Eastern Europe* (pp. 814–1179). Wroclaw, Poland: KEW. Kindle e-book locs.

Holmes, L. (2016). *Advanced introduction to organised crime*. Cheltenham, England: Elgar.

Howard, M. (2003). *The weakness of civil society in post-communist Europe*. Cambridge, England: Cambridge University Press.

Il Fatto Quotidiano. (2017). United mafias of Europe. *Il Fatto Quotidiano*. Retrieved from https://www.ilfattoquotidiano.it/longform/mafia-and-organized-crime-in-europe/map/.

IRBC. (2014). *Serbia: Organized crime; corruption in the police force and other government agencies; government response; state protection available to victims and witnesses of crime (2012–May 2014) [SRB104865.E]*. Ottawa, Canada:

Immigration and Refugee Board of Canada. Retrieved from https://www.ecoi.net/en/document/1256733.html.
JHA. (2011, June 9). Bulgaria, Romania denied Schengen entry. *Euractiv—Justice and Home Affairs*. Retrieved from https://www.euractiv.com/section/justice-home-affairs/news/bulgaria-romania-denied-schengen-entry/.
Kan, P. R., Bechtol, B., & Collins, R. (2010). *Criminal sovereignty: Understanding North Korea's illicit international activities*. Carlisle, PA: Strategic Studies Institute.
Kelly, R. (2016, March 16). North Korea as a 'mafia state'. *The Interpreter*. Retrieved from https://www.lowyinstitute.org/the-interpreter/north-korea-mafia-state.
Lale-Demoz, A., & Lewis, G. (Eds.). (2013). *Transnational organized crime in East Asia and the Pacific: A threat assessment*. Bangkok, Thailand: United Nations Office on Drugs and Crime.
Lee, R. (1998). *Smuggling armageddon: The nuclear black market in the former Soviet Union and Europe*. New York, NY: St. Martin's.
Lintner, B. (2002). *Blood brothers: Crime, business and politics in Asia*. Crows Nest, NSW, Australia: Allen and Unwin.
Matthews, C. (2014, September 20). Fortune 5: The biggest organized crime groups in the world. *Fortune Magazine*, 1.
Mavrikos-Adamou, T. (2014). Rule of law and the democratization process: The case of Albania. *Democratization, 21*(6), 1153–1171.
McCormick, T. (2013, December). The Darknet. *Foreign Policy, 203*, 22–23.
Michaletos, I. (2012, November 26 and 2016, March 6). *Southeastern European organized crime and extremism review*. Serbianna. Retrieved from http://serbianna.com/analysis/archives/1706.
Mladenovic, N. (2012). The failed divorce of Serbia's Government and organized crime. *Journal of International Affairs, 66*(1), 195–209.
Morselli, C. (2009). *Inside criminal networks*. New York, NY: Springer.
Morselli, C. (Ed.). (2014). *Crime and networks*. New York, NY: Routledge.
Murray, D. (with Qin B-Q.) (1994). *The origins of the Tiandihui: The Chinese triads in legend and history*. Stanford, CA: Stanford University Press.
Nanto, D. (2009). *North Korean counterfeiting of U.S. currency*. Washington, DC: Congressional Research Service.
NCA. (2014). *National strategic assessment of serious and organised crime 2014*. London, England: National Crime Agency.
Ngoc, A. C., & Wyatt, T. (2013). A green criminological exploration of illegal wildlife trade in Vietnam. *Asian Journal of Criminology, 8*(2), 129–142.

NIDA. (2019). *Overdose death rates*. Bethesda, MD: National Institute on Drug Abuse. Retrieved from https://www.drugabuse.gov/related-topics/trends-statistics/overdose-death-rates.

Nikolić-Ristanović, V. (2004). Organised crime in Serbia—Media construction and social reaction. In G. Meško, M. Pagon, & B. Dobovšek (Eds.), *Policing in central and eastern Europe: Dilemmas of contemporary criminal justice* (pp. 685–694). Ljubljana, Slovenia: University of Maribor.

Nikolov, J. (1997). Crime and corruption after communism: Organized crime in Bulgaria. *East European Constitutional Review, 6*(4), 80–84.

OCCRP. (2018, November 19). *UK: Human trafficking surge linked to Albanian gangs*. Organized Crime and Corruption Reporting Project. Retrieved from https://www.occrp.org/en/daily/8933-uk-human-trafficking-surge-linked-to-albanian-gangs.

Ogawa, A. (Ed.). (2018). *Routledge handbook of civil society in Asia*. Abingdon, England: Routledge.

Ohmae, K. (1990). *The borderless world: Power and strategy in the interlinked economy*. New York, NY: Harper Business.

OMRI. (1996, January 23). *Serbia to crack down on economic crime?* Open Media Research Institute Daily Digest II, No. 16, Retrieved from http://www.hri.org/news/balkans/omri/1996/96-01-23.omri.html#5.

OSCE (Organisation for Security and Cooperation in Europe). (2011, July 15). *OSCE fights against organized crime in Serbia*. Retrieved from https://www.osce.org/serbia/80986.

Parliament of the Commonwealth of Australia. (1995). *Asian organised crime in Australia: A discussion paper by the Parliamentary Joint Committee on the National Crime Authority* (Canberra, Australia: Commonwealth of Australia). Retrieved from https://fas.org/irp/world/australia/docs/ncaaoc1.html.

Pavlovska-Hilaiel, S. (2015). The EU's losing battle against corruption in Bulgaria. *Hague Journal on the Rule of Law, 7*(2), 199–217.

Perl, R. (2004). State crime: The North Korean drug trade. *Global Crime, 6*(1), 117–128.

Perry, A. (2018, November 22). Organised crime in the UK is bigger than ever before. Can the police catch up? *Guardian*. Retrieved from https://www.theguardian.com/uk-news/2018/nov/22/uk-organised-crime-can-police-catch-up-national-crime-agency-lynne-owens.

Petrova, V. (2007). Civil society in post-communist eastern Europe and Eurasia: A cross-national analysis of micro- and macro-factors. *World Development, 35*(7), 1277–1305.

Plywaczewski, E. (2002). *Chinese organized crime in Western and Eastern Europe*. Paper delivered at the 3rd annual symposium 'crime and its control in greater China', June 21–22, 2002, University of Hong Kong, PRC. Retrieved from https://strategicanalysis.wordpress.com/2006/10/26/chinese-organized-crime-in-western-and-eastern-europe/.

Rademeyer, J. (2016). *Beyond borders: Crime, conservation and criminal networks in the illicit rhino horn trade*. Geneva, Switzerland: Global Initiative Against Transnational Organized Crime.

Rujevic, N. (2018, July 31). *Mafia murders shock Serbia, reveal web of corruption*. DW (Deutsche Welle). Retrieved from https://www.dw.com/en/mafia-murders-shock-serbia-reveal-web-of-corruption/a-44902334.

Sala-i-Martin, X. (Ed.). (2004). *The global competitiveness report 2003–2004*. New York, NY: Oxford University Press.

Schloenhardt, A. (2010). *Palermo in the Pacific: Organised crime offences in the Asia Pacific region*. Leiden, the Netherlands: Martinus Nijhoff.

Schoenmakers, Y., Bremmers, B., & Kleemans, E. (2013). Strategic versus emergent crime groups: The case of Vietnamese cannabis cultivation in the Netherlands. *Global Crime, 14*(4), 321–340.

Schwab, K. (Ed.). (2010). *The Global Competitiveness Report 2010–2011*. Geneva, Switzerland: World Economic Forum.

Schwab, K. (Ed.). (2014). *The Global Competitiveness Report 2014–2015*. Geneva, Switzerland: World Economic Forum.

Schwab, K. (Ed.). (2017). *The Global Competitiveness Report 2017–2018*. Geneva, Switzerland: World Economic Forum.

Schwab, K., & Porter, M. (Eds.). (2006). *The Global Competitiveness Report 2006–2007*. Geneva, Switzerland: World Economic Forum.

Serio, J. (2008). *Investigating the Russian mafia*. Durham, NC: Carolina Academic Press.

Shelley, L. (2014). *Dirty entanglements: Corruption, crime and terrorism*. New York, NY: Cambridge University Press.

Siegel, D. (2012). *Vory v Zakone*: Russian organized crime. In D. Siegel & H. van de Bunt (Eds.), *Traditional organized crime in the modern world* (pp. 27–48). New York: Springer.

Siegel-Rozenblit, D. (2011). *Asian organized crime in the European Union*. Brussels, Belgium: European Parliament Directorate-General for Internal Policies. Retrieved from http://www.europarl.europa.eu/RegData/etudes/note/join/2011/453191/IPOL-LIBE_NT%282011%29453191_EN.pdf.

Silverstone, D., & Savage, S. (2010). Farmers, factories and funds: Organized crime and illicit drug cultivation within the British Vietnamese community. *Global Crime, 11*(1), 16–33.

Simon, K. (2013). *Civil society in China: The legal framework from ancient times to the 'new reform era'*. New York, NY: Oxford University Press.

Smith, G. (2007). The procuracy, Putin, and the rule of law in Russia. In F. Feldbrugge (Ed.), *Russia, Europe, and the rule of law: Russia, Europe, and the rule of law* (pp. 1–14). Leiden, the Netherlands: Martinus Nijhoff.

Spires, A. (2018). China. In *Ogawa 2018* (pp. 49–65).

Szalontai, B., & Choi, C. (2014). Immunity to resistance? State–society relations and political stability in North Korea in a comparative perspective. *North Korean Review, 10*(1), 55–70.

Talalayev, G. (1993, February 12). *Boris Yeltsin addresses all-Russia conference on problems of the fight against organized crime and corruption: Full text of speech*. ITAR-TASS.

Thomas, D. (2005, January 6). From Russia with malice: Organised online crime has risen dramatically in the former Soviet Union—And it's still growing. *Computing*. Retrieved from https://www.computing.co.uk/ctg/analysis/1830051/from-russia-malice.

Townsend, M. (2019, January 13). Kings of cocaine: How the Albanian mafia seized control of the UK drugs trade. *Guardian*. Retrieved from https://www.theguardian.com/world/2019/jan/13/kings-of-cocaine-albanian-mafia-uk-drugs-crime.

US Attorneys. (2013, August 20). *49 Members and associates of an international ethnic-Albanian organized crime syndicate convicted of drug trafficking crimes*. New York, NY: Department of Justice, U.S. Attorney's Office, Eastern District of New York.

US Department of State. (2018). *Trafficking in persons report—June 2018*. Washington, DC: Department of State.

US Senate Sub-Committee. (1992). *Asian organized crime: Hearing before the permanent subcommittee on investigations of the Committee on Governmental Affairs, United States Senate, one hundred second Congress, first session*. Washington, DC: US Department of Justice.

Volkov, V. (2014). The Russian mafia: Rise and extinction. In L. Paoli (Ed.). *The Oxford handbook of organized crime* (pp. 159–176). New York, NY: Oxford University Press.

Wang, P. (2013). The rise of the Red Mafia in China: A case study of organised crime and corruption in Chongqing. *Trends in Organized Crime, 16*(1), 49–73.

Wang, P. (2017). *The Chinese mafia: Organized crime, corruption, and extra-legal protection*. Oxford, England: Oxford University Press.

Wang, P., & Blancke, S. (2014). Mafia state: The evolving threat of North Korean narcotics trafficking. *RUSI Journal, 159*(5), 52–59.

Webster, W. (Ed.). (1997). *Russian organized crime: Global organized crime project*. Washington, DC: Center for Strategic and International Studies.

Wee, S.-L. (2018, December 3). Trump says China will curtail fentanyl. The U.S. has heard that before. *New York Times*. Retrieved from https://www.nytimes.com/2018/12/03/business/fentanyl-china-trump.html.

Wikileaks. (2005, July 7). *(U) Bulgarian organized crime (C-CN5-00054)*. Retrieved from https://wikileaks.org/plusd/cables/05SOFIA1207_a.html.

Wing Lo, T., & Kwok, S. I. (2012). Traditional organized crime in the modern world: How triad societies respond to socioeconomic change. In D. Siegel & H. van de Bunt (Eds.), *Traditional organized crime* in the *modern world* (pp. 67–89). New York: Springer.

Wischermann, J., & Phuong, D. T. V. (2018). Vietnam. In *Ogawa 2018* (pp. 129–142).

Worden, T. (2012, March 23). Serbian gangsters killed rival, ate him for lunch in a stew and disposed of body using a MEAT GRINDER. *Daily Mail Australia*. Retrieved from https://www.dailymail.co.uk/news/article-2119103/Serbian-gangsters-killed-rival-ate-disposed-body-using-MEAT-GRINDER-dumping-remains-river.html.

World Justice Project. (2019). *Rule of law index 2019*. Washington, DC: World Justice Project.

Xinhua. (2018, December 31). *1,000 mafia-style gangs removed in China's organized crime crackdown*. Xinhuanet. Retrieved from http://www.xinhuanet.com/english/2018-12/31/c_137710286.htm.

Yun, M., & Kim, E. (2010). Evolution of North Korean drug trafficking: State control to private participation. *North Korean Review, 6*(2), 55–64.

Zhao, S. (2016). Xi Jinping's Maoist revival. *Journal of Democracy, 27*(3), 83–97.

Zhilla, F., & Lamallari, B. (2015). Albanian criminal groups. *Trends in Organized Crime, 18*(4), 329–347.

Zhilla, F., & Lamallari, B. (Eds.). (2016). *Evolution of Albanian organized crime*. Tirana, Albania: Open Society Foundation for Albania. Retrieved from https://www.academia.edu/35335836/Evolution_of_Albanian_Organized_Crime.

Part II

Values, Security and Foreign Policy in Russia

6

U.S.–Russia Relations in the Last 30 Years: From a Rapprochement to a Meltdown

Victoria V. Orlova

The Cold War Paradigm

The Cold War paradigm has served as a conventional blueprint for U.S.–Russian relations based on a long-term confrontation. The polarised relationship between Moscow and Washington has turned out to be an alternative to the bipolar world order. There is neither the Iron Curtain nor a clash of ideologies, but patterns of the Cold War still affect global politics, and a gap between old adversaries is growing exponentially, destabilising a bilateral political process. In recent years, U.S.–Russia relations have progressively deteriorated. NATO expansion, the Ukraine crisis, the Syria campaign, allegations of Russia's meddling in the U.S. presidential election have become turning points in the complex geopolitical play of world powers.

Over the last three decades, U.S.–Russian relations have developed in the context of tectonic shifts in world politics, economy, technology and communications. In contrast with the bipolar system, a rapidly

V. V. Orlova (✉)
Lomonosov Moscow State University, Moscow, Russia

© The Author(s) 2020
A. Akimov and G. Kazakevitch (eds.), *30 Years since the Fall of the Berlin Wall*, Palgrave Studies in Economic History, https://doi.org/10.1007/978-981-15-0317-7_6

changing multipolar world is chaotic and unpredictable. The United States and Russia, obsessed with a spiralling confrontation, are unlikely to secure the international order. The reasons for this confrontation are straightforward: Russia rejects American supremacy and U.S. unilateral policy associated with interventions, proxy wars and democracy promotion campaigns, especially in the post-Soviet space; the United States refuses to consider Russia as a major power, diminishes its status and condemns Russia for its geopolitical ambitions (Rumer & Sokolsky, 2019). A sophisticated matrix of U.S.–Russian relations cannot be interpreted without a deep understanding of historical context, national interests and geopolitical strategies of both countries.

Since the second half of the twentieth century, relations between the United States and Russia have been defined by the specifics of strategic rivalry. During the Cold War, the main areas of competition included control over geopolitical spheres of influence, a conventional and nuclear arms race and space exploration as well. After World War II, the United States and the Soviet Union began to struggle for global influence as the leaders of polar blocs representing capitalist and communist ideologies. The Cold War dichotomy involved the Western Bloc controlled by the United States and the Eastern Bloc supervised by the Soviet Union. The bipolar world order attained the equilibrium due to the balanced system of confrontation based on nuclear parity and the policy of deterrence and containment.

In terms of the bipolar system, the world order was balanced and predictable enough except some events when a nuclear catastrophe seemed imminent as it happened during the Cuban missile crisis in 1962. Despite an explicit threat of mutual destruction of the United States and the Soviet Union, the Cold War was regarded as the era of strategic stability provided by bilateral arms control. Both the United States and the Soviet Union pursued a military buildup and developed the strategic military alliances, NATO and the Warsaw Pact, to protect the Western and Eastern camps. "The confrontation helped cement a world dominated by Superpowers, a world in which might and violence—or the threat of violence—were the yardsticks of international relations…" (Westad, 2017, "World making", para. 2). After World War II, security dilemma, based on fear of military power of a rival, defined a rapid transformation of the

United States and the Soviet Union when both states turned into superpowers with political, military and ideological arsenals. Former anti-fascist allies became uncompromising adversaries in a struggle for global influence and leadership. Zbigniew Brzezinski (1992) noted, "Geopolitically the struggle, in the first instance, was for control over the Eurasian landmass and, eventually, even for global preponderance. Each side understood that either the successful ejection of the one from the western and eastern fringes of Eurasia or the effective containment of the other would ultimately determine the geostrategic outcome of the contest".

The United States, except for the period of the Great Depression from 1929 to the late 1930s, remained a wealthy, stable and relatively invulnerable nation. After World War II, which devastated and destructed the Soviet Union, Europe, and much of Asia, the territory of the United States was intact, so America had a definite competitive advantage. Pursuing geopolitical and economic leadership, the United States supported Western Europe, launching the Marshall Plan and transferring to Europe more than 12 billion dollars (Westad, 2017, "Europe's asymmetries", para. 51). It was a solid investment in the consolidation of the West to counter the Eastern Bloc and the main adversary—the Soviet Union. Brzezinski (1998, p. 3) stated that "[i]n the course of a single century, America has transformed itself—and has also been transformed by international dynamics—from a country relatively isolated in the Western Hemisphere into a power of unprecedented worldwide reach and grasp". In contrast with the United States, throughout the twentieth century, Russia suffered heavy casualties during the revolution, the civil war, Stalin's repressions and world wars. The Second World War turned out to be the most devastating for the Soviet Union, taking at least 27 million lives. Every time Russia had to rise from the ashes. After World War II, the Soviet Union managed to restore the country and strengthened the communist empire. The competition with the United States was a strong stimulus for Soviet progress and expansion. As *The Economist* ("Not a Cold War", 2007) notes, "For much of the 20th century, the chief object of Russian admiration and revulsion has been the United States—the country that, with its combinations of fissiparous diversity and fierce patriotism, insularity and messianic sense of destiny, Russia arguably most resembles".

Exceptionalism and messianism have become the main driving forces for the national identities of both states. Throughout history, America remained monolithic in its ideology, whereas Russia had to revise the system of values and ideology to find new pathways for building its national identity. Nevertheless, Russia is a messianic nation, and Russian messianism, associated with heroic sacrifice and patriotism, has been a leitmotif in Russia's history and consciousness. After World War II, the United States and the Soviet Union transformed into "supercharged empires with a growing sense of international mission" (Westad, 2017, "Starting points", para. 1) and claimed their exceptional right to decide the world's fate, taking responsibility for world order. This right in the context of the Cold War became a catalyst for the confrontation between superpowers and a determining factor in foreign policy as well.

The equilibrium of the bipolar system was based on nuclear parity: a massive nuclear arsenal as a primary means of deterrence equalised the strength of both states. "Deterrence by nuclear threat was one way that each superpower tried to prevent the other from gaining advantage and hence upsetting the balance of power between them" (Nye & Welch, 2017, p. 147). In terms of security dilemma, a growing nuclear arsenal is regarded as a competitive tool for retaining the status of a great world power. After the end of the Cold War, nuclear security has remained a critical issue on the agenda of world leaders, highlighting a threat of a nuclear conflict between the United States and Russia: "[t]wo sides remain locked into the threat of mutually assured destruction (MAD), with short decision times in the event of a military escalation, accident, or misperception" (Kuchins, 2016, p. 4).

American–Soviet relations developed in accordance with a complex scenario based on sophisticated strategies of U.S. and Soviet leaders, politicians and scholars. Apart from deterrence aimed at preventing an armed conflict, a geopolitical palette included a policy of containment to control the expansionism of a rival state, détente for a relaxation of strained relations as well as strategies of rollback and proxy conflicts to manage military conflicts, intelligence operations and regime change in strategically important states and regions. George F. Kennan (1947), an American diplomat and a Cold War strategist, elaborated a policy of "long-term, patient but firm and vigilant containment of Russian expansive tendencies" that was extrapolated to the Truman Doctrine and the Marshall Plan. Containment turned out to be a long-term strategy used by the United States against the Soviet Union to restrict communism's expansion. Another architect of the Cold War, Zbigniew Brzezinski, was one of the most influential political figures affecting foreign policy of many American presidents and specialised in hawkish strategies against the Soviet Union. His credo was the strategic deterioration of American relations with the Soviet Union, and he contributed significant efforts to destroy the communist camp (Brzezinski, Scowcroft, & Ignatius, 2008, p. 20). Apart from the policy aiming at the disintegration of the Soviet empire, Brzezinski proposed sophisticated geopolitical schemes including a strategy of U.S. military and financial support of Afghan *mujahedeen* during the Soviet–Afghan War, challenging the Soviet military operation in Afghanistan (Garfinkle, 2008).

In the last thirty years, there were five main periods remarkable for dramatic events in U.S.–Russia relations: 1989–1991—from a breakthrough in Soviet–American relations to the collapse of the Soviet Union and the dissolution of the Eastern Bloc; 1992–1999—from the Yeltsin-Clinton rapprochement to NATO expansion and the Serbia bombing; 2000–2007—from the U.S.–Russian partnership in the war on terror to the Munich speech of Vladimir Putin, blaming the U.S.-led world order; 2008–2013—from the Russo-Georgian war to the Syria policy; 2014–present—from the Ukraine crisis to accusations of Russia's meddling in the U.S. presidential election. Interestingly, there was a steady pattern in U.S.–Russia relations: a new U.S. administration that came to power usually assessed the relationship with Russia as disastrous and tried to find pathways to a rapprochement. However, results of any reset were predetermined: affected by disruptive circumstances, seemingly promising relations, after a short period of mutual understanding, quickly turned into a deep frustrating crisis, and, in the end, almost collapsed (Rumer & Sokolsky, 2019).

The Fall of the Soviet Empire

The period from 1989 to 1991 was a time of tectonic shifts: the fall of communism in Europe, the dissolution of the Eastern Bloc and the collapse of the Soviet Union. There have been several turning points in international affairs, dramatically changing the world order, but, undoubtedly, the demise of the Soviet Union as an ideological, political and military adversary of the United States is one of the most dramatic events in modern history. Historically, it was the second meltdown of Russia in the twentieth century—the first one happened in 1917, after the Russian revolution, which led to the destruction of the Tsar Empire and the oppression of the Russian Orthodox Church. Despite many conventional explanations, it was unclear how the Soviet Union could break up so quickly. Perhaps, the effect of "imperial overstretch" turned out to be profound and irreversible; or the massive military buildup significantly weakened the economy of the Soviet Union; or the decline of communism ideology deeply affected a rigid political system (Nye & Welch, 2017, p. 173). Besides, American long-term geopolitical and military strategies, along with soft power tools, contributed to the Soviet Union's erosion and collapse.

Undoubtedly, the central figure of the Soviet makeover was Mikhail Gorbachev. His liberal policy of new thinking, *glasnost* and *perestroika* resulted in deep transformations inside the U.S.S.R. and the Soviet bloc. As Engdahl (2009, p. 3) noted, "The Cold War ostensibly ended with Mikhail Gorbachev's decision in November 1989 not to order Soviet tanks to East Germany to block the growing nonviolent anti-government candlelight protest movement and let the Berlin Wall, the symbol of the 'Iron Curtain' dividing Eastern from Western Europe, fall down". Indeed, Gorbachev brought about a revolution in U.S.-Soviet relations, impressing American leaders, Ronald Reagan and George H. W. Bush, with his ideas and intentions of changing the U.S.S.R and the world. As a result of remarkable progress in the U.S.-Soviet relationship, American and Soviet leaders reached agreements of historical importance—the INF Treaty on the elimination of intermediate-range and shorter-range missiles in 1987 and START I—Strategic Arms Reduction Treaty in 1991.

Despite innovative approaches to domestic politics, Gorbachev did not cope with a deep crisis inside the country. Being an idealist, inspired by Western social democratic ideas, Gorbachev believed in the Soviet Union's democratisation. He did not expect that his liberal reforms "snowballed into a revolution" (Nye & Welch, 2017, p. 174). Besides, economic problems were crucial. The exhausted Soviet economy was about to collapse: it "had been literally bled to the bone in order to feed an endless arms race with its arch-rival and Cold War opponent" (Engdahl, 2009, p. v). The United States did not support the dying Soviet Union when Gorbachev appealed to Western partners for economic assistance at the G7 summit in 1991 (Sachs, 2018, p. 70). When irreversible political and economic transformations reached a peak, the Soviet Union had ceased to exist.

After the Soviet Union's collapse, Russia needed to solve issues of national identity and the dilemma of its diminishing status. Russia underwent tremendous transformations, including total changes in ideology, politics, economy, social life and culture. Political and economic instability had inevitably led to the loss of Russia's influence in geopolitically vital regions. The status dilemma in the destroyed Soviet empire was acute, given that "Russia's national identity is deeply rooted in its sense of being a great power" (Kuchins, 2016, p. 14). For reborn Russia, it has been an essential task to restore the status and the standing on the world scene to be able to protect national interests and provide state security.

NATO Expansion

After the end of the Cold War, U.S.–Russia relations developed in the context of U.S. dominance and unipolarity. Experiencing devastating consequences of the Soviet meltdown, both politically and economically, Russia tried to adjust its broken system to new conditions. The Clinton administration promised to support Russia and enhance the bilateral partnership. The United States provided Russia with funds for democratic and market reforms; however, these measures turned out to be insufficient. Despite warm relations between U.S. and Russian presidents, Bill Clinton and Boris Yeltsin, a rapprochement was affected by political turmoil and the harmful effects of economic shock therapy in Russia.

Seeking for the integration with the West, Russia signed agreements with the European Union, became a member of the Council of Europe, joined G8, and, as it seemed, these steps strengthened Russia's position in the world. Despite many challenges, westernisation was an essential part of Russian foreign policy, and the American factor remained critical in shaping Russia's political priorities. "The Cold War legacy of bipolarity is the main reason for the ingrained Western-centrism of Russian foreign policy; Russia's ruling elite grew up during an era when Moscow and Washington largely directed the fate of the world" (Mankoff, 2009, p. 16). In 1993–1996, Moscow and Washington tackled many problems, including issues concerned with weapons of mass destruction, terrorism and regional conflicts. However, as Robert Legvold (2007, p. 5) noted, "Russian policy had lost the simple positive dynamism inherited from the Gorbachev years". In the second half of the 1990s, the idea of strategic partnership with the United States faded, and Russia began to focus on multipolarity, considering relations with China and India as promising and beneficial.

The U.S. policy towards Russia had remained controversial: The United States pursued NATO enlargement and, in 1997, invited the first group of former Soviet allies—Poland, Czech Republic and Hungary—to join the Northern Alliance. It became a turning point in U.S.–Russia relations, although the United States tried to tread softly. "In order to reassure the Russians that enlargement is not a military threat, NATO declares that it has 'no intention, no plan and no reason' to deploy nuclear weapons, or to station permanently 'substantial combat forces' on the territory of new members" ("A new European order", 1997). Nevertheless, the negotiations on NATO enlargement, initiated by Madeleine Albright, then U.S. secretary of state, inevitably led to a chill in relations between Moscow and Washington. In Western mass media, the decision on NATO expansion was regarded as a significant geopolitical failure of Russia which "admitted that several countries once in its sphere of influence could join what had been for a half-century a hostile coalition, the West's NATO alliance" ("A new European order", 1997).

The United States ignored Moscow's concerns over NATO's threats to Russian national security. In terms of Germany reunification, U.S. state secretary James Baker promised Mikhail Gorbachev that NATO would not expand "not one inch eastward" ("Gorbachev was promised",

2017). Western leaders also guaranteed that they would not promote NATO expansion "ensuring a non-aligned buffer zone between NATO' eastern border and Russia" (MccGwire, 1998). But those promises were quickly forgotten. The United States offered Russia a special status in NATO; however, it was just an appeasing step to mitigate Russia's frustration. Russia did not receive any credentials and power, so it was not able to affect NATO's decisions.

Although U.S. policymakers consider NATO enlargement as "the principal instrument of U.S. security policy in Europe and Eurasia" (Rumer & Sokolsky, 2019), it remains a highly controversial issue. A key turning point in this regard occurred in 1999, when NATO's decision to bomb Yugoslavia without a U.N. Security Council mandate in order to resolve the Kosovo crisis, led to a deep crisis in relations between Moscow and Washington. The Clinton administration supposed that the Moscow reaction would be angry given that, historically, Russia maintained geopolitical interests in the Balkans and had close ties with Serbs. When in April 1999, Al Gore, the American vice president, informed Yevgeny Primakov, the Russian prime minister, who was en route to Washington, about the bombing of Yugoslavia, Primakov had ordered his pilots to make a U-turn in the sky over the Atlantic Ocean and return to Moscow (Broder, 1999). There were fears that the Serbia bombing could lead to "a wider conflict in Europe or even a third world war" ("A new Cold War?", 1999). The NATO bombing of Yugoslavia signalled Moscow that the United States could act unilaterally, ignoring any rules (Rumer & Sokolsky, 2019).

Expanding NATO, the United States showed Russia that it remained a potential adversary, not a partner. At the same time, former Soviet republics and states-satellites, gripped by fear of possible Russia's expansion, tended to seek for protection of the West, particularly, the NATO membership. Apart from Poland, Czech Republic, and Hungary, which became NATO's members, there were three waves of NATO enlargement: Bulgaria, Latvia, Lithuania, Estonia, Romania, Slovakia and Slovenia joined NATO in 2004, Albania and Croatia—in 2009, Montenegro—in 2017. George F. Kennan (1997) warned about NATO expansion that it "would be the most fateful error of American policy in the entire post-cold-war era" because it could "inflame the nationalistic, anti-Western and militaristic tendencies in Russian opinion; to have an adverse effect on the development of Russian democracy; to restore the atmosphere of the cold war to East-West relations, and to impel Russian foreign policy in directions decidedly not to our liking". Indeed, it was NATO expansion that made Russia reassert its military and geopolitical strength and led to the resurgence of Russia's power. Dmitri Trenin (2016, p. 27), director of the Carnegie Moscow Center, remarked that "over the years Russia had drawn a number of red lines to its partners, which they chose to ignore. Finally, this provoked Moscow's pushback".

The NATO bombing of Yugoslavia became a turning point in American–Russian relations. Symbolically, the U-turn of the Russian aeroplane in the sky over the Atlantic Ocean meant growing estrangement between the United States and Russia. The rapprochement evaporated, and mentions of a new cold war appeared in the media. Continuing to fortify its positions, the United States relished the period of unipolarity and sought for global supremacy, whereas Russia, trying to integrate with the West, found out that its interests were ignored by the West. Andrew Kuchins (2016, p. 13) pointed out that the Soviet Union's demise dramatically changed U.S.–Russian relations: "Before the [Soviet Union's] collapse, the United States was negotiating with a weakening but equal partner that had a shared vision of transforming European and global security. With the disappearance of the Soviet Union..., Russia and its neighbours became 'a project' for Washington. This was a dramatic paradigm shift for the relationship..."

This "paradigm shift" inevitably affected Russia's foreign policy and geopolitical priorities when the new Russian leader appeared on the world stage. Under the leadership of Vladimir Putin, Russia has changed dramatically, reviving after a decade of severe economic and political crisis. Lost in the transition to democracy, Russia needed to restore its status and reputation after a volatile period of the 1990s (Graham, 2017). This task became the highest priority for the Russian president who intended to achieve stability and reinvent Russia's foreign policy. It was challenging, given that during the Putin era, U.S.–Russia relations developed under the presidency of four U.S. leaders: Bill Clinton, George W. Bush, Barack Obama and Donald Trump.

The War on Terror

At the beginning of the new millennium, on 11 September 2001, the unprecedented terrorist attacks on the United States that destroyed the World Trade Center and the west side of the Pentagon became offensive symbols of the new age. Vladimir Putin was the first world leader who expressed his support and offered assistance to the American president, George W. Bush. In that dramatic moment, Russia and the United States found common ground for cooperation. In 2002, in terms of Russia's renewed partnership with the United States, the NATO-Russia Council was created that allowed both nations to coordinate intelligence and military activities. It seemed that acting together against a common threat, the United States and Russia could establish a long-term strategic partnership, but it did not happen (Tsygankov, 2009, p. 3–6). The war on terror resulted in extensive military campaigns: the U.S.-led counterterrorism operation in Afghanistan and the Iraq war. As for the counterterrorism operation in Afghanistan, Russia entirely supported America, providing military bases in Central Asia and intelligence assistance. However, the next U.S. initiative—the invasion of Iraq in 2003 without the resolution of the U.N. Security Council—provoked Moscow's negative reaction. The Iraq war resulted in the overthrow of Saddam Hussein's regime, multiple terrorist attacks as well as the rapid expansion of terrorist organisations and radical Islamist groups. As Angela Stent (2014, p. 82) stated, "U.S.-Russian relations began to fray as two issues became particularly contentious: the use of military force to effect regime change and the legitimacy of undertaking military intervention without United Nations sanction". When it became clear that the United States provided the faulty evidence of Hussein's weapons of mass destructions as the rationale for the war, it had led to a deep crisis of trust. Other explanations of the United States, such as protection of human rights and democracy promotion in Iraq only strengthened Moscow's scepticism.

In the 2000s, terrorism threats were acute in Russia; however, the United States did not support Russia as it was expected in terms of joint counterterrorism activities (Graham, 2017). Russia experienced several terrorist attacks, including the most devastating incidents—the Moscow theatre hostage crisis in October 2002 and the Beslan school massacre in September 2004. After the Beslan tragedy, the Russian leader took measures on enhancing the Kremlin's power. Blaming some "foreign powers" for their exploitation of terrorists against Russia (Trenin, 2014), Vladimir Putin decided to concentrate power to hold Russia's regions under strict control as well as to tackle security issues in the North Caucasus. The Bush administration criticised anti-democratic trends in Russia, including the elimination of direct gubernatorial elections that led to an erosion of political pluralism.

During the Bush presidency, Russia was annoyed by growing American influence in the post-Soviet space. In 2004, seven countries, including the three Baltic states, joined NATO. Besides, the so-called colour revolutions—in Georgia (the Rose revolution) in 2003, Ukraine in 2004 (the Orange revolution) and Kyrgyzstan in 2005 (the Tulip revolution)—intensified Russia's suspicions about U.S. covert intentions to impose rules of their game in Russia's zones of influence. Moreover, after the U.S. withdrawal from the Anti-Ballistic Missile (ABM) Treaty in 2002, which was a guarantee of strategic stability for Russia, George W. Bush announced that the United States would deploy a missile defence system in Poland and Czech. Not surprisingly, these geopolitical and military ambitions made Moscow reassess U.S. foreign policy.

On 10 February 2007, Vladimir Putin, in his speech at the Munich Security Conference, outlined the main issues of U.S. foreign policy and criticised the U.S.-led unipolar order: "It is world in which there is one master, one sovereign… [T]his is pernicious not only for all those within this system but also for the sovereign itself because it destroys itself from within" (Putin, 2007). The Russian leader highlighted the most controversial Washington initiatives such as the deployment of the anti-missile defence system in Europe and NATO enlargement. "I think it is obvious that NATO expansion does not have any relation with the modernisation of the Alliance itself or with ensuring security in Europe. On the contrary, it represents a serious provocation that reduces the level of mutual trust. And we have the right to ask: against whom is this expansion intended?" (Putin, 2007). It was a decisive moment for the Russian leader who intended to stand up for his vision of international affairs, Russia's foreign policy and further developments in relations with the United States. As Angela Stent (2014, p. 136) noted, "While Washington appeared to be floundering, Russia for the first time in fifteen years began to project the image of a rising power". The Munich speech deeply impressed U.S. and Western policymakers, and, not surprisingly, comments in Western media were mostly unfavourable. "After the rushed, giddy embrace of American ideas in the 1990s, the anti-Western impulse has again become increasingly conspicuous during the presidency of Vladimir Putin", wrote *the Economist* ("Not a Cold War", 2007). Indeed, this "anti-Western impulse" has turned into an essential element of Russia's foreign policy.

U.S. interference in Russia's spheres of influence, including former Soviet republics and satellites, has been one of the most challenging issues in Moscow's relations with Washington. At the same time, Russia did not manage to use soft power tools enough to change its standing in the post-Soviet space, especially in former Soviet republics seeking for their national identities outside Russia's influence. Russia was perceived as the Soviet Union's successor with expansionist ambitions, so its image in post-Soviet countries remained controversial. The United States took into account this controversy and used it in its interests, offering military protection to some former Soviet republics, understanding that such initiatives were unacceptable for Moscow. When, in 2008, U.S. officials began to promote the possible NATO membership for Ukraine and Georgia, not surprisingly, they crossed Russia's red line (Sachs, 2018, p. 73). In the context of U.S. plans to deploy missile bases in Poland and the Czech Republic, further NATO's eastward promotion for Georgia and Ukraine seemed like an aggressive action against Russia. Later, Thomas Graham (2017) admitted that "there was a great deal of unease about the United States trying to insert itself into Georgia by undermining Russia's own presence". That is why the Georgian–Ossetian conflict in August 2008 turned out to be a serious geopolitical challenge. In response to this conflict, Russia launched a military operation against Georgia, and this short but intense war ended with Georgia's defeat. In a moment, Russia was blamed by the West as the main culprit. When Russia recognised the independence of South Ossetia and Abkhazia, it caused a fierce reaction of the United States, condemning Russia for the redrawing of the world map. In turn, Russia accused the United States of orchestrating the Georgia crisis.

The Russo-Georgian War resulted in a severe crisis in U.S.–Russia relations drifting towards a long-term confrontation. However, Russia demonstrated that it would defend its spheres of influence in the post-Soviet space, so, in this sense, Russia managed to strengthen its position as an independent actor on the global stage (Mankoff, 2009). The Russo-Georgian war became a final chord in U.S.–Russian relations under the Bush administration. The implications were profound, first of all for Russia, which was punished by the withdrawal of foreign investment that affected the Russian economy. More significantly, this war revealed "the failure of political leaders in both Western countries and Russia to overcome the main institutional legacies of the Cold War" (Pitty, 2010, p. 40). The next period under the presidency of Barack Obama, Dmitry Medvedev and Vladimir Putin brought new challenges.

Reset vs Overload

The Obama presidency started with a promising initiative to reload strained U.S.–Russia relations. Symbolically, Hillary Clinton, the U.S. secretary of state, and Sergei Lavrov, the Russian foreign minister, during the official meeting on reloading of U.S.–Russian relations activated a pushing button where instead of the Russian word "perezagruzka" meaning "reset", the word "peregruzka"—"overload"—was written. It was prophetic: the reset turned into the overload. Nevertheless, Dmitry Medvedev and Barack Obama achieved some positive results in bilateral relations: They launched the Obama-Medvedev commission for effective U.S.–Russia cooperation and communication as well as reached an essential agreement for global security, New START—Strategic Arms Reduction Treaty.

The geopolitical context, however, was complicated, especially when Hillary Clinton pursued a tough policy in international affairs. Playing "the realist hawk" in the Obama administration, Hillary Clinton had a profound impact on the American president (Hirsh, 2013). She maintained relationships with influential political actors and launched major initiatives in foreign policy, including a NATO-led intervention in Libya and support of the Arab Spring. In March 2011, Dmitry Medvedev, then the Russian president, granted the United States a legal opportunity for military operations in Libya refusing to put a veto on U.N. Security Council Resolution. As Charles Grant (2012), director of the Center for European Reform, stated, "That decision—opposed by Prime Minister Putin and much of the Russian security establishment—gave the United States and its allies the legal cover to intervene militarily in Libya". The U.S.-led NATO military action in Libya resulted in the dismantling of the Qaddafi regime and the brutal murder of the Libyan leader, Muammar Qaddafi. The Libya debacle became a key point of disagreement inside the ruling tandem of Vladimir Putin and Dmitry Medvedev, and, in the longer term, affected Russia's foreign policy to prevent a repeat of the Libyan scenario in Syria.

The period from 2011 to 2012 became a litmus test for U.S.–Russia relations when Russia faced mass protests against the ruling party *Edinaya Rossiya* (United Russia) and Vladimir Putin. The protests intensified just before the presidential election in Russia. Moscow, disturbed by outcomes of the Arab Spring igniting the Greater Middle East, presumed that the United States could evoke rebellious moods in Russia. Tensions escalated when Vladimir Putin blamed Hillary Clinton for "inciting unrest in Russia", supported by the U.S. Department (Herszenhorn & Barry, 2011). The Russian leader became more suspicious of American policymakers, striving for "eliminating foreign political influence in the country and ensuring that Moscow's special interests in its former borderlands are recognised" (Trenin, 2014).

The reset, in the end, failed and resulted in disappointment and frustration for both sides. Some incidents added fuel to the fire—the Magnitsky case and U.S. sanctions against Russian officials, and the Snowden case, when Russia granted asylum for Edward Snowden, the American whistleblower, rejecting his extradition to the United States. In response, Barack Obama cancelled the U.S.–Russian summit in 2013.

The Syria campaign turned out to be especially frustrating for the American president who was irritated by Russia's growing influence and assertiveness in this geopolitically vital region. In Syria, Russia steadily resisted U.S. attempts to overturn the Bashar al-Assad regime. Robert Legvold (2016, p. 109) argued, "On the heels of the Libyan intervention, the U.S. campaign against Bashar al-Assad in the Syrian civil war was perceived as more of the United States recklessly toppling regimes without considering the chaos that would follow". To save Assad, Russia vetoed several UN resolutions on Syria backed by the United States and other members of the UN Security Council, including Britain and France. In 2013, Vladimir Putin skillfully prevented a U.S. strike against the Syrian leader just shortly before a decisive vote in the U.S. Congress on Obama's decision to attack Bashar al-Assad, blamed for using chemical weapons. Then the Russian leader offered Syria to remove or destroy its chemical weapons under the control of the United Nations. As a result, Russia and the United States reached an unprecedented agreement on Syria's chemical disarmament (Gordon, 2013). In 2015, Russia launched a military operation in Syria, challenging the U.S.-led order in this region (Trenin, 2016, p. 17). Geopolitically, the Russian military campaign in Syria is supposed to be far-reaching for Russia's perspectives in the Greater Middle East as well as for Russia's strategic competitiveness in the region where multiple interests of various political actors are intersected.

Deep Freeze

The Syria campaign was only a prelude to a geopolitical turmoil engaging Ukraine, Russia, and the West. The Ukraine crisis has become a crucial turning point in Russia's relations with the United States and the West. For the first time in post-Cold War history, a strategic rivalry between major powers has reached its highest point leading to a full-scale confrontation. Clashes of geopolitical interests have broken out in a vulnerable post-Soviet place—Ukraine, unfolding on the unpredictable scenario, followed by a long-term hybrid war in Eastern Ukraine, provocations and dramatic events in the conflict zone involving Donetsk and Lugansk. Matthew Rojansky (2017), director of the Kennan Institute at the Wilson Center, explained different approaches of both states to the Ukraine crisis: "Where Americans saw Russian aggression and violation of basic international norms in Ukraine, Russians described a necessary counter-offensive against hostile European and American intervention to pull Ukraine into an anti-Russian alliance". This conflict has poisoned Russia's relations with Ukraine and the West, so it seems incredibly challenging to come to a reconciliation. Geopolitically, Ukraine is one of the most vital regions for Russia, as Zbigniew Brzezinski clearly described this phenomenon in his book "The Grand Chessboard" (1998, p. 46), "Ukraine… is a geopolitical pivot because its very existence as an independent country helps to transform Russia. Without Ukraine, Russia ceases to be a Eurasian empire". Russia's annexation of Crimea (in Russian interpretation, the reunification with Crimea) became the point of no return for Moscow, resulted in further Russia's alienation from the West and heavy economic sanctions.

In 2016, when Donald Trump came to power, the United States accused Russia of meddling in the presidential election. The Russia case was under a special investigation, conducted by U.S. special counsel Robert Mueller, who, in the end, did not find any evidence of a criminal conspiracy between the Trump administration and Russia ("Mueller report", 2019). Russia's meddling in U.S. elections has become one of the most discussed themes in the American media and outweighed essential issues in domestic politics. "Not surprisingly, "the fog of suspicion" is chilling, even freezing, public discourse about worsening U.S.—Russian relations, which should be a compelling media subject", believes Stephen F. Cohen (2019, "The fog of suspicion", para. 3). It seemed to be a climax in a hyperreal postmodernist story when *The New York Times* (Goldman, Schmidt, & Fandos, 2019) reported that the F.B.I. thoroughly investigated whether American president Donald Trump was a Russian agent working "on behalf of Russia against American interests". Remarkably, Russia has been exploited as "a meme in U.S. politics" (Lukyanov, 2018), and this trend has reflected increasing political polarisation in American society. In 2016–2019, the Trump-Russia saga was one of the main political and media shows, surprising and frustrating the public. No doubt, the so-called Russiagate has damaged U.S.–Russian relations, and the Trump presidency has turned out to be challenging for Moscow. Severe economic and diplomatic sanctions, imposed on Russia by the United States and the European Union, have contributed to the escalation of tensions between Russia and the West. Geopolitically, in response to these challenges, Russia has cultivated relations with other world players, including China, Saudi Arabia, Turkey, Egypt and Israel, and extended its influence in strategically important areas.

In terms of global security, Donald Trump's policy toward Russia remains controversial. National Security Strategy, developed by the Trump administration, considers Russia as "one of the most geopolitical threats to the United States" (Rumer & Sokolsky, 2019). In this regard, the issue of nuclear proliferation highlighted on the agenda of world leaders seems to be essential for global security. The United States, blaming Russia for testing and deploying new cruise missiles, decided to terminate the Intermediate-Range Nuclear Forces Treaty (INF), the historical agreement on the elimination of intermediate-range and shorter-range missiles, signed by Ronald Reagan and Mikhail Gorbachev in December 1987, after several years of U.S.–Russian negotiations ("America tears up an arms treaty", 2018). In symmetrical response, Russia announced that it also would pull out the INF treaty. Ramifications of the INF treaty demise are likely to be detrimental: from an uncontrollable nuclear arms race to global nuclear disaster. Being a cornerstone of nuclear security, the treaty allowed to control nuclear players. "Consumed by their New Cold War, Russia and the United States are dismantling the last pieces of the arms control framework they laboriously negotiated over a half-century", resumes Robert Legvold (2018, p. 15). These developments reveal that nuclear security, undoubtedly, remains an acute issue on the global agenda and demands a greater responsibility of the United States and Russia in terms of growing threats of a nuclear catastrophe. In today's complex multipolar world, states can exploit nuclear proliferation for strategic manoeuvres in foreign policy (Trenin, 2018). Many experts believe that a doomsday scenario is highly probable if a nuclear catastrophe can be triggered by a conventional military conflict or subversive activities of non-state actors. In this sense, a military confrontation between the two major powers can be disruptive for global security; on the contrary, U.S.–Russian collaboration can minimise risks of nuclear disaster.

Conclusion

For the last 30 years, U.S.–Russia relations have been affected by various factors such as clashes of geopolitical and national interests, the strategic rivalry in wars and conflicts, military ambitions and sophisticated information techniques. Until now, the United States and Russia have pursued a conventional policy of confrontation. However, it becomes clear that the old paradigm is outdated. It is difficult for a new generation to find sense and logic in the existential struggle between the former Cold War rivals. Despite political turbulence and uncertainty, world leaders have to tackle global challenges such as terrorism, nuclear proliferation, cyber warfare, natural disasters and climate changes. In this regard, Russian–American cooperation can be beneficial for world security, stability and development. Some options for a strategic partnership between Moscow and Washington are worth considering. First, there is a need for a joint policy in the field of global security, including nuclear and cybersecurity. Second, the United States and Russia need to balance their national interests in geopolitical spheres of influence, particularly in the post-Soviet space. Third, the two states can optimise business and science cooperation, including projects in such areas as artificial intelligence and space exploration. There is only one way to reach a breakthrough in U.S.–Russia relations: A common willingness to end the confrontation and derive benefits from the partnership.

Acknowledgements I would like to express my deep gratitude to distinguished scholars of international relations Philip Seib, Roderic Pitty and Roger Markwick for their valuable advice, insights and comments.

References

America tears up an arms treaty and harms itself. (2018, October 27). *The Economist*. Retrieved from https://www.economist.com/united-states/2018/10/25/america-tears-up-an-arms-treaty-and-harms-itself.

A new Cold War? (1999, April 15). *The Economist*. Retrieved from https://www.economist.com/leaders/1999/04/15/a-new-cold-war.

A new European order. (1997, May 15). *The Economist*. Retrieved from https://www.economist.com/europe/1997/05/15/a-new-european-order.

Broder, J. M. (1999, March 24). Conflict in the Balkans: The Russians; a phone call from Gore and a U-turn to Moscow. *The New York Times*. Retrieved from https://www.nytimes.com/1999/03/24/world/conflict-balkans-russians-phone-call-gore-u-turn-moscow.html.

Brzezinski, Z. (1992, Fall). The Cold War and its aftermath. *Foreign Affairs*. Retrieved from https://www.foreignaffairs.com/articles/russia-fsu/1992-09-01/cold-war-and-its-aftermath.

Brzezinski, Z. (1998). *The grand chessboard: American primacy and its geostrategic imperatives*. New York: Basics Books.

Brzezinski, Z., Scowcroft, B., & Ignatius, D. (2008). *America and the world: Conversations on the future of American foreign policy*. New York: Basic Books.

Cohen, S. F. (2019). *War with Russia? From Putin & Ukraine to Trump & Russiagate*. New York: Hot Books.

Engdahl, F. W. (2009). *Full spectrum dominance: Totalitarian democracy in the new world order*. Wiesbaden: Edition. Engdahl.

Garfinkle, A. (2008, 1 May). Zbigniew Brzezinski: "I'll do it again". *The American Interest*. Retrieved from https://www.the-american-interest.com/2008/05/01/id-do-it-again/.

Goldman, A., Schmidt, M. S., & Fandos, N. (2019, January 11). F.B.I. opened inquiry into whether Trump was secretly working on behalf of Russia. *The New York Times*. Retrieved from https://www.nytimes.com/2019/01/11/us/politics/fbi-trump-russia-inquiry.html.

Gorbachev was promised NATO would not expand east–declassified docs. (2017, December 14). RT. Retrieved from https://www.rt.com/news/413029-nato-gorbachev-expansion-promises/.

Gordon, M. R. (2013, September 14). U.S. and Russia reach deal to destroy Syria's chemical arms. *The New York Times*. Retrieved from https://www.nytimes.com/2013/09/15/world/middleeast/syria-talks.html.

Graham, T. (2017, June 19). Interview with Michael Kirk. Frontline. PBS. Retrieved from https://www.pbs.org/wgbh/frontline/interview/thomas-graham/.

Grant, C. (2012, April 4). Will Putin delete the reset? *The New York Times*. Retrieved from https://www.nytimes.com/2012/04/05/opinion/will-putin-delete-the-reset.html.

Herszenhorn, D. E., & Barry, E. (2011, December 8). Putin contends Clinton incited unrest over vote. *The New York Times*. Retrieved from https://www.nytimes.com/2011/12/09/world/europe/putin-accuses-clinton-of-instigating-russian-protests.html.

Hirsh, M. (2013, May/June). The Clinton legacy. *Foreign Affairs*. Retrieved from https://www.foreignaffairs.com/articles/united-states/2013-04-03/clinton-legacy.

Kennan, G. F. "X" (1947, July). The sources of Soviet conduct. *Foreign Affairs*. Retrieved from https://www.foreignaffairs.com/articles/russian-federation/1947-07-01/sources-soviet-conduct.

Kennan, G. F. (1997, February 5). A fateful error. *The New York Times*. Retrieved from https://www.nytimes.com/1997/02/05/opinion/a-fateful-error.html.

Kuchins, A. C. (2016, December). *Elevation and calibration: A new Russia policy for America*. Center on Global Interest. Retrieved from http://globalinterests.org/wp-content/uploads/2016/12/CGI_A-New-Russia-Policy-for-America_Andy-Kuchins.pdf.

Legvold, R. (Ed.). (2007). *Russian foreign policy in the twenty-first century and the shadow of the past*. New York: Columbia University Press.

Legvold, R. (2016). *Return to Cold War*. Malden: Polity Press.

Legvold, R. (2018, May 29–June 3). U.S.–Russian relations: The price of Cold War. In *U.S.–Russia relations: Policy challenges in a new era*. Washington, DC: The Aspen Institute. Congressional Program. Retrieved from https://assets.aspeninstitute.org/content/uploads/2018/06/Helsinki-2018-Conference-Report.pdf.

Lukyanov, F. (2018, December 18). Russia is being used as a meme in U.S. politics. *The Moscow Times*. Retrieved from https://themoscowtimes.com/articles/the-view-from-moscow-63872.

Mankoff, J. (2009). *Russian foreign policy: The return of great power politics*. New York: Rowman & Littlefield Publishers.

MccGwire, M. (1998, January). NATO expansion: 'A policy error of historic importance'. *Review of International Studies, 24*, 1.

Mueller report: Trump cleared of conspiring with Russia. (2019, March 25). *BBC News*. Retrieved from https://www.bbc.com/news/world-us-canada-47688187.

Not a Cold War, but a cold tiff. (2007, February 15). *The Economist*. Retrieved from https://www.economist.com/international/2007/02/15/not-a-cold-war-but-a-cold-tiff.

Nye, J. S., Jr., & Welch, D. A. (2017). *Understanding global conflict and cooperation: An introduction to theory and history*. New York: Pearson.

Pitty, R. (2010, October). Russian views about the Cold War and its legacies. *Cold War Dossier. 28*.

Putin, V. (2007, February 10). *Speech and the following discussion at the Munich Conference on Security Policy.* The Presidential Press and Information Office Department. Retrieved from http://en.kremlin.ru/events/president/transcripts/24034.
Rojansky, M. (2017). Rapporteur's summary. In *U.S.–Russia relations: Policy challenges in a new era.* Washington, DC: The Aspen Institute. Congressional Program. Retrieved from https://assets.aspeninstitute.org/content/uploads/2017/10/2017-Berlin-Conference-Report.pdf.
Rumer, E., & Sokolsky, R. (2019). *Thirty years of U.S. policy toward Russia: Can the vicious circle be broken?* The Carnegie Moscow Center. Retrieved from https://carnegieendowment.org/2019/06/20/thirty-years-of-u.s.-policy-toward-russia-can-vicious-circle-be-broken-pub-79323.
Sachs, J. D. (2018). *A new foreign policy: Beyond American exceptionalism.* New York: Columbia University Press.
Stent, A. E. (2014). *The limits of partnership: U.S.–Russian relations in the twenty-first century.* Princeton: Princeton University Press.
Trenin, D. (2014, December). *Russia breakout from the post-Cold War system: The drivers of Putin's course.* Carnegie Moscow Center. Retrieved from https://carnegie.ru/2014/12/22/russia-s-breakout-from-post-cold-war-system-drivers-of-putin-s-course-pub-57589.
Trenin, D. (2016). *Should we fear Russia?* Malden: Polity Press.
Trenin, D. (2018, October 24). *Back to Pershings: What the U.S. withdrawal from 1987 INF treaty means.* Carnegie Moscow Center. Retrieved from https://carnegie.ru/commentary/77568.
Tsygankov, A. P. (2009). *Russophobia: Anti-Russian lobby and American foreign policy.* New York: Palgrave Macmillan.
Westad, O. A. (2017). *The Cold War: A world history.* New York: Basic Book.

7

Russia's Growing Relationship with Iran: Strategic or Tactical?

Ian Parmeter

A Troubled Past

Russian–Iranian bilateral ties have a troubled history, including wars and bitter territorial disputes over centuries. It's worth noting briefly how humiliating its interactions with Russia were for Iran.[1]

As the Russian empire expanded southwards in the seventeenth, eighteenth and nineteenth centuries, it absorbed what were then Persia's northern territories, which today are Dagestan, Georgia, Armenia and Azerbaijan. Consequent anti-Russian sentiment led to the massacre of the Russian ambassador and his staff by a Persian mob in 1829. At the same time Persia was squeezed from the south as the British, Portuguese and Dutch competed for its territory.

---

[1] For detail on the way in which past frictions in the Russia–Iran relationship affect present ties, see Vatanka (2018).

I. Parmeter (✉)
Australian National University, Canberra, ACT, Australia
e-mail: Ian.Parmeter@anu.edu.au

© The Author(s) 2020
A. Akimov and G. Kazakevitch (eds.), *30 Years since the Fall of the Berlin Wall*, Palgrave Studies in Economic History, https://doi.org/10.1007/978-981-15-0317-7_7

By the end of the nineteenth century the central government in Tehran was under the joint control of the Russian and British consulates there. Before the First World War Russia and Britain had effectively divided Iran between them.

A new era in Russian–Iranian ties seemed to be emerging after the 1917 Russian revolution. In 1921 the Bolshevik government returned parts of northern Iran through the Russo-Persian Treaty of Friendship. Despite this, the Soviet Union and Britain invaded Iran in 1941, ignoring Iran's formal neutrality.

After World War II the US moved quickly to end Soviet influence in Iran and supplant Britain's role there in order to make Iran part of the anti-Communist bloc. The US-British orchestrated coup in 1953 to remove nationalist Prime Minister Mohammad Mosaddegh generated bitterness among Iranians that still resonates today.

Iran with Saudi Arabia became the twin pillars of the US strategy to dominate the Middle East, constituting important elements in its Cold War policy of "containment" of the Soviet Union. This twin pillar concept worked brilliantly for the US—including through helping to satisfy the US economy's seemingly insatiable demand for Middle East oil—until one half of the strategy collapsed with the Iranian revolution of 1979.

But the Islamic rulers of now fully-independent Iran, whose territory was (and remains) among the most strategically valuable regions on the planet, had good reason to distrust all foreign powers. Though the Soviet Union was the first foreign government to recognise the new dispensation in Tehran, the new regime's "neither West nor East" doctrine meant Moscow scarcely benefitted from the change—except in the sense that the US had suffered a major foreign policy setback.

Spurned by Iran's new leadership, Moscow tilted to Saddam Hussein during the Iran–Iraq war (1980–1988)—further alienating Tehran. And following the collapse of the Soviet Union in 1991, President Boris Yeltsin's early attempts to woo the US and win economic benefits for Russia ruled out significant Russian ties with Iran.

A Cloudy New Dawn

But it became gradually clear from the mid-1990s that the US, while delighted with the demise of the Soviet enemy, was putting limits on its dealings with the new Russia. And it quickly became equally clear the US had no intention of bailing out Russia's bankrupt economy through a new Marshall Plan, which in the early 1990s many Russians had hoped for.

So Yeltsin and especially his successor, Vladimir Putin, turned to foreign policy options that did not involve rapprochement with the US. NATO's expansion eastwards from 1999 confirmed Moscow in this thinking, which culminated in Putin's address to the Munich Security Conference in 2007, in which he accused the US of seeking a monopolistic dominance in global relations.

In that context Russia and Iran discovered that they had a number of mutual interests.

Since the start of Putin's presidency, Russia's relations with Iran have been part of Russia's struggle with the US. Iran's Supreme Leader, Ali Khamenei, despite suspicion of Putin's motives in reaching out to him, recognised they had a shared interest in undermining US power.

But there was a fundamental mismatch: Tehran was mainly interested in the regional dimension of this anti-US objective, while Moscow's interest was in the global dimension.

It helped to build the relationship early in the Putin era that Russia was Tehran's only provider of arms and nuclear technologies. And because of Russia's veto in the UN Security Council (UNSC), it could (when it chose) shield Tehran from Washington's attempts to use UN mechanisms to step up pressure on Iran.

Russia's "Instrumentalism"

But under Yeltsin and then Putin, Russia developed an instrumental approach to its relations with Iran—which meant limiting or downgrading its assistance to Tehran when that might assist Russia's larger interests.[2]

---

[2]This instrumentalism is set out in detail in Rodkiewicz (2017, p. 41).

In 1995 Moscow concluded a secret agreement with the US in which Russia undertook not to export any arms or military technology to Iran after 1999. In return the US exempted Russia from US sanctions over weapons Russia supplied to Iran under contracts already in place (Rodkiewicz, 2017, p. 39).

Putin withdrew from this agreement in the autumn of 2000—thus signalling to Tehran that Moscow would not be willing to limit its relations with Iran at US behest (for then, at least). Russia then resumed sales of arms and military equipment to Iran.

In 2003 when credible information emerged that Iran was working to develop nuclear weapons, Russia found itself under US and other international pressure to restrict its nuclear cooperation with Iran. So Russia juggled its Iranian interests.

Russia continued its nuclear cooperation with Iran but formulated new conditions in order to deflect Western criticism (Iran's return of spent nuclear fuel and refraining from enriching uranium to weapons-grade). At the same time Russia voted for three UNSC resolutions banning export of nuclear technologies to Iran and imposing sanctions on persons associated with Iran's nuclear programme (UNSC, 2006, 2007, 2008). But it claimed to Iran to have mitigated the scope and severity of these resolutions. It also carried on the delayed construction works on the Bushehr nuclear plant on the western Iranian coast.

Under the Obama Administration's "reset" of relations with Russia from 2009, Russia backed a new UNSC (2010) resolution imposing further sanctions on Iran. Then-President Medvedev further expanded the ban to include S-300 surface-to-air missile systems, which Russia had contracted to sell to Iran in 2007.

The missile ban had real consequences for Iran which was then under threat of airstrikes from Israel and the US over its continuing nuclear enrichment. This revision was part of the deal whereby the Obama administration scrapped plans to deploy elements of the US missile shield in Central Europe and signed the new START treaty.

Unsurprisingly, Iran was furious over these several examples of Russia's willingness to "trade" aspects of their relationship for other benefits—causing a marked cooling of mutual relations. Tehran brought a lawsuit against Russia for breaching the S-300 contract.

Middle East Catalysts

But then the "Arab Spring" from late 2010 provided an incentive for serious rapprochement between the two. Both Russia and Iran saw the upheavals as a potential threat to their internal orders and geopolitical positions in the Middle East. In particular, they feared that the uprisings could lead to:

* a strengthening of the US in the region, or
* an activation of radical Sunni movements, which could strengthen Saudi Arabia, Iran's main geopolitical rival in the region.

Moreover, the hostile US and broader Western reaction to Russia's annexation of Crimea in 2014 and its active support for Ukrainian rebels in eastern Ukraine put on hold any chance of another Russian quid-pro-quo with the US over Iran.

The upshot was that both Russia and Iran became involved in defending the Assad regime, both materially and, for Iran, with troops on the ground. And when Russia launched its direct military intervention in September 2015, Russia and Iran became de facto allies in the war.

Though the war started as an internal conflict in Syria, it rapidly became also a regional and global cockpit for foreign powers supporting the different sides in the civil war. The US, Turkey and Saudi Arabia backed often-different elements of the rebels, with the US focusing after 2014 mainly on defeating Islamic State, while Turkey sought to ensure that Syrian Kurds were unable to mount operations inside Turkey. Russia, Iran and Lebanese Hizballah sought primarily to preserve the Assad regime.

As a result, the intensity of political and military liaison between Russia and Iran reached an unprecedented level.

* Joint military operations required contacts to be developed between the military and security services.
* In January 2015 the defence ministers of Russia and Iran had signed a cooperation agreement providing for joint drills, contacts between military staffs and exchange of intelligence. These intensified after September 2015.

- Two joint centres for military information exchange and operational coordination were created in Damascus and Baghdad.
- Joint exercises by the Iranian and Russian navies in the Caspian Sea were increased.
- Russian cooperation with Iran on military technology was reinforced.
- In April 2015 Putin repealed Medvedev's decree banning the export of S-300 anti-aircraft missiles to Iran. In early 2016, Russia delivered the first batch of these missile systems to Iran (with the contract providing for Russia to deliver four in all).
- Iran gave consent for Russian bombers to use the Hamadan air base in Western Iran for operations in Syria. This was a particularly significant gesture, given that the Iranian constitution prohibited use of Iranian territory by foreign military forces.

The Balance

Does all this amount to a strategic relationship?

Iran's chequered history with Tsarist Russia and the Soviet Union before 1991 and then with post-Soviet Russia, along with Russia's ambivalent dealings with Iran since 1991, suggest not.

And though Russian and Iranian officials have described their bilateral relations as strategic since the early 1990s, much has occurred in recent years to deepen Iranian mistrust of Russia.

- Apart from the secret 1995 agreement with the US on limiting Russian arms sales to Iran, Iran believed Russia deliberately delayed completion of the Bushehr nuclear power reactor. Though the contract was signed in 1995, Bushehr was not operational until late 2011, about 10 years after the original deadline. Iran interpreted the delay as Russia bowing to Western pressure. Tehran also assessed that Russia wanted to use the reactor as a card to play in Russian dealings with Western states, including exacting concessions from Washington.
- As noted, Russia's delayed delivery of the S-300 missile system caused major friction in the relationship.

- Before the signing of the Joint Comprehensive Plan of Action (JCPOA—the Iran-P5+1 agreement to limit Iran's nuclear programme) in 2015, Russia participated in sanctions against Iran imposed by the UNSC. Moreover, Russia did not veto or abstain on the resolutions authorising these sanctions. Russia told Iran that Moscow had worked behind the scenes to water down the resolutions, but Tehran never openly accepted that explanation. Ahmadinejad when Iranian President (2005–2013) accused Russia of playing "good cop" to the US's "bad cop" on this issue (Vatanka, 2018, p. 91).
- In 2007 Supreme Leader Khamenei told the then-head of the Russian Security Council, Igor Ivanov, that Tehran wanted to form a "strategic alliance against common adversaries" and proposed that the two countries share between them responsibility for the future of the Middle East and Central Asia. Khamenei followed up by sending his foreign policy adviser, Ali Akbar Velayati, to Moscow with a detailed plan. Russia did not respond. For Moscow the need to have a working relationship with the US—despite tensions caused by, for example, Russia's intervention in Georgia—far outweighed the advantages of strategic ties with Iran (Vatanka, 2018, p. 91).
- That said, at a tactical level, when policy objectives were narrower, cooperation has been relatively good.
- After the Soviet withdrawal from Afghanistan in 1989, Tehran and Moscow were de facto partners in supporting the Northern Alliance against the Pakistani- and Saudi-backed Taliban movement in the Afghan civil war.
- Tehran and Moscow were also on the same side in the civil war in Tajikistan in the 1990s.
- Similarly Russia and Iran both wanted to counter Turkish inroads in the South Caucasus, where Ankara was backing Azerbaijan against Armenia, which both Moscow and Tehran supported.
- Iran has been careful not to upset Russian interests in the former Soviet south—Russia's "near abroad". Tehran, as a large Muslim state, played an accommodating role in the context of Russia's two bloody military interventions in Muslim-populated Chechnya. Despite much condemnation in the Islamic world, Tehran used its chairing role in the Organisation of the Islamic Council (OIC) to moderate

organisational criticism in that forum. Iran indicated it was ready to "collaborate with Russia to establish stability in the North Caucasus, including Chechnya"—far from censure of Russia.

Misunderstandings and Suspicions

Russia's and Iran's joint venture in Syria is their most important claim to a strategic alliance.

But even the Iranian-Russian compact over Syria has not been without problems and misunderstandings. The Iranian regime, though welcoming Russian military assistance, seemed to harbour suspicions that Moscow might reach separate understandings with the US or Turkey.

Such doubts have been fuelled by unilateral Russian actions. In January 2016 Moscow announced that it was pulling out of Syria—a step apparently not coordinated with Tehran. The withdrawal did not materialise, but Moscow subsequently revealed unilaterally that it was using the Hamadan airbase for its operations in Syria. This was extremely embarrassing to the Iranian regime for reasons set out above. Iranian Defence Minister Hossein Dehghan called the Russian indiscretion a "betrayal".

Not surprisingly, Iran continues to monitor Russia's Syria agenda nervously. They are military partners in Syria, and they jointly sponsor the Astana peace process. But Iran knows that Russia has a freer hand than Iran in seeking to cut deals with an array of other actors—the US, Turkey, Israel and even the Gulf Arabs.

The IRGC v Rouhani

The calculus in Tehran concerning Russia is affected also by rivalries within the regime.

The Islamic Revolutionary Guard Corps (IRGC), the political-military guardian of the Islamic Republic, is pro-Moscow, and speaks of "strategic overlap" of Iranian interests with Russia concerning rolling back US power in the Middle East and combatting Sunni terrorism. The IRGC values the flow of Russian arms, intelligence cooperation and other practical benefits from Russia—and is not worried about any dent from this to Iran's Islamic credentials.

The Rouhani government appears to have a less rosy view of Russia. Since 2013 it has looked at the renewed US–Russia tensions as an opportunity not to move closer to Moscow per se, but to play the Russia card in an effort to prod Washington to reassess its overall posture towards Iran.

Moreover, Rouhani is focused mainly on improving Iran's economy, and in this respect the Russian relationship is of little use.

No economic bounce

The enhancements to military and security ties resulting from joint hostility towards the US and their cooperation in Syria have not been reinforced by closer economic relations, despite the two sides stated intentions to this effect at government level.

Russian companies have not benefitted from absence of competition from Western businesses kept out of Iran by Western sanctions (which Russia does not recognise). This is due to the absence of trade and economic complementarities but also because, paradoxically, many Russian companies have seen the West as a more valuable market than Iran and have not wanted to put their dealings there at risk (Thomas, 2018).

In 2017 Iran was the 47th ranked destination for Russian exports, totalling $1.3 billion. In that year Iran was the 61st ranked source of Russian imports—just $393 million. Russia was Iran's 18th ranked export market, and 8th largest source of imports. Unsurprisingly, China was the dominant export market and import source for both Russia and Iran (IMF, 2019).

A 2014 barter agreement on the exchange of Iranian oil for Russian industrial products has produced few results. The agreement was for 500,000 barrels of oil per month, but Iran had been able to export to Russia only 100,000 barrels per month by 2017 (Rodkiewicz, 2017, p. 43).

A further economic, as well as political, irritant was that Moscow shamelessly exploited the restrictions on Iran's oil exports so that Russia could sell more of Russia's oil on the global market.

The effective failure of negotiations to create a free trade zone between Iran and the Eurasian Economic Union also demonstrates the scale of difficulties in negotiating mutually beneficial economic deals between Russia and Iran. The free trade concept has had to be downgraded to a trade liberalisation agreement, which will involve customs rates that are yet to be agreed.

Before the advent of Donald Trump as US President, the Russians, too, would have had grounds for suspicions about Tehran's game plan. President Rouhani's *sotto voce* overtures to the West from 2013, and President Obama's apparent receptiveness, may have created doubt in Moscow about Iran's reliability as an anti-Western partner. The Rouhani government's conspicuous preference for Western goods and services is a sore point in Moscow. In one case a Russian minister cancelled a visit to Tehran in anger over Iran's preference for Boeing and Airbus over Russian-made aircraft (Vatanka, 2018, p. 99).

But that's presumably in the past. Trump's extreme hostility towards Iran and reneging on the JCPOA would have reassured Moscow that a turnaround in Iran's relations with the US and the West in general is not on the cards. Trump's approach to Iran has also benefitted the IRGC and other regime hardliners vis-à-vis Rouhani in their domestic power struggle.

Fatal Flaw

The problem in the Russian–Iranian relationship is that Moscow and Tehran have different priorities and expectations. Russia's policy in the Middle East is part of a wider strategy aimed at creating an international order which would shield Russia against Western interference in its internal affairs and would guarantee it an equal footing with the US.

In practice, that means Russia's Middle East policy is subordinated to the Kremlin's global strategy towards Washington.

Moscow seeks to create in the Middle East a regional variant of what it believes to be the best model of the international order: a concert of powers that would include, apart from Russia and China, regional

7 Russia's Growing Relationship with Iran: Strategic or Tactical?

powers Turkey and Iran. The US can be part of this provided it shows willingness to cooperate with Russia on an equal footing.[3]

In addition, Putin's deft outflanking of the US in the Middle East has the domestic benefit of reinforcing Moscow's claims to great power status in the eyes of both the Russian elite and the Russian population at large.

Iran fits well into this strategy. Both states have the shared priority of undermining the US position in the region. For this reason, Moscow and Tehran view each other as valuable partners in the Middle East.

But Russia has other regional partners it is wooing: particularly Israel, Turkey and Saudi Arabia.[4] Unsurprisingly Iran looks askance at Russia's attempts to develop these relationships.

Iran for its part values Russia for the support Russia provides to Tehran's regional objectives and the diplomatic cover Moscow can provide in international fora. Iran judges Russia as an essential building block in the anti-Western global front that Iran has wanted to see emerge to challenge the Western-dominated international system.

The crux is that Russia is more important to Iran than Iran is to Russia. They are neighbours with a troubled history, which both remember and which affects their capacity to trust each other. But despite this they can work well together when they have major interests in common. Syria is for now the glue in the relationship. But as their interests change, the incentives to maintain this close relationship will diminish.

Tehran would be unwise to assume that Moscow will take any significant action to offset the sanctions regime the Trump Administration is progressively tightening on Iran. Russia is a net beneficiary from

---

[3]Australian scholar Lo (2015) sets out this Russian approach in detail—see especially Chapter 3. He sees the most serious weakness of this approach in the fact that it is rooted in an idealised version of the past, a revamped Concert of Great Powers, rather than looking to a new model of international relations that reflects the changing dynamics of power and influence in the contemporary international situation.

[4]Russian scholar Kozhanov (2016) examines this conundrum in detail in Chapter 6 "The Marriage of Convenience: Russian-Iranian Cooperation in Syria". On p. 89 he describes Israel as Russia's "silent partner" in the Middle East. Kozhanov concludes emphatically that the Russian-Iranian relationship is far from an alliance.

the sanctions—it stands to benefit from helping to fill the gap left by the shortfall in Iranian oil exports. And Moscow need not fear adverse repercussions in its relations with Iran: Iran has nowhere else to go. This is a tactical, not a strategic, relationship.

References

IMF. (2019). *Direction of trade statistics—Ranking by partners*. Retrieved from http://data.imf.org/?sk=9D6028D4-F14A-464C-A2F2-59B2CD424B85.
Kozhanov, N. (2016). *Russia and the Syria conflict*. Berlin: Gerlach Press.
Lo, B. (2015). *Russia and the new world disorder*. London: Chatham House.
Rodkiewicz, W. (2017). *Russia's Middle East policy—Regional ambitions, global objectives*. Warsaw: Centre for Eastern Studies (OSW).
Thomas, A. (2018, April 12). Russia's trade with the west surges even as sanctions mount. *Wall Street Journal*.
UNSC. (2006). Resolution 1737 of 23 December 2006.
UNSC. (2007). Resolution 1747 of 24 March 2007.
UNSC. (2008). Resolution 1803 of 3 March 2008.
UNSC. (2010). Resolution 1929 of 9 June 2010.
Vatanka, A. (2018). "Iran's Russian Conundrum", Chapter 4 of Theodore Karasik and Stephen Blank (Eds.), *Russia in the Middle East*. Washington: Jamestown Foundation.

8

Energy Integration in Eurasian Economic Union: Preliminary Study on Progress and Policy Implications

Elena Shadrina

Introduction

Energy integration initiatives of the Eurasian Economic Union (EAEU) have been given insufficient scholarly attention. Meanwhile, the EAEU's projected common energy markets (CEMs) appear to deserve scrutiny. The EAEU, owing to Russia and Kazakhstan, produces almost 5% of the world's electricity. It holds nearly 19% of the world's total proved gas reserves, 18% of the world's gas output and 31% of the world's gas exports. The EAEU possesses more than 8% of the world's oil reserves, 14.2% of the world's crude production and 15% of the world's crude exports. Furthermore, the EAEU runs more than 7% of the world's oil refining capacity and 13.5% of the word's petroleum products exports (BP, 2018).

The chapter presents a preliminary comparative exercise on energy integrations in Eurasia and Europe. To begin with, integration may involve

This research was supported by Waseda University grant-in-aid BARD00523801 and 2019R-069.

E. Shadrina (✉)
Waseda University, Tokyo, Japan

several dimensions: sectoral, vertical (distribution of competencies among integrated institutions in respective integrated sector) and horizontal (territorial extension of sectoral and vertical integration resulting in transfer of competencies from a nation-state to supranational polity). Neofunctionalism traditionally examines sectoral integration, intergovernmentalism addresses vertical integration, while supranationalism theoretically underpins horizontal integration. Neofunctionalism sees integration as the process wherein national political actors shift their loyalties, expectations and political activities towards a new supranational entity (Haas, 1958, 1961; Lindberg & Scheingold, 1970; Nye, 1971; Schmitter, 1969). Intergovernmentalism argues that the process of integration is under the control of member-state governments, who determine the speed and substance of integration, therefore, integration strengthens the nation-state (Hoffmann, 1966, 1982; Milward, 1984, 1992; Moravcsik, 1998, 1999). Representatives of supranationalism, Stone Sweet and Sandholtz (1997) reinterpret neofunctionalism explaining integration as a result of transactional exchange which raises social demand for international regulation and leads to the formation of the supranational institutions. Created by member-states, the supranational institutions trigger a self-reinforcing process of further integration that exercises a transformative impact on the identity of member-states. Supranationalism is underpinned by rationalist and constructivist theories with the former originating primarily in historical institutionalism and the latter in the theories of socialisation (Schimmelfennig & Rittberger, 2005; Stone Sweet & Fligstein, 2001).

In this chapter, the Eurasian and European energy integrations are examined upon a plain analytical framework consisting of three elements: the ideational component of energy integration (ideas); the motivational aspect of member-states to engage into energy integration (interests); and the institutional form of integration (institutions). The political economy studies often employ the notions of ideas, interests and institutions for the analysis of policy transformation (Hall, 1997; Schirm, 2016). Out of these three, ideas tend to be the most static component; they are path-dependent and value-based collective expectations about a particular policy issue. Interests can be explained as material considerations (in the form of costs- benefits equations) of the national actors that evolve to match the dynamic environment. Institutions, which in the most generic form are defined as "humanly devised constraints that structure political, economic and social interaction" (North, 1990, p. 97), are influenced by the type of economic system (Greif, 2006; Hall & Soskice, 2001; Maszczyk & Rapacki, 2012; Nolke & Vliegenthart, 2009). North, Wallis, and Weingast (2009) identify two principal types of institutional environments: open access orders (OAO) and limited access orders (LAO). The former relies on efficient impersonal institutions guaranteeing inclusiveness, ensuring the rule of law, reducing the opportunities for rent-seeking and promoting the Schumpeterian creative destruction. In contrast, the LAOs are based upon personal relationships, the principal goal of which is creating and capturing the rents. Because the stability of institutional setting secures the continuity of rent flows, the LAOs resist institutional changes. Naturally, building supranational institutions in the process of integration requires a certain degree of compatibility among the nations' sets of ideas, interests and institutions (Blockmans, Kostanyan, Remizov, Slapakova, & van der Loo, 2017; Rustemova, 2011; Shadrina, 2018).

As is known, the very inception of the European integration *idea* back in the 1950s was linked to the initiation of supply policies' coordination in the coal and nuclear power sectors. The contemporary Energy Union of the European Union is a qualitatively novel project involving the shift from supranational governance towards supranational policy. Before 2014, the market-led policy was a dominant course for energy integration in the EU. The Ukrainian crisis prompted the traditional external security concerns in the EU leading to the conception of the Energy Union aimed "to end Russia' energy stranglehold" (Blockmans, 2019). Furthermore, the traditional security agenda was supplemented by the ideas of sustainability, solidarity/coordination of external action of the member-states and innovations. In turn, in Eurasia, energy has emerged on the integration agenda during the Eurasian Customs Union (Lukashenko, 2011; Nazarbaev, 2011; Putin, 2011). The joint energy initiatives were revealed by Belarus, Kazakhstan and Russia in their Declaration on Eurasian Economic Integration. The advancement of Eurasian energy integration shall be perceived in a broader context. Having encountered with the western targeted sanctions, Russia started to promulgate a novel concept of Greater Eurasia.[1] In other words, in a changed geopolitical and geoeconomic context, the importance of the EAEU as one of the immediate conduits towards the materialisation of a Greater Eurasia project has dramatically grown to Russia. In its contemporary form, the Eurasian concept of energy integration is reminiscent of the EU's early energy integrative undertakings for its rather functionalist and technical design. It envisions the formation of the CEMs to ensure energy security, enhance competition (in its idiosyncratic mode implying the maintenance of state-owned enterprises and natural monopolies with only some pockets of competition permitted), and, perhaps most importantly, strengthen the Eurasian integration itself. Conceptually, the Eurasian CEMs do not imply policy coordination, nor do they envisage the harmonisation of an external component of the member-states energy policies. Rather, the CEMs are concerned to homogenise regulation in specified energy markets and liberalise transactions among the national energy sectors.

Intuitively, a member-state's *interest* in energy integration is shaped by its energy profile. An economy lacking energy resources is more likely to engage in integrative initiatives while exploring other avenues along the way. By the same token, the energy-endowed economy would consider integration as one of the options for energy export diversification. Differentiating between low politics and high politics aspects, Andersen, Goldthau, and Sitter (2017) generalise that the energy policy of some nations is dominated by the pursuance of market values, while other nations prioritise the security of energy supply. As is discussed further, the member-states' interests tend to be not finely convergent in either the EU or the EAEU case. Nonetheless, the variety of interests in the realm of energy integration can be analysed as being influenced by the logic of path dependency, or path change. The latter is a result of a transition triggered by domestic or/and external factors at a critical juncture. A somewhat more consolidated motivation of the EU member-states for energy integration was fuelled by the aftermaths of

---

[1]Kompas pobiditelei. (2016, June 19). *Rossiiskaya gazeta*. Retrieved from https://rg.ru/2016/06/19/regszfo/vladimir-putin-proekt-bolshoj-evrazii-otkryt-i-dlia-evropy.html.

the Russian–Ukrainian gas conflicts in 2006 and 2009 and the Crimean crisis in 2014 (Andersen et al., 2017; Andoura & Vinois, 2015; Maltby, 2013), albeit the harmonisation of external energy policy of the member-states remains a challenge for the EU (Jegen, 2014; Kustova, 2017). The Eurasian nations interests in energy integration seem to be shaped by the remnants of the Soviet-era attitudes and the pursuance of LAO. Belarus, for example, seeks to prolong energy subsidies extended by Russia, although such behaviour contradicts the market logic. Likewise, instead of modifying their national institutional designs towards something more efficient, large economies Russia and Kazakhstan prefer transplanting their existing institutions to other Eurasian economies and having them endorsed as universal norms for the EAEU. Most telling illustration is a natural monopoly, which in the energy sector is almost exclusively a state-owned company (SOEC). The SOECs are loyal to their national governments for they depend on the government for energy rents distribution. In turn, the governments not only gain control over the domestic energy sectors but also strengthen their ability to influence the foreign energy importing economies.

The EU's has passed through a long process of mastering multiple embeddedness of member-states for the supranational institution-building (Beyers, 2005). The formation of the supranational institutions became possible with the internalisation of state representatives within a supranational institution after they became able to set aside their national preferences and act for the common good (Howorth, 2012). The EU has ample expertise on the member-states' engagement into supranational entrepreneurship (Cram, 1997; Maltby, 2013; Moravcsik, 1999; Sandholtz & Zysman, 1989) and institutional activism (Howarth & Ross, 2017). Institutionally, the Eurasian integration is complete, albeit it differs in many ways from the European case. For one, the EAEU does not have the supranational legislative body (Shadrina, 2018). The institutionalisation of energy integration began after the launch of the EAEU in 2015. At times, it still stumbles over the member-states' pursuance of self-centred interests. Overall, the character of national institutional environments influences the nature of the supranational institutions. If not ready for the institutional shifts, a nation defending LAO domestically will not seek an authentic integration with an OAO economy. The points of reference here are the compatibility of institutional settings across the EAEU economies and the incompatibility of those in the EAEU and EU. The politicisation of gas supplies to the European markets by export monopoly SOEC Gazprom and, a result of this, at times escalated tensions between Russia and the EU are the side-effects of the transactions between institutionally incompatible systems.

With the above observations incorporated, the chapter is organised as follows. First, it explains the ideational and motivational frames of the Eurasian energy integration. Then, it details the EAEU's energy integration project and characterises the institutional environment for energy integration in the EAEU. Similarly, the chapter discusses the evolution of ideas, interests and institutions for the case of Energy Union in the EU. The concluding section summarises the arguments and offers some policy implications.

Eurasian Energy Integration

(Dis-)Integrative Power of Energy in EAEU

A significant part of energy infrastructure in the EAEU member-states was constructed during the Soviet era. Because energy infrastructure was primarily designed to satisfy the needs of the unified Soviet economic system, in modern times, the EAEU countries have unevenly developed domestic energy infrastructure. Speaking of gas pipeline segment (Table 8.1), in Kazakhstan, nearly 98% of gas reserves are located in

Table 8.1 Connectivity to gas pipeline network in EAEU member-states, share of population with access to pipeline gas, 2016, %

Armenia	Belarus	Kazakhstan	Kyrgyzstan	Russia
95	99	uneven: 79.9–96.4 in the west; 19.1–63.4—in the south; the north (except for Kostanay region) and the east have no access	22	67.2 (highly uneven, eastern regions have largely no access)

Source Author based on Gazprom and EAEU statistics

the west and only about 40% of the population has access to the pipeline gas (Parkhomchik, 2016). Kyrgyzstan is the least interconnected among the EAEU gas markets. Relatively low access ratio for Russia can be explained by the peculiarities of its geographic, demographic and economic profiles: vast eastern territories with a low density of population and limited economic activity are largely not connected to the gas pipelines.

As per the intra-EAEU gas pipelines, Russia and Belarus are connected by the Yamal—Europe pipeline, which enables Russia's exports to Belarus as well as to the EU. Although the Nord Stream I removed certain transit volumes in part of Russian gas exports to Germany (Heinrich, 2017), Belarus still keeps 22% of Russian gas transit (Ellinas, 2019). Russia is a single gas supplier of Belarus. More than 90% of Belarus's electricity and heat is generated by gas-fired power plants relying on Russian gas. Gazprom controls the Yamal–Europe transit and after the acquisition of the Belarusian pipeline operator Beltransgaz in 2011, it owns almost the entire Belarusian gas pipelines (Williams, 2018). Kazakhstan is linked with Russia via the Soviet-era built Central Asia Center (CAC) gas pipeline system. Controlling the CAC, Gazprom has long brokered Central Asian (especially Turkmen) gas exports to the European markets acquiring significant benefits.[2] Kyrgyzstan has a 3.9 bcm annual capacity gas link with Uzbekistan and Kazakhstan, but Gazprom has exclusive rights for gas importation and owns the national gas transmission and distribution systems through its subsidiary Kyrgyzgaz.[3] Natural gas plays an important role in Armenia, accounting for half of winter heating and more than a quarter of electricity generation. Lacking hydrocarbon resources, Armenia is in an especially difficult situation. Additionally, the logistics for its energy import is complicated by the economic blockade imposed by Azerbaijan to the East and Turkey to the West over the Nagorno-Karabakh conflict. Gazprom Armenia, owned by Russian Gazprom, holds the gas pipeline network and retains a monopoly over

---

[2]The purchases of Turkmen gas were stopped in 2016 over a mix of reasons, but in late 2018 Gazprom announced the resumption of the trade from 2019.
[3]Retrieved from www.gazprom.com/about/production/projects/deposits/kyrgyzstan/.

the import and distribution of natural gas. Gazprom continues to supply Armenia with about 2 bcm of natural gas annually via a pipeline that passes through Georgia. Inaugurated in 2009 Iran–Armenia gas pipeline of projected annual capacity 2.3 bcm is not fully utilised.[4]

Unlike in the gas segment, Belarus controls domestic oil infrastructure, including the part of Russia's Druzhba oil pipeline. Yet, Belarus' role as a transit country has been diminishing lately over Russia's efforts to open alternative export routes. The Baltic Pipeline System (BPS), for instance, redirected Russian oil exports to the Baltic Sea ports. Kazakhstan's oil pipelines are concentrated in the west. In the east, the Omsk-Pavlodar-Shymkent-Chardzhou pipeline crosses the country from north to south (Chichkin, 2019). The existing pipelines deliver Kazakhstani crude oil to domestic refineries (Atyrau, Shymkent and Pavlodar), as well as to the refineries in Russia's south. Major crude oil export pipelines include the Caspian Pipeline Consortium (CPC) pipeline to the Black Sea port of Novorossiysk, the Kazakhstan–China pipeline, and the Uzen-Atyrau-Samara pipeline to Russia. A portion of Kazakhstani oil is shipped by the Caspian Sea to be transported via the Baku-Tbilisi-Ceyhan (BTC) pipeline or the Northern Route pipeline (Baku-Novorossiysk) for onward transportation to Europe. Before the collapse of the USSR, Armenia had been receiving Russian oil by the railway via Georgia. After the Abkhazia-Georgia border was closed, the fuel is transported across the Black Sea to Georgia from where it is delivered to Armenia by rail.

In the electricity sector, the Soviet-era built United Energy System of Central Asia (UESCA), which enabled resource sharing between water-rich and hydrocarbon-rich nations in the region (exchange of water and hydroelectricity in summer for fossil fuels and power in winter), ceased to operate in 2009 (Shadrina, 2019a). The UESCA was also designed to ship hydroelectricity generated in Siberia to the Central Asian republics and the central part of Russia (via the Kazakhstani grids). After formerly established cooperation waned, the unutilised capacity of the

---

[4]Ministry of Energy Infrastructures and Natural Resources of the Republic of Armenia. Retrieved from http://www.minenergy.am/en/page/540.

Table 8.2 Share of energy trade in intra-EAEU trade, 2017, %

	EAEU	Armenia	Belarus	Kazakhstan	Kyrgyzstan	Russia
Share of trade in fossil fuels, crude oil and petroleum products	15.48	–	1.14	3.82	0.83	23.38
Share of gas trade	6.88	–	0.14	2.89	0.01	10.36
Share of electricity trade	0.48	0.48	0.00	2.06	0.02	0.44

Source Author, based on statistics of the Eurasian Economic Commission, http://eec.eaeunion.org/ru/act/integr_i_makroec/dep_stat/tradestat/tables/intra/Pages/2017/12-.aspx

Siberian system reached some 1100 kWh, an equivalent to US$ 18 mn loss annually. The newly initiated economic openness of Uzbekistan permits the resumption of negotiations on the revival of UESCA, as well as its connection to the Central Asia—South Asia electricity grid (CASA-1000) (Shadrina, 2019b). Provided two cascades—the Kambar-Ata-1 and Verkhne-Narynsky—are constructed, Kyrgyzstan can become a large hydroelectricity exporter.[5] For its electricity generation, Armenia relies on Russian gas and nuclear fuel for the Metsamor nuclear power plant. The latter generates over 30% of electricity but is scheduled to be shut down in 2026.

Thus, in the fossil fuel segment, the roles of suppliers and consumers in the CEMs are clear (Table 8.2). Provided electricity segment is unified and developed, Russia and Kyrgyzstan will have sufficient volumes of hydroelectricity for intra-regional exports.

Energy cooperation among the economies at study was established in the Soviet period but it weakened following the dissolution of the Soviet Union. Nowadays, energy integration in the EAEU, according to the founding documents reviewed below, is being pursued in order to enhance

---

[5]Sem' vajnyh proektov, kotorye nikak ne mogut realizovat' v Tsentral'noi Azii (2018, February 5). *CA-portal*. Retrieved from http://www.ca-portal.ru/article:40646.

sustainable economic development of the EAEU member-states; ensure their energy and ecological security; improve economic efficiency and reliability of the national energy sectors; enhance the member-states' competitiveness; and accelerate economic integration within the EAEU.

Institutionalisation of Eurasian Energy Integration

Various aspects of the EAEU formation have been examined by Vinokurov and Libman (2012a, 2012b), Dragneva and Wolczuk (2012, 2013), Kirkham (2016), Verdiyeva (2018), among other scholars. Energy integration within the EAEU has been subject to limited research. Among the valuable analyses are the studies by Pastukhova and Westphal (2018) and Zemskova (2018).

The formation of the CEMs is coordinated by the Ministry of Energy and Infrastructure of the Eurasian Economic Commission and the respective divisions within the departments of Energy and Transport and Infrastructure (Fig. 8.1).

The Energy Department of the Eurasian Economic Commission functions in collaboration with respective national government entities on three competencies: economy, energy, and antitrust regulation and competition.

The EAEU's energy integration initiative implies the establishment of the Common Electric Power Market (CEPM) by July 2019, the Common Gas Market (CGM) and the Common Market for Oil and Petroleum Products (CMOPP), both by 2025 (EAEU Treaty, arts 81, 83 and 84). According to the EAEU Treaty Art. 104, a separate international treaty is to be concluded for each energy market to become operational. The respective concept and programme documents have been already adopted in preparation for the establishment of the CEMs.[6]

---

[6] O kontseptsii formirovaniya obshchego electroenergeticheskogo rynka Yevraziiskogo ekonomicheskogo soyuza (2015, May 8); O kontseptsii formirovaniya obshchego rynka gaza Yevraziiskogo ekonomicheskogo soyuza (2916, May 31); O kontseptsii formirovaniya obshchikh rynkov nefti i nefteproduktov Yevraziiskogo ekonomicheskogo soyuza (2016, May 31). Retrieved from http://www.eurasiancommission.org/ru/act/energetikaiinfr/Pages/default.aspx.

8 Energy Integration in Eurasian Economic Union …

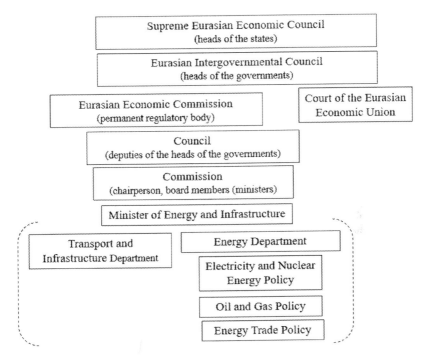

Fig. 8.1 Institutions for energy integration in the EAEU (*Source* Shadrina [2018, p. 119])

The legal foundations for the CEM are laid out by Chapter 20 of the EAEU Treaty[7] (Fig. 8.2, Appendix). The relevant to energy integration aspects of competition and natural monopolies are articulated in Chapters 18 and 19, respectively. Separate protocols to the EAEU Treaty, the Annexes 21, 22 and 23, contain the principal provisions for the formation of the CEPM, the CGM and the CMOPP, respectively.

In July 2019, the CEPM will integrate the electricity systems of the EAEU member-states. The formation of the CEPM is assumed to actualise large hydro potential of Siberia enhancing the intra-EAEU electricity trade and enabling electricity exports to third countries.

---

[7]Dogovor o Yevraziiskom Ekinomicheskom Soyuze. (2014, May 29). English version: Treaty on the Eurasian Economic Union. Retrieved from https://www.wto.org/english/thewto_e/acc_e/kaz_e/WTACCKAZ85_LEG_1.pdf.

Treaty on the EAEU (May 29, 2014), Chapter 20 "Energy"
Art. 79 "Interaction of the member states in the energy sector"
Art. 80 "Indicative (estimated) balances of gas, oil and petroleum products"
Art. 81 "Formation of a common electric power market"
Art. 82 "Providing an access to services of natural monopolies in electricity sector"
Art. 83 "Formation of a common gas market and providing access to the services of natural monopolies in the field of gas transportation"
Art. 84 "Formation of a common markets of oil and petroleum products and providing access to the services of natural monopolies in the sector of oil and petroleum products transportation"
Art. 85 "The Eurasian Economic Commission's authority in energy sector"

Chapter 18 "Common Rules and Principles of Competition"
Chapter 19 "Natural Monopolies"
Chapter 27 "Transitional Provisions"
Art. 104 "Transitional provisions in relation to Chapter 20"

Agreement on the methodology for the formation of indicative (estimate) balances of gas, oil and petroleum products

---

Annex 21 to the EAEU Treaty "Protocol on providing access to the services of natural monopolies in electric power sector, and the principles of pricing and tariff policy"

Annex "The methodology for the interstate transmission of electricity"

The Concept for the Common Electric Power Market (May 8, 2015)

The Program for the Formation of the Common Electric Power Market (December 8, 2016)

The EAEU Treaty on the Formation of the Common Electric Power Market, including the rules of access to services of natural monopolies in electricity sector (to be effective no later than July 1, 2019)

The concepts and programmes are effective until the respective treaties come to force

---

Annex 22 to the EAEU Treaty "Protocol on the rules of access to the services of natural monopolies in gas transporting sector via gas transporting systems, and the principles of pricing and tariff policy"

The Concept for the Common Gas Market (May 31, 2016)

The Program for the Formation of the Common Gas Market (December 6, 2018)

The EAEU Treaty on the Formation of the Common Gas Market, including the rules of access to gas transmission systems located on the territories of the member states (to be effective no later than January 1, 2025)

Annex 23 to the EAEU Treaty "Protocol on organisation, management, operation, and development of the Common Markets for Oil and Petroleum Products"

The Concept for the Common Markets for Oil and Petroleum Products (May 31, 2016)

The Program for the Formation of the Common Markets for Oil and Petroleum Products (December 6, 2018)

The EAEU Treaty on the Formation of the Common Markets for Oil and Petroleum Products, including the rules of access to the oil and petroleum products transportation systems located on the territories of the member states (to be effective no later than January 1, 2025)

Fig. 8.2 Principal legal provisions for energy integration in the EAEU (*Source* Author)

It is estimated that electricity integration will result in 1.5-2-fold growth in electricity trade and a 7% increase in the usage of existing generating capacities. The overall synergy effect of CEPM formation is assessed at US$ 7-7.5 bn GDP growth across the EAEU economies (Volgin, 2018). Among the considered models for electricity integration in the EAEU there were such as: to apply the Russian wholesale electricity market as a model; to create regional electricity markets in Russia like those in Kazakhstan and Belarus; or to follow the EU's model for continental electricity market that allows the formation of a common electricity market while preserving national markets. The latter model has been agreed upon by the EAEU member-states. Formation of the CEPM will require relevant domestic reforms. While the Russian, Kazakhstani, Kyrgyz and Armenian electricity markets are liberalised and partially operated by private companies, the Belarusian power sector is under the full state control. The CEPM envisions higher flexibility of electricity supplies via the day-ahead as well as the transactions in the capacity market via the commodity exchanges. There are three entities specialising in electricity trading in the EAEU. One is: Kazakhstan Electricity and Capacity Market Operator (KOREM JSC). Two others are Russian companies—Administrator of the Wholesale Electricity Market Trading System (ATS) and St. Petersburg International Commodity Exchange. The EAEU member-states are the least unified in terms of their ideational and physical approaches to gas integration, therefore the formation of the CGM appears to be the most challenging task.

Asymmetry of Interests in Eurasian Energy Integration

It should be noted that the progress with integration in three markets—oil and petroleum products, gas and electricity—differs greatly. The CEPM is the most advanced and least prone to the conflicts over the pace and forms of integration, whereas the CGM repeatedly proved to be the hardest to reach the consensus.[8] The national electricity sectors

---

[8]Lukashenko prizval "provesti revisiyu" doqovora o Yevrazes (2016, October 28). *Ria Novosti*. Retrieved from https://ria.ru/economy/20161028/1480193958.html.

are more liberalised and historically have been interlinked into a united grid. Even though the national gas and oil segments also have common infrastructure since the Soviet era, throughout the post-Soviet transition they have been shaped by vested interests of the dominating SOECs, domestic ones in Kazakhstan, Russia, and to some degree Belarus, and mainly Russian in Armenia and Kyrgyzstan.

The EAEU member-states reveal divergent preferences for the scope, pace and sequence of energy integration (Abdraimov, 2019; Shustov, 2019). Whereas energy-sufficient Russia and Kazakhstan have been more discreet about the pace of energy integration, Belarus lobbied heavily for rapid energy integration, attempting to stipulate the continuation of its membership in the EAEU by the preferred sequence of integration initiatives (Verdiyeva, 2018). Belarus has long had certain leverage over Russia for it hosts the passage for Russian Europe-bound oil and gas (Balmaceda, 2015). Russia's dependence on Belarus for transit helped the latter bargain over gas and oil prices. The conclusion of the Russia-Belarus Economic Union activated export duty exemptions for Russian crude oil, although the processed products are being re-exported to third countries. Furthermore, Belarus is granted gas price equivalent to that for Russia's domestic customers in Yamal-Nenets Okrug (the region of gas origin) plus transport tariff incurred to ship gas to Belarus (Kucherov, 2019). That makes Belarus' import gas prices two-fold lower than the average Russian prices for Germany and 2.5 times smaller than those for Ukraine (Shadrina, 2018). The Russian energy subsidies (in the form of waived oil export duties and lower hydrocarbons prices) to the Belarussian economy have been large. Throughout 2001–2016, Belarus is assessed to had been subsidised by Russia for more than US$ 100 bn, which is double of Belarus' GDP (Tkachyov & Feinberg, 2017). The tax reforms in the Russian oil sector[9] helped reduce the losses to the Russian budget from RUR 341 bn in 2014 to 195 bn in 2015, 114 bn in 2016 and RUR 111 bn, or US$ 1.7

---

[9] The so-called tax manoeuvre is designed to improve the efficiency of the Russian oil sector. In essence, the export duties are replaced with the severance tax. Effectively, this means that Belarus will not be able to enjoy lower—export duties exempt—oil price.

bn in 2017 (Ezhov & Tyrtov, 2018, p. 12). However, Belarus repeatedly expressed its dissatisfaction with oil price increase disregarding the fact that this is a result of Russia's domestic tax reform (Derkul, 2019).

The discrepancies over the pricing and technical standards of gas, crude oil and petroleum products are significant among the EAEU member-states. To a large extent, this is a result of the differences between the national regulations in respective areas. Russia, for instance, links its pricing for oil and petroleum products to the international price quotes, and, accordingly, suggests this practice be adopted in the EAEU. Belarus (surprisingly joined by Kazakhstan) lobbies for an odd pricing model, whereby gas, oil and petroleum products' prices would be discounted for the costs of transportation across the EAEU and purification towards a unified technical standard. Such proposal aims to reduce the price for consumers/buyers (especially, Belarussian refineries processing Russian crude and exporting petroleum products to third countries) but is unacceptable to producers/(Russian) suppliers. To the proposal to ensure the unified quality standard of gas, oil and petroleum products shipped through the territory of the EAEU, Russia points to high costs of quality monitoring in the context of geographical (distance) and geological (diverse chemical characteristics of hydrocarbons extracted at different fields) realties. In the brotherly Soviet and post-Soviet traditions, Russia seems to be expected by the EAEU member-states to accept larger costs of energy integration, while granting the resultant bonuses to other EAEU economies. Such anticipations appear to be inappropriate as contradicting the very nature of the CEMs.

Energy Union of European Union

Institutionalisation of Energy Integration in EU

The early designs for supranational energy governance in Europe were formulated at the inception of the European integration. In 1951, Belgium, France, Germany, Italy, Luxemburg, and the Netherlands established the European Coal and Steel Community (ECSC). Article 3 of the ECSC Treaty introduced the notion of security of supply for the members of the European Community (EC).[10] In 1957, the European Economic Community and the European Atomic Energy Community (Euratom) were established. Article 52 of the Euratom Treaty established a Supply Agency (since 1960) and permitted the regulator's intervention to ensure that all members in the EC receive a regular and equitable supply. An upper limit equal to 20% of uranium supply from a single non-EC state was stipulated. Article 53 granted the Supply Agency an exclusive right to conclude contracts relating to supplies.[11] In 1964, the need for a common energy policy for the entire Community was emphasised and this became one of the activities of the European Council.[12] In 1968, the Commission endorsed the Community Energy Policy, where it outlined the dependency concerns.[13] As early as in 1968, the EC stated that coordinated energy policy would help integrate energy sectors of the nation-states into a common market offsetting the risks of dependency on imports and poor diversification of the sources of supply. Thus, it is historically accurate to acknowledge the importance of energy in the process of the European Union foundation and emphasise that common energy policy was one of the earliest designs of the supranational governance.

Despite the awareness of the risks of high import dependency and low diversification, the EC member-states were not actively pursuing the stated objectives and principles of the common energy policy (Buchan & Keay, 2015). Even the 1973 crisis did not lead to a comprehensive united approach; the solidarity principle was often traded for the easier to implement individual solutions (Maltby, 2013, p. 438). The attitude has started to change in the 1990s. While Belgium

---

[10]European Coal and Steel Community (ECSC) Treaty. (1951, April 18). Treaty establishing the European Coal and Steel Community, Paris.

[11]Euratom Treaty. (1957, March 25). Treaty Establishing the European Atomic Energy Community, Rome.

[12]Council of the European Union. (1964, April 21). Protocol of Agreement on Energy Problems. Official Journal 069: 1099–1100. Brussels: European Council.

[13]European Commission. (1968, December 18). First Guidelines for a Community Energy Policy: Memorandum Presented by the Commission to the Council. COM (68) 1040 Final. Brussels: European Commission.

historically had its electricity mostly privately owned, and Germany started the privatisation early (during the 1960s), most of the European economies deregulated their national electricity in the 1980s. Austria and Spain started deregulation in 1988. England and Wales commenced privatisation of electricity in 1988, and completed it by 1996. Other EU countries launched privatisation in the 1990s. Yet, France resisted the liberalisation concerned to protect the incumbent operator (Clifton, Comín, & Fuentes, 2006). Among others pursuing privatisation in the electricity sector were: Sweden (1991), Finland (1994), Portugal (1997), Italy (1999), the Netherlands (1999), Denmark (2000) and Greece (2003). As European economies were advancing the deregulation of their domestic energy sectors, they began to seek an extension of such policies to the larger European energy sector.

The Maastricht treaty, signed in 1992, tasked the European Union with establishing and developing a transnational network in the areas of transport, telecommunications and energy. In 1996, the Trans-European Networks for Energy (TEN-E) was developed as part of the EU's single market.[14] Currently, the TEN-E focuses on nine projects significant for the connectivity across the entire EU: four electricity corridors, four gas corridors and one oil corridor.[15]

The European Commission proposed a directive to extend a Single European Market to the electricity and gas sector in 1990. In 1996, the European Union adopted the first directive on the liberalisation of the energy market. In 1998, a directive on the liberalisation of the gas market was issued. Yet, the Community actions through the endorsed Maastricht (1992), Amsterdam (1997) or Nice (2001) Treaties did not have the external dimension for the common energy policy. From January 2001, the Commission had regular energy dialogue with its key gas supplier Russia. The Commission embarked on a strategy of exporting the EU legislation promoting the principles of rule-based market multilateralism. The Energy Charter Treaty (ECT) uniting fifty-one country in Asia and

---

[14]Retrieved from https://ec.europa.eu/energy/en/topics/infrastructure/trans-european-networks-energy.

[15]Retrieved from https://ec.europa.eu/energy/en/topics/infrastructure/trans-european-networks-energy.

Europe became such legal framework advancing the principles of market governance and offering provisions for regulation of third-party access, transit and supply of energy, investment, efficiency[16] and dispute resolution.[17] Russia initially signed although did not ratify the ECT but eventually withdrew its provisional application in August 2009.[18] The most principal disagreement between Russia and the EU occurred over the ECT provisions for transit and third-party access.

The second legislative package was endorsed in 2003 and implemented in 2004–2007. However, it was not until the Lisbon Treaty of 2009 that the EU defined competencies in energy policy. Article 194 of the Treaty grants a member-state a sovereign right to design its energy mix but states that the EU ensures the functioning of the internal market and security of supplies, promotes energy efficiency and saving and unification of energy networks.[19] The elaboration of unified policies was exacerbated by the gas supply crisis of 2006, which was not intentionally staged to harm the European consumers, but disrupted between Russia and Ukraine over their disagreement on the terms of transit. The 2009 crisis repeated in a similar fashion but caused more severe consequences for the European customers. That made the EU categorically wary of the security of Russian gas supply and accelerated its actions towards the establishment of an Energy Union. Failing to achieve solidarity in their attitude to the Russian gas supplies, the EU members were often finding themselves exploring opposite strategies. Some invested in building the interconnectors on the existing pipelines delivering Russian gas to Europe, others expedited the construction of

---

[16]Protocol on Energy Efficiency and Related Environmental Aspects. (1994, December 17). Retrieved from https://energycharter.org/process/energy-charter-treaty-1994/energy-efficiency-protocol/.

[17]The International Energy Charter Consolidated Energy Charter Treaty with Related Documents. Transparency Document (With Annex W, Modified into a Positive List of the Applicable WTO Provisions). Retrieved from https://energycharter.org/fileadmin/DocumentsMedia/Legal/ECTC-en.pdf.

[18]Russia signed the ECT in 1994 but did not ratify it, having, however, provisionally applied it in 1994–2009. Belarus did not ratify the ECT but provisionally applies it.

[19]The Lisbon Treaty, Article 194. Retrieved from http://www.lisbon-treaty.org/wcm/the-lisbon-treaty/treaty-onthe-functioning-of-the-european-union-and-comments/part-3-union-policies-and-internal-actions/title-xxi-energy/485-article-194.html.

LNG terminals to enable non-Russian supplies (Lithuania and Poland), yet others enthusiastically worked towards getting non-transit gas from Russia. Germany started importing gas via Nord Stream in 2009. Italy, Bulgaria, Hungary, Serbia and Slovenia supported, albeit inconsistently, the South Stream project. Energy became the key area where deep controversies among the EU member-states have been occurring.

Endorsed in 2009, the Third Energy Package was envisioned to facilitate the completion of a harmonised, competitive energy market within the EU. It strengthened the rule of unbundling (separating production and turnover of gas fuels and energy from transmission and distribution). The Third Package complicated business prospects for Russian SOEC Gazprom. The Package, specifically the unbundling requirements of Article 9 of the Gas Directive,[20] allows the EU to deny the transmission licence to a company controlled by an entity from a third country in case such a company does not comply with the unbundling rules and its activity jeopardises the EU's supply security. The Agency for the Cooperation of Energy Regulators (ACER) was created in 2011 to facilitate the implementation of liberalisation in the electricity and gas markets.

The authorship of the EU's Energy Union[21] project is being rivalled. Fischer and Geden (2015, p. 2) point that as early as in 2010, then President of the European Parliament Jerzy Buzek and the former Commission President Jacques Delors "called for a politicisation of EU energy policy, which they saw as focused too narrowly on the internal market, through the creation of a 'European Energy Community'". Ringel and Knodt (2018) credit the then president of the European Commission Jean-Claude Juncker with the Energy Union initiative proposed in 2014. Łada, Skłodowska, Szczepanik, and Wenerski (2015) attribute the idea (allegedly presented the same year) to the then prime minister of Poland Donald Tusk.

---

[20]Directive 2009/73 concerning the common rules for the internal market in natural gas and repealing Directive 2003/55, OJ L211/94, art 11(3)(a).
[21]Energy Union and Climate. Retrieved from https://ec.europa.eu/commission/priorities/energy-union-and-climate_en.

Ideas and Realities of European Energy Integration

From the outset, the Energy Union was envisioned as the project to address three aims, those of security of energy supply, sustainability and competitiveness. The EU especially emphasises the need for improving cooperation among the member-states; in the terminology of Ringel and Knodt (2018), between the North and West, and Centre and East. The North and West been swiftly advancing their national low carbon transitions and advocating a common approach for the entire EU, while the latter attempted to protect their sovereignty over the national energy-mix decisions and prioritised most of all the agenda of security of supply. In February 2015, the European Commission endorsed the Energy Union Package[22] concerning five policy areas:

- the assurance of energy security in the context that Russia is no longer considered a reliable supplier;
- the enhanced internal connectivity to enable competition among energy providers;
- the improved energy efficiency for the reduction of pollution and lower demand for energy imports;
- the reduction of greenhouse gas emissions by 40% by 2030 from 1990s levels; and
- the encouragement of advanced research and innovation in low-carbon technologies.

Transition to a low-carbon society became one of the focal themes for the Energy Union, which even added "Climate" to its title (to become "Energy Union and Climate"). The Clean Energy Package for All Europeans[23] and the proposals on low-emission mobility presented were developed in 2016 and 2017, respectively. In November

---

[22]Energy Union Package. (2015, February 25). A Framework Strategy for a Resilient Energy Union with a Forward-Looking Climate Change Policy. Brussels: European Commission. Retrieved from https://ec.europa.eu/commission/priorities/energy-union-and-climate_en.

[23]Retrieved from https://ec.europa.eu/energy/en/topics/energy-strategy-and-energy-union/clean-energy-all-europeans.

Table 8.3 The EU's targets for energy and climate, %

	Reduction of greenhouse gas emissions	Share of renewable energy in energy mix	Improvements in energy efficiency	Interconnection
2020	20	20	20	10
2030	≥ 45*	≥ 27	≥ 30	15
2050*	≥ 60	≥ 32	≥ 32.5	

Source Based on Third Report on the State of the Energy Union. (2017, November 23). European Commission. Brussels. Retrieved from https://ec.europa.eu/commission/publications/third-report-state-energy-union-annexes_en; (*) A Clean Planet for all A European strategic long-term vision for a prosperous, modern, competitive and climate neutral economy. (2018, November 28). European Commission. Brussels. Retrieved from https://ec.europa.eu/clima/sites/clima/files/docs/pages/com_2018_733_en.pdf

2018, the European Commission presented a long-term vision called Climate Neutral Europe by 2050.[24] This was done in line with the Paris Agreement[25] and under the Clean Energy for All Europeans package. Even more ambitious targets for energy and climate change policy were set forth (Table 8.3). The new regulatory framework introduced the first long-term national energy and climate plans (2021–2030), thereby making regulatory environment conducive to the investments that are so essential for the aspired energy shifts.

The Council adopted the regulation On Energy Performance in Buildings in June 2018, and the regulations on Renewable Energy, Energy Efficiency and Governance in December 2018. Electricity Regulation, Electricity Directive, Regulations on Risk Preparedness and establishing the European Union Agency for the Cooperation of Energy Regulators are at the stage of inter-institutional negotiations.[26]

While energy transition appears to be a focal agenda for the EU, Harjanne and Korkonen (2019) hold that (universally) inconsistent conceptualisation of renewable energy renders the EU's ambitious

---

[24]Retrieved from https://ec.europa.eu/energy/en/topics/energy-strategy-and-energy-union/2050-long-term-strategy.

[25]Retrieved from https://ec.europa.eu/clima/policies/international/negotiations/paris_en.

[26]Retrieved from https://ec.europa.eu/energy/en/topics/energy-strategy-and-energy-union/clean-energy-all-europeans.

goals for sustainability unattainable. Assessing the adequacy of the EU's decarbonisation targets, Stern (2019) argues that the EU's gas industry is not vigorous enough to materialise business models and strategies that could activate the opportunities of natural gas as of an expected intermediary in the EU's grand energy transition towards a low-carbon economy.

The Energy Union of the EU is a result of an over six-decade institutionalisation process, which at different stages embraced the evolutionary incremental changes before entering the path-breaking transformations. The EU has been advancing domestic and external energy policies upon different principles: the market thinking has been dominant in the former, while the security concerns influenced the latter (Andoura & Vinois, 2015).

Asymmetry of Interests in European Energy Integration

Albeit the title of this section suggests a broader discussion (Fischer & Geden, 2015; Kustova, 2017; Łada et al., 2015; Ringel & Knodt, 2018; Szulecki, Fischer, Gullberg, & Sartor, 2016), we focus on the asymmetry of interests as it relates to energy relations between the EU and EAEU member-states.

While the EU's indigenous oil and gas production declines (BP, 2018), significant export volumes keep Russia the EU's largest supplier (Fig. 8.3). This is despite the 2016 energy security package provisions, which stipulated the disclosure of the price terms of business gas deals and the ban on the intergovernmental agreements between the EU member-state and the third-state if these potentially jeopardise the EU's common energy security (Georgiou & Rocco, 2017). The Russia–Ukraine gas dispute in 2009 cost Russia great reputational damage leading many to claim that the Russian government is using gas as a political weapon. Within the framework of Russia-EU Energy Dialogue,[27] the two parties developed the Early Warning Mechanism to prevent the disruption of supply in the future. Under such

---

[27]Put on hold in 2014 at the initiative of the EU in the aftermath of Crimea.

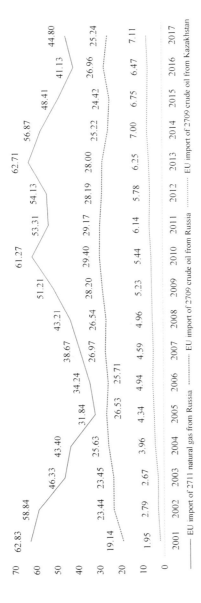

Fig. 8.3 Share of Russia's oil and gas and Kazakhstan's oil in EU-28 imports, % (*Source* Author, based on ITC Trade Map data retrieved from https://www.trademap.org. Note calculated based on value in US$)

Table 8.4 Share of Russia in national extra-EU imports of oil and gas, share of trade in value, 2018, %

Share	Oil imports	Gas imports
0–25	Austria, Cyprus, Denmark, Ireland, Greece, Spain, France, Italy, Latvia, Luxemburg, Malta, Portugal, Slovenia, UK	Belgium, Denmark, Ireland, Spain, France, Croatia, Cyprus, Luxemburg, Malta, Portugal, Sweden, UK
25–50	Belgium, Croatia, Germany, the Netherlands, Romania, Sweden	Italy, the Netherlands
50–75	Czech Republic, Lithuania, Hungary, Poland	Germany, Greece, Lithuania
75–100	Bulgaria, Estonia, Finland, Slovakia	Austria, Bulgaria, Czech Republic, Estonia, Finland, Latvia, Hungary, Poland, Romania, Slovenia, Slovakia

Source EU imports of energy products—recent developments. (2018, November 19). Retrieved from https://ec.europa.eu/eurostat/statistics-explained/pdfscache/46126.pdf
(*)—number of countries in the respective category

circumstances, Kazakhstan, the EU's 5th largest oil supplier, started to be considered as one of the desired alternative suppliers.[28]

Dependency of European economies on Russia tends to be higher for gas; both dependencies, however, vary greatly by country (Table 8.4).

A member of the ECT, Kazakhstan is better posited to engage in a multilateral framework for cross-border energy cooperation. Meanwhile, Russia faces growing regulatory barriers to energy cooperation with the EU.

Like the earlier Nord Stream 1, the Nord Stream 2 (Fig. 8.4) appears to be dividing the EU members (Beckman, 2017; Coelho & Grojec, 2018; Gurzu, 2015). The Baltic states and Poland are opposing the project. Finland, Sweden and Denmark turned out to be open to negotiation. German business circles find the project commercially attractive, actively support it, participate in it, and point out that if the German government decides to side with the opponents for the matter

---

[28]Retrieved from https://ec.europa.eu/energy/en/topics/imports-and-secure-supplies/supplier-countries.

8 Energy Integration in Eurasian Economic Union … 175

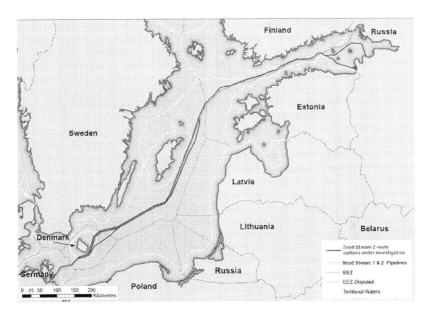

Fig. 8.4 Route of the Nord Stream 2 (*Source* https://www.nord-stream2.com/en/pdf/document/125/)

of solidarity, it will be nothing else but politically motivated position (William, 2019).

The opponents of the Nord Stream 2 maintain that although it is an offshore pipeline, it should be subject to the Third Energy Package, including the provisions relating to the ownership unbundling and third-party access. This implies that Gazprom should not be able to exploit the pipeline to its full capacity and would need to let other suppliers use it (Barnes, 2019; Berkhahn & Kruse, 2019). This appears to be unacceptable to Gazprom and is objectively difficult to implement, as there are no third countries' suppliers to export gas through the pipeline originating in Russia. The only scenario could be the dismantling Gazprom's export monopoly and liberalisation of pipeline gas export in Russia itself. The supporters maintain that the Nord Stream 2 is an import pipeline, and like other operating import pipelines—the Nord Stream 1, Trans Adriatic Pipeline (Khatinoglu, 2019) and the pipelines in the Mediterranean—it should be exempted from the Third Energy

Package regulation. The connection to Nord Stream 2 on German territory, called Eugal pipeline, shall be subject to the Third Energy Package rules, just like the Opal pipeline linked to the Nord Stream 1. It is emphasised that the Nord Stream 2 is a private project financed by a consortium comprising Gazprom and five European companies: Uniper and Wintershall (Germany), OMV (Austria), Engie (France), and Royal Dutch Shell (the Anglo-Dutch oil major). Overall, there are 28 European companies from 11 countries that are directly involved in the Nord Stream; some are engaged very substantially. German's Europipe, for example, supplies almost half of the large-diameter pipes that the Nord Stream 2 needs.

The opponents to Russian supplies are pursuing various strategies to ensure their energy security. To boost gas import from elsewhere (foremost, from the United States), Poland and Lithuania constructed the LNG terminals of annual import capacity of 5 bcm and 4 bcm, respectively. 100%-dependent on Russian gas supply, Finland is building the Balticconnector with Estonia (Nosovich, 2018). A new gas pipeline linking Inkoo and Paltiski, respectively, will bring North American and other non-Russian gas to Finland (the interconnector can equally be used to ship Russian gas to Estonia). Lithuania has been consistently pursuing a common Baltic LNG market based on the terminals in Lithuania and Estonia and the underground gas storage facility in Latvia. In electricity sector, the three Baltic states progressed with unplugging their grids from the Russian electric power system. The ultimate goal is to synchronise their grids with the system of Continental Europe via the LitPol Line power interconnection with Poland. The LitPol is the final link in the EU's Baltic Ring initiative interconnecting the electric power systems of Baltic states, Poland, Germany, Denmark, Norway, Sweden and Finland.

The EU member-states struggle to speak with one voice on the issues involving Russian supplies. Overall, the post-Soviet and post-communist countries of the EU tend to approach energy relations with Russia with a more pronounced political attitude.

Table 8.5 Two paths for energy integration

	CEMs of the EAEU	EU of the EU
Ideas	•sustainable economic development •energy and ecological security •economic efficiency and reliability of the national energy sectors •economic competitiveness •acceleration of economic integration	•security of energy supply •sustainability of energy •competitiveness in energy markets
Interests	•enhanced integration •export expansion vs demand security •commercially viable pricing vs external subsidisation •asymmetry in preference for integration sequence	•energy business expansion •external energy supply security •benefits of R&D spillover •asymmetry of interests of EU member-states concerning to energy relations with EAEU (Russia)
Institutions	•Eurasian Economic Commission/ Transport and Infrastructure and Energy Departments •respective Concepts (2015, 2016), Programmes (2016, 2018), Treaties •insignificant institutional changes, regulatory norms of major suppliers dominate	•European Commission/ACER •Energy Packages (1996–1998, 2003, 2009, 2016), Directives •path-breaking institutional changes (ETS)

Source Author

Conclusion and Policy Implications

As has been detailed, energy integration in the EAEU is still in the making, therefore there are more aspects to contemplate than those to analyse. We summarise by putting our findings in perspective of the earlier suggested "ideas – interests – institutions" model (Table 8.5).

Unquestionably, the ideational dimension of the two energy integrations is different. The EU's Energy Union is appealing to the shared values of the member-states—sustainability, green growth, efficiency—while the EAEU is tackling the technical task of founding the CEMs.

The CEMs' ideational component is not highlighted, as the EAEU does not address, at least not at the current stage, the agenda of climate change, external action coordination or other shared ideas. The diversity of motivations of the member-states to engage in energy integration occurs in both cases. When presented with a task of joint problem solving for energy integration, the EAEU member-states' representatives reveal that they did not fully adopt the supranational concepts and norms, which is not surprising, given that the EAEU's supranationalism started in only 2015. The prioritisation of national interests by the EAEU member-states[29] often transforms in their attempts to reproduce the existing (or even the past) modes of cooperation. This path dependency logic is highlighted by Belarus' demands for the continued energy subsidies and exemptions to be extended by Russia.[30] Belarus unduly demands Russia's compensations for the increase in crude oil prices, albeit the latter is the result of Russian tax reform (shift from export duties to the taxation of production). Meanwhile, the EU member-states more often reveal the variability of interests in the realm of path-breaking innovative transformations of energy goods, services, technologies, markets and actors.

The CEMs and the Energy Union demonstrate the importance of institutional complementarity within their respective integrations revealing, however, marked institutional discrepancy between them. Market principles, liberalisation and competition underpin institution building in the EU, while the EAEU member-state replicate their national idiosyncratic institutions guaranteeing the appearance of the equally flawed supranational constructions. To be fair, the EAEU draws on the EU's early approaches to energy markets regulation, as well as the World Trade Organisation (WTO) rules. Yet, the interaction between the two energy integrations is complicated by the incompatibility of their respective institutional environments at the absence of shared

---

[29]Itogi VEES: odobreny programmy formirovaniya obshchikh rynkov gaza, nefti i nefteproduktov. (2018, December 7). Retrieved from http://www.eurasiancommission.org/ru/nae/news/Pages/07_12_2018_1.aspx.

[30]Obshchii rynok energoresursov EAES – muki rozhdeniya. (n.d.). Retrieved from http://eurasian-studies.org/archives/7432.

regulative mechanisms. Hypothetically, the interregional EAEU-EU energy dialogue and cooperation could have been enhanced upon the ECT mechanism. While the ECT trade arrangements allow Belarus (non-member of the WTO) to apply respective provisions in the energy sector, Russia's non-participation in the ECT cancels out its applicability. Also, unlike the rest of the EAEU members-states, Russia is not a partner of the EU INOGATE. The INOGATE is the programme for enhancing energy security and convergence of member-state energy markets based on the EU's internal energy market principles, supporting sustainable energy development, and attracting investment for energy projects of common and regional interest. Since 2011, the only member of the EAEU Armenia is an observer in the EU's Energy Community aiming to enhance the EU's energy policy towards South-Eastern Europe and the Black Sea basin through the creation of a stable regulatory model, development of a united energy market, enhancement of energy supply security and promotion of climate change policy.

Considering mutual implications of the energy integrations at hand, it seems that in the short-run the Eurasian energy integration will not have a negative effect on the European energy markets. When implementing energy transactions, the endorsed provisions for the CEMs stipulate the following hierarchy of priorities: national; third parties under the agreed contracts; and the interests of the EAEU member-states'. The EU is absolutely important for Russia and increasingly significant for Kazakhstan, therefore it is highly unlikely that EAEU would approve any regulatory changes that may be unfavourable to the EU.

Within the CEMs, transplanting the Russian energy sector regulation is envisioned (e.g., natural monopolies in electricity and gas). By the same token, the liberalisation of CEMs may start following the institutional changes in the Russian energy sector. One of the strong impulses for the domestic deregulation may be Gazprom's already modifying business strategy for Europe. The diffusion of market principles in the Russian gas sector will bring about long-awaited liberalisation of gas export.

Russia will continue to experience the EU's new liberal mercantilism (Andersen et al., 2017) with the Ukrainian transit being one of the prime agendas for the year 2019. Consequently, Russia's endeavours to expand transit-free exports will be increasingly challenged by the opponents of enhanced energy cooperation with Russia within the EU as well as outside, especially the United States. On the other hand, the CEMs may improve Kazakhstan's bargaining position vis-à-vis Russia for additional supplies to the European oil and potentially gas markets. The Convention on the legal status of the Caspian Sea (2018) supports such prospects.

Meanwhile, in the absence of comprehensive EAEU-EU bilateral formats for energy cooperation, the EAEU member-states shall actively use other existing institutional frameworks (WTO, ECT, INOGATE) for more diversified energy cooperation, especially in renewable energy, energy R&D and ICT.

Appendix

Overview and Interpretation of Principal Legal Provisions for Common Energy Markets of Eurasian Economic Union

The legal foundations for the CEM are laid out by Chapter 20 of the EAEU Treaty. Separate protocols to the EAEU Treaty, the Annexes 21, 22 and 23, contain the principal provisions for the formation of the Common Electric Power Market (CEPM), the Common Gas Market (CGM) and the Common Market for Oil and Petroleum Products (CMOPP).

Annex 21 provides the principles and terms for access to the services of natural monopolies in electricity. Art. 3 stipulates that the CEPM interlinks the national electric grids, which are operated upon the member-states regulation. According to Art. 5 containing the references to Chapters 18 and 19, the member-states are oriented at gradual harmonisation of their legislation with a principal course being towards fair competition and liberalisation of the national electricity markets. Arts. 7, 8 and 9 explain various aspects of the interstate transmission of electric power with the key point being that the legislation of a member-state through whose territory such transmission takes place is to be applied. Art. 11 stipulates that the pricing and tariff policy are determined by the national legislation of a member-state through whose territory electricity is transmitted, but such prices and tariffs cannot be higher than those effective in the domestic electricity market of a respective member-state. The embedded Appendix contains the methodology for the interstate transmission of electricity.

The Concept for the formation of the CEPM (2015) concretises its goals and objectives (Chapters 2 and 3); characterises the forms of trade, such as trade under the bilateral interstate agreements, as well as trade among market agents, including trading at the exchanges (Chapter 5); specifies the subjects of the CEPM (Chapter 6); elucidates the price and tariff aspects in a way that the national legislation is effective only for the cases when natural monopolies are concerned (but the prices and tariffs cannot be higher than those effective for the national market), otherwise market and market actors define pricing and tariffs (Chapter 9); and sets the timeline for the market formation and stipulates that it shall become fully operational by July 2019 (Chapter 13). The Concept contains the special opinion of Belarus that the CEPM shall be operated as fully competitive only after the CGM is created. This reflects the difficulties in reaching the consensus in the process of CEPM formation.

The Program for the Formation of the CEPM (2016) elaborates the provisions of the Arts. 81 and 82 of Chapter 20, Annex 21 and the CEPM Concept. The Program confirms the timeline for the CEPM formation, defines the principles of interstate electricity trade and transmission and stipulates their forms (Chapter 3); describes the organisation of trade in electricity (Chapter 4); explains the functioning of capacity market (Chapter 5); and specifies the regulation of CEPM (Chapter 6).

The Protocol on the Amendments to the EAEU Treaty in Respect to the Formation of the CEPM (September 7, 2018) clarifies further details on the formation and functioning of the CEPM. Art. 4 of Chapter 2 emphasises that the CEPM respects the rules of fair competition and functions upon market principles. The Memorandum on Cooperation between the Eurasian Economic Commission and the Electric Power Council of the Commonwealth Independent States (October 30, 2018) envisages consultative, non-binding, nature of the interaction between the two electricity systems on a range of related issues.

Concerning the CGM, the Annex 22 addresses the principles and conditions for the EAEU member-states' access to the services of natural monopolies in gas transporting sector and the principles of pricing and tariff policy. The Art. 3.1 of the Annex affirms principles for the formation of the common natural gas market, including non-application of import or export duties. Arts. 3.4 and 3.5 affirm that the member-states intend to harmonise their legal systems and ensure ecological safety. Arts. 5 and 6 of Annex 22 state that the CGM shall operate at the market, preferably equally profitable for gas sellers, prices. This provision has already created significant debates among the member-states. Art. 7 of Annex 22 addresses the commercial conditions for the third-party non-discriminatory access to the transportation of natural gas implying that such matters shall be regulated by the member-states based on the provisions of their national legislations. This implies that the EAEU has no supranational authority over the prices and tariffs of natural gas transportation.

Chapter 3 of the Concept for the Common Gas Market (2016) outlines the principles and objectives of its formation (such as enhanced energy security, improved efficacy of the national gas transportation systems, adoption of market pricing, use of national currencies in gas trade, among others). Chapter 4 defines the timeline for the launch of the CGM. The preparatory stage continues till 2020 when the legal and technical harmonisation shall be implemented, the gas balance shall be formed and the bottlenecks for the CGM functioning shall be examined and attended. By 2022, the access to the transportation systems shall be ensured to the subjects implementing shipments in the fulfilment of gas balance, gas exchanges shall become operational and investment into the gas sector, including infrastructure, shall materialise. From 2025, the CGM shall become operational upon market pricing and equally profitable prices in intra-CGM trade. Chapter 5 provides that trade in gas will be implemented under a direct bilateral contract or run through a gas exchange. According to Chapter 6, the member-states' legislation will regulate the matters of gas transportation in a respective territory ensuring that the interests of gas consumers, producers and natural monopolies are met.

The Program for the Formation of the Common Gas Market (2018) confirms that the CGM will be effective from 2025. The Program reemphasises the importance of market pricing and non-discriminatory access to the gas transporting systems, among other things. Chapter 1 specifies various organisational forms of trade, such as supply under the bilateral agreements, long- and short-term contacts, and exchange trading. The Program presents a range of actions towards the materialisation of the CGM, such as the development of gas exchanges, adoption of rules for the access to the gas transporting systems, as well as pricing and tariff policy.

In the oil sector, Annex 23 is dedicated to the organisation, functioning, governance and development of the CMOPP. Annex 23 outlines the CMOPP's principles, which are similar to those for the CGM. Art. 7 of Annex 23 provides that tariffs for the transportation services of oil and petroleum products are determined upon the national legislation of member-states, but these tariffs cannot be higher than those for the domestic economic entities through the territory of which such oil and petroleum products are transported. Art. 9 states that the regulation of internal markets of oil and petroleum products is implemented by the national authorities of the member-states.

The Concept for the CMOPP (2016) reiterates the importance of the principles of market pricing and non-discriminatory access to the transportation systems, but nearly cancels out these statements by the provision that natural monopolies preserve their practices on pricing, tariffs and access rules in accordance with the national legislation of a respective member-state. The Concept specifies two forms of trade: under bilateral (or multilateral) contract and at the oil and petroleum products exchange, and describes other forms of activities in the CMOPP, such as transit, extraction, transportation and processing of oil. The Concept envisions a range of measures towards the implementation of the CMOPP, such as the harmonisation of technical standards of oil and petroleum products, harmonisation of national legislation, and investment in production, transportation and processing, among others.

The Program for the Formation of the CMOPP (2018) reaffirms the establishment of the common market by 2025 presenting a set of measures scheduled into three stages: 2018–2021, 2024 and 2025.

By 2021, it is expected to develop legislation for the regulation of the CMOPP (trade, in particular), access to the transportation systems, technical standards for oil and petroleum products, organisation of the system and procedures for information exchange, and harmonisation of respective national legislations of the member-states, among other things. The international treaty on CMOPP shall be coordinated among the member-states by 2024 so that it would become effective by 2025.

References

Abdraimov, A. (2019, July 8). *Kakaya dinamika tsen na rossiiskii gaz mozhet ozhifat' Armeniyu? Ritm Yevrazii.* Retrieved from https://www.ritmeurasia.org/news–2019-07-08–kakaja-dinamika-cen-na-rossijskij-gaz-mozhet-ozhidat-armeniju-43675.

Andersen, S., Goldthau, A., & Sitter, N. (2017). *Energy Union: Europe's new Liberal Mercantilism.* Basingstoke, UK: Palgrave Macmillan.

Andoura, S., & Vinois, J. A. (2015). *From the European Energy Community to the Energy Union: A policy proposal for the short and the long term.* Series Report. Series New Decision-Makers, New Challenges. Jacquez Delores Institute.

Balmaceda, M. (2015). *The politics of energy dependency: Ukraine, Belarus, and Lithuania between domestic oligarchs and Russian pressure.* Toronto: University of Toronto Press.

Barnes, A. (2019, January 21). The latest amendment to a directive only add to the legal muddle. *Natural Gas World.* Retrieved from https://www.naturalgasworld.com/ggp-the-romanian-revision-makes-a-bad-directive-worse-67387.

Beckman, K. (2017, November 16). The European Commission's last-ditch effort to stop Nord Stream 2: How likely is it to succeed? *Energypost.eu.* Retrieved from https://energypost.eu/european-commissions-last-ditch-effort-stop-nord-stream-2-likely-succeed/.

Berkhahn, A., & Kruse, M. (2019, February). Fourth revision of the proposed amendment of the gas directive further muddying of the waters? *Arthur D. Little global report.* Retrieved from http://www.adlittle.com/en/fourth-revision-proposed-amendment-gas-directive.

Beyers, J. (2005). Multiple Embeddedness and Socialization in Europe: The Case of Council Officials. *International Organisation, 50,* 899–936.

Blockmans, S. (Ed.). (2019). *What comes after the last chance commission? Policy priorities for 2019–2024* (p. 104). Brussels: Centre for European Policy Studies.

Blockmans, S., Kostanyan, H., Remizov, A., Slapakova, L., & van der Loo, G. (2017). *Assessing European neighbourhood policy perspectives from the literature.* Brussels and London: CEPS & Rowman and Littlefield International.

BP Statistical Review of World Energy. (2018, June). *67th edition* (pp. 14 and 28). Retrieved from https://www.bp.com/content/dam/bp/en/corporate/pdf/energy-economics/statistical-review/bp-stats-review-2018-full-report.pdf.

Buchan, D., & Keay, M. (2015). *Europe's long energy journey: Towards an energy union?.* Oxford: Oxford University Press.

Chichkin, A. (2019, January 16). Tranzitny separatism na neftyanom prostranstve EAEU/ CIS dominiruet. *RitmYeavrazii.* Retrieved from https://www.ritmeurasia.org/news–2019-01-16–tranzitnyj-separatizm-na-neftegazovom-prostranstve-eaes-sng-dominiruet-40554.

Clifton, J., Comin, F., & Fuentes, D. D. (2006). Privatisation in the European Union. *Journal of European Public Policy, 13*(5), 736–756.

Coelho, C., & Grojec, W. (2018, September 12). Pipeline from hell? Nord Stream 2 and why it's so contentious. *Radio Free Europe.* Retrieved from https://www.rferl.org/a/29486007.html.

Cram, L. (1997). *Policy-Making in the European Union: Conceptual Lenses and the Integration Process.* New York: Routledge Research in European Public Policy.

Derkul, O. (2019, March 12). Soyuzny dogovor Rossii i Belorussii: ryvok ili stagnatsiya? *Ritm Yevrazii.* Retrieved from https://www.ritmeurasia.org/news–2019-03-12–sojuznyj-dogovor-rossii-i-belorussii-ryvok-ili-stagnacija-41525?fbclid=IwAR3wwI1PyFgJ-Uo_Y-Ksg5HHBn0vmlM8aeCiK-7w0YoTpC2BIuBm1uRKDPME.

Dragneva, R., & Wolczuk, K. (2012). Russia, the Customs Union and the EU: Cooperation, stagnation or rivalry? *Chatham house briefing paper REP BP, 1.*

Dragneva, R., & Wolczuk, K. (2013). The Eurasian Customs Union: Framing the analysis. In R. Dragneva & K. Wolczuk (Eds.), *Eurasian economic integration: Law policy and politics.* Cheltenham, UK: Edward Elgar Publishing Ltd.

Ellinas, C. (2019). Ukraine: Gazprom's key to flexibility. *Natural Gas World, 4*(5), 27–31.

Ezhov, S., & Tyrtov, E. (2018, November). *Zavershenie nalogovogo manevra. Epizod I – Dempfer. Vygon Consulting.* Retrieved from http://vygon.consulting/upload/iblock/7e7/vygon_consulting_end_of_tax_maneur_ep1.pdf.

Fischer, S., & Geden, O. (2015). Limits of an "Energy Union": Only pragmatic progress on EU energy market regulation expected in the coming months. *SWP Comment 2015/C 28.* German Institute for International and Security Affairs.

Georgiou, N., & Rocco, A. (2017). The energy union as an instrument of global governance in EU-Russia energy relations: From fragmentation to coherence and solidarity. *Geopolitics, History, and International Relations, 9*(1), 241–268.

Greif, A. (2006). *Institutions and the path to the modern economy: Lessons from medieval trade (political economy of institutions and decisions).* Cambridge: Cambridge University Press.

Gurzu, A. (2015, June 10). *Europe's energy (dis)union.* Retrieved from https://www.politico.eu/article/europe-energy-union-community-infrastructure-pipelines-interconnectors-plan-juncker/.

Haas, E. (1958). *The Uniting of Europe: Political, social and economic forces, 1950–1957.* Stanford: Stanford University Press.

Haas, E. (1961). International integration: The European and the universal process. *International Organization, 15,* 366–392.

Hall, P. (1997). The role of interests, institutions, and ideas in the comparative political economy of the industrialized nations. In M. I. Lichbach & A. S. Zuckerman (Eds.), *Comparative politics: Rationality, culture, and structure* (pp. 174–207). Cambridge: Cambridge University Press.

Hall, P., & Soskice, D. (2001). *Varieties of capitalism: The institutional foundations of comparative advantage.* Oxford: Oxford University Press.

Harjanne, A., & Korkonen, J. (2019). Abandoning the concept of renewable energy. *Energy Policy, 127,* 330–340.

Heinrich, A. (2017, September 12). Energy issues in Russia's relations with Belarus. *Russian Analytical Digest, 12*(206), 14–16.

Hoffmann, S. (1966). Obstinate or obsolete? The fate of the nation-state and the case of Western Europe. *Daedalus, 95,* 862–915.

Hoffmann, S. (1982). Reflections on the nation-state in Western Europe today. *Journal of Common Market Studies, 21,* 21–37.

Howarth, D., & Roos, M. (2017). Pushing the boundaries new research on the activism of EU supranational institutions. *Journal of Contemporary European Research, 13*(1), 1007–1024.

Howorth, J. (2012). Decision-making in security and defense policy: Towards supranational inter-governmentalism? *Cooperation and Conflict, 47*(4), 433–453.

Jegen, M. (2014). *Energy policy in the European Union: The power and limits of discourse* (Les Cahiers européens de Sciences Po, n° 2). Centre: D'etudes Europeennes.

Khatinoglu, D. (2019, February 12). Baku ratifies Caspian Convention. *Natural Gas World*. Retrieved from https://www.naturalgasworld.com.

Kirkham, K. (2016). The formation of the Eurasian Economic Union: How successful is the Russian regional hegemony? *Journal of Eurasian Studies, 7*, 111–128.

Kucherov, N. (2019, January 10). Minsk deistviteljno ne ponimaet, chto takoe obshchii rynok gaza s Rossiei, ili delaet vid? *Ritm Yevrazii*. Retrieved from https://www.ritmeurasia.org/news–2019-01-10–minsk-dejstvitelno-ne-ponimaet-chto-takoe-obschij-rynok-gaza-s-rossiej-ili-delaet-vid-40463?fbclid=IwAR1MiD4GaKNXxyO__Oq7WXSUXPt8a-3j_Vl-R9NGir6rfY68YPz6SvPVE7s.

Kustova, I. (2017). Towards a comprehensive research agenda on EU energy integration: Policy making, energy security, and EU energy actorness. *Journal of European Integration, 39*(1), 95–101.

Łada, A., Skłodowska, M., Szczepanik, M., & Wenerski, L. (2015). *The Energy Union: Views from France, Germany, Poland and the United Kingdom*. Warsaw: Institute of Public Affairs European Programme.

Lindberg, L., & Scheingold, S. (1970). *Europe's would-be polity*. Englewood Cliffs, NJ: PrenticeHall.

Lukashenko, A. (2011, October 17). O sudjbakh nashei integratsii. *Izvestiya*. Retrieved from http://www.izvestia.ru/news/504081.

Maltby, T. (2013). European Union energy policy integration: A case of European Commission policy entrepreneurship and increasing supranationalism. *Energy Policy, 55*, 435–444.

Maszczyk, P., & Rapacki, R. (2012). *Varieties of capitalism in transition countries*. Warsaw: Warsaw School of Economics.

Milward, A. (1984). *The reconstruction of western Europe 1945–1951*. London: Methuen.

Milward, A. (1992). *The European rescue of the nation-state*. London: Routledge.

Moravcsik, A. (1998). *The choice for Europe: Social purpose & state power from Messina to Maastricht*. Ithaca, NY: Cornell University Press.

Moravcsik, A. (1999). A new statecraft? Supranational entrepreneurs and international cooperation. *International Organization, 53*(2), 267–306.
Nazarbaev, N. (2011, October 25). Yevraziiskii soyuz: ot idei k istorii budushchego. *Izvestiya*. Retrieved from http://www.izvestia.ru/news/504908.
Nolke, A., & Vliegenthart, A. (2009). Enlarging the varieties of capitalism: The emergence of dependent market economies in East Central Europe. *World Politics, 61*(4), 670–702.
North, D. (1990). *Institutions, institutional change, and economic performance.* Cambridge: Cambridge University Press.
North, D., Wallis, J., & Weingast, B. (2009). *Violence and social orders.* Cambridge: Cambridge University Press.
Nosovich, A. (2018, November 7). Gazoprovod s rossiiskim gazom zamenit Pribaltike litovsky SPG-terminal. *RuBaltic.Ru*. Retrieved from https://www.rubaltic.ru/article/ekonomika-i-biznes/07112018-gazoprovod-s-rossiyskim-gazom-zamenit-pribaltike-litovskiy-spg-terminal/?sfns=mo.
Nye, J. (1971). *Peace in parts: Integration and conflict in regional organization.* Boston, MA: Little Brown.
Parkhomchik, L. (2016). *Natural gas industry of Kazakhstan: Key features and future prospects.* Retrieved from http://eurasian-research.org/en/research/comments/energy/natural-gas-industry-kazakhstan-key-features-and-future-prospects.
Pastukhova, M., & Westphal, K. (2018). Eurasian Economic Union integrates energy markets: EU stands aside. *SWP Comments* C 05. Retrieved from www.swp-berlin.org/fileadmin/contents/products/comments/2018C05_puk_wep.pdf.
Putin, V. (2011, October 3). Novyi integratsionnayi proekt Yevrazii – budushchee, kotoroe rojdaetsya segodnya. *Izvestiya*. Retrieved from http://www.izvestia.ru/news/502761.
Ringel, M., & Knodt, M. (2018). The governance of the European Energy Union: Efficiency, effectiveness and acceptance of the winter package 2016. *Energy Policy, 112,* 209–220.
Rustemova, A. (2011). Political economy of Central Asia: Initial reflections on the need for a new approach. *Journal of Eurasian Studies, 2*(1), 30–39.
Sandholtz, W., & Zysman, J. (1989). 1992: Recasting the European bargain. *World Politics, 42*(1), 95–128.
Schimmelfennig, F., & Rittberger, B. (2005). Theories of European integration: Assumptions and hypotheses. In J. Richardson (Ed.), *European Union: Power and policy-making.* London: Routledge.

Schirm, S. (2016). Domestic ideas, institutions or interests? Explaining governmental preferences towards global economic governance. *International Political Science Review, 37*(1), 66–80.

Schmitter, P. (1969). Three neo-functional hypotheses about international integration. *International Organization, 23,* 61–166.

Shadrina, E. (2018). The common gas market of the Eurasian Economic Union: Progress and prospects for the institutionalisation. *Region: Regional Studies of Russia, Eastern Europe, and Central Asia, 7*(1), 105–137.

Shadrina, E. (2019a). Energy cooperation and security in Central Asia: The possible Synergy between hydrocarbon rich and water rich countries. In F. Taghizadeh-Hesary, N. Yoshino, Y. Chang, & A. Rillo (Eds.), *Achieving energy security in Asia: Diversification, integration, and policy implications.* Singapore: World Scientific Press.

Shadrina, E. (2019b). Renewable energy in Central Asian Economies: Role in reducing regional energy insecurity. In N. Yoshino, F. Taghizadeh-Hesary, Y. Chang, & T.-H. Le (Eds.), *Energy Insecurity in Asia: Challenges, Solutions, and Renewable Energy.* Tokyo: ADBI Press.

Shustov, A. (2019, July 5). *Gaz ili integratsiya? V Moskve i Minske Soyuzny dogovor poka vidyat po-raznomu. Ritm Yevrazii.* Retrieved July 5, 2019 from https://www.ritmeurasia.org/news–2019-07-05–gaz-ili-integracija-v-moskve-i-minske-sojuznyj-dogovor-poka-vidjat-po-raznomu-43635?sfns=mo?print=1?print=1?print=1?print=1.

Stern, J. (2019). Narratives for natural gas in decarbonising European energy markets. *OIES PAPER: NG141.* Oxford, UK: The Oxford Institute for Energy Studies.

Stone Sweet, A., & Fligstein, N. (Eds.). (2001). *The institutionalization of Europe.* Oxford: Oxford University Press.

Stone Sweet, A., & Sandholtz, W. (1997). European integration and supranational governance. *Journal of European Public Policy, 4*(3), 297–317.

Szulecki, K., Fischer, S., Gullberg, A. T., & Sartor, O. (2016). Shaping the 'Energy Union': Between national positions and governance innovation in EU energy and climate policy. *Climate Policy, 16*(5), 548–567.

Tkachyov, I., & Feinberg, A. (2017, April 2). Skrytyi schyot na $100 mlrd: как Rossiya soderzhit belorusskuyu ekonomiku. *RBC.* Retrieved from https://www.rbc.ru/economics/02/04/2017/58e026879a79471d6c8aef30.

Verdiyeva, S. (2018). The Eurasian Economic Union: Problems and prospects. *Journal of World Investment and Trade, 19,* 722–749.

Vinokurov, E., & Libman, A. (2012a). *Eurasian integration: Challenges of transcontinental regionalism*. Basingstoke: Palgrave Macmillan.

Vinokurov, E., & Libman, A. (2012b). Eurasia and Eurasian integration: Beyond the Post-Soviet borders. In *The economics of the Post-Soviet and Eurasian integration*. EDB Eurasian Integration Yearbook. Almaty: Eurasian Development Bank.

Volgin, Y. (2018, March 26). *Formirovanie obshchego elektroenergeticheckogo rynka EAES*. Retrieved from http://eurasian-studies.org/archives/7432.

William, P. (2019, January 14). German gas lobby rebuts US Ambassador. *Natural Gas World*. Retrieved from https://www.naturalgasworld.com/german-gas-lobby-rebuts-us-ambassador-67291.

Williams, N. (2018, October 12). *Russian oil monopoly over Belarus Persists in bilateral trade agreements*. Retrieved from https://www.irinsider.org/easterncentral-europe/2018/10/18/russian-oil-monopoly-over-belarus-persists-in-bilateral-trade-agreements.

Zemskova, K. (2018). The common energy market of the Eurasian Economic Union: Implications for the European Union and the role of the Energy Charter Treaty. *Occasional Paper Series*. Energy Charter Secretariat.

9

Mediating Populist Discourse in Russia via YouTube: The Case of Alexey Navalny

Sofya Glazunova

Introduction

Debates on populism have become commonplace in contemporary political science and political communication research. The phenomenon of a wave of successful populist movements in Western politics recently triggered a series of investigations on populism and its means of communication. The case of Russia, as well as of other non-democratic countries, was sidelined due to the low competitive political environment as well as a manipulative, one-sided style of communication. However, this does not mean that the populist style, discourse, and ideology are not used by politicians in Russia to achieve different political goals. The contradistinction between the "rotten" West and a

This paper is a part of Sofya Glazunova's Ph.D. thesis "Digital media as a tool for anti-systemic opposition in Russia: the case study of Alexey Navalny's populist political communications on YouTube", hosted by Creative Industries Faculty, Queensland University of Technology, Brisbane, Australia (2017–2020).

S. Glazunova (✉)
Queensland University of Technology, Brisbane, QLD, Australia
e-mail: s.glazunova@qut.edu.au

© The Author(s) 2020
A. Akimov and G. Kazakevitch (eds.), *30 Years since the Fall of the Berlin Wall*,
Palgrave Studies in Economic History, https://doi.org/10.1007/978-981-15-0317-7_9

"prosperous" Russia is peculiar to the Russian establishment's discourse, which Russia has inherited from the Cold War. In this context, the corruption accusations towards Putin's elite, which has held power for almost twenty years and have been seen to be opposed to "ordinary people", appear unique to the Russian political environment. Emerging as one of the voices of the Russia's fragmented opposition, the political project of Alexey Navalny has become one of the most successful opposition projects in Russia in recent years.

The mass protests "for fair elections" in 2011–2012 in Russia brought to the fore several opposition activists who were dissatisfied with the political situation in the country. Among them was political activist Alexey Navalny, who by that time had run several projects against corruption in Russia. Later, he became the head of the non-governmental organisation (NGO) Anti-Corruption Foundation (ACF) which investigated and revealed to the public the malicious acts of corruption among several high-ranking Russian officials. In 2015–2016, Navalny and his colleagues actively used digital tools and platforms to communicate their anti-corruption discourse. They created a regular video blog on YouTube and a YouTube channel called *Navalny LIVE*. Their videos discrediting Russian officials reached millions of viewers on YouTube; some of them led to mass protests across major metropolitan areas in Russia. One prominent example includes a video entitled "He is not Dimon to you" created by Navalny in 2017, which thematises the corruption activities of Russian Prime Minister Dmitry Medvedev. After its release, on at least two occasions (in March and June 2017), thousands of people marched the streets, outraged with the corrupt activities of the head of the Russian Government.

The success of Navalny as a member of an anti-systemic opposition who effectively acts online—attracting millions of viewers on YouTube—as well as offline, running for the elections and organising protests, has stimulated my investigation of the content conveyed in Navalny's discourse online. The populist style of communication gives Navalny an advantage compared to his opponents in garnering support both online and offline. Herein, I investigate the main frames of Navalny's discourse on YouTube. Frames which consist of symbols can lead to the triggering of particular emotions in citizens, which can possibly turn into subsequent political participation. Using the framing method, I investigated the English transcripts of YouTube videos posted on Navalny's video blog. The main frames of Navalny's videos included "anti-corruptionism", "elections", "populism" itself, as well as the notion of "truth" and "ways to communicate it".

Political Communication and Digital Media

Research of the populist discourse of Navalny is situated in the field of political communication (PC). This field is located at the intersection of political and communication sciences, exploring the interrelationships of the main PC actors such as political actors, the media, citizens, and public relations structures. PC research was predominantly developed in the first decades after the Second World War by American and British researchers, for example by Blumler and Kavanagh (1999), who divided PC history into three ages in democratic societies. The latest "third age of PC", in which many authors believe we are still living, is associated with different trends affecting the PC sphere (ibid.). It includes intensified professionalisation of political advocacy, an increased competitive environment among mass media, anti-elitist popularisation, populism, and mediatisation of politics (ibid., pp. 213–225).

In the twenty-first century, academic scholarship has shifted towards the existence of the "fourth age of PC". This new era of PC, though, is still defined by features of the "third age" but, at the same time, is rapidly changing (Blumler, 2013). The new emerging features of PC comprise diffusion and utilisation of Internet facilities, the emergence of synchronous communicative networks replacing simple interpersonal communication, and audiences moving from being merely receivers of information to producers of content by themselves, as well as other features (ibid.). New challenges and transformations described by Blumler (2013) and others require a new framework and understanding of PC in the modern world.

Together with the challenges of PC, new actors of communication have emerged in the "fourth age of PC". To some extent, social media can serve as a PC actor too. Recent examples of involvement of social media platforms such as Facebook and Twitter in the electoral campaigns of presidential election in the United States (2016), the Cambridge Analytica scandal and concerns surrounding illegal digital campaign spending during the UK's "Brexit" referendum in 2016 were all testament to the fact that the role of social media in PC is rapidly changing. From its original purpose as a means of communication, social media is turning into a full-value actor with its policies, content and instruments of PC. In this paper, PC is understood as a dynamic network structure which involves the exchange of political messages between politicians, media, citizens, PR specialists, and new emerging actors utilising traditional and digital communication technologies. Navalny's communication strategy fits this definition neatly as he deliberately employs purposeful communication to achieve his political goals, mostly by engaging in digital communication channels such as YouTube.

YouTube, according to Kaplan and Haenlein (2010), is a content community; its main objective is to share media content between users (2010, p. 63). Evans (2016, p. 337) describes its distinctive affordances in PC as follows: "Unlike Facebook or Twitter, YouTube users do not register to receive information from specific sources as followers or friends and therefore are more likely to encounter information serendipitously, rather than being directed towards it by someone with whom they share a similar political or social perspective". More specifically, YouTube affordances allow for the production of investigative videos on the corruption of Russian officials and to subsequently enable the spread to large parts of the population. YouTube remains one of the few social media channels available to opposition leader Navalny, helping the spread of anti-government content for activists despite Russia's well-known restrictions on media freedom (Freedom House, 2017).

Populist Style of Communication

There are different approaches to defining populism comprehensibly. Different authors consider populism as an ideology (Mudde, 2007), a philosophy (Inglehart & Norris, 2016), a logic (Laclau, 2005), a discourse (Laclau, 1977, 1980, 2005; Laclau & Mouffe, 1985), or a political style (Moffitt & Tormey, 2014). In this paper, I subscribe to an understanding of populism as a political style, where it is understood as "the repertoires of performance that are used to create political relations" (Moffitt & Tormey, 2014, p. 387). Moffitt and Tormey (ibid., p. 388) argue that "the contemporary political landscape is intensely mediated and stylised, and as such, the so-called 'aesthetic' or performative features are particularly important". When politicians become pseudo-celebrities, they use "flash mobs, protests, and different types of content to attract the attention of voters using stylistic features" (Moffitt & Tormey, 2014, p. 388). YouTube, in this sense, is a favourable environment for the populist style, allowing the populist leader to perform and appeal to users directly involving the visual, audio and text content. The populist style can bring together different content, messages and themes which create political relations between PC actors.

As Moffitt and Tormey (2014) argue, the main elements of the populist style are an appeal to "the people" as opposed to the elite; a perception of crisis, breakdown, threat; and the "bad manners" of the populist (as an outsider of "normal politics"). These features are inherent to the discourse of Navalny, too; however, the Russian version of populism generally has its distinctive features. Populism in Russia is mostly personalised; different Russian politicians oppose their counter-elite and seek active feedback from the voters. The current leader of the Communist Party of Russia, Gennady Zyuganov, has been expressing the nostalgia of a Communist past; the leader of the Liberal Democratic Party of Russia, Vladimir Zhirinovsky, opposes himself to the "Evil" West. The distinction of "us" and "them" in Putin's rhetoric has undergone several transformations from "them" as terrorists, as the West (and, the United States particularly) and to the opposing liberals known and labelled as "Fifth Column" (Kolesnikov, Kortunov, & Snegovaya, 2018).

Navalny himself uses some of the typical Russian populist features in his discourse, although, his content and channels of dissemination are different from the one ascribed to the establishment. The government deploys conventional instruments for spreading populist rhetoric, including the resources of the mainstream media, which restrict freedom of expression in Russia. Opposition leader Navalny is forced to use social media platforms like YouTube, where the government thus far has little or no control over the international digital platform.

Navalny's Communication: Roles, Purposes, and Messages

As per the introductory words of this chapter, Navalny is an opposition activist, the head of the NGO ACF, and was previously also a presidential candidate for the 2018 presidential election. The combination of these varying roles—an active citizen fighting against corruption; a journalist (a host) producing investigative journalistic content; and a politician entering the political system by participating in the elections—creates different narratives in content disseminated by Navalny.

The anti-corruption activity is the first distinctive narrative of Navalny's communication. As the official website of the ACF states, the NGO "is the only Russia-based NGO that investigates, exposes and fights corruption among high-ranking Russian government officials" (Anti-Corruption Foundation, n.d.). Representing civil society and relying on donations, the NGO ran several campaigns and projects against corruption in the government. Starting from 2015 to 2016, however, the activities of the NGO have been taking place mostly online, specifically in the form of publications on the website, blog posts and, more critically, YouTube videos. The NGO has produced investigative documentary films about the corruption of Russian General Prosecutor Chaika in 2015, Russian Prime Minister Medvedev in 2017 and other high-ranking officials. Sampson (2010, p. 262) considers anti-corruption logic as a whole industry comprising "knowledge, people, money and symbols". As an industry, Sampson argues (ibid.), anti-corruptionism brings a new way of thinking about the world, a new discourse. The ACF in Russia led by activist Alexey Navalny fits this anti-corruption logic neatly, being not only an NGO, whose aim is to fight corruption, but also producing the content and symbols of anti-corruptionism in semi-authoritarian Russia.

Another role of Navalny in a political context is the role of a journalist. He often initiates investigations and production of videos in journalistic formats. He situates himself as the narrator of these documentary films, explaining and outlining the corrupt schemes of officials in detail. Moreover, in 2017, Navalny and his colleagues created a YouTube channel called *Navalny LIVE*, where they discuss political news as experts and journalists. *Navalny LIVE*, together with the creators of investigative videos of the ACF on YouTube, constitute the most significant alternative media content producers in Russia (Glazunova, 2018). Opposed to the mainstream media outlets, sponsored by the government or related business structures, Navalny's media is crowdfunded but also consists mostly of non-professionals, more specifically lawyers and managers who work on these investigative projects (ibid.). These are typical characteristics of alternative journalism as has been described by Atton and Hamilton (2008) as well as Harcup (2013). The alternative format of the media allows for the communication of different agendas, and so reflects on the state of "truth" in the public sphere in Russia. The organisational description of *Navalny LIVE* (n.d.) portrays itself as the only channel in Russia telling the "truth", as opposed to Russian state TV.

Beyond these roles, Navalny has also tried to enter a formal opposition role in Russia's system, participating in elections, including contesting for a position in the State Duma (2011), the mayoral election of Moscow (2013) and the presidential election (2018). He took the second place in the Moscow mayoral election in 2013 (27.4% of votes), and all his attempts to enter the political arena by being elected and act as an opposition figure inside Russia's political system have failed. The Central Election Commission revoked Navalny's nomination as a presidential candidate in 2017 on the grounds of his criminal records. This, however, did little to hamper his popularity, which continued to grow despite the official ban.

Gel'man outlined the state of political opposition in Russia since 2000 (2008, 2013, 2015). At the beginning of the 2000s, as Gel'man (2008) described, the extinction of principal opposition (which requires total control over power resources through radical change) and semi-opposition (which is critical of government policies, but backing its major decisions) took place. As he explained, it happened due to the strengthening of Putin's elite, a rise of its integration and a decrease of the elite's differentiation. The anti-systemic opposition remained in a ghetto until the State Duma elections of 2011, which led to the mass protests "for fair elections" (Gel'man, 2013). At that time, both systemic and anti-systemic opposition movements could effectively activate and mobilise supporters. At the beginning of the 2010s, new opposition figures such as Navalny emerged and became prominent in the fragmented opposition market. Navalny was gaining popularity due to his political and blogger activity, which he had sustained for years. Over the years, however, he failed to position himself as a credible, systemic opposition leader due to attempts by the Russian political regime to "twist the nuts" towards authoritarianism. The symbols of opposition broadcasted to Navalny supporters online continued to maintain the illusion of a real opposition force, which sometimes led to offline actions such as protests or alternative voting patterns.

Overall, in his discourse and activities, Navalny appears as an active citizen, a journalist, and a politician. This skilful combination of roles, as I argue, allows him to attract more supporters dissatisfied with the current government, media, and high-ranking officials. He alternates the type of content and messages, he produces and, instead, diffuses them to peripheral voters. Engaging in relatively low-cost and free digital media allows him to achieve these goals while his populist style of communication helps to unite different content under one "umbrella".

Methodology

Framing

This research identifies the main frames of Navalny's discourse as communicated in his YouTube videos. The primary method which can help to illuminate these categories is known as "framing". According to Entman (1993, p. 52), framing rests on the ability "to select some aspects of a perceived reality and make them more salient in a communicating text, in such a way as to promote a particular problem definition, causal interpretation, moral evaluation, and/or treatment recommendation". Frames in political communication are essential, as they "call attention to some aspects of reality while obscuring other elements, which might lead audiences to have different reactions" (Entman, 1993, p. 55). Texts are the primary data for framing, as they can consist of pieces of information associated with "culturally familiar symbols" (ibid., p. 53). An analysis of transcripts of Navalny's YouTube video is used to identify the main frames in his pre-election communication. Through the word frequencies and word co-occurrences, one can deduce to map the "semantic field of related words, which specify the meaning constructed about the issue" (Van der Meer & Verhoeven, 2013, p. 230).

The process of framing constitutes identifying *concepts*, or collections of words, travelling together within the text (Leximancer Pty Ltd, 2018). Concepts that then appear together in the same pieces of text are clustered into higher-level *themes* (Leximancer Pty Ltd, 2018). Later, through the process of contextual analysis and interpretation, themes are transformed into *frames* themselves, or "the central organising ideas or storylines that provide meaning" (Gamson & Modigliani, 1987, p. 1943). The first two stages of this process can also be referred to as "frame mapping" which helps to identify words that appear jointly within the text with the help of cluster algorithms (Matthes & Kohring, 2008). For these purposes, qualitative software for content analysis, Leximancer, was used. Leximancer performs conceptual and relational analyses measuring the presence of concepts together, with the measurement of relationships between them (Leximancer Pty Ltd, 2018, p. 8) visualised in the form of a concept map. The following process of interpretation brings the meaning and the context for the concept map, highlighting the main frames of Navalny's communication.

Sampling and Extraction

The data for the analysis are the YouTube transcripts of Navalny's videos as the primary source of his discourses. I investigate the period of Navalny's electoral campaigning from his 13 December 2016 announcement, where he made clear that he would contest the 2018 Russian presidential election, up until the inauguration of the elected President Vladimir Putin on 7 May 2018. Usually, the electoral period contains the maximum concentration of populist messages, as such messages help to garner support during the elections. In these 18 months, Navalny posted 146 videos of different lengths on YouTube, each with a different number of user views. The overall mean number of views of these videos is 1,954,422, while the median is 1,600,000 views.[1] To reduce the sample of videos for the analysis, I chose the videos with the views above the median and the videos that contain English transcripts of the texts. Out of 146 videos, 52 met the criteria as mentioned above.

The Analysis of Concepts and Themes

I proceeded to the actual frame mapping with the Leximancer software. I analysed 52 transcripts of Navalny's videos about the connectivity of words and co-occurrence of words within texts. Leximancer can run an automated process of concept mapping, but manual adjustments were needed to exclude stop words. Some of the concepts were merged if they were a singular or plural form of the same word (e.g. election, elections) or different forms of a name (e.g. Putin and Vladimir Putin), as well as other adjustments. The software then identified the texts' main themes and created a concept map, using the principle that "concepts that appear together, often in the same pieces of text, attract one another strongly, and so tend to settle near one another in the map space" (Leximancer Pty Ltd, 2018, p. 12). The theme, according to Leximancer Pty Ltd (2018), "takes its name from the most connected concept within that circle". As per Fig. 9.1, five main themes were identified: *house*, *rubles* (the Russian currency), *Russia*, *truth*, *elections*. The full list of the concepts and themes can be seen in Table 9.1. The following section will provide a detailed analysis of the themes and concepts followed by the author's interpretation.

Elections

Elections were one of the central topics of Navalny's discourse, as he was running as a candidate for the presidential race in 2018. Of the words from

---

[1] These figures relate to the period of data collection (May 2018).

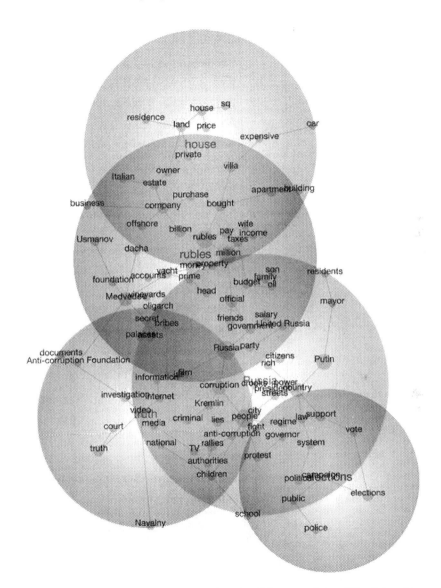

Fig. 9.1 Concept map in Leximancer of 52 English transcripts of YouTube videos of Alexey Navalny (*Source* Image by the author based on the information transcribed from the YouTube videos by Alexey Navalny. *Note* The configuration of the map in Leximancer: theme size—57%; visible concepts—100%)

Table 9.1 Main themes and concepts of 52 English transcripts of YouTube videos of Alexey Navalny

Theme	Concepts
Rubles	Rubles, million, money, Medvedev, official, company, billion, bought, pay, taxes, yacht, apartment, prime, oligarch, secret, Usmanov, budget, offshore, foundation, bribes, vineyards, family, dacha, property, son, business, oil, wife, head, income, accounts
Russia	Russia, people, Putin, corruption, country, rallies, government, city, support, friends, lies, citizens, streets, power, Kremlin, law, anti-corruption, rich, president, United Russia, fight, mayor, regime, party, salary, governor, protest, residents, crooks
Truth	Truth, video, investigation, TV, palaces, Navalny, information, media, assets, authorities, court, children, film, internet, criminal, documents, national, Anti-corruption Foundation, jail
House	House, land, estate, villa, sq, purchase, building, owner, residence, expensive, price, Italian, private, car
Elections	Elections, campaign, vote, political, system, public, school, police

Source Transcribed by the author from YouTube videos by Alexey Navalny

the row "elections" in Table 9.1, some had a political meaning that is specific to a Russian context. Among them are *school* and *police*, which require interpretation if they are to be understood fully by those outside the contemporary Russian milieu. Schools in Russia usually serve as voting stations during the elections. Teachers from these schools are observers, sometimes chairpersons of the polling station commissions. Often, citizens or opposition forces accuse them of falsifying the results of the elections due to the pressure of local or regional authorities (Rybina, 2012). The title and topic of one of the Navalny videos are "Dear teachers, do not do that!" (Navalny, 2018a).

Navalny mentions *police* in the context of elections as one of the forces that sabotaged his participation in elections. Using co-occurrence search of words *elections* and *police* from Leximancer, this is evident from the following fragment: "Because of this, I'd like to make a small announcement about our plans for all of you, as well as for the members of Putin's administration, central **election** commission, **police**, FSB and others who would like to sabotage my nomination" (Navalny, 2017a).

In broad terms, the word *elections* in relation to *system* and *political* can mean an institution as a part of the political system which, after the dissolution of Soviet Union, has become essential to many Russian citizens. For Russian authorities elections serve more as a referendum of approval than as full democratic elections in the traditional sense. This is due to non-removability of elites in Russia's semi-authoritarian political system. In speaking of "elections", Navalny reminds people of the importance of the institution of free and fair elections, as well as articulating his ambitions for entering the political system as institutional oppositional figure. Overall, the frame based on this theme and concepts can also be referred to as "elections".

House

This block of words (see row "house" in Table 9.1) is related to the expensive property or real estate that Russian officials possess, according to Navalny's investigations. Navalny accuses high-ranking Russian officials of buying luxurious estates, expensive cars, and other luxury items through corrupt schemes (Navalny, 2018b).

> So, the house we labelled as "uninteresting" and "unimpressive" a year ago turned out to be literally one of the most expensive objects we have ever filmed. So, we make a fairly obvious conclusion that oligarch Prokhorov bought a villa from a government official for such colossal money because this was not a purchase of the real estate, but a legalised and disguised transfer of money to the deputy prime minister of our country.

Expensive houses, villas, and cars are embedded in the anti-corruption discourse described by Navalny in his documentary films. They symbolise the items of luxury which officials possess by stealing money from ordinary citizens, according to the films' authors. These symbols can provoke emotional reactions from citizens, particularly given the significant economic disparity between rich and poor in Russia. According to a European Parliament report "Russia has more billionaires relative to the size of its economy than any other large country" as well as "huge wealth (estimated at up to 75% of Russia's GDP) hidden in offshore accounts"; conversely, in 2016, 13.8% of Russians (20 million people) lived below the poverty line (European Parliament, 2018). According to the framing map in Fig. 9.1, these are not the only symbols of an anti-corruption industry mentioned in the texts, as the next theme shows.

Rubles

Another group of words was united under the theme *rubles* (see Table 9.1). 31 words represent different aspects of the anti-corruption industry in Russia in a version of Alexey Navalny. I divided them into several groups. The first group represents the financial-fiscal attributes of the anti-corruption industry, such as words *rubles, million, money, billion, bought, pay, taxes, budget, offshore, income, assets, accounts*. These concepts are an essential part of the anti-corruption industry. The second group of concepts is linked to the investigation movie "He is not Dimon to you" about the corruption of Russian Prime Minister Dmitriy Medvedev. This group of concepts includes words *Medvedev, official, company, yacht, prime, oligarch, secret, Usmanov, foundation, bribes, vineyards, dacha*. The movie reached 27 millions views in May 2018, the biggest in the history of Navalny's video blog. It also provoked a series of anti-corruption protests. The movie describes the corruption schemes organised by the Prime Minister, including the work of charity organisations and businesspeople. Navalny mentions the luxury items which, according to Navalny, the Prime Minister supposedly possesses: yachts, vineyards, dacha (country house), and other items (Navalny, 2017b).

The nepotism of Russian elites is represented through the group of the words *family, son, wife*. Usually, Navalny describes the schemes where the members of the officials' families are involved in the corruption (Navalny, 2016): "So, there is no reasonable explanation of how the mayor's **family** found 130 million rubles for their American purchases, although we can make some guesses. Interestingly enough, Karnilin did not mention his **wife** in his latest tax return". Other words such as *apartments, property, business, oil, head* also fit the anti-corruption industry discourse. The overall theme *rubles*, together with the theme *house*, can be coded in our research as the "anti-corruptionism" frame. It represents the multiple symbols of corruption crimes of Russian officials.

Truth

The fourth cluster of words in Leximancer was merged under the theme of "truth" (see Table 9.1). In many videos, Navalny describes himself and his organisations as the suppliers of "truth" as opposed to corrupt elites and TV channels that support them: "Think about it, and subscribe to our channel, because we tell the truth here, unlike your own deceitful and unconstructive TV" (Navalny, 2017c). Part of this cluster is associated with Navalny's version of ways to communicate "truth" in the conditions of the semi-authoritarian regime, where mass media is under government control. My previous discussion noted how Navalny circumvents such controls by using the formats of alternative journalism, but the word *truth* opens a broader perspective. Through discussions of channels, instruments, formats, genres, and other means of communication, Navalny illuminates the symbols of "truthful" communication that are or are not available to his team in modern Russia. These are words like *video, investigation, information, media, TV, film, Internet, documents*. In almost every video, Navalny repeats the same phrase at the end: "Subscribe to our channel, we tell the truth here". Navalny uses the symbols of "truth" to support his claim that his way of communication is the most trustworthy in Russia as opposed to the information provided by mass media and ruling elites. The antagonism of his claims, together with the contraposition of mainstream and biased mainstream media to new journalistic formats, fits his populist paradigm and style of communication.

The rest of the words had little connectivity under this topic; these include *palaces, assets, authorities, children, criminal, national, Anti-corruption Foundation, jail*. So, in order to investigate the theme more in detail, I changed the configuration of the map in Leximancer, switching to the Concept Cloud view, which shows more accurate results of connectivity between words as per Fig. 9.2.

It is evident from Fig. 9.2 that the concepts *palaces, assets* and *Anti-Corruption Foundation* connected to the group of words under the frame of "anti-corruptionism", as described above. The words *national, authorities, children, jail* and *film* are more connected with the nodes

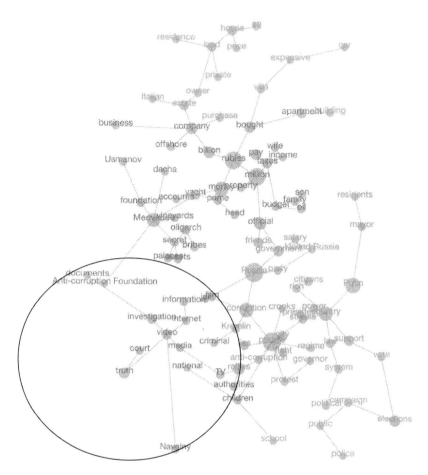

Fig. 9.2 Concept cloud in Leximancer of 52 English transcripts of YouTube videos of Alexey Navalny (*Source* Image by the author based on the information transcribed from the YouTube videos by Alexey Navalny. *Note* The configuration of the map in Leximancer: Visible Concepts: 100%; Theme Size: 57%)

Russia and *people*, which are clustered under theme *Russia* (see Fig. 9.1). I excluded those words from the "truth" cluster, the central theme of this cluster, and added the concept *film*, which is also connected to the "ways of communicating of truth" in Navalny's version.

Russia

The last group of the words merged under the theme *Russia* (see Table 9.1) consists of a larger quantity of words compared to other themes. The words were divided into several thematic groups. First of all, it consists of political actors holding power, such as *Putin, government, Kremlin, president, United Russia, party, mayor, regime, governor, mayor, authorities*. They are also somehow connected with the words *law* and *jail* as instruments that authorities use to hold *power*.

Navalny criticises these actors in his videos as most of them, in his view, constitute the corrupted elite: "This is nonsense, and this makes the Russian regime a structure that represents no one except for a small group of bureaucrats. If you elect me as a president, I will abolish all of these municipal filters and hassles" (Navalny, 2017d). As an element of populist discourse, Navalny matches the symbols of corrupted elites with particular names.

Another group of words is the representation of civic identity, ordinary citizens to whom Navalny appeals (to support him as a candidate, to vote, to protest, to fight corruption). This theme also includes the ways and places of participating in civic life. These can be the words *people, rallies, support, cities, citizens, streets, fight, protest, residents,* and *children*. Children constitute a specific group inside of this theme as journalists and experts argue that, during some of the protests, children and school students were one of the influential groups of Navalny's support during his protests (Human Rights Watch, 2017). Navalny made a separate video for them entitled "To schoolchildren and students!" (Navalny, 2017e). Also, the word *friends* can be related to this group, often Navalny calls his audience as "friends" but, at the same time, it is also used to show the nepotism of Russian elites as in the case containing the words *family, son, wife* from the "anti-corruptionism" frame. National identity is represented in texts by the words *Russia, country,* and *national*.

What results is a clear picture of the main elements of the Russian political system: civil society and its symbols, but also the political actors and governmental institutions which Navalny criticises. The use of emotionally coloured words such as *lies, crooks, rich* in the same group only confirms this fact and further relates to the populist style of communication. The so-called populist "bad manners" (Moffitt & Tormey, 2014) show that he is an "outsider" of the political elite. This block of words represents not only the populist style but the populist discourse itself, consonant with other themes. Navalny appeals to "the people" and their civic identity to fight and hold accountable Putin's elite. The words *corruption* and *anti-corruption*, however, are situated in this block despite the existence of a separate frame called "anti-corruptionism". This fact should lead us to a further investigation of the interconnection between themes in future research.

The Frames of Navalny's Communication

Overall, exploring the most frequent concepts travelling together clustered in themes in texts of Navalny's videos and their interpretation, I revealed four main frames in the English transcripts of Navalny's YouTube videos. These are: "elections", "anti-corruptionism", "populism" and "ways of communicating the truth" as per Table 9.2. The "elections" frame reflects Navalny's pretentions for political power in the conditions of a semi-authoritarian regime. Legally, he is not able to "obtain" power due to the current Russian political elite's monopoly of power. This does not, however, prevent him from communicating these political ambitions verbally through digital instruments.

The "anti-corruptionism" frame consists of symbols of wealth that, according to Navalny, Russian authorities possess; this can be financial-fiscal items or items of property. In the Russian context, this discourse is also connected with the nepotism of elites: when friends and families of officials get the political rent from the regime. The cornerstone of the anti-corruption industry in Navalny's discourse was the investigation of the corruption of Russian Prime Minister Dmitriy Medvedev. The uncovering of concrete corruption cases, together with the embodiment in the high-ranking officials and businesspeople resonated strongly among the Russian anti-corruption community.

The "populism" frame includes the appeal of Navalny to the people, their civic identity, and the political rights of Russian citizens. In this

Table 9.2 Main frames and concepts from 52 English transcripts of Navalny's videos

Frames	Concepts
Elections	Elections, campaign, vote, political, system, public, school, police
Anti-corruptionism	Rubles, million, money, Medvedev, official, company, billion, bought, pay, taxes, yacht, apartment, prime, oligarch, secret, Usmanov, budget, offshore, foundation, bribes, vineyards, family, dacha, property, son, business, oil, wife, head, income, accounts, house, land, estate, villa, sq, purchase, building, owner, residence, expensive, price, Italian, private, car, palaces, assets, Anti-corruption foundation, salary
Populism	Russia, people, Putin, corruption, country, rallies, government, city, support, friends, lies, citizens, streets, power, Kremlin, law, anti-corruption, rich, president, United Russia, fight, mayor, regime, party, governor, protest, residents, crooks, national, authorities, children, jail
Ways of communicating the truth	Truth, video, investigation, TV, Navalny, information, media, court, film, internet, documents

Source Transcribed by the author from YouTube videos by Alexey Navalny

discourse, Navalny opposes himself to a corrupt elite and its monopoly of political power. Moreover, finally, the "ways of communicating the truth" frame describes how Navalny can communicate his truth in Russia. These are crucial digital instruments which are available in the absence of mass media freedom in Russia.

Conclusion

Populism in Russia has its own characteristic features: highly personified, the established version of populism in Russia blames the "Evil" West or the "Fifth column" and penetrates all levels of Russian elites. Mainstream media mostly echoes the populist discourses of ruling elites, operating in a primarily restricted environment. But the populist style of communication is not only deployed by the ruling elites, but also by the anti-systemic opposition. Alexey Navalny has become perhaps not the strongest, but at least the most noticeable opposition project in the Russian political arena over the last ten years.

Navalny actively uses digital media, namely YouTube, to communicate his criticism of the establishment, to develop his anti-corruption industry, and to garner support from voters during the elections. Being an active citizen, a journalist and a politician rolled into one, Navalny uses different messages and symbols embedded in frames to attract more users and attention to his persona across the political arena. As this research shows, these are the frames of "populism" itself, "anti-corruptionism", "elections" and also Navalny's "ways of communicating the truth". These frames fit the populist style of communication as they contain antagonism of ordinary people towards officials ("elections", "populism"), corrupt officials and businesspeople ("anti-corruptionism"), and finally mass media ("ways of communicating the truth"). They correlate with the picture of corruption and a system crisis, where the political system is portrayed as "sick" and "rotten", while Navalny is presented as an alternative to this apocalyptic background. Further to this, Navalny uses specific, emotionally coloured words including, for example, "crooks" as from a newly developed expression in the 2010s "Party of crooks and thieves" used to describe the dominant political party in Russia. All of the above are characteristics of the populist communication style in Moffitt and Tormey's version (2014), which could be explored in detail in future research together with the role of YouTube and its affordances in Navalny's communication.

References

Anti-Corruption Foundation. (n.d.). *About*. Retrieved from https://fbk.info/english/about/.
Atton, C., & Hamilton, J. F. (2008). *Alternative journalism*. London: Sage.
Blumler, J. G. (2013, September 12). The fourth age of political communication [Keynote address]. *Workshop on Political Communication Online*. Berlin: Free University of Berlin. Retrieved from http://www.fgpk.de/en/2013/gastbeitrag-von-jay-g-blumler-the-fourth-age-of-political-communication-2/.

Blumler, J. G., & Kavanagh, D. (1999). The third age of political communication: Influences and features. *Political Communication, 16*(3), 209–230.
Entman, R. M. (1993). Framing: Toward clarification of a fractured paradigm. *Journal of Communication, 43*(4), 51–58.
European Parliament. (2018, April). *Socioeconomic inequality in Russia* [PDF document]. Retrieved from http://www.europarl.europa.eu/RegData/etudes/ATAG/2018/620225/EPRS_ATA(2018)620225_EN.pdf.
Evans, M. (2016). Information dissemination in new media: YouTube and the Israeli-Palestinian conflict. *Media, War & Conflict, 9*(3), 325–343.
Freedom House. (2017). *Freedom of the Press 2017.* Russia. Retrieved from https://freedomhouse.org/report/freedom-press/2017/russia.
Gamson, W. A., & Modigliani, A. (1987). The changing culture of affirmative action. In R. G. Braungart & M. M. Braungart (Eds.), *Research in political sociology* (Vol. 3, pp. 137–177). Greenwich, CT: JAI Press.
Gel'man, V. (2008). Political opposition in Russia: A dying species? *Post-Soviet Affairs, 21*(3), 226–246.
Gel'man, V. (2013). Cracks in the wall: Challenges to electoral authoritarianism in Russia. *Problems of Post-Communism, 60*(2), 3–10.
Gel'man, V. (2015). Political opposition in Russia: A troubled transformation. *Europe-Asia Studies, 67*(2), 177–191.
Glazunova, S. (2018, June). *Alternative journalism in Russia: The case of the Anti-Corruption Foundation.* Paper presented at the Association of International Media and Communications Research Conference, Eugene, Oregon, USA.
Harcup, T. (2013). *Alternative journalism, alternative voices.* Abingdon: Routledge.
Human Rights Watch. (2017, June 11). *Russia: Children, students targeted after protests.* Retrieved from https://www.hrw.org/news/2017/06/11/russia-children-students-targeted-after-protests.
Inglehart, R., & Norris, P. (2016). *Trump, Brexit, and the rise of populism: Economic have-nots and cultural backlash* (HKS Faculty Research Working Paper Series). RWP16-026, 1–52.
Kaplan, A. M., & Haenlein, M. (2010). Users of the world, unite! The challenges and opportunities of social media. *Business Horizons, 53*(1), 59–68.
Kolesnikov, A., Kortunov, A., & Snegovaya, M. (2018, May 21). *Ssha, Evropa, Rossiya: Takie raznye populizmy* (USA, Europe, Russia: Such different populisms) [Audio recording]. Round table at Carnegie Moscow Center, Moscow. Retrieved from http://carnegie.ru/2018/05/21/ru-event-6896.
Laclau, E. (1977). Towards a theory of populism. In *Politics and ideology in Marxist theory* (pp. 143–200). London: New Left Books.

Laclau, E. (1980). Populist rupture and discourse. *Screen Education, 34*(99), 87–93.
Laclau, E. (2005). *On populist reason.* London: Verso.
Laclau, E., & Mouffe, C. (1985). *Hegemony and social strategy: Towards a radical democratic politics.* London: Verso.
Leximancer Pty Ltd. (2018, April 12). *Leximancer user guide* [PDF document]. Retrieved from https://doc.leximancer.com/doc/LeximancerManual.pdf.
Matthes, J., & Kohring, M. (2008). The content analysis of media frames: Toward improving reliability and validity. *Journal of Communication, 58*(2), 258–279.
Moffitt, B., & Tormey, S. (2014). Rethinking populism: Politics, mediatisation and political style. *Political Studies, 62*(2), 81–397.
Mudde, C. (2007). *Populist radical right parties in Europe.* Cambridge: Cambridge University Press.
Navalny LIVE. (n.d.). *About.* Retrieved from https://www.youtube.com/channel/UCgxTPTFbIbCWfTR9I2-5SeQ/about.
Navalny, A. (2016, December 26). *Mer i ego tainye kvartiry v Maiami (The mayor and his secretive apartments in Miami)* [Video file]. Retrieved from https://www.youtube.com/watch?v=q8GvCG0t7Fo&t=1s.
Navalny, A. (2017a, December 18). *Vybory objavleny: Nashi blizhaishie plany (The elections are announced: Our upcoming plans)* [Video file]. Retrieved from https://www.youtube.com/watch?v=Cd0EbzegNH0.
Navalny, A. (2017b, March 2). *On vam ne Dimon (He is not Dimon to you)* [Video file]. Retrieved from https://www.youtube.com/watch?v=qrwlk7_GF9g&t=62s.
Navalny, A. (2017c, July 11). *Otvechayu Vladimiru Putinu: O konstrucktive (Answering to Vladimir Putin: About constructive)* [Video file]. Retrieved from https://www.youtube.com/watch?v=_8FKdlfj7yc&t=1s.
Navalny, A. (2017d, July 19). *Na cherta nam takie vybory? (Why the hell we need this election?)* [Video file]. Retrieved from https://www.youtube.com/watch?v=sjmLR5TzLDA.
Navalny, A. (2017e, June 7). *Shkolnikam I studentam (To schoolchildren and students)* [Video file]. Retrieved from https://www.youtube.com/watch?v=eLkWEpbQspE.
Navalny, A. (2018a, March 15). *Dorogie uchitelya! Ne delaite etogo! (Dear teachers! Do not do this!)* [Video file]. Retrieved from https://www.youtube.com/watch?v=ntnyMlGASZc.

Navalny, A. (2018b, April 26). *Oligarkch pokupaet chinovnika: Pokazyvaem kak (The oligarch buys the official: Showing how)* [Video file]. Retrieved from https://www.youtube.com/watch?v=hWKRaIISr_M.

Rybina, L. (2012, February 2). Zamministra: "Ya ne znayu zachem na uchitelei davyat pered vyborami" (Deputy minister of education: "I do not know why teachers are pressured before the elections"). *Novaya Gazeta*. Retrieved from https://www.novayagazeta.ru/articles/2012/02/02/48027-zamministra-obrazovaniya-171-ya-ne-znayu-zachem-na-uchiteley-davyat-pered-vyborami-187.

Sampson, S. (2010). The anti-corruption industry: From movement to institution. *Global Crime, 11*(2), 261–278.

Van der Meer, T. G., & Verhoeven, P. (2013). Public framing organizational crisis situations: Social media versus news media. *Public Relations Review, 39*(3), 229–231.

Part III

Economy and Society in Central Asia

10

Why Uzbekistan and Kazakhstan Are Not Singapore: Comparing the First 25 Years of Reforms

Alexandr Akimov

Introduction

This year we are approaching the significant milestone of thirty years since the fall of the Berlin Wall. The world now is very different from that of thirty years ago. No longer is there a competition between two 'poles' of global affairs—the USA and the USSR. Indeed, after the collapse of the USSR, the hegemony of the remaining 'pole'—the USA—is being challenged, whether it is by China, Putin's Russia, or internally by President Trump's administration.

Against this backdrop, two ex-Soviet countries, Kazakhstan and Uzbekistan, that have transitioned towards authoritarian regimes under the leaderships of their respective presidents, have faced new challenges. Uzbekistan's president, Islam Karimov, who had led the country since independence, died in September 2016, while Kazakhstan's first president, Nursultan Nazarbayev, stepped down from his role in March 2019.

A. Akimov (✉)
Department of Accounting, Finance and Economics,
Griffith University, Brisbane, QLD, Australia
e-mail: a.akimov@griffith.edu.au

© The Author(s) 2020
A. Akimov and G. Kazakevitch (eds.), *30 Years since the Fall of the Berlin Wall*,
Palgrave Studies in Economic History, https://doi.org/10.1007/978-981-15-0317-7_10

The countries they ruled shared many things in common—geographic location, cultural traditions, religion, language and a post-Soviet heritage. Similarly, the two statesmen shared many things: a career in the Communist Party and Soviet industry, a vision for the prosperity of the countries they led and, to a certain degree, an approach to nation-building. Both leaders have rejected the idea of implementing Western-style democratization, claiming its unsuitedness to the mentality of their local populations. In this regard, they are not dissimilar to prominent Singaporean leader Lee Kuan Yew, to whose style both leaders explicitly or implicitly aspire.

The approach to economic and governance reforms in Uzbekistan and Kazakhstan has differed, which has led to variation in outcomes for the economic development of the two countries. What is clear, though, is that reforms under neither leader have brought the Singaporean-style economic prosperity they envisioned for their countries in the early years of independence.

This chapter aims to assess the legacy of both leaders from a political economy point of view, with Lee Kuan Yew's leadership and the economic outcomes in Singapore serving as a benchmark. The chapter consists of five main parts. In the next section, the appropriateness of benchmarking Karimov's and Nazarbayev's leaderships against that of Lee Kuan Yew is discussed. In particular, the initial political, economic, demographic and social conditions in these countries at the time of independence are reviewed, followed by examination of the main leadership ideas adopted. In the third section, the key criteria for successful reform in Singapore in terms of political changes, governance and economic reforms are established. In the fourth section, Uzbekistan's and Kazakhstan's reforms are assessed against these key criteria. Finally, the economic and social outcomes in Kazakhstan and Uzbekistan following 25 years of transition are summarized and the main reasons for not achieving their aspirational goals are hypothesized. In conclusion, I consider whether the legacy of Lee Kuan Yew is still alive in Uzbekistan and Kazakhstan, and whether there is an opportunity to 'reset' the reform agenda.

Are Uzbekistan and Kazakhstan Comparable to Singapore?

To be able to analyse the successes or failures in any comparative work, one essential component is the choice of an appropriate benchmark. Unfortunately, perfect benchmarks are a rarity in the real world, and this is especially true when we want to compare countries; no two countries have the same history, demographics, climate, natural resources and economic or legal environments. Leaders in both Uzbekistan and Kazakhstan chose personal political domination in the landscapes of their respective countries as their modus operandi. Akimov (2015) used Wintrobe's (1998) classification to assess the authoritarian regimes in Kazakhstan and Uzbekistan, concluding that Karimov's leadership matched most closely to a 'totalitarian regime', whereas Nazarbayev's had elements of both 'timocracy' and 'totalitarianism', with a gradual tendency to the latter as time progressed. Therefore, from the political economy point of view, it would be appropriate to compare the first 25 post-independence years with a country or countries that have been successful while also having an authoritarian leader in charge. Although there was an abundance of the latter, the choice of those that could also be deemed a success was very limited. The country that appears to offer the best fit is Singapore, which leapt from being 'a Third World country' at the time of separation from Malaysia to become a 'First World' country in the 1990s under the strong leadership of Lee Kuan Yew. There is a debate among some authors (e.g. Josey, 1980, p. 232; Milne & Mauzy, 1990, p. 105) as to whether Lee Kuan Yew's term in office should be classified as a dictatorship or could be regarded as a team effort, albeit a team he built around himself. However, there is no doubt that Lee's style of leadership has been rather authoritarian and has created the closest regime that we have had in recent history to what we could call a 'benevolent dictatorship' (Wintrobe, 1998, p. 14).

In his approach, President Nazarbayev has openly aspired to the leadership style of Lee Kuan Yew, mentioning Singapore's founding leader as a 'personal example' to him (Nazarbayev, 2006, p. 11). Moreover, Nazarbayev (2006, pp. 28, 30, 39, 205) emphasized on numerous occasions that he was keen to learn many aspects of Singapore's transformation strategy. By contrast, President Karimov of Uzbekistan never explicitly mentioned Singapore as a prime model for Uzbekistan's development path, but has cited the impressive growth of the newly industrialized economies, which include Singapore, as an important experience to study. Moreover, he emphasized the important role of government in promoting economic growth and ensuring social stability in such countries (Karimov, 1996e, p. 276). The principle has been adopted in Karimov's own 'model for economic reforms' (Karimov, 1996d, pp. 166–167; 1996e, pp. 294–299). Moreover, Karimov's rejection of Western liberal democracy in its purest form for Uzbekistan is very similar to that of Lee Kuan Yew. Karimov, from the outset, emphasized that the democratic principles to be adopted should be adjusted to national culture and traditions (Karimov, 1996f, p. 44). This resonates well with Lee's view of Singapore's Confucian values and how democratic principles should be aligned with those values in countries like Singapore (Lee, 2000, pp. 490–496).

Initial Conditions

At the time of independence, Uzbekistan and Kazakhstan enjoyed many similarities with Singapore. Firstly, the way in which the countries became independent was not dissimilar.

Prior to independence, Singapore was a colony of the British Empire. Nationalistic movement in the 1950s resulted in greater independence from the British, especially after the election into government in 1959 of the People's Action Party (PAP) led by Lee Kuan Yew. At that time, the Singaporean leadership did not envision Singapore as an independent state but rather a part of a larger, independent Malaya. This became a reality with the Malaysia Agreement of 1963.

Prior to the communist revolution in 1917, the territories of Kazakhstan and Uzbekistan were part of the Russian Empire. They became republics of the Soviet Union following Lenin's national delimitation policy in the 1920s. At the end of the 1980s, not dissimilarly to the rest of the Soviet Union, nationalist movements for greater autonomy occurred in both republics. Despite the de facto secession of the

Baltic States in 1991, both Nazarbayev and Karimov, then leaders of the Communist Party in their respective republics, saw themselves in a revised union with Russia (in the form of the Union of Sovereign States). The rapid disintegration of the Soviet Union in 1991 came as a surprise to many, including the leaders of both republics, and meant that they had to start a process of nation-building from the beginning without any preparation. The story was similar in Singapore, where an unexpected independence arrived after the sudden expulsion of the region from the union with Malaysia in 1965.

At independence, Singapore had to deal with tricky ethnic issues. The country was multi-ethnic, with large Chinese, Malay and Tamil groups. An important task was to maintain inter-ethnic peace and stability in the country. Moreover, these large ethnic groups felt strong allegiances to neighbouring China and Malaysia. A key challenge was to make all groups feel Singaporean.

Both Kazakhstan and Uzbekistan were multi-ethnic communities too. Sizeable ethnic minorities, especially Russians who had a strong sense of allegiance to Russia, also posed a challenge for the respective republics in their efforts to maintain unity. The problem was particularly pronounced in Kazakhstan where ethnic Russians accounted for nearly half of the pre-independence population. What was different in these republics, in contrast to Singapore, was that their ethnic majorities were indigenous to the region.

The process of disintegration is never without harmful effects on trade and economy. Singapore had to deal with deteriorated trade relationships with Malaysia and inherited tensions with Indonesia, its primary neighbours. Moreover, the gradual withdrawal of British political and economic interests was posing additional difficulties to the country.

Likewise, both Kazakhstan and Uzbekistan suffered from broken economic ties with other Soviet republics, because all such republics' economies had been elements in the flow of goods and services designed by Soviet planners. Although there were no major political obstacles to continuing trade relationships between the countries, technical problems resulting from new borders and a lack of unified enforceable rules harmed the economies of the republics dramatically.

As well as such similarities, key differences should be noted too. Singapore had long served as an entrepôt in the South-East Asian region and was therefore exposed to varying cultures, having trade ties with many countries both inside and outside of the region. The economy of the region was based on market forces, with good legal institutions and public administration to support the market economy inherited from the British. In contrast, Kazakhstan and Uzbekistan had hardly any experience of trading with the outside world, because all external trade flows had to be processed through relevant departments in Moscow. After more than 70 years of communism, there was little left that resembled a market economy, and no institutions to support one. Both the populations and the leaderships of the republics effectively had to learn about market principles from scratch.

Geographic location was also highly favourable to Singapore, it being a natural hub for regional trade routes in shipping and air transport. Its natural deep-sea port was a major reason for British interest in establishing a trading post there in the first place. This geographic advantage has allowed Singapore to rapidly mitigate its awkward relationships with Malaysia and Indonesia immediately following independence. In contrast, both Kazakhstan and Uzbekistan lack access to the sea, which constrains their ability to trade with the rest of the world. Moreover, instability in next-door Afghanistan rendered routes to southern ports unavailable for trade. Northern and north-western trading routes had to go through Russia, which was itself in economic turmoil. The only alternative, at the time, was a new eastern route and trade with China, albeit through its less developed regions. Uzbekistan, in particular, suffered from being a double-landlocked country, having to cross two borders to access any ports: trading routes to its north and east had first to go through Kazakhstan before they could reach Russia or China.[1]

There is also a vast difference in size between Singapore and Kazakhstan and Uzbekistan, both in terms of population but even more so in terms of land area, Singapore effectively being a city-state. Thus, Deng Xiaoping, in conversation with Lee Kuan Yew, commented,

---

[1]China can also be reached via mountainous regions in Kyrgyzstan or Tajikistan.

'If I had only Shanghai, I might be able to develop Shanghai as quickly [as Singapore]. But I have the whole of China!' (Lee, 2000, p. 602). Furthermore, Uzbekistan and Kazakhstan had to deal with their unevenly developed regions and local peculiarities, as well as with the socioeconomic problems of rural communities and their migration to the cities.

However, in contrast to Singapore, which had no natural resources, Uzbekistan and, in particular, Kazakhstan were generously endowed with mineral resources. Moreover, as a result of universal schooling, healthcare and housing policy in the ex-USSR, both Uzbekistan and Kazakhstan had near-perfect literacy ratios and no pressing housing problems to manage. This allowed both countries the opportunity to address more pressing issues.

Key Principles of Successful Reforms in Singapore

Academic commentators have pointed at a variety of drivers that enabled the successful transition of Singapore from a Third World colonial region to a prosperous First World country (Lee, 2000; Neo & Chen, 2007; Root, 1996; Wirtz & Chung, 2006; Yusuf & Nabeshima, 2002). However, the influence of the following factors is unequivocal:

i. good governance and political stability;
ii. investments in human capital;
iii. smart growth-oriented economic policies.

A premise for any government in undertaking difficult reforms is its legitimacy and political stability. Lee Kuan Yew used existing British-based political institutions to come to power in 1959 on an anti-colonial platform as one of the leaders of the PAP. Originally, the party was a mixture of people with a variety of ideas, united by anti-colonialism. It had a strong communist faction, including trade union leaders and members. Being himself a moderate, Lee had to ensure that his party's ideas appealed to a public with whom communist ideas were very popular at the time. However, over time, Lee succeeded in removing extreme leftists from the party ranks. From independence in 1965, Lee and the PAP's leadership pursued a so-called 'survival' ideology, based on the principles of pragmatism, meritocracy, multiracialism and Asian values (Tremewan, 1996, p. 105). Until Lee Kuan Yew's retirement in 1991, the party won all the elections with a supermajority and no more than two seats going to the opposition. This dominance, unusual for liberal democracies, came from the genuine popularity of the PAP as a result of effective government policies, strong economic performance, political stability and lack of corruption. As Milne and Mauzy (1990, p. 96) noted, 'Elections in Singapore have the reputation of being scrupulously honest, which enhances legitimacy. There is no ballot-rigging, intimidation of voters, inaccurate or slow counting of ballots, or fiddling with the registration rolls to produce so-called phantom voters or multiple voters'. From the outset, Lee made the government's performance a key election platform by which the public should decide whether or not to vote for the PAP. He maintained that 'The PAP is the Government and the Government is the PAP' (Lew Kuan Yew, as quoted in Milne and Mauzy [1990, p. 85]).

Lee Kuan Yew's governance strategy was based largely on three principles: keep politics out (of economic management), keep performance accountable and keep the government clean (Root, 1996).

A distinct division of labour was created between the PAP parliamentarians and technocratic government. Bureaucrats had to resign before they could become members of the parliament. Civil servants were not allowed to have any relationships with the private sector. A well-structured system of accountability was set in place to ensure that public funds were not wasted or misused.

One of the key priorities for the Singaporean government from the outset was 'keeping the government clean'. Lee (1998, 2000) viewed corruption as a major obstacle to political stability and governmental effectiveness: 'Only by upholding the integrity of the administration can the economy work in a way which enables Singaporeans to clearly see the nexus between hard work and high rewards' (Lee Kuan Yew, as quoted in Lim [1998]).

Clean government was a premise Lee's PAP used to maintain dominance in Singapore's political arena. Lee believed that this, in turn, would allow the government to focus on the tasks of the country's economic management. One important component of the clean government policy was to pay government employees and politicians good wages to discourage rent-seeking behaviours. Good salaries were also an important component of the strategy to attract top talent into civil service jobs. The focus of the anti-corruption body, the Corrupt Practices Investigation Bureau (CPIB), has been on the higher echelons of power, with a few high-level officials caught and successfully prosecuted. For lower-level corruption, the government focused on streamlining processes and removing decision-making powers, where possible, from lower-level officials. Anti-corruption laws were tightened to help successful prosecution of corruption cases.

One key component of successful governance is ensuring administrative competence at all levels of government and public service. Singapore has put a strategy in place whereby talented individuals were, for example, identified in their university years and attracted into the government sector. The principle of meritocracy was set and rigorously enforced at all levels of government and public service. The criteria for a successful career in government were set beyond good academic results alone. As Lee Kuan Yew put it in a 1965 speech, 'Singapore must get some of its best in each year's crop of graduates into the government. When I say the best, I don't mean just academic results. His … university degree will only tell you his power of analysis. This is only one third of the helicopter quality. You've then got to assess him for his sense of reality, his imagination, his quality of leadership, his dynamism. But most of all, his character and his motivation, because the smarter a man is, the more harm he will do to society' (Han, Fernandez, & Tan, 1998, pp. 331–342). The task of recruiting the best people to public service, as well as managing such personnel to their best use, was entrusted to the Public Service Commission.

Lee Kuan Yew described his leadership style as one similar to 'a conductor of an orchestra'. He credits his loyal colleagues in the government, particularly founding members of the PAP, Goh Keng Swee, Sinnathamby Rajaratnam and Toh Chin Chye, with the success of the government he led (Lee, 2000). The latter three were all very capable individuals, holding senior positions in government for many years.

However, they have not challenged Lee's leadership of the party, which ensured the smooth and efficient operation of the government, free of internal infighting.

With people being a principal resource, the government pushed to ensure that adequate technical training opportunities were created to service a growing manufacturing sector. The number of technical and vocational training places grew rapidly from 1961 to 1967, offering a broad range of courses (Neo & Chen, 2007). Over time, the need for upskilling to service higher-value sectors brought about the creation of the Skills Development Fund. The fund's purpose was to help employers with the retraining and upskilling of their employees. Much effort was dedicated to strengthening school education, especially in technical disciplines. Students were streamed according to their academic performance and their ability to cope with two languages (English and ethnic language). Particular attention was paid to English, as a language of multiracial communication. Moreover, Lee's government has encouraged study of the Mandarin language within the Chinese community in Singapore in preference to supporting the several regional dialects prevalent at that time. This was a strategic move to ensure an effective channel of communication with China as it emerged as a superpower.

Lee also saw English as a language of cutting-edge technology and trade, and actively supported the idea that university education had to be delivered in English. The only Chinese-language university switched to English as a language of instruction in 1975 and later merged with the University of Singapore to form the National University of Singapore. Moreover, efforts were made to improve university standards. Talented youth was encouraged to study overseas, with funding made available to support the most promising students in studying in prestigious universities in the USA, the UK, Australia and elsewhere.

Chen (1984) has reported a 20-fold increase in government expenditure on education over the period from 1960 to 1982, with only a 30% increase in student numbers for the same period, a great indicator of the emphasis placed on the development of human capital in Singapore.

Singapore's economic policy in the 1960s was largely driven by three external forces: merger and separation from Malaysia with no prospect of a common market, a poor relationship with Indonesia and the planned withdrawal of the British military that contributed about 20% to national employment. Following the advice of the Dutch economist Albert Winsemius, the government adopted a strategy of rapid industrialization by encouraging foreign manufacturers to set up manufacturing facilities in Singapore. To achieve this, the government created the Economic Development Board (EDB), a 'one-stop shop' for foreign investors to deal with all government bureaucracy. Moreover, actions were taken to keep labour costs under control, provide tax incentives, set up designated industrial estates, improve the technical skills of labourers and ensure free movement of capital (Rodan, 1989). Although any investment was welcome, the government soon realized that the best opportunities in terms of more modern equipment, know-how and marketing techniques came from American multinational corporations (MNCs), and they became a primary target (Lee, 2000; Minchin, 1986). In the absence of a regional market, they hoped American (and other) MNCs would use Singapore as an offshore production facility, and assist the country with its export-oriented strategy. By the early 1970s, the strategy had started to pay off, gradually reducing the unemployment rate from 14% in 1963 to less than 4.5% by 1974 (Rodan, 1989; World Bank, 2019).

To support government investment in the economy, the government set up the Central Provident Fund (CPF), a compulsory social security scheme for retired workers in Singapore. The scheme has allowed government to access significant funds at below-market rates. It also helped Singaporeans to save for housing, medical expenses and retirement (Beng & Chew, 2002). The government showed great flexibility in using CPF in its labour policy, increasing contribution rates to boost savings for the necessary expenses, but also lowering rates at times of recession to support the disposable income of the population.

The government ensured that it made good use of the savings. Several government-funded enterprises were set up to support economic growth and employment. A notable feature of these projects was a strict adherence to the principles of commercial viability.

One of the industries to which Prime Minister Lee paid particular attention was finance. The goal was to set up a financial centre that would contribute to the 24-hour global financial market, and would complement Europe (particularly London), the USA (New York) and Japan (Tokyo). The Monetary Authority of Singapore, which was established in the 1970s and served as an equivalent to a Singaporean central bank, developed modern rules and regulations to ensure confidence and the integrity of the market. To attract international financial institutions, the government abolished income tax on interest earned by non-resident depositors. Moreover, Singapore started an offshore Asian dollar market with all the Asian dollar deposits exempt from liquidity and reserve requirements. As Lee (2000, p. 73) noted, 'The foundations for the financial centre were the rule of law, an independent judiciary, and a stable, competent, and honest government that pursued sound macroeconomic policies'. These efforts allowed Singapore to become almost the largest financial centre in Asia, only slightly behind Tokyo.

One of the key achievements of Lee's government has been to establish effective relationships with trade unions. The government worked closely with the National Trades Union Congress (NTUC) to ensure that wage growth in Singapore moved in line with productivity improvements. This was critical in attracting and retaining foreign investors' businesses in Singapore. A National Wage Council was set up in 1972 with representatives of government, unions and employers to ensure that workers would receive appropriate compensation without triggering wage spirals.

Assessing Reforms in Uzbekistan and Kazakhstan Vis-à-Vis Singapore

Uzbekistan and Kazakhstan became independent as a result of the dissolution of the Soviet Union in 1991. Being a part of the Russian Empire and then the Soviet Union, both nations participated fully in the communist experiment that built from the communist revolution of 1917. One of the challenges both countries had to face upon independence was the implementation of market-oriented reforms. Over 70 years of communist ideology and centrally planned economic management meant that there was no expertise in managing a free market economy, very little such expertise in the academic community either, and no experience of the people in either country in living in anything resembling Western democracy with relevant institutions. This represents a stark contrast to Singapore, where British institutions were operational at the time of independence. Although the Singaporean government had to work hard to fend off pressures from communists, the latter were unable to make serious inroads into the rule of law, the independent judiciary or commercial contract enforcement principles.

Unfortunately, neither Uzbekistan nor Kazakhstan, in their first 25 years of reforms, were able to establish effective institutions to support a market economy. The European Bank for Reconstruction and Development (2016) provided an assessment of institutional reforms in various sectors of economy: Uzbekistan and Kazakhstan score a lowly 1.59 and 2.25 respectively, where 1 represents no change from a centrally planned economy and 4.3 is the standard associated with an industrialized country.

The Lee Kuan Yew-led government and its PAP, despite their dominance in Singapore since independence, had to face regular elections and prove their merits to the electorate on a regular basis. In Uzbekistan and Kazakhstan, with no history of multi-party elections and no associated experience within the electorate, the communist leaders of the respective republics got elected with relative ease. Karimov, in his first presidential election of December 1991 gained 86% of the vote, while Nazarbayev was elected unopposed in the same month (Akimov, 2015; Minahan, 1998). Arguably, this first election in Uzbekistan has been the only one with a real opposition. All presidential elections thereafter were against hand-picked candidates, while only pro-presidential parties ran in parliamentary elections. Any serious opposition parties and candidates were crushed and not allowed to stand. In those circumstances, all elections in Uzbekistan became a formality, and consequently did not play any role in making the Uzbek government accountable. Similarly, in Kazakhstan, Nazarbayev had consolidated power in his hands by the mid-1990s. Any opposition to the establishment of a strong presidential republic led by him was overcome by repeated dissolution of the parliament, in 1993 and 1995, while attempts to challenge presidential powers by the more liberal Prime Minister, Kazhegeldin, were successfully fended off. Since then,

Nazarbayev and pro-presidential parties have faced little opposition in presidential and parliamentary elections. Here too, democratic elections have not played a significant role in keeping government and the president accountable to the people. Both Uzbekistan and Kazakhstan have consistently ranked poorly in Freedom House's (2016) political freedom and civil liberties ratings, with Uzbekistan having the lowest possible scores (7—the least free) in both categories, and Kazakhstan scoring only marginally better with scores of 6 for political freedom and 5 for civil liberties. Singapore has had higher scores (of 4) since the inception of the index (Freedom House, 1991).

Trade unions have never threatened political stability in either Kazakhstan or Uzbekistan. During the Soviet era, they effectively became instruments for the distribution of perks, such as subsidized travel packages to sought-after destinations, access to sanatoria and free entertainment tickets. They had no ability to consolidate workers against their employers. These trade unions, if anything, became even weaker post-independence. Both countries maintained many aspects of Soviet-style labour laws, and were not configured to provide the flexible work arrangements expected in modern economies.

Lee Kuan Yew's idea of 'keeping politics out' of the economic management of the country has been fully adopted by President Karimov, being emphasized in his books (Karimov, 1996d, p. 63; 1996f, p. 166) and rigorously implemented; Karimov was the only person to speak on political matters publicly. In contrast, accountability has never been high on the agenda; the economic statistics were either withheld or notoriously unreliable (Akimov & Dollery, 2009). The annual performance reports dedicated to discussion of the year-end results were generally full of praise for the achievements of the preceding period. Finally, there has been little effort to combat the problem of corruption in the early years of independence. Thus, on the one hand, Karimov has emphasized the danger of corruption for the country from his earliest speeches (Karimov, 1996a, p. 199; 1996c, p. 221) but, on the other hand, the government formally rehabilitated those accused in the so-called 'Cotton case',[2] sending a mixed message to bureaucrats. As a result, corruption became widespread, with a strong impact on all spheres of the economy (US Department of State, 2009b). The country first appeared in the Corruption Perceptions Index in 1999 when it was ranked 94th out of 99 countries with a score of 1.8 (out of 10), and has since remained consistently near the bottom of the index (Transparency International, 2019). The US Department of State's *2009 Investment Climate Report*, together with its subsequent reports, have repeatedly cited corruption in Uzbekistan as a major obstacle to attracting foreign direct investment. Singapore's strategy of good remuneration for public sector officers has not been adopted in Uzbekistan; bureaucrats' low pay and red tape are often cited as precursors of widespread corruption.

Similarly, in Kazakhstan, corruption has been publicly acknowledged as a problem and a threat, and been deplored (Nazarbayev, 2006). Kazakhstan was the first country in the Central Asian region to adopt an Anti-Corruption Act, in 1998. However, the effectiveness of the legislation was limited. As in Uzbekistan, public sector employees remain poorly paid, thus creating an incentive for bribery and red tape. The country has also been consistently low-ranked in the Corruption Perceptions Index, although it has scored better than Uzbekistan in most of the reported years. The 2003 bribery scandal involving Nazarbayev's economic adviser has stained Nazarbayev's reputation and undermined anti-corruption efforts (Akimov, 2015). Despite the highlighting of corruption issues (US Department of State, 2009a), Kazakhstan has been able to attract foreign direct investment, albeit mainly into the oil and gas sector. Figure 10.1 illustrates the trends in Corruption Perceptions Indices for Kazakhstan, Uzbekistan and Singapore from the index's inception in 1999 through to 2016.

Perhaps among the most damaging obstacles to effective governance and public service is the inability of most capable employees to build their careers in the public sector because of inefficiencies, nepotism, cronyism and corruption. Despite public calls from both leaders to avoid

---

[2]A legal case, which publicly revealed the extent of corruption in cotton production and reporting in the Uzbek Soviet Republic in the 1980s.

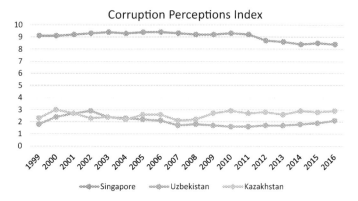

Fig. 10.1 Corruption in Singapore, Kazakhstan and Uzbekistan (*Source* Author's creation based on Transparency International [2019])

nepotism and corruption and promote the most able workers (Karimov, 1996b, p. 66; Kazinform, 2014; Nazarbayev, 2017, pp. 210–211), neither country was able to establish a strong principle of meritocracy. A practice of public rebukes and sackings of regional governors and other high-level officials for mismanagement was popular in Karimov's Uzbekistan, only for those individuals to be re-appointed elsewhere shortly thereafter. In Kazakhstan, the successful public service career of Nazarbayev's daughter, as well as the senior posts held by his two sons-in-law, looked to the public like an 'unofficial' acceptance of nepotism as the norm. Arguably, Nazarbayev has been more systematic and successful in appointing competent and reform-driven personnel to high positions, notably Kazhegeldin in the prime ministerial role in the early 1990s, and Marchenko in leading financial sector reform as the Chief of the National Bank of Kazakhstan.

Education in Kazakhstan was widely regarded as a neglected and less-than-successful area of government activity. Expenditure on education from the national budget dropped to 3–4% of GDP between 1993 and 2004. With a few exceptions, Kazakhstan's educational institutions were grossly under-resourced and inadequate, especially for a country that aspired to be in the top 50 most competitive economies by 2030. Teachers' skills and morale are at low levels and bribery is widespread (Aitken, 2009; Pomfret, 2019). The notable exception was the Bolashak programme, launched in 1994, which provided scholarships to talented youth to study in Western institutions. Many of its graduates returned to Kazakhstan and are pursuing successful careers in business and government. Moreover, a new Nazarbayev University was set up in Astana (now Nursultan) with the assistance of Duke University, with foreign-trained academics delivering Western-style higher education in English. In addition, in 1993, the government allowed establishment of private educational institutions, with a number providing an alternative to poor-quality state universities. Higher education was increasingly delivered in the Kazakh language, which has not encouraged modernization due to the lack of modern scientific literature in the language and delays in translation. Although English-based education grew to 2.6% of the total, it remains almost negligible (Ahn, Dixon, & Chekmareva, 2018).

By contrast, Uzbekistan has maintained much higher spending on education than Kazakhstan. Most of this spend was directed to school education, with limited resources allocated to universities. By the end of the 1990s, the government had announced several educational reforms, replacing the eleven-year compulsory school system with a nine-year programme. This was to be complemented by three-year education in technical colleges or academic lyceums as a pathway to university entry. The government spent considerable resources on building new colleges. However, teacher training, textbooks and equipment were inadequate and lagged behind. Moreover, complaints of inefficiency, corruption and falling standards started to emerge (Pomfret, 2019). The government maintained a strong grip on education and was reluctant to allow private providers to enter the market. Notable exceptions were a small number of foreign university branches, particularly Westminster International University in Tashkent (WIUT). The government ran a similar programme to Bolashak in the late 1990s and early 2000s. However, this 'Umid' foreign-study programme was effectively closed with the opening of WIUT in 2002. Because of government restrictions, tertiary enrolment has remained low in comparison to other countries (Ruziev & Burkhanov, 2018).

In addition, the shifting of education to the Uzbek language and the Latinisation of the Uzbek alphabet put a great burden on the resources required to regenerate educational materials. With limited resources and personnel, it was impossible to do quickly, further restricting modernization in the sector.

Post-independence, Uzbekistan has adopted a very gradual approach to economic reform. Karimov's goal was to maintain and/or restore manageability of an economy facing the breaking of links with other countries of the Soviet Union. Prices were gradually liberalized, and by 1996 housing and small enterprises had been privatized. Inflation remained a problem throughout the 1990s (Akimov & Dollery, 2009; Pomfret, 2006). There was little success in attracting foreign direct investment because so many restrictions remained in place.

After the resumption of foreign-exchange controls in 1997, Uzbekistan's pursuit of an import-substitution policy became more open. Although industrialization was on the government agenda, with flagship projects such as the Daewoo automotive plant in Asaka, many older manufacturing facilities were either scaling down or closing. The share of manufacturing in the economy declined from 28% in 1987 to 9% in 2010 (Pomfret, 2019).

Agriculture remained an important sector of the economy with cotton-farming being one of the most significant, despite being a declining source of export revenue for the government. Mining, particularly for gold and natural gas, was another important source. The financial sector was dominated by state-owned banks, particularly the National Bank of Uzbekistan, with little competition in the sector and a lack of trust on the part of the population (Akimov & Dollery, 2006). There have not been any serious attempts to reform the pension system in Uzbekistan; the system remains largely tax-funded, with individual contributions to personal pension accounts too small to make a substantial difference.

The outcome of these economic reforms has been mixed. The cautious and gradual approach to reforms in the early 1990s paid off in the fastest recovery of the post-Soviet countries. However, the reform reversals from 1997 onwards and a lack of substantive reforms in the 2000s led to slower economic growth than in some other countries in the region. Clearly, in terms of economic indicators such as GDP per capita, Uzbekistan lagged ever further behind neighbouring Kazakhstan, and did not bear comparison with countries like Singapore.

The business environment remained subdued as country remained at the bottom section of the World Bank (2015) *Ease of Doing Business Ranking* until Karimov's death. The country was ranked 141th out of 189 in 2015. Rapid population growth and a lack of economic opportunities inside Uzbekistan led to a mass migration of labour from Uzbekistan to Russia, Kazakhstan and other countries (Kakhkharov, Akimov, & Rohde, 2017).

Kazakhstan's approach to economic reforms was less gradual than Uzbekistan's. It moved faster in terms of liberalization of prices and privatization of enterprises. Privatization of the oil and gas sector in the 1990s was associated with widespread corruption but delivered substantial foreign direct investment (Pomfret, 2006). The government used a practice of management contracting in which foreign managers were invited in to run large enterprises, especially in the oil and gas industry. The GDP share for the private sector grew rapidly, from 25% in 1995 to 65% in 2002 (European Bank for Reconstruction and Development, 2003).

Such changes in the oil and gas industry, including revenue-sharing arrangements with foreign owners, created an excellent platform from which to benefit from rapidly rising hydrocarbon prices in the 2000s and to deliver fast economic growth to Kazakhstan. However, the often opaque and unfair privatization of the industry may have had negative longer-term consequences for the establishment of the rule of law (Pomfret, 2019).

After the early years of chaos, the financial sector had been strengthened by the end of the 1990s (Akimov & Dollery, 2008). Kazakhstan was the first post-Soviet republic to introduce a privately funded pension programme, in 1998. The reform helped to boost development of the financial sector and enabled the opening of private pension funds. The reform was partially reversed after the Global Financial Crisis, which saw private pension funds closed and citizens' accounts incorporated into the public pension fund.

In contrast to Uzbekistan, Kazakhstan also faced a large population decline in the 1990s, mainly caused by the emigration of well-educated ethnic Russians and Germans. This trend, although relieving the separatist moods in the country's northern regions, then dominated by ethnic Russians, had a strong negative impact on the manufacturing sector.

Kazakhstan benefitted greatly from its natural resource endowment and policies that stimulated investments in the sector, which resulted in double-digit economic growth in the 2000s. Despite a slow start in the 1990s, the country became the regional leader in the early 2000s, bringing improvements in living standards. However, the global financial crisis has shaken confidence in the strategy. Falling energy prices led to reduced state revenues, while the financial sector was hit hard by reckless lending practices and a reliance on cheap foreign short-term debt. The share of the value-added mining sector (as a percentage of GDP) grew from 15.39% in 1995 to a peak of 29.28% in 2010, before falling back to 20.65% in 2016. Manufacturing has been registering a steady decline since 1995. The government, to its credit, recognized the problem and put an effort in improving the business environment, which has reflected in the improved scores in the World Bank (2006, 2016) *Ease of Doing Business Ranking*. The country has moved from 86th place in 2006 to 41th in 2016.

Comparative statistics for the post-independence economic performance of Singapore, Kazakhstan and Uzbekistan are presented in Table 10.1. The data for Singapore covers the period under the leadership of Lee Kuan Yew, from 1965 to 1990, whereas that for Kazakhstan and Uzbekistan covers the period of 1991 to 2016.

As is evident from Table 10.1, Singapore has been able to achieve much more impressive economic growth rates, with a 5.52-fold growth in GDP per capita compared to around twofold for both Kazakhstan and Uzbekistan. It has done this initially through better investments in manufacturing facilities, and latterly in cutting-edge services. Thanks to its unique location on a maritime crossroads and its small size, Singapore had no viable choice but to develop an export-oriented economy, where trade plays a much greater role. Economic growth in Singapore brought improvements in social standards and human development, moving it from a Third World economy to a First World one. Having had higher human development levels at independence, social development indicators in Kazakhstan and Uzbekistan have shown far less improvement, due to lower expenditure in social services (in Kazakhstan) or ineffective use of resources and inconsistent quality of services such as education and healthcare (in both countries).

Table 10.1 Comparative post-independence economic performance of Singapore and Kazakhstan and Uzbekistan

	1965 [1991]	1970 [1996]	1975 [2001]	1980 [2006]	1985 [2011]	1990 [2016]	Change %
GDP per capita (constant 2010 US$)							
SG	4088	6787	9674	13534	16633	22572	552
KZ	5210	3814	5107	7917	9603	10583	203
UZ	977	731	842	1061	1452	1909	195
Foreign direct investment, net inflows (% of GDP)							
SG	–	4.84	5.18	10.39	5.46	15.42	
KZ	0.40[a]	5.41	12.72	9.40	7.14	12.54	
UZ	0.07[a]	0.65	0.73	1.00	3.56	2.03	
Gross fixed capital formation (% of GDP)							
SG	20.95	32.12	34.89	39.52	40.79	31.72	10.77
KZ	30.43[a]	17.23	23.73	30.20	21.46	22.72	−7.71
UZ	43.93[a]	23.00	26.82	21.63	25.71	22.83	−21.10
Industry, value-added (% of GDP)							
SG	22.15	26.93	31.21	34.88	32.17	30.86	8.71
KZ	38.97[a]	25.59	36.14	39.36	37.27	31.98	−6.99
UZ	36.68	26.08	19.95	26.84	29.92	24.14	−12.54
Services, value-added (% of GDP)							
SG	69.20	65.02	63.08	59.90	63.14	64.18	−5.02
KZ	25.12[a]	58.04	49.37	51.64	48.89	57.86	32.73
UZ	26.54	37.12	38.21	37.96	43.68	35.77	9.23
Trade (% of GDP)							
SG	257.54	271.06	283.57	410.94	304.14	344.33	
KZ	149.34[a]	71.27	92.85	91.45	73.12	60.31	
UZ	–	–	56.78	67.47	63.49	29.75	
Life expectancy at birth, total (years)							
SG	67.09	68.28	70.22	72.19	73.89	75.30	8.21
KZ	67.98	64.11	65.77	66.16	68.98	72.30	4.32
UZ	66.42	66.49	67.37	68.66	70.32	71.31	4.89

Source World Bank (2019)
[a]Data for 1992

Conclusion

At the time of independence, the Central Asian republics of Kazakhstan and Uzbekistan dismissed the idea of building Western-style liberal democracies, arguing that they would not fit well with local cultural traditions and values. Instead, they looked to the experiences of successful Asian economies for inspiration. Thus, Singapore's impressive transformation under the authoritarian leadership of Lee Kuan Yew might serve as a useful vehicle of comparison. Kazakhstan's Nazarbayev, explicitly citing Lee Kuan Yew as one of his early mentors, has indeed adopted a number of similar economic policies, in particular, attracting foreign direct investment. Uzbekistan's Karimov, although not specifically citing the Singaporean leader as an example, voiced many ideas that resembled those adopted by Lee. However, some of the key ingredients in the economic success of Singapore were not implemented in either of these countries.

Neither Karimov nor Nazarbayev were able to keep their governments clean. Corruption grew out of control in the early years of independence and remains a major challenge to any reforms. Both Uzbek and Kazakh leaders were able to achieve political stability through their domination of the political landscape. However, unlike Singapore, this was not through fair and democratic elections, which also serve as a good tool of discipline when it comes to holding governments and leaders accountable for their actions.

After 25 years of reforms, Kazakhstan and, in particular, Uzbekistan continue to face serious human resource shortages. At the time of independence, the lack of market institutions and of competent administrators capable of introducing market reforms were objective challenges. Unfortunately, due to widespread nepotism, neither country was able to nurture a large enough pool of talented and capable managers and public servants to address such challenges. Given this absence of meritocratic career prospects, many have left their countries in search of better opportunities abroad.

In terms of economic policies, Uzbekistan and Kazakhstan have not adopted export-oriented industrialization strategies. This was a partial consequence of unfavourable geographical location, with no direct access to maritime routes and their distance from major consumer markets. Kazakhstan used its vast mineral resources to its advantage in the 2000s, but was largely unable to build alternative industries. Uzbekistan has done even worse as its import-substitution and protectionist policy failed to create internationally competitive industries besides the extraction of some mineral resources and sales of agricultural products.

After the death of Karimov in 2016, the new Uzbek president, Mirziyoyev, appears to have chosen a different approach and reversed the policy of isolationism. He put significant efforts into improving relationships with neighbours and travelled extensively in search of foreign investors. Moreover, a series of liberalizing reforms have been introduced, although no talk of establishing a Western-style liberal democracy is expected. Instead, the approach of economic pragmatism seems to be his adopted modus operandi. In that sense, Lee Kuan Yew's legacy is still alive in Uzbekistan.

The new Kazakh president, Tokayev, elected after Nazarbayev's retirement in early 2019, has not yet signposted any significant shifts from current policies. Because Nazarbayev's influence on politics and decision-making remains significant, it may take time for the new Kazakh leadership to manifest its intentions.

References

Ahn, E. S., Dixon, J., & Chekmareva, L. (2018). Looking at Kazakhstan's higher education landscape: From transition to transformation between 1920 and 2015. In J. Huisman, A. Smolentseva, & I. Froumin (Eds.), *25 years of transformations of higher education systems in post-Soviet countries: Reform and continuity* (pp. 199–227). Cham: Palgrave Macmillan.

Aitken, J. (2009). *Nazarbayev and the making of Kazakhstan*. London: Continuum.

Akimov, A. (2015). The politcal economy of financial reforms in authoritarian transition economies: A comparative study of Kazakhstan and Uzbekistan. In K. Ruziev & N. Perdikis (Eds.), *Development and financial reform in emerging economies* (pp. 125–148). London: Pickering & Chatto.

Akimov, A., & Dollery, B. (2006). Uzbekistan's financial system: Evaluation of twelve years of transition. *Problems of Economic Transition, 48*(12), 6–31.

Akimov, A., & Dollery, B. (2008). Financial system reform in Kazakhstan from 1993 to 2006 and its socioeconomic effects. *Emerging Market Finance and Trade, 44*(3), 81–97.

Akimov, A., & Dollery, B. (2009). Financial development policies in Uzbekistan: An analysis of achievements and failures. *Economic Change and Restructuring, 42*(4), 293–318.

Beng, C. S., & Chew, R. (2002). Managing the Singapore economy. In K. T. Liou (Ed.), *Managing economic development in Asia: From economic miracle to financial crisis* (pp. 65–92). Westport: Praeger.

Chen, P. S. (1984). Social change and economic planning. In P. S. You & C. Y. Lim (Eds.), *Twenty-five years of development* (pp. 315–338). Singapore: Nan Yang Xing Zhou Lianhe Zaobao.

European Bank for Reconstruction and Development. (2003). *Transition report 2003: Integration and regional cooperation.* London: EBRD.

European Bank for Reconstruction and Development. (2016). *Transition report 2016–17. Transition for all: Equal opportunities in an unequal world.* London: EBRD.

Freedom House. (1991). *Freedom in the world: Political rights & civil liberties 1990–1991.* New York: Freedom House.

Freedom House. (2016). *Freedom in the world 2016. Anxious dictators, wavering democracies: Global freedom under pressure.* Washington, DC: Freedom House.

Han, F. K., Fernandez, W., & Tan, S. (1998). *Lee Kuan Yew: The man and his ideas.* Singapore: The Straits Times Press.

Josey, A. (1980). *Lee Kuan Yew: The struggle for Singapore* (3rd ed.). Singapore: Angus & Robertson.

Kakhkharov, J., Akimov, A., & Rohde, N. (2017, January). Transaction costs and recorded remittances in the post-Soviet economies: Evidence from a new dataset on bilateral flows. *Economic Modelling, 60,* 98–107.

Karimov, I. (1996a). Economic reforms: The crucial stage. Speech in front of Bukhara Regional Council of Deputies on 18 March 1994. In *Our aim is free and prosperous motherland* (pp. 174–201). Tashkent: Uzbekiston.

Karimov, I. (1996b). The motherland's interests are above all: Speech at Syrdarya Council of Deputies on 9 October 1993. In *Our aim is free and prosperous motherland* (pp. 56–68). Tashkent: Uzbekiston.

Karimov, I. (1996c). Our path is the path of indepent statehood and progress. Speech on 15th session of Supreme Council of Republic of Uzbekistan on 5 May 1994. In *Our aim is free and prosperous motherland* (pp. 210–231). Tashkent: Uzbekiston.

Karimov, I. (1996d). *Uzbekistan: On the way of deepening of economic reforms*. In *The motherland must be holy for everyone* (pp. 164–348). Tashkent: Uzbekiston.
Karimov, I. (1996e). *Uzbekistan: Own model of transition to market relations*. In *Uzbekistan: Nation's independence, economy, politics and ideology* (pp. 263–343). Tashkent: Uzbekiston.
Karimov, I. (1996f). *Uzbekistan: Own way for revival and progress*. In *Uzbekistan: Nation's Independence, Economy, Politics and Ideology* (pp. 36–81). Tashkent: Uzbekiston.
Kazinform. (2014, October 6). *Kazakh president warns officials against nepotism in hiring staff.* BBC Monitoring Central Asia.
Lee, K. Y. (1998). *The Singapore story: Memoirs of Lee Kuan Yew*. Singapore: Prentice Hall.
Lee, K. Y. (2000). *From third world to first. The Singapore story: 1965–2000.* New York: HarperCollins.
Lim, S. G. (1998). *Integrity with empowerment: Challenges facing Singapore in combating corruption in the 21st century*. Retrieved from https://www.csb.gov.hk/mobile/pdf/english/conference_meterials/1998_lim.pdf.
Milne, R. S., & Mauzy, D. K. (1990). *Singapore: The legacy of Lee Kuan Yew*. Boulder: Westview Press.
Minahan, J. (1998). *Miniature empires: A historical dictionary of the newly independent states*. New York: Routledge.
Minchin, J. (1986). *No man is an island: A study of Singapore's Lee Kuan Yew*. Sydney: Allen & Unwin.
Nazarbayev, N. (2006). *The Kazakhstan's way*. Karaganda: Arko. (in Russian).
Nazarbayev, N. (2017). *Era of Independence*. Astana: Segoe UI Light.
Neo, B. S., & Chen, G. (2007). *Dynamic governance: Embedding culture, capabilities and change in Singapore*. Singapore: World Scientific Publishing.
Pomfret, R. (2006). *The Central Asian economies since independence*. Princeton: Princeton University Press.
Pomfret, R. (2019). *The Central Asian economies in the twenty-first century: Paving a new Silk Route*. Princeton: Princeton University Press.
Rodan, G. (1989). *The political economy of Singapore's industrialization: National state and international capital*. Basingstoke: Macmillan.
Root, H. (1996). *Small countries, big lessons: Governance and the rise of East Asia*. Hong Kong: Oxford University Press.
Ruziev, K., & Burkhanov, U. (2018). Uzbekistan: Higher education reforms and the changing landscape since independence. In J. Huisman, A. Smolentseva, &

I. Froumin (Eds.), *25 Years of transformations of higher education systems in post-Soviet countries: Reform and continuity* (pp. 435–459). Cham: Palgrave Macmillan.

Transparency International. (2019). *Corruption Perceptions Index.* Retrieved from https://www.transparency.org/research/cpi/cpi_early/0.

Tremewan, C. (1996). *The political economy of social control in Singapore.* Basingstoke: Macmillan.

US Department of State. (2009a). *2009 investment climate statement—Kazakhstan.* Retrieved from https://2009-2017.state.gov/e/eb/rls/othr/ics/2009/117170.htm.

US Department of State. (2009b). *2009 investment climate statement—Uzbekistan.* Retrieved from https://2009-2017.state.gov/e/eb/rls/othr/ics/2009/117170.htm.

Wintrobe, R. (1998). *The political economy of dictatorship.* Cambridge: Cambridge University Press.

Wirtz, J., & Chung, C. (2006). Singapore: Marketing, macro trends, and their implications for marketing management for 2005 and the years beyond. In A. Pecotitch & C. Shultz II (Eds.), *Handbook of markets and economies: East Asia, Southeast Asia, Australia, New Zealand.* New York: M.E. Sharpe.

World Bank. (2006). *Doing business 2006: Creating jobs.* Washington, DC: World Bank. Retrieved from: https://www.doingbusiness.org/content/dam/doingBusiness/media/Annual-Reports/English/DB06-FullReport.pdf.

World Bank. (2015). *Doing business 2015: Going beyond efficiency.* Washington, DC: World Bank. Retrieved from: https://www.doingbusiness.org/content/dam/doingBusiness/media/Annual-Reports/English/DB15-Full-Report.pdf.

World Bank. (2016). *Doing business 2016: Measuring regulatory quality and efficiency.* Washington, DC: World Bank. Retrieved from: https://www.doingbusiness.org/content/dam/doingBusiness/media/Annual-Reports/English/DB16-Full-Report.pdf.

World Bank. (2019). *World Development Indicators online.* Retrieved from https://databank.worldbank.org/reports.aspx?source=world-development-indicators.

Yusuf, S., & Nabeshima, K. (2002). *Some small countries do it better: Rapid growth and its causes in Singapore, Finland, and Ireland.* Washington, DC: World Bank Publications.

11

Money Can't Buy Me Love, but It Can Buy Apples: An Analysis of Fruit and Vegetable Demand in Uzbekistan

Alisher Ergashev

Introduction

Since 1991, horticultural production has been expanding in Uzbekistan in terms of area and quantities (FAOSTAT, 2015). As a result, per capita national supply of fruit and vegetables—as derived from the Food Balance Sheets of the Food and Agriculture Organization of the United Nations (FAO)—exceeds the recommended amount of 400 grams by more than two times.

It is, however, misleading to conclude a saturation of fruit and vegetables in actual consumption, which might be lower than the quantities shown, as food availability may vary because of the magnitude of food losses along the marketing chain, food wastage within the household, cooking and storage losses (Nichols et al., 2012). In fact, individual-level intakes—as derived from the survey conducted for this study—remain inadequate with a strong seasonal pattern (Table 11.1).

A. Ergashev (✉)
Queensland Department of Agriculture and Fisheries,
Brisbane, QLD, Australia
e-mail: Alisher.Ergashev@daf.qld.gov.au

© The Author(s) 2020
A. Akimov and G. Kazakevitch (eds.), *30 Years since the Fall of the Berlin Wall*, Palgrave Studies in Economic History, https://doi.org/10.1007/978-981-15-0317-7_11

Table 11.1 Per capita supply and intake of fruit and vegetables in Uzbekistan, grams per day

	Recommended intake (WHO 2003)	National supply (FAOSTAT 2015)		Actual intake (2014 & 2015 Food consumption survey)
			Summer 2014	Winter 2014/2015
Fruit	180	150	94	72
Vegetables	220	660	251	61
Total	400	810	345	133

Source Author's calculations based on the cited sources

Micronutrient deficiency is a global problem and hidden hunger affects far more people than hunger (WHO, 2006). In Uzbekistan, the nutritional profile shows high rates of stunting in children and overweight in all population (NLiS, 2015). Figures from the Global Burden of Disease Study 2017 showed that within the European Region of the World Health Organization (WHO), unhealthy eating is deadliest in Uzbekistan: 394 diet-related deaths per 100,000 people (Meier et al., 2019). Such elements as a 'diet low in fruit' and a 'diet low in vegetables' lead the group of dietary risk factors attributable to the disease burden in Uzbekistan, as expressed in per cent of a total number of years of life lost (IHME, 2018).

Meanwhile, fruit and vegetables provide an easily available source of micronutrients (WCRF & AICR, 2007) and are linked with reduced risk of chronic diseases (Lock, Pomerleau, Causer, Altmann, & McKee, 2005), obesity and type 2 diabetes (Ball et al., 2003). Given the importance of a healthy diet and especially fruit and vegetables, this paper therefore quantitatively identifies the determinants of fruit and vegetable consumption among the Uzbek population.

Conceptual Framework

The conceptual framework on Fig. 11.1 succinctly summarises the key assumptions and hypotheses of the interactions between fruit and vegetable supply and demand and their effect on nutrition and health. For the sake of the current analysis, the focus lies on the demand side of

11 Money Can't Buy Me Love, but It Can Buy Apples ...

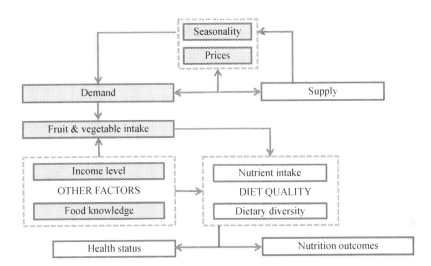

Fig. 11.1 Conceptual framework (*Source* Adapted from Bouis, Raney, and McDermott [2013], Gillespie, Harris, and Kadiyala [2012], Masset, Haddad, Cornelius, and Isaza-Castro [2011], Ruel [2002]. *Note* Interactions between the shadowed boxes are analysed explicitly while outlining the white box linkages in the Supply-Demand-Diet-Nutrition-Health nexus)

the equation. For instance, seasonality in supply influences decisions on consumption via prices and other factors. It is noteworthy that interaction between supply and demand goes both ways, as the horticultural industry is attempting to react efficiently to changes in consumer demand, while supply shortages/surpluses are the signals for consumers' behaviour. According to a theory of reciprocal determinism, consumption of fruit and vegetables (being a person's behaviour) both influences and is influenced by personal factors, such as knowledge and wealth, and social environment (Bere & Klepp, 2005; Cullen et al., 2003; Granner et al., 2004).

The limited fruit and vegetable intake, therefore, affects individual's diet quality and it is assumed that there is a positive association between dietary diversity and nutritional outcomes in children, which might also lead to better health. In sum, improving fruit and vegetable supply, in order to match the population demand, should improve diets and reduce micronutrient deficiencies and stunting that, in turn, will result in better health outcomes.

Data

Data availability remains a constraining factor in analysing agricultural economics in Uzbekistan, as authorities have a reluctant attitude in sharing the data and making them publicly available. Other data sources rarely exist in the country.

Therefore, all analyses are largely based on the primary data, which were purposely collected in the research area among various target groups. This study's focus lies in Tashkent province, which is located in the northeast of Uzbekistan. The choice of the research area was based on the fact that the province is a leading region in terms of horticultural production. Being a case study analysis, this paper does not serve as a country- or region-representative research.

Food Consumption Survey

The food consumption survey was performed in the form of structured face-to-face interviewing, including 24-hour food recall and physical measurements. The target sample size for this survey was calculated as 200 households or 1040 people. A multi-stage cluster sampling procedure was chosen as a sampling design.

In the first stage, the population was split into five strata, each representing a selected district of Tashkent province (Fig. 11.2). Each stratum was allocated 40 households that are a disproportional allocation of a total number of 200 households among five districts.

In the second stage, the target population was divided into two domains—urban and rural—in each stratum, resulting in ten final strata. The sample allocation of households in these strata was done proportionally to the distribution of the urban/rural population. As a result, 94 households were selected in urban areas, whereas 106 households in rural areas.

During the third stage, the primary sampling units (PSU) were chosen with probability proportional to their size (PPS) from the list of small territorial units within the strata. In this survey, administrative units were regarded as the PSUs: in urban areas—towns and urban

Fig. 11.2 Research area: food consumption survey, Tashkent province, Uzbekistan (*Source* Author's compilation)

settlements, and in rural areas—village assemblies of citizens. Due to budget and time restrictions, it was decided to select 10 PSUs in each district with equal probabilities: four PSUs in urban areas and six PSUs in rural areas. As a result, a total of 50 PSUs were selected.

In Uzbekistan, the *mahalla* (local neighbourhood community) serves as a territorial unit of households and plays a great role in organising the social life of its inhabitants. Therefore, for this survey, it was decided to take advantage of the availability of the *mahalla* level of disaggregation and use it as a secondary sampling unit (SSU) for the fourth stage of sampling.

Finally, in the fifth stage, in each SSU the required households were selected at random. Prior to actual interviews, the updated lists of households were obtained from the village assemblies of citizens and/or local *mahalla* committees. Such updated lists were used as the frames for the fifth stage of sampling. For that, the households were sequentially numbered from one to n (the total number of households in each enumeration area).

The actual survey was conducted in two waves: first in August–September 2014 and second in February–March 2015. During both waves 200 households were interviewed, 193 of which were the same, the remaining seven were not available during the winter period, as they moved out. As a result, the information on food consumption and other variables both in summer 2014 and winter 2014/2015 is available for 931 people in 193 households.

During the survey, the person mainly responsible for food preparation and distribution was interviewed for most of the questions. In answering questions related to individual-level diet, the main respondent was consulting with each available family member.

The survey questionnaire was designed using the WHO's STEPS methodology (WHO, 2008) and based on the 2006 Uzbekistan Multiple Indicator Cluster Survey and other sample questionnaires (in particular, FEHD 2010). The questionnaire was translated into Uzbek and Russian languages and pre-tested in one urban area of Tashkent city (Mirabad district) and one rural area of Kibray district of Tashkent province before fieldwork.

Fruit and Vegetable Market Survey

For the market price analysis, the data come from 2014 & 2015 Fruit and vegetable market survey, which was implemented by the author in three big markets of Tashkent province (Chirchik, Kuylik and Parkent). The choice of these markets was explained by their equidistant proximity to the SSU and sample households, as shown on Geographic Information System map in Fig. 11.3.

Qualitative and quantitative data were obtained from structured face-to-face interviews conducted with randomly selected horticultural retailers and wholesalers as well as key resource experts such as market staff members. As a result, collected information includes quarterly data on fruit and vegetable retail and wholesale prices for 2013 and 2014. For each traded product, an average price was taken based on at least three bids, representing a general price trend in the respective market.

Field visits took place in April 2014 and March 2015. Necessary permissions were obtained from local governments and market directorates. Challenges included lack of recorded information on sales, the reluctant attitude of some traders and inconvenient working time of wholesalers.

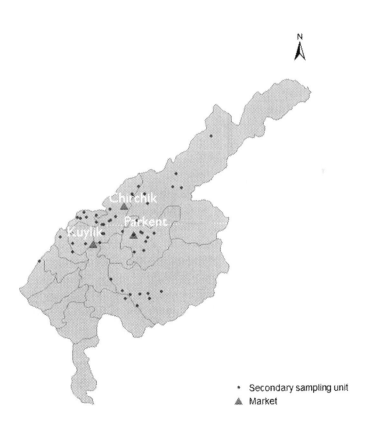

Fig. 11.3 Research area: fruit & vegetable market survey, Tashkent province, Uzbekistan (*Source* Author's compilation)

Methods

The empirical estimation involves three steps. The food consumption data allow calculating individual-level intakes of fruit and vegetables, which would then lay a basis for dependent variable in the econometric model of fruit and vegetable intake. The second step involves quantification of the independent variables. Special attention is given to such variables as income, market prices and food knowledge. Finally, an econometric model is constructed and analysed to investigate the role of each factor on fruit and vegetable consumption.

Fruit and Vegetable Intake Level

In the current study, the definitions of fruit and vegetables relate to their nutritional qualities, and therefore are defined as 'low-energy-dense foods relatively rich in vitamins, minerals and other bioactive compounds as well as being good sources of fibre' (Agudo, 2005).

'Vegetables' include fruited vegetables, leafy vegetables, onions and roots, but exclude legumes, pulses, potatoes and other starchy tubers. Fruit jams, nuts, seeds and cereals are classified as differing from the fruit category, while pome fruit, stone fruit, berries, currants, citrus fruit, grapes and tropical fruit, as well as 100% derived fruit juices, are classified as 'fruit' (SAFEFOOD, 2013).

Based on the survey results, it was possible to estimate individual fruit and vegetable intake in both summer and winter seasons. The questionnaire was structured by meals in chronological order, starting from the first breakfast and ending with the last dinner. The actual intake of each food item was expressed in grams, following a calculation procedure given the daily frequency and portion size, as outlined in Fig. 11.4.

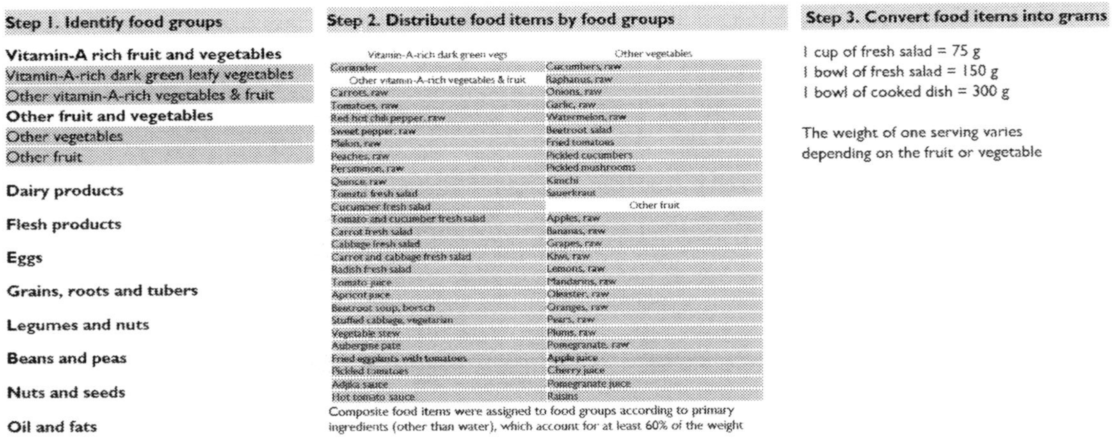

11 Money Can't Buy Me Love, but It Can Buy Apples ...

Fig. 11.4 Procedure of calculation of fruit and vegetable intake (Adapted from Martin-Prevel et al. [2015], Herrador et al. [2015], WHO [2008])

Household Income Level

Being partly food security research, this study tries to capture the role of affordability in healthy eating. The piloting phase of the fieldwork showed that the respondents were reluctant to share the information regarding their income status in absolute terms. Keeping in mind this attitude, there was a five income categories' breakdown provided in the questionnaire. Given the fact that there is no official statistics on the income level either at the individual or household level in Uzbekistan, the threshold values for each category were calculated based on previous research and official statistics. Below there is an explanation of how these five categories were chosen: lowest income, low-to-middle, middle, middle-to-high and highest income (Table 11.2).

Following household expenditure statistics among various income groups by Musaev, Yakshilikov, and Yusupov (2010) (who, in turn, used the data from the World Bank's Uzbekistan Regional Panel Survey 2006), total expenditures per capita for middle-income group—25,251 Uzbek soums (UZS)—was taken as a reference for calculating the relative ratios of total expenditures per capita for other income groups. Assuming that the real income pattern follows the pattern of total expenditures linearly, the values of real income per capita for all income groups were calculated given that an official aggregate real income per capita for 2011 (UZS 1,992,400 per annum, or UZS 166,033 per month) was assumed to be associated with the middle-income group. Household-level data were calculated as a product of household size and real income per capita of each respective income group. Then, the values of 2011 data were expressed in 2014 prices using Consumer Price Indices. Finally, the values of real income per household were rounded up to serve threshold values for identification of each income group.

Fruit and Vegetable Price Index

During the study period, clear seasonal price variations of some fruit crops (apples, grapes, apricots, cherries, plums) and vegetables

Table 11.2 Calculation of threshold values for household income groups

	Lowest income	Low-to-middle	Middle income	Middle-to-high	Highest income
Household size[a]	6.5	6.1	5.6	5	3.6
Total expenditures per capita per month in 2005, UZS[a]	12,028	18,233	25,251	37,425	87,468
Ratio of expenditures per capita to the middle-income group value	0.48	0.72	1.00	1.48	3.46
Real monthly income per capita in 2011, UZS[b]	79,090	119,887	166,033	246,084	575,132
Real income per HH per month in 2011, UZS	514,084	731,313	929,787	1,230,419	2,070,474
Peal income per HH per month, in 2014 prices, UZS[c]	586,382	834,161	1,060,547	1,403,459	2,361,655
Income group thresholds, UZS	<500,000	500,000–1,000,000	1,000,000–1,500,000	1,500,000–2,000,000	>2,000,000

Source Author's calculations based on [a]Musaev et al. (2010), [b]Goskomstat (2012), and [c]CER (2014)

(tomatoes, cucumbers, radish) were observed across quarters as substantiated in peaking prices during the winter season.

Based on the interviews with fruit and vegetable market retailers, there were two main sources of supply: home-grown products and those purchased from farmers or wholesalers for further reselling. Wholesalers normally buy fresh foodstuffs from farmers via pickup from the fields. All retailers sell the products to individual consumers at the same market at retail prices, whereas wholesalers sell to retailers at the same market at wholesale prices, and occasionally they sell to individual consumers at retail prices. Prices, in general, can be bargained.

For the current analysis an aggregate index was generated, equalling to an average price for a basket of fruit and vegetables typically available in the area such as apples, grapes, tomatoes and cucumbers. The dynamics of this index in three sample markets is depicted in Fig. 11.5.

It was assumed that these four basic foodstuffs would represent the price dynamics of the general fruit and vegetable category. This assumption was confirmed by exploration of the food consumption survey data, which showed the dominant role of these four crops in domestic consumption in both seasons.

Unfortunately, the absence of primary data on prices for food groups other than fruit and vegetables did not allow controlling for food substitution effects. Seasonal movements and price differences were examined using tabular analyses and t-tests, conducted in Microsoft Excel.

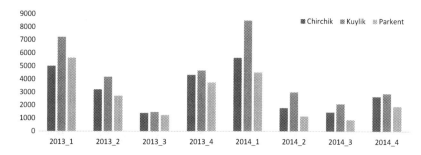

Fig. 11.5 Dynamics of fruit and vegetable retail price index in 2013–2014, UZS per kilo (*Source* Author's representation based on the Fruit and vegetable market survey)

Food Knowledge Index

In order to capture the individual's knowledge of healthy eating habits, a self-designed index was constructed based on the answers of the person responsible for food preparation and distribution. While developing this index, previous international studies were considered. For example, Parmenter and Wardle (1999) constructed and validated a nutrition questionnaire tool, which was tested among British adults and included four sections, two of which were adopted for constructing the current food knowledge index: awareness of dietary recommendations, and awareness of diet-disease associations. These two components were also found in a three-dimensional health and nutrition knowledge index used by Mancino and Kinsey (2010) in the United States, which also captured the knowledge of how many servings should be consumed.

The data for the food knowledge index used in this study come from the answers to the five questions, covering such modules as food variety, fruit and vegetables, oils and fats and diet-disease associations (Table 11.3). Since the index covers only a limited area of diet awareness and lacks important information on, for example, sources of nutrients, it therefore cannot be appropriate for use in measuring the overall nutrition knowledge.

Fruit and Vegetable Intake Model

Intuitively, economic factors are very important when making decisions regarding fruit and vegetable consumption. Naturally, more income and lower prices should lead to higher intake. Although this relates to all socio-economic groups, it tends to be more of a concern among those with smaller incomes (Azagba & Sharaf, 2011; Dibsdall, Lambert, Bobbin, & Frewer, 2003).

Sociodemographic factors have been observed to influence fruit and vegetable consumption in various studies. For example, being married might predispose an individual to better access to fruit and vegetables (Franchini, Poínhos, Klepp, & Vaz de Almeida, 2013), while being employed would lead to better knowledge about their benefits for human health (Thompson, Margetts, Speller, & McVey, 1999).

Table 11.3 Structure of the food knowledge index

Module	Questions	Answers
Food variety	1. Do you think health experts recommend that people should be eating more/less of these 10 foods? 1. Fruit & vegetables, 2. Meat & meat products, 3. Fish & seafood, 4. Oil & fat products, 5. Milk & dairy products, 6. Eggs, 7. Cereals & bakery products, 8. Legumes, 9. Salty foods, 10. Sweets	1 = More 2 = Less 3 = Doesn't matter 4 = Don't know
Fruit and vegetables	2. How many servings of fruit and vegetables should be consumed daily by an average person of your age and sex to maintain good health?	
	3. Do you know any diseases or health problems, which are related to low intake of fruit and vegetables?	1 = Yes 2 = No 3 = Don't know
Cooking oil	4. What do you think, how useful are the following five types of oil and fat products in cooking? 1. Cottonseed oil, 2. Vegetable oil, 3. Animal fat, 4. Butter, 5. Margarine	1 = More healthy 2 = Less healthy 3 = Don't know
	5. Do you know any diseases or health problems, which are related to consuming too much oil and fat products?	1 = Yes 2 = No 3 = Don't know
Total		

Source Adapted from Parmenter and Wardle (1999), Mancino and Kinsey (2010)

It is rather interesting that intake decreases with age for children (Rasmussen et al., 2006), while it increases for adults (Oliveira, Maia, & Lopes, 2014).

Food knowledge has been positively associated with intake of fruit and vegetables, as found elsewhere (Beydoun & Wang, 2008; Brug, Tak, te Velde, Bere, & De Bourdeaudhuij, 2008; Lin, Yang, Hang, & Pan, 2007; Yeh et al., 2008).

Thus, based on the quantified variables, representing summer and winter seasons, it was possible to use them for multiple linear regression analysis, by means of ordinary least squares to examine the determinants of fruit and vegetable intake. Similar estimations have been conducted elsewhere (Agudo & Pera, 1999; Ahlstrom, 2009; Amo-Adjei & Kumi-Kyreme, 2014).

The functional form of the model can be expressed as follows:

$$\ln Y_{it} = \beta_{0i} + \beta_1 W_{it} + \beta_2 \ln P_{it} + \beta_2 E_{it} + \beta_4 Z_{it} + \beta_5 Season_{it} + \varepsilon_{it},$$

Y_{it} Intake of fruit and vegetables, log transformed
W_{it} Household income level (Base: Lowest income)
P_{it} Fruit and vegetable price index, log transformed
E_{it} Food and nutrition knowledge index
Z_{it} Confounding factors: household size, age, marital status, occupation
   (Base: Unemployed)
Season Data collection season (Base: Summer 2014)
ε_{it} Error term.

In order to control the heterogeneity of different age groups, three focal groups were identified and treated separately: infants aged six months or older and below four years, children aged four years or older and below 15 years and adolescents and adults aged 15 years or older.

Given the panel nature of the sample data and time-invariant personal characteristics such as sex and residence, fixed effects model was employed. All analyses were conducted with STATA statistical software (version 13), using a statistical significance level of 0.05 or less for all tests.

Results and Discussion

There was a significant difference in the total fruit and vegetable intakes between summer 2014 ($M=345$, $SD=11.6$) and winter 2014/2015 ($M=133$, $SD=5.5$); $t(1860)=16.48$, $p=0.0000$. There was a statistical variance in summer intake between urban ($M=372$, $SD=16.6$) and rural ($M=307$, $SD=15.3$) residents: $t(929)=-2.81$, $p=0.0051$. This difference, however, vanished in winter.

The found significant seasonal difference is in line with most studies conducted in similar settings. For example, one study found drastic seasonal fluctuations in daily per capita intake of fruit (from 263 grams in summer to 143 grams in winter) and vegetables (221 grams versus 145, respectively) among Iranian households (Toorang, HoushiarRad, Abdollahi, Esmaili, & Koujan, 2013).

Figure 11.6 shows a comparison between recommended and actual levels of fruit and vegetable intakes across different population groups. While average intake in summer 2014 was slightly higher than the mean recommended level, in winter 2014/2015 this indicator was much lower. In the summer period, adult males consumed slightly lower than recommended amounts, whereas children's consumption was above recommended thresholds. In winter, however, consumption was significantly lower than it should be in all age categories.

There was no significant gender difference in the total fruit and vegetable intakes between males ($M = 236$, $SD = 10.5$) and females ($M = 241$, $SD = 9.0$); $t(1860) = 0.3609$, $p = 0.7182$. However, straightforward analysis of mean intakes shows that in both seasons, girls consume larger amounts than do boys of the same age, as well as do female adolescents and adults in winter season compared to their male counterparts. The observed gender difference is similar to what has been found in Sweden, the UK and Norway (Rasmussen et al., 2006).

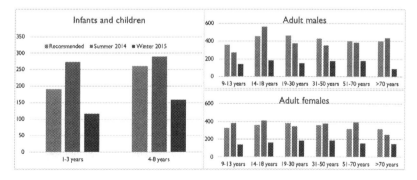

Fig. 11.6 Actual and recommended intakes of fruit and vegetables, grams/day/person (*Source* Author's illustration based on the food consumption survey and the recommendations from WHO [2003])

Table 11.4 Summary statistics of the model variables

	Average	Summer 2014	Winter 2014/2015
Intake of fruit and vegetables (grams/day/person)	239	345	133
Household income level (prevalence: total number and %)			
Lowest income	131 (14%)	155 (17%)	108 (12%)
Low-to-middle	400 (43%)	435 (47%)	365 (39%)
Middle income	280 (30%)	256 (27%)	303 (33%)
Middle-to-high	83 (9%)	77 (8%)	89 (10%)
Highest income	37 (4%)	8 (1%)	66 (7%)
Fruit and vegetable price index (UZS/kg)	4014	1367	6661
Food and nutrition knowledge index (0-to-6 range)	4.3	4.3	4.2
Household size	6.4	6.3	6.4
Age	31	31	31
Employment status* (prevalence: total number and %)			
Unemployed (unemployed, retired, and housewives)	230 (34%)	235 (34%)	224 (33%)
Employed (formally employed, private sector workers, students & seasonal labour)	455 (66%)	450 (66%)	461 (67%)
Marital status* (prevalence: total number and %)			
Not married (single, divorced, widowed)	351 (51%)	343 (50%)	358 (52%)
Married (de facto, de jure)	334 (49%)	342 (50%)	327 (48%)

Source Author's calculations based on the food consumption survey
Note Reported values for variables with asterisk (*) only for adolescents and adults aged 15 years and older

Descriptive statistics of the regression variables are presented in Table 11.4. Overall summary statistics are complemented by the seasonally grouped data.

The socio-economic profile of households remains the same across two seasons, and the sample data show a predominance of households below the middle-income group, with very few rich families. The food knowledge index does not vary across seasons and exhibits a rather adequate level of 4.3 out of 6. On the contrary, the fruit and vegetable price index shows a five-fold increase in winter compared to summer, which might partially explain the observed high seasonality pattern in fruit and vegetable intakes.

Whereas half of the adult population was married, one third was unemployed. Average household size of 6.4 is rather large, suggesting possible issues with intra-household food distribution. The average age of the sample is 31 years, reflecting the prevalence of a young population in the national age distribution.

As shown in Table 11.5, the fixed effects model indicates that the fruit and vegetable consumption is quite sensitive to economic factors' change, which is consistent with classical demand theory, especially for adult females and infants. Being in the 'highest income' category compared to the 'lowest income' category leads to a tremendous 350% increase in intake of fruit and vegetables in children. This income elasticity is even more striking for infants: a five times increase in intake is associated with being raised in a rich family, all other factors being constant. A similar association (4.6) is found in female adolescents and adults. For this category, any improvement in income leads to higher probability of consuming more fruit and vegetables.

The present study reveals the strong role of socio-economic status in food consumption within Uzbekistan. In their analysis of the results of the World Bank's 2005 Uzbekistan Regional Panel Survey, Musaev et al. (2010) argued that the diet of the poorest households was mostly comprised of cereals (an inexpensive source of nutrients) and much less consumption of fruit.

The found socio-economic gradient in fruit and vegetable consumption pattern is also in line with the results of studies conducted in countries with similar fruit and vegetable intake: in the United Kingdom (Dibsdall et al., 2003), Norway (Bere & Klepp, 2004), Finland (Roos, Hirvonen, Mikkilä, Karvonen, & Rimpelä, 2011) and Sweden (Höglund, Samuelson, & Mark, 1998).

As expected, fruit and vegetable prices serve as another important economic factor in consumption. For instance, for adult females, a 1% increase in fruit and vegetable price index is associated with a 6% decrease in intake of fruit and vegetables, other variables being equal. Similar to income variable, prices affect consumption even greater if it

Table 11.5 Parameter estimates of the fruit and vegetable intake regression model

	Infants (6mo–4 yr)	Children (4–15 yr)	Adolescents and adults (>15 yr) Males	Females
Household income (Base: Lowest income)				
Low-to-middle	0.508	1.155	1.387**	2.087***
	(2.088)	(0.784)	(0.671)	(0.552)
Middle income	1.134	1.214	1.148	1.407**
	(2.329)	(0.779)	(0.733)	(0.597)
Middle-to-high	0.751	1.047	1.079	1.901***
	(2.695)	(0.909)	(0.809)	(0.668)
Highest income	4.862*	3.472**	3.173***	4.586***
	(2.637)	(1.487)	(1.111)	(0.969)
Fruit and vegetable price index (log)	−17.44**	−1.174	−2.981	−5.868**
	(6.989)	(2.675)	(2.603)	(2.335)
Food and nutrition knowledge index	0.843	0.251	0.292*	0.229*
	(0.539)	(0.246)	(0.168)	(0.169)
Household size	−0.718	0.534	0.945***	0.705**
	(0.577)	(0.466)	(0.334)	(0.354)
Age	−18.29	−13.65	−9.196*	−25.47***
	(15.21)	(8.384)	(5.533)	(6.301)
Employment status (Base: Unemployed)			−0.240 (0.356)	0.376 (0.305)
Marital status (Base: Not married)			0.0324 (0.274)	0.181 (0.319)
Season (Base: Summer 2014)	35.67**	6.878	7.461	19.56***
	(14.45)	(7.734)	(5.625)	(5.829)
Constant	174.4***	133.9	373.6*	1,060***
	(64.13)	(92.97)	(219.5)	(260.9)
Observations	118	374	624	746
Number of groups	59	187	312	373
R-squared (within)	0.297	0.212	0.238	0.294
F-value	2.027*	5.063***	7.448***	10.75***

Source Author's calculations based on the food consumption survey
Note Dependent variable is log transformed fruit and vegetable intake
The reported are fixed effects regression coefficients and the robust standard errors in parentheses
*Significant at 10%; **significant at 5%; and ***significant at 1%

comes to children under four: a more than 17% reduction in intake results from increasing price index by 1 at 5% significance level, ceteris paribus.

Being a nutrient-dense diet, fruit and vegetables are far more costly than energy-dense foods (Darmon & Drewnowski, 2008). In fact, due to cold winters in Uzbekistan, the costs for horticultural growing are extremely high in the off-season, resulting in drastic seasonality of supply (Ali et al., 2006). Strong state control systems over the horticultural volumes and prices limits the flexibility of farmers and, as noted by Bobojonov and Lamers (2008), the lack of information on prices results in poor decision-making activities, given a shortage of knowledge regarding their comparative advantages.

The food knowledge index is statistically significant and positively associated with fruit and vegetable consumption: one unit increase in food knowledge index leads to a 23% (for females) and 30% (for males) increase in intake, with other variables being constant.

The strong correlation observed between knowledge and intake highlights the importance of food and nutrition knowledge, found in other studies too. For example, the study by De Bourdeaudhuij et al. (2008) showed a strong effect of knowledge (awareness of national recommendations) on children's fruit and vegetable intake in nine European countries.

A straightforward bivariate correlation test showed that household income level narrowly correlates with food knowledge: $r(193) = -0.05$ in summer 2014 and $r(193) = 0.16$ in winter 2015, suggesting that even richer families might have a low level of awareness about a healthy diet.

The size of the family positively affects consumption in adults: an additional family member is associated with more than 70% (for females) and almost 95% (for males) increase in intake, ceteris paribus. This positive association possibly reflects the greater wealth often associated with household size and economies of scale because of less waste and the possibility to purchase in bulk associated with larger family size, as found by Robin (1985) in France. While understanding that it is not the household size per se but the dependency ratio within a household that plays an important role in determining the intake levels, in this analysis, however, the dependency ratio was not included in the model due to the complexity of its measurement.

In adolescents and adults, age has a strong negative influence on decisions regarding fruit and vegetable consumption, especially for females. This can be related to the inter-household distribution of healthy food, such as fruit and vegetables, from elder to younger family members. Given the limited sources, adults would care more about the children's health, limiting their own diet. This finding should be taken with caution, as the age-consumption link is not this straightforward and needs more detailed disaggregation. Obviously, the more age/sex specification, the more precise would be the conclusion. For example, one study by Oliveira et al. (2014) showed that inadequate fruit and vegetable consumption was more frequently found in younger women and men (<40 years) compared to older people (>=65 years).

Seasonality had a surprisingly strong positive effect on intake of infants and women, meaning a significant increase in winter season compared to summer. It can be due to changes in the composition of total fruit and vegetable intakes between seasons as a result of substitution effect. In fact, the survey data showed that such winter fruit as persimmon and quince, as well as such vegetable products as pickles increased considerably in winter. It might be true that the winter season does increase consumption of fruit and vegetables in women and infants in relative terms, because in most cases being better aware of health benefits of fruit and vegetables, women are responsible for health and diet in the family, and therefore they try to increase the winter intake in order to smoothen a year-long consumption. This hypothesis is supported by the survey data showing that female adults are indeed consuming larger amount of fruit and vegetables in winter compared to men. The positive association between winter season and intake can also be related to possible flaws with the use of the generic price index. In particular, any association between season and intake disappears after separating price effects into grapes and cucumber prices.

For adults, the effects of being married and employed on fruit and vegetable intake are not statistically significant, while age, food knowledge and household size are statistically non-significant for infants and children.

Conclusion

For this analysis, a food consumption survey was conducted for the first time in the last 30 years, filling an important geographic gap in the dietary analysis, as Uzbekistan remains one of the countries where determinants of fruit and vegetable consumption have been understudied.

It is hoped that the results from this evidence-based study will lay the ground for future research on food demand in the Central Asian region. Being in line with the work by Mirzabaev (2013), who found that the Uzbekistan households' food consumption is quite sensitive to agricultural income changes, this paper underlines the strong role of economic factors in people's diet.

This conclusion should give rise to a more balanced and harmonious policy approach to tackle nutrition and well-being issues in Uzbekistan. An expected negative effect of market prices on individual-level intake demonstrates a high price elasticity of nutrient-dense diet, which would give a greater emphasis on the importance of measures on improving a year-long fruit and vegetable supply, including protected cultivation and post-harvest handling technologies.

The fact that income and price elasticities were found the strongest in infants compared to older children and adults, should gain a particular attention for policy-making, given the crucial significance of healthy diet at this age for further physical development.

The positive association between food knowledge and intake of fruit and vegetables, found in adults, highlights the importance of raising awareness about a healthy diet. This should eventually result in encouraging healthier eating habits among children.

In order to increase demand for fruit and vegetables, the state policies should consider providing subsidies and other incentives to help low-income families purchase more fruit and vegetables, with particular focus on children's diet. According to DiSogra (2014), such strategies include free fruit and vegetable snacks and vouchers for students from low-income families.

Although the study showed the overall good knowledge about a healthy diet, the awareness of some aspects requires improvement. In addition, there is a lack of basic education and training in food hygiene and safety at technical and educational institutions, as well as inadequate information services and a lack of resources for programmes studying nutrition.

In this regard, educational programmes, which would aim at building capacity in dietary recommendations and implications for human health, will be useful in reaching appropriate dietary change. There is a need for public campaigns that give advice on improving variety, increasing healthy foods (such as fruit and vegetables) and cutting down unhealthy meals.

References

Agudo, A. (2005). *Measuring intake of fruit and vegetables*. Geneva, Switzerland: World Health Organization.

Agudo, A., & Pera, G. (1999). Vegetable and fruit consumption associated with anthropometric, dietary and lifestyle factors in Spain. *Public Health Nutrition, 2*(03), 263–271. https://doi.org/10.1017/S136898009900035X.

Ahlstrom, D. (2009). *Social cognitive predictors of college students' fruit and vegetable intake*. All Graduate Theses and Dissertations (Paper 433). Utah State University.

Ali, M., Mavlyanova, R., Wu, M., Farooq, U., Lin, L., & Kuo, C. (2006). Setting research and development priorities for market-oriented vegetable production systems in Central Asia and the Caucasus. *Increasing market-oriented vegetable production in Central Asia and the Caucasus through collaborative research and development. AVRDC publication number 06-679. AVRDC–The World Vegetable Center, Shanhua, Taiwan. 250*, 105.

Amo-Adjei, J., & Kumi-Kyereme, A. (2014). Fruit and vegetable consumption by ecological zone and socioeconomic status in Ghana. *Journal of Biosocial Science, 47*, 613–631. https://doi.org/10.1017/S002193201400025X.

Azagba, S., & Sharaf, M. F. (2011). Disparities in the frequency of fruit and vegetable consumption by socio-demographic and lifestyle characteristics in Canada. *Nutrition Journal, 10*(118), 1–8. https://doi.org/10.1186/1475-2891-10-118.

Ball, S. D., Keller, K. R., Moyer-Mileur, L. J., Ding, Y. W., Donaldson, D., & Jackson, W. D. (2003). Prolongation of satiety after low versus moderately high glycemic index meals in obese adolescents. *Pediatrics, 111*(3), 488–494. https://doi.org/10.1542/peds.111.3.488.

Bere, E., & Klepp, K. I. (2004). Correlates of fruit and vegetable intake among Norwegian schoolchildren: Parental and self-reports. *Public Health Nutrition, 7*(08), 991–998. https://doi.org/10.1079/PHN2004619.

Bere, E., & Klepp, K. I. (2005). Changes in accessibility and preferences predict children's future fruit and vegetable intake. *International Journal of Behavioural Nutrition and Physical Activity, 2*(1), 15. https://doi.org/10.1186/1479-5868-2-15.

Beydoun, M. A., & Wang, Y. (2008). Do nutrition knowledge and beliefs modify the association of socio-economic factors and diet quality among US adults? *Preventive Medicine, 46*(2), 145–153. https://doi.org/10.1016/j.ypmed.2007.06.016.

Bobojonov, I., & Lamers, J. (2008). Analysis of agricultural markets in Khorezm, Uzbekistan. In P. Wehrheim, A. Schoeller-Schletter, & C. Martius (Eds), *Continuity and change: Land and water use reforms in rural Uzbekistan. Socio-economic and legal analyses for the region Khorezm* (pp. 165–182). Halle/Saale: IAMO. ISSN 1436-221X.

Bouis, H., Raney, T., & McDermott J. (2013). *Priorities for public sector research on food security and nutrition.* Mimeo.

Brug, J., Tak, N. I., te Velde, S. J., Bere, E., & De Bourdeaudhuij, I. (2008). Taste preferences, liking and other factors related to fruit and vegetable intakes among schoolchildren: Results from observational studies. *British Journal of Nutrition, 99*(S1), S7–S14. https://doi.org/10.1017/S0007114508892458.

Center for Economic Research [CER]. (2014). *Inflation and prices in Uzbekistan, information and analytical bulletin for January–September 2014.* Tashkent.

Cullen, K., Baranowski, T., Owens, E., Marsh, T., Rittenberry, L., & de Moor, C. (2003). Availability, accessibility, and preferences for fruit, 100% fruit juice, and vegetables influence children's dietary behavior. *Health Education & Behavior, 30*(5), 615–626. https://doi.org/10.1177/1090198103257254.

Darmon, N., & Drewnowski, A. (2008). Does social class predict diet quality? *The American Journal of Clinical Nutrition, 87*(5), 1107–1117.

De Bourdeaudhuij, I., te Velde, S., Brug, J., Due, P., Wind, M., Sandvik, C., et al. (2008). Personal, social and environmental predictors of daily fruit and vegetable intake in 11-year-old children in nine European countries. *European Journal of Clinical Nutrition, 62*(7), 834–841.

Dibsdall, L. A., Lambert, N., Bobbin, R. F., & Frewer, L. J. (2003). Low-income consumers' attitudes and behaviour towards access, availability and motivation to eat fruit and vegetables. *Public Health Nutrition, 6*(2), 159–168. https://doi.org/10.1079/PHN2002412.

Disogra, L. (2014). *Global strategies to increase fruit & vegetable consumption: Aligning public health and agriculture goals*. Report for 2014 Grand Challenges Meeting. Seattle, United States. Available at: http://worldfoodcenter.ucdavis.edu/docs/gates_pres/disogra_gates.pdf. Accessed 4 May 2017.

FAOSTAT. (2015). *Statistics division of the food and agriculture organization of the United Nations*. Available at: http://faostat3.fao.org/home/E. Accessed 18 Jan 2019.

Food and Environmental Hygiene Department [FEHD]. (2010). *Hong Kong population-based food consumption survey 2005-2007 final report*. Hong Kong: FEHD. Available at: http://cfs.fehd.hksarg/english/programme/programme_firm/files/FCS_final_report.pdf.

Franchini, B., Poínhos, R., Klepp, K., & Vaz de Almeida, M. (2013). Fruit and vegetables: Intake and sociodemographic determinants among Portuguese mothers. *Annals of Nutrition & Metabolism, 63*(1–2), 131–138. https://doi.org/10.1159/000351987.

Gillespie, S., Harris, J., & Kadiyala, S. (2012). *The agriculture-nutrition disconnect in India: What do we know?* (No. 1187). Washington, DC: International Food Policy Research Institute (IFPRI). http://ebrary.ifpri.org/cdm/ref/collection/p15738coll2/id/126958.

Granner, M., Sargent, R., Calderon, K., Hussey, J., Evans, A., & Watkins, K. (2004). Factors of fruit and vegetable intake by race, gender, and age among young adolescents. *Journal of Nutrition Education and Behaviour, 36*(4), 173–180. https://doi.org/10.1016/S1499-4046(06)60231-5.

Herrador, Z., Perez-Formigo, J., Sordo, L., Gadisa, E., Moreno, J., Benito, A., & Custodio, E. (2015). Low dietary diversity and intake of animal source foods among school aged children in Libo Kemkem and Fogera Districts, Ethiopia. *PLoS one, 10*(7). https://doi.org/10.1371/journal.pone.0133435.

Höglund, D., Samuelson, G., & Mark, A. (1998). Food habits in Swedish adolescents in relation to socioeconomic conditions. *European Journal of Clinical Nutrition, 52*(11), 784–789. https://doi.org/10.1038/sj.ejcn.1600644.

Institute of Health Metrics and Evaluation [IHME]. (2018). *GBD Compare— Data Visualizations of the Global Burden of Disease study*. Institute of Health Metrics and Evaluation, University of Washington. Retrieved January 18, 2019, from https://vizhub.healthdata.org/gbd-compare/.

Lin, W., Yang, H., Hang, C., & Pan, W. (2007). Nutrition knowledge, attitude, and behavior of Taiwanese elementary school children. *Asia Pacific Journal of Clinical Nutrition, 16*, 534. https://doi.org/10.6133/apjcn.2007.16.s2.04.

Lock, K., Pomerleau, J., Causer, L., Altmann, D. R., & McKee, M. (2005). The global burden of disease attributable to low consumption of fruit and vegetables: Implications for the global strategy on diet. *Bulletin of the World Health Organization, 83*(2), 100–108. https://doi.org/10.1590/S0042-96862005000200010.

Mancino, L., & Kinsey, J. (2010). *Is dietary knowledge enough? Hunger, stress, and other roadblocks to healthy eating.* ERR-62, U.S. Department of Agriculture, Economic Research Service.

Martin-Prevel, Y., Allemand, P., Wiesmann, D., Arimond, M., Ballard, T., Deitchler, et al. (2015). *Moving forward on choosing a standard operational indicator of women's dietary diversity.* FAO. 226 p.

Masset, E., Haddad, L., Cornelius, A., & Isaza-Castro, J. (2011). *A systematic review of agricultural interventions that aim to improve nutritional status of children.* London: EPPI-Centre, Social Science Research Unit, Institute of Education, University of London.

Meier, T., Gräfe, K., Senn, F., Sur, P., Stangl, G. I., Dawczynski, C., et al. (2019). Cardiovascular mortality attributable to dietary risk factors in 51 countries in the WHO European Region from 1990 to 2016: A systematic analysis of the Global Burden of Disease Study. *European Journal of Epidemiology, 34*(1), 37–55. https://doi.org/10.1007/s10654-018-0473-x.

Mirzabaev, A. (2013). *Climate volatility and change in Central Asia: Economic impacts and adaptation.* Dissertation, Zentrum fuer Entwicklungsforschung.

Musaev, D., Yakshilikov, Y., & Yusupov, K. (2010). *Food security in Uzbekistan.* Tashkent, Uzbekistan: United Nations Development Programme.

Nichols M., Townsend N., Luengo-Fernandez R., Leal J., Gray A., Scarborough P., & Rayner M. (2012). *European Cardiovascular Disease Statistics 2012.* European Heart Network, Brussels, European Society of Cardiology, Sophia Antipolis.

Oliveira, A., Maia, B., & Lopes, C. (2014). Determinants of inadequate fruit and vegetable consumption amongst Portuguese adults. *Journal of Human Nutrition & Dietetics, 27*(s2), 194–203. https://doi.org/10.1111/jhn.12143.

Parmenter, K., & Wardle, J. (1999). Development of a general nutrition knowledge questionnaire for adults. *European Journal of Clinical Nutrition, 53*(4), 298–308.

Rasmussen, M., Krølner, R., Klepp, K. I., Lytle, L., Brug, J., Bere, E., & Due, P. (2006). Determinants of fruit and vegetable consumption among children and adolescents: A review of the literature. Part I: Quantitative studies. *International Journal of Behavioral Nutrition and Physical Activity, 3*(1), 22. https://doi.org/10.1186/1479-5868-3-22.

Robin, J. (1985). *Price of goods and consumer behavior: The case of food.* Manuscript. Paris: Inst. National de la Recherche Agronomique.

Roos, E. B., Hirvonen, T., Mikkilä, V., Karvonen, S., & Rimpelä, M. (2001). Household educational level as a determinant of consumption of raw vegetables among male and female adolescents. *Preventive Medicine, 33*(4), 282–291.

Ruel, M. (2002). *Is dietary diversity an indicator of food security or dietary quality?* (No. 140). International Food Policy Research Institute (IFPRI).

SAFEFOOD. (2013). *Consumer focused review of fruit and vegetables: Fruit and vegetable supply chain.* Co Cork, Ireland.

The Nutrition Landscape Information System [NLiS]. (2015). World Health Organization. Retrieved January 18, 2019, from http://apps.who.int/nutrition/landscape/report.aspx?iso=UZB&rid=161&template=nutrition&goButton=Go.

The State Committee on Statistics of the Republic of Uzbekistan [Goskomstat]. (2012). *Statistical yearbook of Uzbekistan social development and living standards.* Tashkent.

Thompson, R., Margetts, B., Speller, V., & McVey, D. (1999). The health education authority's health and lifestyle survey 1993: Who are the low fruit and vegetable consumers? *Journal of Epidemiology and Community Health, 53*(5), 294–299. https://doi.org/10.1136/jech.53.5.294.

Toorang, F., HoushiarRad, A., Abdollahi, M., Esmaili, M., & Koujan, S. E. (2013). Seasonality in Iranian fruit and vegetable dietary intake. *Thrita, 2*(4), 58–63. https://doi.org/10.5812/thrita.11634.

World Cancer Research Fund [WCRF], & American Institute for Cancer Research [AICR]. (2007). *Food, nutrition, physical activity, and the prevention of cancer: A global perspective* (Vol. 1). Washington, DC: Amer Institute for Cancer Research.

World Health Organization [WHO]. (2003). *Diet, nutrition and the prevention of chronic diseases.* WHO Technical Report Series: Report of a joint WHO/FAO Expert consultation. Geneva 916 (i–viii).

World Health Organization [WHO]. (2006). *Guidelines on food fortification with micronutrients* (L. Allen, B. Bruno, O. Dary, & R. Hurrell Edts, Eds.). Geneva: World Health Organization.

World Health Organization [WHO]. (2008). *WHO STEPS surveillance manual.* Geneva: World Health Organization.

Yeh, M. C., Ickes, S. B., Lowenstein, L. M., Shuval, K., Ammerman, A. S., Farris, R., et al. (2008). Understanding barriers and facilitators of fruit and vegetable consumption among a diverse multi-ethnic population in the USA. *Health Promotion International, 23*(1), 42–51. https://doi.org/10.1093/heapro/dam044.

12

Squandering Remittances Income in Conspicuous Consumption?

Jakhongir Kakhkharov and Muzaffar Ahunov

Introduction

Remittances that is money and/or goods that migrant workers employed outside their home countries send to their homeland have been under scrutiny of researchers, because of their sheer size and potential impact on development. A large number of studies specifically focus on the impact of remittances on household-level consumption and investments. However, literature that investigates the way remittances impact conspicuous consumption that is purchase of goods and services for demonstrating social status remains limited and inconclusive.

J. Kakhkharov (✉)
Flinders University, Adelaide, SA, Australia
e-mail: jak.kakhkharov@flinders.edu.au

M. Ahunov
Woosong University, Daejeon, South Korea

One transition country that has seen large inflows of remittances during the last two decades is Uzbekistan. With 32 million inhabitants, the country is the most populous in Central Asia and one of the leading sources of migrant workers in the former Soviet Union. Most labour migrants from Uzbekistan travel seasonally to Russia and Kazakhstan. The Yegor Gaidar Institute for Economic Policy in Russia estimates the number of Uzbek labourers in Russia in 2017 as about 1.9 million (Bobylev et al., 2017), and the number of Uzbek migrants who were living temporarily in Kazakhstan in that year stood at 800,000 (Seidakhmetov, 2017). Most Uzbek labourers migrate because of limited job opportunities in Uzbekistan and a large wage differential between that available at home and that in destination countries, so the number of families that depend on remittances is large. The economic downturn in Russia took its toll, and remittances from this source country declined from its peak of US$6.6 billion (approximately 12% of Uzbekistan's GDP) in 2013 (Central Bank of Russia, 2014) to US$2.7 billion in 2016 (Central Bank of Russia, 2016). The volume of recorded remittances from Kazakhstan appears to be relatively modest—US$189 million (National Bank of Kazakhstan, 2016)—but the common border with Kazakhstan and the visa-free regime may result in significant underestimation of the figures for remittances. In fact, many migrants prefer to carry their earnings in their pockets and/or to pass them through their network of friends who are traveling back home from Kazakhstan (Kakhkharov & Akimov, 2015).

Despite the recent decline, the flow of remittances to Uzbekistan remains significant, so they have a major influence on household expenditures. Whether remittances are spent on consumption or investment is important to policymaking because long-term economic effects depend on these expenditure patterns. If remittances finance enhancements in human capital, education, health outcomes, or small business development, their contribution to economic growth is maximized (Acosta, 2011). On the other hand, if remittances are spent primarily on consumption of status-oriented goods, their effect is less productive to the economy as a whole.

The body of research that investigates how remittances impact the consumption and investments of households in remittance-receiving countries has risen with the increasing size of international remittances. However, this impact remains little explored in Uzbekistan, even though the country presents a unique transition and development case in which a gradual approach to transition resulted in relatively good performance in the first decade of transition that became less positive in the second (Pomfret, 2010). A review of the literature shows an abundance of research on many remittance-receiving countries and how migrants and their families use remittances. However, the focus is on major consumption categories like education, health, and food. In particular, the literature fails to consider remittances' impact on expenditures on traditional and cultural ceremonies and status-oriented activities, which could be substantial in traditional societies. For example, Irnazarov (2015) estimates the cost of a wedding in Uzbekistan at around US$10,000, even though the average wage of an Uzbek migrant labourer from Uzbekistan in Russia is only about US$500 a month (Petrova, 2017). Finally, Uzbekistan's experience could be relevant to other transition countries in the region that are at a similar stage in their path to a market economy, that share a common history and culture, and that are alike in terms of exposure to remittances.

This paper bridges this gap in the research using unique household-level survey data collected by the German Agency for International Development (GIZ) and the World Bank in 2013, the 'Uzbekistan Jobs, Skills, and Migration Survey'. The data from the survey, which covers around 1500 households from all parts of Uzbekistan, allows us to scrutinize the impact of remittances on household expenditures on food, non-food consumer goods, health, education, and traditional ceremonies. We compare mean expenditures of households receiving remittances and those that do not to identify the differences in the expenditure patterns. The results provide evidence that households that receive remittances tend to spend these hard-won earnings on traditional ceremonies, wedding gifts, and non-food expenditures. The majority of these expenditures are aimed at increasing the household's social status and could be classified as manifestations of conspicuous consumption to display wealth and income, rather than to cover the consumer's investment needs. The paper also recommends policy measures that could help to rectify this situation.

The rest of the paper is organized as follows: section "Literature Review" reviews the literature on the topic, while section "Data Description and Methodology" presents the data and the research methodology. Section "Results" focuses on the results, and section "Conclusion and Policy Recommendations" draws conclusions and discusses policy implications.

Literature Review

The reasons migrants send remittances are central to the study of how households spend remittances. Lucas and Stark (1985) examine these motivations and create a theoretical framework for micro-level research on remittances. These authors identify three primary motivations at the household-level: 'pure altruism', 'pure self-interest', and 'tempered altruism or enlightened self-interest'. However, in many cases, these motives could account for the same type of migration and remittance behaviours. While a body of research attempts to distinguish on what motivations remittance behaviours depend, the process is difficult because survey data is not always sufficiently detailed.

Classical and neo-classical economic models view migrants as self-interested agents who leave their places of origin in search of new economic opportunities. Migrants' remittances represent the largest observable impact of migration on the migrant-sending areas. The New Economics of Labour Migration (NELM), which was developed by Stark (1991) and Stark's followers and colleagues, links remittance behaviour to migration decisions. According to the NELM, migration decisions are a 'calculated strategy' of households to improve the family's well-being, rather than an 'act of desperation or boundless optimism' (Stark, 1996, p. 26). By sending a member of a household to work in another country, the household seeks to maximize joint income and status and to minimize risks. The NELM also offers insight into migration decisions by linking labour migration with public policy and capital market failures in the labour-source countries. In making the decision to migrate for work, households in these countries design their own strategy to cope with the absence of appropriate credit, insurance instruments, and public protection. Remittances from a family member abroad provide an additional source of funding, insurance in case the main source of family income falters, and financial protection for a rainy day. As such, migration can be seen as risk aversion. As these findings show, the NELM is an innovative, realistic, and useful framework, and it is widely applied in recent migration studies.

Research on remittances in transition countries applying panel data techniques finds that a reduction in transaction costs and a depreciation of the currency in the host country are the main factors that influence the growth of recorded remittances (Kakhkharov, Akimov, & Rohde, 2017). Transfer fees charged by money transfer operators and banks remain a very important factor influencing the volume of formal remittances. Kakhkharov et al. (2017) conclude that inverse relationship between transaction costs and recorded remittances is due to the fact that migrants switch from informal channels to formal channels to send remittances when costs are low. Thus, lower transfer fees for remittances may help curb the proportion of informal flows and lead to increased use of remittances in the formal economy (Kakhkharov et al., 2017). In addition, it is also found that remittances impact financial development positively (Kakhkharov & Rohde, 2019). This is despite the fact that financial systems of countries in transition economies receiving significant part of remittances is less developed (Kakhkharov & Akimov, 2018).

A number of cross-country empirical studies on the effects of remittances show that remittances reduce poverty in migrant-sending countries (Acosta, Calderon, Fajnzylber, & Lopez, 2008; Adams & Page, 2005; Gupta, Pattillo, & Wagh, 2009). Adams and Page (2005) use one of the broadest set of countries, seventy-one developing nations, while Acosta et al. (2008) investigate the impact of remittances on poverty in ten Latin American countries, and Gupta et al. (2009) assess the poverty-mitigating effect of remittances in sub-Saharan Africa. All of these authors use OLS as a baseline estimation and augment the results with instrumental variable regressions to control for endogeneity. Acosta et al. (2008) also employ a two-stage Heckman model to control for selection, but the extent of poverty reduction in these estimations is only 3–5%. Country-specific analysis using household survey data also finds evidence that international remittances reduce poverty in Ghana (Adams, 2006), Nepal (Lokshin, Bontch-Osmolovski, & Glinskaya, 2010), Nicaragua (Barham & Boucher, 1998), Tonga (Jimenez-Soto & Brown, 2012), and Mexico (Lopez-Córdova, 2006; Taylor & Mora, 2006).

Many studies find that international remittances are predominantly spent on non-food items. For instance, Castaldo and Reilly (2007) for Albania and Tabuga (2007) for the Philippines find that families that receive remittances invest in durable goods, while Adams and Cuecuecha (2010), Fajnzylber and López (2008), and Taylor and Mora (2006) use household survey data for Guatemala, seven Latin American countries, and Mexico, respectively, to report that households that receive remittances allocate a smaller share of income to food relative to what they would spend without remittances.

Remittances also appear to improve health outcomes in the households that receive remittances. Several studies that use data for Mexico find evidence of this outcome in their empirical research (Duryea, Loīpez-Coīrdova, & Olmedo, 2005; Hildebrandt, McKenzie, Esquivel, & Schargrodsky, 2005; Lopez-Córdova, 2006). De and Ratha (2012) show that remittances benefit children's health in Sri Lanka; Amuedo-Dorantes and Pozo (2011), Amuedo-Dorantes, Sainz, and Pozo (2007), Valero-Gil (2009), and Fajnzylber and López (2008) report a rise in health expenditures among households in Mexico that receive remittances; and Cardona Sosa and Medina (2006) document a positive impact of international remittances on health expenses in Colombia.

Evidence on whether remittances increase household spending on education is mixed. For example, Cox-Edwards and Ureta (2003), Calero, Bedi, and Sparrow (2009), and De and Ratha (2012) report a beneficial influence of remittances on children's education in El Salvador, Ecuador, and Sri Lanka, respectively. Adams and Cuecuecha (2010) in Guatemala, Kifle (2007) in Eritrea, Cardona Sosa and Medina (2006) in Colombia, and Yang (2008) in the Philippines also conclude that households that receive remittances spend more on education than do households that do not receive remittances. However, Fajnzylber and López (2008) use data from seven Latin American countries to find a positive impact of remittances on education spending for El Salvador, Guatemala, the Dominican Republic, and Peru, while reporting the opposite impact for Jamaica and no impact for Mexico and Nicaragua. In investigating the effect of remittances in Albania, Cattaneo (2012) concludes that remittances have no influence on education spending, while McKenzie and Rapoport (2011) and Lopez-Córdova (2006) report that remittances have a significant negative effect on the school attendance of teenagers in Mexico.

Despite pessimistic concerns that significant proportions of remittances are spent on status-oriented consumption goods, diverting funds from productive investment activities (Airola, 2007; Carling, 2008; Zarate-Hoyos, 2004), the empirical evidence of this effect is scant, perhaps because the detail in the household data is not sufficient. Some examples of conspicuous consumption are found from interviews with migrant households (Day & Içduygu, 1999). To the best of our knowledge, the only recent empirical study that finds evidence of remittance-receiving households engaging in conspicuous consumption is in the case of the Philippines (Tabuga, 2007).

Empirical research in Uzbekistan says little about the consumption patterns of families that send labour migrants. A common problem for researchers is the lack of reliable data on labour migration and the families left behind. As a result, the studies are mainly descriptive or based on small-scale surveys with non-representative samples. For example, Radnitz (2006) uses a survey of 200 people in Tashkent, Uzbekistan. Another research uses data from the Uzbekistan Jobs, Skills, and Migration Survey, which was developed and conducted jointly by the German Society for International Cooperation (GIZ) and the World Bank in 2013–2014, to find that remittances have a significant positive effect on non-food and healthcare expenditures and a negative impact on food spending among families that receive remittances compared to those that do not (Ahunov, Kakhkharov, Parpiev, & Wolfson, 2015). This research applies the Engel curve framework, supplemented by instrumental variable estimations, to correct for endogeneity. Since this strategy relies on the robustness of available instruments, the results are highly sensitive to the quality of the instruments (Adams, 2011). Kakhkharov (2019) finds that households receiving remittances may invest in family business only when this inflow is supplemented with sufficient income or savings. Finally, based on interviews with labour migrants, Juraev (2012) notes that survival is no longer the main reason for labour migration in Uzbekistan, as remittances are spent mainly on the purchase of non-essentials like real estate and cars.

One of the few rigorous empirical studies of the impact of remittances on household expenditures in a Central Asian country (Tajikistan) is (Clément, 2011), which uses PSM analysis to find that households that receive remittances spend more on food, non-food items, and health than do households that do not receive remittances. However, Clément (2011) finds no evidence of a significant effect of remittances on education expenditures.

Data Description and Methodology

Data

This study uses data from a survey of the jobs, skills, and migration patterns of citizens in Uzbekistan, the Uzbekistan Jobs, Skills, and Migration Survey, to explore the link between remittances and investment. The survey collected comprehensive information not typically captured by traditional household surveys and is representative at the national, regional (Oblast), and urban/rural levels. Two instruments are employed in the survey: a core questionnaire and a skills questionnaire. The sample size of the core questionnaire is 1500 households (8622 individuals). One adult individual per household ($N=1500$) was randomly selected to partake in the skills questionnaire. The second questionnaire's sample consisted of 1500 individuals.

The core questionnaire contains modules that focus on education, employment, migration, health expenditure, remittances, government transfers, financial services, subjective poverty, housing conditions, and household expenditures, while the skills questionnaire contains detailed modules on labour and work expectations, migration and preparation for migration, language skills, and technical skill training.

12 Squandering Remittances Income in Conspicuous Consumption?

Table 12.1 Descriptive statistics

	Obs.	Mean	SD	Min.	Max.
Households that declare remittances as part of their income	1432	0.28	0.45	0	1.00
Households that declare that remittances constitute at least 50% of their income	1432	0.21	0.41	0	1.00
Household size (number of household members)	1432	5.71	2.32	1	17.00
Number of female members aged 16–60	1432	1.83	0.96	0	5.00
Share of children under 7 years old	1432	0.12	0.14	0	0.67
Household members 60 and older	1432	0.53	0.76	0	4.00
Members aged 16–60	1432	3.63	1.67	0	10.00
Dummy: 1 = migrant-sending household, 0 otherwise	1432	0.26	0.44	0	1.00
Self-employed with hired labour	1432	0.81	0.98	0	6.00
Self-employed, as a share of members aged 16–60	1432	0.25	0.58	0	5.00
Members employed in an occasional job	1432	0.17	0.52	0	6.00
Members employed in a temporary job	1432	0.19	0.53	0	5.00
Members employed in a permanent job	1432	0.94	1.04	0	6.00
Members employed in an informal job	1432	0.96	1.13	0	7.00
Dummy: 1 if a household is in a rural area, 0 otherwise	1432	0.63	0.48	0	1.00
Dummy: 1 if a household head is a female, 0 otherwise	1432	0.23	0.42	0	1.00
Dummy: 1 if a household head is married, 0 otherwise	1432	0.75	0.97	0	1.00
Dummy: 1 if a household head is an agricultural worker, 0 otherwise	1432	0.14	0.35	0	1.00
Dummy: 1 if a household head has a higher education, 0 otherwise	1432	0.18	0.39	0	1.00
Dummy: 1 if a household head speaks Russian, 0 otherwise	1432	0.76	0.43	0	1.00
Dummy: 1 if a household head belongs to an ethnic minority, 0 otherwise	1432	0.13	0.34	0	1.00

Source Calculated using the survey data collected by the authors

The descriptive statistics in Table 12.1 show that 28% of households revealed that they receive remittances and that remittances for 21% of all household constitute at least half of their income. Only 26% of households said they had sent a migrant overseas, so it appears that predominantly migrant households have access to remittances, while a smaller number of households may be receiving remittances

Table 12.2 Households with and without migrants

	Non-migrants	Migrants	Total
Number of children under age 5	0.47	0.61	0.52
	(0.73)	(0.85)	(0.78)
Number of children under age 10	1.00	1.14	1.05
	(1.12)	(1.22)	(1.16)
Household size (number of household members)	5.37	6.45	5.75
	(2.24)	(2.34)	(2.33)
Education			
None	0.02	0.01	0.02
	(0.14)	(0.11)	(0.13)
Primary	0.02	0.02	0.02
	(0.13)	(0.13)	(0.13)
Basic	0.07	0.06	0.06
	(0.25)	(0.23)	(0.24)
Secondary	0.38	0.44	0.40
	(0.49)	(0.50)	(0.49)
Secondary special	0.24	0.28	0.26
	(0.43)	(0.45)	(0.44)
Secondary technical	0.06	0.06	0.06
	(0.25)	(0.24)	(0.24)
Higher education	0.20	0.14	0.18
	(0.40)	(0.35)	(0.38)
Graduate school	0.00	0.00	0.00
	(0.03)	(0.00)	(0.03)
Observations	1432		

Source Calculated using the survey data collected by the authors
Notes Mean coefficients; standard deviation in parentheses

from extended family members, friends, or distant relatives. The mean household size of 5.71 members and the average number of household members aged 60 or older (0.53 members) are signs of high dependency ratio that could be pushing labour migrants overseas in search of higher income to sustain dependents. In addition, the descriptive statistics suggest that most of the households that participated in the survey—and since the survey was nationally representative most of the households in Uzbekistan (63%)—are in rural areas.

Table 12.2 compares households in terms of whether they sent a labour migrant to another country. Since sending a migrant to work is closely associated with the receipt of remittances, this characteristic could be interpreted as a comparison of households that receive and do not receive remittances. It appears that households that sent migrants tend to have more children under age 5 and age 10 and overall larger household sizes. In addition, members of these households have greater secondary or secondary specialized (vocational tertiary) education and less higher education, confirming that most labourers from Uzbekistan go to work in Russia to do '3D' jobs–dirty, dangerous, and demeaning. In general, it appears that households receiving remittances and those that do not have similar characteristics probably due to location in the same market with quite homogenous structure.

Methodology

The method we use to identify the impact of remittances on household expenditures in this research is juxtaposing the means of the outcomes of interest for remittance recipients and non-recipients to see the differences between these two types of households. This method assumes the recipient and non-recipient households are randomly assigned, as in a controlled experiment, or that their characteristics are identical. We acknowledge that households that send a family member overseas and receive remittances may differ from households that do not. For example, that one household has more dependents than another might affect the outcome variables and make it difficult to ascertain whether the differences in the observable outcomes are due to exposure to remittances or to the difference in the number of dependents. Nevertheless, since as descriptive statistics show, in this country case study the characteristics of remittance recipient and non-recipient households appear to be similar, comparing means could give interesting insights on how households, whose exposure to remittances differs, spend their income.[1]

---

[1] The authors intend to further develop their analysis by using propensity score matching methodology in future.

Table 12.3 Mean differences in household spending for certain items (in logs of Uzbek soums)

Expenditure	Households with no remittances as a source of income (1)	Households with remittances part of their income (2)	Mean difference (2) − (1) (3)	Households whose remittances constitute at least 50% of their income (4)	Mean difference (4) − (1) (5)
School fees/tuition	3.45 (2.47)	3.31 (2.52)	−0.14 (0.16)	3.41 (2.51)	−0.04 (0.18)
Private tutoring	0.34 (1.08)	0.30 (0.99)	−0.04 (0.07)	0.34 (1.02)	0.00 (0.08)
Food	3.07 (0.64)	2.91 (0.55)	−0.16*** (0.04)	2.91 (0.57)	−0.16*** (0.04)
Dining out	1.51 (1.02)	1.43 (1.06)	−0.08 (0.13)	1.39 (1.02)	−0.12 (0.15)
Non-food	4.29 (1.41)	4.57 (1.61)	0.28*** (0.09)	4.63 (1.62)	0.35*** (0.10)
Maintenance and repair of personal vehicles	5.46 (1.28)	5.47 (1.20)	0.01 (0.17)	5.53 (1.17)	0.07 (0.20)
Home improvements	5.58 (1.60)	6.07 (1.37)	0.49*** (0.19)	6.09 (1.37)	0.51*** (0.21)
Small electric appliances	6.68 (1.33)	7.21 (1.42)	0.53*** (0.15)	7.29 (1.44)	0.61*** (0.16)
Vehicle, land, and property tax	3.61 (0.75)	3.60 (0.80)	0.00 (0.11)	3.61 (0.76)	0.00 (0.13)
Wedding gifts	4.50 (0.59)	4.55 (0.59)	0.05 (0.04)	4.61 (0.54)	0.11*** (0.05)
Ceremonies	4.99 (1.11)	5.09 (1.06)	0.10 (0.07)	5.13 (1.05)	0.14* (0.08)
Observations	1497	1497		1387	

Source Calculated using the survey data collected by the authors
Notes Standard errors are in parentheses. *p<0.1, **p<0.05, ***p<0.01

Results

Table 12.3 compares the means of some household expenditures in logs of Uzbek soums. Using data from the Uzbekistan Jobs, Skills, and Migration Survey, this comparison is made for households that receive remittances and those that do not receive remittances and for households whose remittances constitute more than 50% of their income and those that do not receive remittances. It appears that both categories of households that receive remittances spend less on food and more on non-food items than do households that do not receive remittances. They also tend to spend greater amounts in Uzbek soums on home improvement and small electric appliances. In addition, households that generate more than 50% of their income from remittances spend 2.4% more on wedding gifts and 2.8% more on traditional rites/ceremonies (e.g., weddings, birthdays) than do households that do not receive remittances.

Conclusion and Policy Recommendations

Remittances have become a very important international flow of funds affecting many macro-and micro-economic parametres in the recipient economies. Estimating the impact of remittances on household expenditures could be crucial for policymaking as the way how these funds are spent has vital economic consequences. In the present research endeavour, we compare average expenditures of households receiving remittances with those that do not using GIZ/World Bank household survey data. The main purpose is to investigate the impact of remittances on household expenditures in Uzbekistan. This straightforward comparison of expenditures patterns indicates that households in Uzbekistan that receive remittances engage, despite their relatively meagre incomes, in conspicuous consumption by spending more on marriage gifts and wedding ceremonies.

Our research's findings show policymakers how remittances are spent by recipient households, so they can encourage channelling these resources into productive investments, rather than wedding gifts and ceremonies. For example, public policy measures could be designed to teach households about the benefits of investment in human and business capital versus the illusory advantages of increasing social status.

One limitation of the present research is that the method comparing mean expenditures in logs of local currency assumes the recipient and non-recipient households are identical. Although the summary statistics of the survey indicate that these two sets of households are similar, they are not identical. In other words, households receiving remittances may have a number of characteristics that make them different from those households that do not. These differences may include educational attainment, marital status of the household head and many other community and social attributes. Obviously, the presence of these differences makes it difficult to ascertain whether the differences in the mean expenditures are due to exposure to remittances or to the differences in the individual, social, or community characteristics.

Finally, migration and remittances research elsewhere shows that the best way to stimulate efficient use of remittances is to create an economic environment that facilitates development in general, presents favourable conditions for conducting business, and offers a well-functioning financial system. An education and vocational system that focuses on helping households develop entrepreneurial skills would also help to induce migrants to invest in their home economies and reap the benefits of remittances more efficiently.

References

Acosta, P. (2011). School attendance, child labour, and remittances from international migration in El Salvador. *Journal of Development Studies, 47*(6), 913–936.

Acosta, P., Calderon, C., Fajnzylber, P., & Lopez, H. (2008). What is the impact of international remittances on poverty and inequality in Latin America? *World Development, 36*(1), 89–114.

Adams, R. H. (2006). *Remittances and poverty in Ghana*.

Adams, R. H. (2011). Evaluating the economic impact of international remittances on developing countries using household surveys: A literature review. *Journal of Development Studies, 47*(6), 809–828.

12 Squandering Remittances Income in Conspicuous Consumption?

Adams, R. H., & Cuecuecha, A. (2010). Remittances, household expenditure and investment in Guatemala. *World Development, 38*(11), 1626–1641.

Adams, R. H., & Page, J. (2005). Do international migration and remittances reduce poverty in developing countries? *World Development, 33*(10), 1645–1669.

Ahunov, M., Kakhkharov, J., Parpiev, Z., & Wolfson, I. (2015). *Socio-economic consequences of labor migration in Uzbekistan* (Discussion Paper Series in Economics, Griffith University, Department of Accounting, Finance and Economics, 201507).

Airola, J. (2007). The use of remittance income in Mexico. *International Migration Review, 41*(4), 850–859.

Amuedo-Dorantes, C., & Pozo, S. (2011). New evidence on the role of remittances on healthcare expenditures by Mexican households. *Review of Economics of the Household, 9*(1), 69–98.

Amuedo-Dorantes, C., Sainz, T., & Pozo, S. (2007). *Remittances and healthcare expenditure patterns of populations in origin communities: Evidence from Mexico* (Working Paper ITD. Documento de Trabajo ITD; 25). BID-INTAL.

Barham, B., & Boucher, S. (1998). Migration, remittances, and inequality: Estimating the net effects of migration on income distribution. *Journal of Development Economics, 55*(2), 307–331.

Bobylev, Y., Firanchuk, A., Florinskaya, Y., Khromov, M., Knobel, A., Mkrtchyan, N., & Tsukhlo, S. (Producer). (2017). Мониторинг Экономической Ситуации в России. Тенденции и Вызовы Социально-Экономического Развития [Monitoring of Russia's economic outlook: Trends and challenges of socio-economic development]. Retrieved from http://www.iep.ru/files/text/crisis_monitoring/2017_12-50_June.pdf.

Calero, C., Bedi, A. S., & Sparrow, R. (2009). Remittances, liquidity constraints and human capital investments in Ecuador. *World Development, 37*(6), 1143–1154.

Cardona Sosa, L., & Medina, C. (2006). *Migration as a safety net and effects of remittances on household consumption: The case of Colombia.* Borradores de Economia 414, Banco de la Republica de Colombia, Bogota. Retrieved from http://repositorio.banrep.gov.co/bitstream/handle/20.500.12134/5432/BORRADOR%20414.pdf?sequence=1.

Carling, J. (2008). Interrogating remittances: Core questions for deeper insight and better policies. In *Migration and development: Perspectives from the south* (pp. 43–64). Geneva: International Organization for Migration.

Castaldo, A., & Reilly, B. (2007). Do migrant remittances affect the consumption patterns of Albanian households? *South-Eastern Europe Journal of Economics, 5*(1), 25–54.

Cattaneo, C. (2012). Migrants' international transfers and educational expenditure. *Economics of Transition, 20*(1), 163–193.

Central Bank of Russia. (2014). *Cross-border remittances via money transfer operators and post offices in breakdown by countries 2013*. Available from Central Bank of Russia cross-border remittances via money transfer operators and post offices in breakdown by countries from Central Bank of Russia. http://cbr.ru/statistics/print.aspx?file=CrossBorder/Rem_countries_13.htm&pid=svs&sid=TGO_sp_post.

Central Bank of Russia. (2016). *Cross-border remittances of individuals in breakdown by countries 2016 from Central Bank of Russia*. http://cbr.ru/statistics/?PrtId=svs.

Clément, M. (2011). Remittances and household expenditure patterns in Tajikistan: A propensity score matching analysis. *Asian Development Review, 28*(2), 58–87.

Cox-Edwards, A., & Ureta, M. (2003). International migration, remittances, and schooling: Evidence from El Salvador. *Journal of Development Economics, 72*(2), 429–461.

Day, L. H., & Içduygu, A. (1999). Does international migration encourage consumerism in the country of origin?—A Turkish study. *Population and Environment, 20*(6), 503–525.

De, P. K., & Ratha, D. (2012). Impact of remittances on household income, asset and human capital: Evidence from Sri Lanka. *Migration and Development, 1*(1), 163–179.

Duryea, S., Loīpez-Coīrdova, E., & Olmedo, A. (2005). *Migrant remittances and infant mortality: Evidence from Mexico*. Washington: Inter-American Development Bank.

Fajnzylber, P., & López, J. H. (2008). The development impact of remittances in Latin America. In P. Fajnzylber & J. H. Lopez (Eds.), *Remittances and Development: Lessons from Latin America* (pp. 1–21). Washington, DC: World Bank.

Gupta, S., Pattillo, C. A., & Wagh, S. (2009). Effect of remittances on poverty and financial development in Sub-Saharan Africa. *World Development, 37*(1), 104–115.

Hildebrandt, N., McKenzie, D. J., Esquivel, G., & Schargrodsky, E. (2005). The effects of migration on child health in Mexico [with comments]. *Economia, 6*(1), 257–289.

Irnazarov, F. (2015). *Labour migrant households in Uzbekistan: Remittances as a challenge or blessing* (The Central Asia Fellowship Papers, No. 11).
Jimenez-Soto, E. V., & Brown, R. P. (2012). Assessing the poverty impacts of migrants' remittances using propensity score matching: The case of Tonga. *Economic Record, 88*(282), 425–439.
Juraev, A. (2012). *Labor migration from Uzbekistan: Social and economic impacts on local development*. University of Trento.
Kakhkharov, J. (2019). Migrant remittances as a source of financing for entrepreneurship. *International Migration.* https://doi.org/10.1111/imig.12531.
Kakhkharov, J., & Akimov, A. (2015). Estimating remittances in the former Soviet Union: Methodological complexities and potential solutions. In *Neotransitional economics* (pp. 337–362). Bingley: Emerald Group Publishing Limited.
Kakhkharov, J., & Akimov, A. (2018). Financial development in less-developed post-communist economies. *Problems of Economic Transition, 60*(7), 483–513.
Kakhkharov, J., Akimov, A., & Rohde, N. (2017). Transaction costs and recorded remittances in the post-Soviet economies: Evidence from a new dataset on bilateral flows. *Economic Modelling, 60,* 98–107.
Kakhkharov, J., & Rohde, N. (2019). *Empirical Economics.* https://doi.org/10.1007/s00181-019-01642-3.
Kifle, T. (2007). Do remittances encourage investment in education? Evidence from Eritrea. *GEFAME Journal of African Studies, 4*(1). Retrieved from http://hdl.handle.net/2027/spo.4761563.0004.101.
Lokshin, M., Bontch-Osmolovski, M., & Glinskaya, E. (2010). Work-related migration and poverty reduction in Nepal. *Review of Development Economics, 14*(2), 323–332.
Lopez-Córdova, J. E. (2006). *Globalization, migration and development: The role of Mexican migrant remittances* (Working Paper ITD = Documento de Trabajo ITD; n. 20, Vol. 20). BID-INTAL.
Lucas, R. E., & Stark, O. (1985). Motivations to remit: Evidence from Botswana. *Journal of Political Economy, 93*(5), 901–918.
McKenzie, D., & Rapoport, H. (2011). Can migration reduce educational attainment? Evidence from Mexico. *Journal of Population Economics, 24*(4), 1331–1358.
National Bank of Kazakhstan. (2016). *Payment systems: International and local remittances.* http://nationalbank.kz/?docid=502&switch=english.

Petrova, N. (2017). Мигрант с натуры [Migrants in nature]. *Kommersant*. Retrieved from https://www.kommersant.ru/doc/3380376.
Pomfret, R. (2010). Constructing market-based economies in Central Asia: A natural experiment? *The European Journal of Comparative Economics, 7*(2), 449.
Radnitz, S. (2006). Weighing the political and economic motivations for migration in post-Soviet space: The case of Uzbekistan. *Europe-Asia Studies, 58*(5), 653–677.
Seidakhmetov, B. (2017). Трудовая миграция меняет вектор [Labour migration changes direction]. *Exclusive resources for professionals*.
Stark, O. (1991). *The migration of labor*. Cambridge, MA: Basil Blackwell.
Stark, O. (1996). On the microeconomics of return migration. In *Trade and development* (pp. 32–41). Vienna: Springer.
Tabuga, A. D. (2007). *International remittances and household expenditures: The Philippine case*. PIDS Discussion Paper No. 2007-18, Philippine Institute for Development Studies, Makati City. Retrieved from https://www.econstor.eu/bitstream/10419/127952/1/pids-dps2007-18.pdf.
Taylor, J. E., & Mora, J. (2006). *Does migration reshape expenditures in rural households? Evidence from Mexico* (Vol. 3842). Washington, DC: World Bank Publications.
Valero-Gil, J. N. (2009). Remittances and the household's expenditures on health. *Journal of Business Strategies, 26*(1), 119.
Yang, D. (2008). International migration, remittances and household investment: Evidence from Philippine migrants' exchange rate shocks. *The Economic Journal, 118*(528), 591–630.
Zarate-Hoyos, G. A. (2004). Consumption and remittances in migrant households: Toward a productive use of remittances. *Contemporary Economic Policy, 22*(4), 555–565.

13

Equal Citizenship, Language, and Ethnicity Dilemmas in the Context of the Post-Socialist Legal Reforms in Central Asia

Aziz Ismatov

Introduction

Citizenship is a highly controversial concept with no generally recognized definition. Yet, it is one of the most essential elements of sovereignty which defines the initial body of the state. Presently, citizenship is considered to be a key instrument for the enjoyment of rights which remain unavailable for stateless persons or non-nationals. Traditionally, international law posed no concrete limitations in respect to citizenship, considering it to be an independent matter for each state. In turn, states are very reluctant to share their sovereignty with international law in terms of citizenship. Those few existing limitations address mainly avoidance of de jure statelessness or undetermined status for spouses and children. Scholars and practitioners involved into the topic often question the effectiveness of such limitations. In fact, when one

A. Ismatov (✉)
Nagoya University, Center for Asian Legal Exchange (CALE), Nagoya, Japan
e-mail: ismatov@law.nagoya-u.ac.jp

takes a closer look into actual situation, it is evident that existing practice provides very few cases in which citizenship-related disputes have been successfully resolved by international rules. Furthermore, it is necessary to address a variety of sources in order to find out more about those rules, namely to answer the question; what are the existing international limitations (Pilgram, 2011, p. 2).

The regulation of citizenship becomes more complicated in situations where two or more states are involved. When a federal entity is dissolved into sovereign states, apart from the unpredictable internal effect, new citizenship laws might extend beyond territorial borders and result in negative interstate relations or even in conflict (Tishkov, 2007, p. 241). Above all, they may negatively impact on individuals who suddenly find themselves in a legal limbo or face considerable difficulty in establishing a legal status. Another problem in cases of dissolution is the difficulty of determining particular rights or international obligations of old and new states in relation to citizens or those who compose groups of potential citizens.

In the post-Soviet space, the problem of Baltic non-nationals, especially in Latvia and Estonia became the first problem to draw significant international attention from various international actors. The new political elites in these two countries headed toward the restoration of preoccupied statehood and therefore, within the context of state continuity doctrine reintroduced the prewar citizenship laws which automatically excluded significant number of Russian-speaking population who came to these countries during the USSR period (Ziemele, 2005, p. 386). Subsequently, failed policies on compatriots caused citizenship-related problems in the Russian Federation—a successor of the USSR.

This paper asserts that when CA republics were catapulted into independence, their authorities have quite unpreparedly initiated citizenship reforms which, however, compared to the Baltics, contained only minor components based on nationalistic views. On the other hand, reforms generated laws on language which gave priority to titular languages. The new governments also started placing representatives of titular nations in high governmental positions. In the years following independence, together with restored culture and history, the new authorities in each CA state promoted the idea of a restored titular nation.

In such circumstances, the growing wave of nationalism questioned the place of minorities in the future nation-states.

The scope of the present paper is geographically and objectively limited to the CA states. It aims to analyze the domestic citizenship laws in texts and states' receptivity toward international human rights norms amid the collapse of the federative state. While analyzing rules and policies which govern citizenship policies in each of the states, the research also focuses on such sensitive elements as language laws and ethnicity in order to find out about existing legal and social distinctions between "insiders" and "outsiders" or in other words, examine the inclusive and exclusive components of the citizenship laws. The main question which the discussion in this research attempts to answer refers to the issues of post-socialist citizenship and language reforms. Namely, have the choices integrated in the citizenship laws of the CA states been aimed at including or excluding the nonethnic component of their populations from own citizenship, and thus reducing their rights and freedoms in these countries? Do citizenship and language solutions comply with applicable rules of international law?

Terminological Axiom

It should be noted that international citizenship law presently suffers from terminological chaos in the form of the different usages of "nationality" and "citizenship." The Western approach equally addresses nationality and citizenship. The terms are considered as synonyms, and therefore most of the laws are called—nationality acts. In the Russian context, however, such terms do not have the same meaning. In particular, the term "nationality" has an equal significance with the "ethnicity" (ethnic background) of the person. On the other hand, the term citizenship (*grazhdanstvo*) specifies legal and political bond between state and individual.

In terms of the present research, such linguistic axioms may create wrong perceptions since the CA states regard citizenship and nationality as entirely different concepts. In their passport systems, some of these states use citizenship—to show the legal and political link with a state and, simultaneously, nationality—to show the ethnic background of the person (Smith, Law, Wilson, Allworth, & Bohr, 1998, p. 119). At present, these terms have not been carefully examined by researchers and are still differently addressed throughout the literature in the area. In order not to mislead the reader, the present research will use words citizenship and avoid using the term nationality (Some explanation is available in Brubaker, 1992).

The Regulation of Citizenship in the Central Asian States

Constitutional and Statutory Provisions

A detailed concept of implementing zero-option in all five Central Asian republics appeared between 1990–1995 in their constitutions and pioneer citizenship statutes (Ismatov, 2014, p. 197). This concept automatically recognized as citizens those people who by the critical dates had USSR citizenship and registered permanent residence in the country (Art. 4, the 1992 Citizenship law of Uzbekistan; Art. 39, the 1992 Citizenship law of Turkmenistan; Art. 3, the 1991 Citizenship law of Kazakhstan; Art. 3, the 2017 Citizenship law of the Kyrgyz Republic [and also outdated 1993 and 2007 laws]). The critical date was associated with the date of adoption of the new citizenship laws by the respective national parliaments. The former USSR passports with stamps specifying residence details of the bearer, including *propiska*, enabled the authorities to ascertain the place of habitual residence on the critical date (Ismatov, 2014, p. 131).

The law in Uzbekistan, Kazakhstan, and Kyrgyz Republic specified citizenship as a legal and political bond between the individual and the state, whereas the Tajik and Turkmen laws omit the word political. In Uzbekistan, the law separately stated that Uzbek citizenship was conferred on the residents of Kara-Kalpak Autonomy which is a part of Uzbekistan (Art. 2, the 1992 Citizenship law of Uzbekistan). This moment separately makes a notion that Uzbekistan is a state with the elements of federalism.

Hence, the constitutions and citizenship statutes in all five CA republics maintained that citizenship of their respective individuals is determined on the basis of the principle of state succession. This, indeed, puts them in a position entirely different from Baltic republics such as Latvia and Estonia, which implemented the principle of state continuity and denied zero-option in their respective citizenship laws. Based on such conditions, one may assert that CA states adopted inclusive citizenship concepts and codified them in relevant statutes which are in line with the general principles of international law regarding the dissolution of federal state and regulation of citizenship of population in the respective territory.

Language and Other Naturalization Requirements

Naturalization policy in Uzbekistan requires five years of permanent residency and renunciation of any other existing citizenship (Art. 17, the 1992 Citizenship law of Uzbekistan; Sec. II, the 1992 Regulation No. UP-500). The residency requirement is not applied in cases where the applicant can demonstrate that one of his parents or grandparents was born in the territory of Uzbekistan (Art. 17, the 1992 Citizenship law of Uzbekistan; Sec. II, the 1992 Regulation No. UP-500). There are no legal provisions for simplified naturalization for compatriots such as former USSR citizens or co-ethnics. The Uzbek law does not require language exam for naturalization. With certain amendments, the authorities have also started requiring a medical certificate which proves that the applicant is free of HIV/AIDS (Art. 4, chapter II (b)(1), the 1992 Regulation No. UP-500).

In the Kyrgyz Republic, the most recent 2017 law on citizenship offers the most detailed set of rules specifying various modes of naturalization for former USSR citizens, stateless, foreigners, and other categories including co-ethnics. For example, this law recognized as citizens the USSR passport-holders residing in the country for five years without applying for the citizenship of another state (Art. 14 (2), the 2017 Citizenship law of Kyrgyz Republic). The same residency period is applied for foreigners and stateless persons (Art. 17, 22–25; Art. 10, the

2007 Regulation No. 473). This requirement might be shortened from five to three years for certain persons who meet individual criteria outlined in law, which is usually ability to invest into various sectors (Art. 20–24, the 2007 Regulation No. 473). The Kyrgyz law also requires the knowledge of the state or official languages which are, respectively, Kyrgyz or Russian. The language requirement lies in the ability to make an individual understood him/herself and ability to interact with the society (Art. 13, I (2), the 2007 Regulation No. 473). The language sufficiency however not required from Kyrgyz co-ethnics willing to naturalize (Art. 25, the 2007 Regulation No. 473). The provision on language is very vague as law does not specify in concrete terms how to evaluate the language competence.

The naturalization procedure in Kazakhstan similarly requires the residence period of five years (Art. 16, the 1991 Citizenship law of Kazakhstan; the 1996 Regulation No. 3120). However, this might be lifted for co-ethnics, for example—*Oralman*, and persons repressed by the Soviet regime (Art. 16-1 (1, 2, 3), the 1991 Citizenship law of Kazakhstan). Usually, they are exempted from various fees and do not have to follow the five-year residency requirement (Para 15 (9), the 2002 Order No. 556). The Kazakh law also offers a simplified naturalization for former USSR citizens in case if they have at least one relative who is a citizen of Kazakhstan regardless of the residence period (Art. 16, the 1991 Citizenship law of Kazakhstan). Similarly, to Uzbekistan, the Kazakh law also does not require language exam for naturalization.

A pioneer citizenship law of Tajikistan also required five or three-year residence for naturalization. Former USSR citizens have a priority for a simplified naturalization in which the residence requirement may be lifted entirely (Art. 22–23, the 1995 Citizenship law of Tajikistan). Tajik law also poses no language exam requirement.

The Turkmen citizenship law is obviously the most restrictive among other CA states as apart from the five-year residence it also requires the knowledge of the Turkmen language (ability to communicate at a daily level) and legal sources of income (Art. 12, the 1992 Citizenship law of Turkmenistan). The residence requirement can be lifted in cases when co-ethnics, namely, Turkmen and their descendants, and former

USSR citizens who have a relative in Turkmenistan (Art. 12, the 1992 Citizenship law of Turkmenistan).

With exception of Turkmen law's provision on Turkmen language and partly, Kyrgyz Republic's requirement of Kyrgyz or Russian, other CA states pose no language requirements. Whereas laws in Turkmenistan, Kyrgyz Republic and Kazakhstan offer specific naturalization priorities for co-ethnics, Tajik and Uzbek laws do not stipulate similar clauses. Simultaneously, while four states offer preferences for the former USSR citizens, the Uzbek law contains no similar norms.

While the citizenship laws in CA republics designate specific bodies in charge of the citizenship affairs, it is only the Kazakh law which gives an explicit provision for due process guarantees and legal remedies to review the decisions of such body. The Kazakh law also guarantees that decisions regarding the loss of citizenship do not come in force until the person concerned has been informed. Relevant legislation also allows individuals to seek a reconsideration of the presidential decision on nationality (Art. 28–32, the 2000 Regulation). Procedural violations can be appealed through the court (Art. 41, the 1991 Citizenship law of Kazakhstan).

In case of other CA republics, laws do not clearly stipulate legal provisions on the rights or remedies to seek information about the status and the outcome of application. The absence of proper provisions and mechanisms to seek information and to appeal the decision on citizenship increase the risk of maladministration and poor protection of individual rights. Simultaneously, while some norms briefly mention about the right to seek reconsideration of the authorities' decision, there is no provision on review of naturalization process. Furthermore, constitutional principle of *actio popularis,* often used in European and some Asian jurisdictions, still remains widely unknown in CA region.

General Statutory Prohibition of Discrimination

The constitutions and relevant statutory regulations in all CA states provide a right to acquire citizenship irrespective of racial, ethnic, linguistic, and cultural origin. Hence, any discrimination on the basis of ethnicity and language are de jure outlawed. There is a particular discrepancy between the constitutions, laws on citizenship, and essential statutory regulations regarding their lists on the grounds for nondiscrimination. For example, the clause on language raises well-grounded concerns regarding the requirement of the Turkmen citizenship law on Turkmen language. Simultaneously, except the Tajik law, the rest of the mentioned countries provide in their laws a separate provision of equal citizenship for all individuals regardless its acquisition (Art. 2, the 1992 Citizenship law of Uzbekistan; Art. 5, the 1991 Citizenship law of Kazakhstan; Art. 4, the 1992 Citizenship law of Turkmenistan; Art. 8 Citizenship law of Kyrgyz Republic). While the contradictions between constitutions, principal statutes, and regulations may exist, according to the principles of CA states' legal systems, the right to acquire citizenship would apply without any discrimination listed either in the constitution and relevant statutes. Hence, the basic principles for naturalization in legal texts of CA republics, with the exception of certain vague provisions on language in Turkmenistan and Kyrgyz Republic, seem to comply with the general international standards, and to some extent, even extra inclusive because some states go beyond and do not require any language proficiency exam. It is however, often the case, that regulations and orders bureaucratize heavily the procedural matters and restrict individuals to obtain information on the status of their applications. Seeking legal remedy in such cases is usually burdensome and complicated.

Ethnic Minorities and Their Rights in the Context of Citizenship

In the initial years of independence, all CA republics held a considerable minority population (S. Abashin in Bassin & Kelly, 2012, p. 150). Notably, Kazakhstan and Kyrgyz Republic hosted the largest Slavic population in comparison to their own population, whereas the minority groups in Turkmenistan, Uzbekistan, and Tajikistan composed mainly non-Russians (Fierman, 2006, p. 1088) As an example, the population of Uzbekistan by 1990 comprised more than 23 million people. "The titular majority was over 17 million people, but there were representatives of more than 100 nationalities (ethnicities) in the republic. Besides Uzbeks, there were more than million Tajiks and approximately the same number of Russians and Kazakhs, 420,000 KaraKalpaks, up to 300,000 Tatars, about 200,000 Koreans, more than 170,000 Kyrgyz, over 150,000 Ukrainians, and approximately the same number of Turkmen and Armenians" (Mesamed, 1996, pp. 20–26). Such a heterogeneous ethnic composition, not only in Uzbekistan but also in neighboring states was mainly created by the Soviet practices of human resources movement, deportations, and also evacuations during the Second World War. Some aspects of migration were also echoed in the Tsarist migration policies in Turkestan (*Pereselencheskaya politika*). As the Soviets created the present borders in CA artificially, sometimes the whole territories which once hosted different ethnic and language groups were transferred under jurisdiction of particular Soviet CA republic (Refer for details to Ubiria, 2015).

Although the CA states hosted various groups of minorities, they initially demonstrated signs of denying the pluralist concept of a multiethnic state (Schoeberline-Engel, 1996, pp. 12–20). In addition, many political parties, to gain popularity, made promising manifestoes about a future mono-ethnic vision of the state. Such developments widely resembled to the initial scenario of nationality politics in the Baltic region and raised serious concerns about the future of ethnic minorities and Russian-speaking groups in CA region. Nevertheless, these states took on itself an obligation to de jure grant equal citizenship and passports to all former USSR citizens who resided permanently in their territory by 1990, regardless ethnicity, race, religion, culture, or language. Generally speaking, citizenship laws made no direct reference to the past Soviet history, as it was done in Baltics, and reflected a liberal principle of granting equal access to citizenship to every individual. Probably, this development came in the context of foreign legal assistance and pioneer steps of building a sovereign nationhood when former CA socialist republics started making their initial steps toward recognizing international legal norms and obligations. In such context, it seemed that a multiethnic vision of nationhood prevailed in the formal political agenda as a sort of positive human rights record.

The Principle of Reduction of Statelessness

All five states apply in their citizenship policy the principle of *jus sanguinis* inherited from the old Soviet law. Recently, some provisions also demonstrate a sporadic application of *jus soli* principle, for example, in case of abandoned foundlings who are also automatically considered as citizens (For ex. Art. 14 or 16, the 1992 Citizenship law of Uzbekistan). Children born in wedlock between citizens and stateless persons are also automatically considered as citizens, irrespective of the place of birth. In the case of both parents being stateless, most states require valid residence permit for considering a child as a citizen. As existing practice shows, the absence of such a permit may lead to the high risk of statelessness because the respective authorities deny the issuing of a birth certificate to children of stateless parents without permanent residency. As yet, the data on the stateless population in CA is incomplete as the UNHCR office and mission have been restricted in some regions or do not have access to the adequate statistical data (Farquharson, 2011, p. 12).

In Uzbekistan, all applicants are required to submit a confirmation of their non-belonging to the citizenship of another state in the form of confirmation of renunciation together with an application for naturalization. No later renunciation is accepted (Art. 17, the 1992 Citizenship law of Uzbekistan). Therefore, applicants are left stateless at least during the naturalization period, while there are no legal guarantees for positive decisions on the application. Before 2007, although Kyrgyzstan implemented a zero-option principle in its state citizenship law, international human rights actors frequently reported on the problems of statelessness because the first 1993 citizenship law created a gap for certain groups of people and caused statelessness for technical reasons. With financial support from donor organizations, the state elaborated in 2007 the law on citizenship which addressed a wide range of problematic issues related to addressing statelessness. It lifted many barriers and enabled many stateless persons to legalize their stay. In particular, it enabled the naturalization of all former Soviet citizens who did not change their citizenship status on time. Thus, the country could decrease its stateless population, which by 2007 had reached almost 13,000 persons (UNHCR, 2009, p. 32).

By 2013, the UNCHR mission in Kazakhstan officially registered close to 7300 stateless people (UNHCR, 2013). There is a more complicated situation in this country with refugees and asylum seekers from neighboring, non-former USSR countries as they usually comprise a so-called gray area of people with uncertain status. Up to date, Turkmenistan is the only state in CA which is a state-party to the statelessness conventions and has been working toward creating a framework to ensure every person's right for citizenship (The 1954 and 1961 Statelessness Conventions).

Sub-conclusion

The post-1990 citizenship laws in CA countries were initially based on liberal principles of state succession and reflected fundamental human rights for citizenship. In fact, these states demonstrated an excellent example of adopting into the law a zero-option principle and thus avoided the mass statelessness problem caused by ethnicity or language concerns. In general terms, in the first years after the breakup of the USSR, the citizenship laws as such did not raise any heavy critics from the international human rights watchdogs. Simultaneously it should be mentioned here that citizenship laws of the CA republics share many similar and different points. The origin of the similarities, such as *jus sanguinis*, residency requirement, procedural matters can be traced back to the former Soviet laws on citizenship, which indeed, contributed in the socialist era to the mixed ethnic composition of CA states. On the other hand, legal evolution of the citizenship laws in CA republics demonstrates that they gradually obtain certain individual characteristics. Such tendency is especially visible in elective approaches by states to the issues of statelessness, dual citizenship, language laws for the naturalization, and the so-called ethnic factors for the simplified naturalization. Such uneven development can be characterized by a set of factors related to the political agenda, migration and out-migration statistics, and receptivity toward internationally recognized norms and practices in the field of citizenship.

The Regulation of Language in the Central Asian States

Similarities and Variations of Language Policies Across the Region

After 1989, all CA republics adopted their language laws to promote the official status of their titular languages (The 1989 State Language law of Uzbekistan; the 1989 State Language law of Kyrgyzstan, the 1989 Language law of Kazakhstan). These laws required persons employed in state organs, public administration, law enforcement agencies, and wide range of organizations and educational institutions to have a fluent command of the titular languages. Simultaneously, these laws secured for Russian the status of an interethnic communication language (*Yazik mejetnicheskogo obsheniya*). In Uzbekistan and Turkmenistan subsequent amendments, however, abolished the special status of Russian as an interethnic tool of communication and replaced the widely used Cyrillic script with Latin which was quite unknown for the local population (The 1989 State Language law of Uzbekistan with 2011 amendments). Similar intentions also existed in Kyrgyz Republic and Kazakhstan. As an example, in Kazakhstan, it was initially hard to decide whether to give the preference to Kazakh language, which was considered as the language of the titular nationality or whether to continue usage of Russian, which had the status of *lingua franca*. The complicated character of the issue is explained by the mere fact that the majority in Kazakhstan in the early years of its independence used Russian as their native language, while, simultaneously, nationalist senses demanded for the rebirth of the Kazakh language as a living symbol of the future state. Due to the fact these two states hosted the highest proportion of non-titular Russian-speaking population, Russian's role as a language of interethnic communication has been maintained in their laws (Fierman, 1998, p. 180). Similarly, if initially constitutions in Kyrgyz Republic and Kazakhstan prioritized their titular languages, later they also secured official role for Russian (The 1993 Constitution of Kyrgyzstan). Later, with the revision of existing legal framework, these two countries also codified the status of Russian alongside with own titular languages in respective constitutional statutes (The 2004 State Language law of the Kyrgyz Republic).

In contrast to Russian which is a dominantly used language, the laws in all CA republics make somewhat symbolic provisions for other minority languages. As an example, Kazakh law states, "state takes care of the creation of conditions conductive to the learning and development of the languages of the people of Kazakhstan" (Art. 6 of the renewed 1997 Languages law of Kazakhstan). Some reports show that the state provides at least school education in places of concentrated residence of different minorities, basically for Uzbeks and Uyghurs. However, the problematic issue is that while primary education is available in their native languages, higher education is only limited to the titular language or, sporadically, Russian. It eventually makes many young people who wish to continue their education to flee the country to other states (Oka, 2007, pp. 98–99).

Current Constitutional and Statutory Provisions

A legal status of Russian language bears specific differences across CA republics. Similarly, to Baltic states, in Uzbekistan and Turkmenistan, Russian has no specially codified legal status and exceptional constitutional guarantees and, therefore, is de jure a foreign language. These countries only recognize as official their own titular languages, Uzbek and Turkmen respectively, and leave minimal legal space for using Russian, for example, provisions enabling citizens to request notarized papers in Russian or similar.

On the other hand, the three remaining Central Asian republics while formalizing in their constitutions' titular languages, simultaneously codified the status of Russian. The Tajikistan's 1994 Constitution reflected somewhat common factual approach to Russian in the post-Soviet Space and addresses it as the language of interethnic communication (*Russkiy yazyk yavlyaetsya yazykom mejnatsional'nogo obsheniya*. Art. 2, the 1994 Constitution of Tajikistan). Both the 1993 and, subsequently, the 2010 constitutions of Kyrgyz Republic kept Kyrgyz as official and, simultaneously stated that Russian is "used as an official language" (Art. 5, the 1993 Constitution of Kyrgyz Republic, Art. 10; the 2010 Constitution of Kyrgyz Republic) The most detailed constitutional provision on Russian is codified in Kazakhstan's constitution. It states that "Russian language officially used in state organizations and organs of local self-government (*Organy mestnogo samoupravleniya*) on a par with Kazakh" (Art. 7, the 1995 Constitution of Kazakhstan) Notably, on the request of the group of the parliament members of Kazakhstan, the Constitutional Council of Kazakhstan has reviewed this provision in 1997 and in 2007. In its interpretation, the Constitutional Council has reiterated the legality of the article 7 and stated that "Russian language officially used in state organizations and organs of local self-government on a par with Kazakh without any exceptional circumstances" (*Postanovlenie Konstitutsionnogo Soveta RK, N 10/2*, 1997).

Sub-conclusion

Adoption of language laws in 1989 signaled of diminishing perspective of the Russian vis-à-vis the titular languages of the newly emerging independent states in CA region. It was thought that rise in legal status of titular languages would inevitably cause the decline of Russian and other minority languages (Fierman, 2006, p. 1092). This could have also affected the citizenship laws, as for example, it did in Baltic countries (notably, Latvia and Estonia) and thus restrict access to obtain citizenship for minorities. The issue of citizenship was not, however, the case in CA.

What could be observed from the subsequent developments in the field of language politics in the CA region—is an unbalanced and differentiated approach toward Russian in terms of social and political perspectives. The legal status of Russian as official language in Kazakhstan and Kyrgyzstan is substantially different from Turkmenistan, Uzbekistan, and Tajikistan. Russian has practically disappeared as a working language from legislative, judicial, and governmental institutions in Turkmenistan. In 1995, Uzbekistan adopted the state language law which mandated the exceptional use of Uzbek in the top governmental level. Despite constitutional codification, Tajikistan adopted a similar law on Tajik language in 2009 and since then, has been limiting the office work in its organs to titular language. This move was viewed by many as a step to undermine the status of Russian as a tool for interethnic communication. Simultaneously, national elites considered such development as protection of own identity and paving the way for the development of titular languages.

Social Practices

Upon the collapse of the USSR, the political power concentrated mainly in the hands of titular elites who widely advocated for the creation of a new identity based on the mono-ethnic state vision. In such circumstances, many non-titular groups feared becoming second-class citizens and viewed post-Socialist reforms in CA states with a reasonable degree of anxiety and potential discrimination. On the other hand, the nationalist elites viewed it as an achievement that would lead to the creation of citizenship based on titular ethnic identity. Notably, such citizenship struggle trend was quite common in 1990 in most of the former USSR states. For example, in Baltic states which rejected zero-option, the ethnicity, and language identity played crucial factor in determining eligibility for citizenship. Even though similar appeals on ethnicity and rigorous language exams for non-titular language speaking persons existed in CA states, such nationalist agenda did not affect their citizenship laws as such.

Indeed, all CA states have de jure provided the citizenship to all residents, including all nonethnic minorities. With exception of certain provisions offering benefits to co-ethnics, the citizenship concept design in all five countries was rather inclusive. Hence, in terms of succession in relation to citizenship, CA states fulfilled their international responsibilities within the context of the state succession to provide all residents with a legal status. The phenomenon that took place in these states regardless of their inclusive citizenship laws, is however, a substantial out-migration—an entirely opposite issue compared to Baltics.

In particular, initially, a sizeable Russian-speaking population in CA were not unconditionally required to shift to titular languages in their employment and education activities. In the working environment where many skilled professionals educated and trained in Russian were unprepared to switch into titular languages, they continued using Russian as *lingua franca*. Notably, the significant part of the political elites who formed newly independent governments in the CA republics had very limited mastery of titular languages because they were trained in the realities of the Soviet education system, mainly in Russian.

However, these new language laws de facto prioritizing titular languages and gradually restricting modes of Russian questioned the mere fact of future perspectives for both titular and non-titular Russian-speaking groups in CA region. Accompanying economic disadvantages, concerns about the quality of education and employment opportunities eventually made the Russian-speaking population to consider alternative solutions in the form of out-migration. Hence, the ethnic structure has undergone changes in all five CA states particularly since 1995. The most dramatic decrease occurred in Tajikistan during the civil war, when many people fled the country. In the subsequent years, there was a horrendous exodus of people which a bit later resulted in a protracted brain drain as most of those leaving were qualified technicians, scientist, and teachers (Landau & Kellner-Heinkele, 2011; Peyrouse, 2008). The new national ideologies of independent CA states made it difficult not only for the Slavic population but also Russian educated people to see equal social opportunities, which eventually affected their perception of equal citizenship.

Conclusion

The nationalist movements which brought local elites into power in the wake of independence were not only observed in the Baltic region. In CA, citizenship laws theoretically established a liberal approach as they were based on the zero-option principle. Unlike the Baltic states, there was not even a single case in any of the CA republics where a person's citizenship was disputed by the state on the ground of ethnic or linguistic identity. Notably, the CA states were the most ethnically heterogeneous among the other post-Soviet republics as they included not only Russians but also a large number of other ethnicities who were forcibly or voluntarily transferred there.

On the other hand, the social practices of the independence period in all five newly emerged republics demonstrated the prioritization of local ethnicities over those who were resettled in CA states during the Soviet era. Such prioritization was apparent in various sectors, including; high appointments in public administration, justice, education, and many other sectors. People who belonged to other ethnicities and did not speak a titular language were often viewed as potential emigrants and therefore, were less competitive compared to titular ethnicities.

Another issue of concern has been language legislation in individual states. Although language was never considered as a precondition for granting citizenship or naturalization, in practice, it served as a legal barrier which prevented minorities from taking high positions in state offices. It also became a prerequisite for the gradual displacement of other languages from public use or education. The last became the reason for the predominantly Russian-speaking population to flee CA states because of the unclear future perspectives. The subsequent social practices in all CA states demonstrate a politics of gradual underrepresentation of minorities in the political and other spheres and active promotion of titular majority groups. Thus, although the general citizenship concept design among CA states integrates the ideas of multiethnicity, their architects de facto have all emphasized the unity and special place of the titular ethnicity. Such approach eventually questions the de facto equal citizenship that some CA states presently claim to have.

References

Bassin, M., & Kelly, C. (2012). *Soviet and post-Soviet identities*. Cambridge: Cambridge University Press.
Brubaker, W. R. (1992). Citizenship struggles in Soviet successor states. *International Migration Review, 26*(2), 269–291.

Farquharson, M. (2011). *Statelessness in Central Asia* (p. 12). UNHCR. www.unhcr.org/4dfb592e9.html.
Fierman, W. (1998). Language and identity in Kazakhstan: Formulations in policy documents 1987–1997. *Communist and Post-communist Studies, 31*(2), 180.
Fierman, W. (2006). Language and education in post-Soviet Kazakhstan: Kazakh-medium instruction in urban schools. *The Russian Review, 65*(1), 98–116.
Ismatov, A. (2014). *Citizenship regulation in the republics of the former USSR territory: An international legal study in nationality and statelessness* (pp. 1–220) (Monograph). Nagoya University Repository.
Landau, Jacob M., & Kellner-Heinkele, B. (2011). *Language politics in contemporary Central Asia: National and ethnic identity and the Soviet legacy.* London: I.B. Tauris.
Mesamed, V. (1996). Interethnic relations in the Republic of Uzbekistan. *Central Asia Monitor, 6,* 20–26.
Oka, N. (2007). *Managing ethnicity under authoritarian rule: Trans-border nationalisms in post-Soviet Kazakhstan* (pp. 98–99). JETRO: Institute of Developing Economies.
Peyrouse, S. (2008). *The Russian minority in Central Asia: Migration, politics, and language.* Washington, DC: Woodrow Wilson International Center for Scholars.
Pilgram, L. (2011). *International law and European nationality laws.* EUDO citizenship observatory. http://eudocitizenship.eu/docs/Pilgram.pdf.
Schoeberline-Engel, J. (1996). The prospects for Uzbek national identity. *Central Asia Monitor, 6,* 12–20.
Smith, G., Law, V., Wilson, A., Allworth, E., & Bohr, A. (1998). *Nation-Building in the post-Soviet borderlands: The politics of national identities* (p. 119). Cambridge University Press; Central Asian republics inherited in their new citizen's passports the infamous Soviet fifth graph—(*pyataya grapha*) which requires a bearer to specify own ethnic identity.
Tishkov, V. (2007). *Ethnicity, nationalism and conflict in and after the Soviet Union: The mind aflame* (p. 241). London: United Nations Research Institute for Social Development, International Peace research Institute and Sage Publications.
Ubiria, G. (2015). *Soviet nation-building in Central Asia: The making of the Kazakh and Uzbek nations.* London: Routledge.

UNHCR. (2009). *A place to call home: The situation of stateless persons in the Kyrgyz Republic* (p. 32). Bishkek: Findings of the Survey Commission by the UNHCR.
UNHCR 2014-2015. (2013, January). *Global Appeal, Central Asia.*
Ziemele, I. (2005). *State continuity and nationality: The Baltic states and Russia: Past present and future as defined by international law.* Leiden: M. Nijhoff.

Legal Data

Convention relating to the Status of Stateless Persons, United Nations Treaty Series, vol. 360, 1954.
Convention on the Reduction of Statelessness, United Nations Treaty Series, vol. 989, 1961.
The 1992 Constitution of Republic of Uzbekistan, *989-XII*.
The 1992 Constitution of Republic of Turkmenistan.
The 1993 Constitution of Republic of Kyrgyzstan, *N 1 185-XII*, (replaced by the 2010 Constitution of Republic of Kyrgyzstan).
The 1994 Constitution of Republic of Tajikistan.
The 1995 Constitution of Republic of Kazakhstan, *2454*.
The Law on Citizenship of the Republic of Kazakhstan, N 1017-XII, 1991.
The Law on Citizenship of the Republic of Uzbekistan, N 632-XII, 1992.
The Law on Citizenship of the Republic of Turkmenistan, N 9-71, 1992.
The Law on Citizenship of the Kyrgyz Republic, 1333-XII, 1993 (replaced by the 2017 Law on Citizenship of the Kyrgyz Republic.
The Law on Citizenship of the Republic of Tajikistan, 1995 (replaced by the 2015 Law on Citizenship of the Republic of Tajikistan 1208.
The 1992 Regulation No. UP-500 on the Procedure for Concerning Issues related to the Citizenship of Republic of Uzbekistan.
Regulation No. 473 on the Procedure for Considering Issues related to the Citizenship of the Kyrgyz Republic.
The 1996 Regulation No. 3120 of the Republic of Kazakhstan.
The 2002 Instruction on the Issues related to the Citizenship of Kazakhstan, Order of the Minister of Interior No. 556.
The 1989 Law on State Language of the Republic of Uzbekistan, Supreme Council, No. 26-28.
The 1995 Law on State Language of Uzbekistan, No. 168-1.

Zakon Respubliki Uzbekistan O Vneseniy i Dopolneniy v Zakon Respubliki Uzbekistan o Gosudarstvennom Yazike, Vedomosti Oliy Majlisa, 1995, No. 12 St, 257, s izmeneniyami I dopolneniyami ot 2010 i 2011 goda. (The amendments to the 1995 Law on State Language, with modifications on 2010 and 2011.)

The 1989 Law of the Kyrgyz SSR on State Language, the Supreme Soviet of Kyrgyz SSR, *N17.*

The 2004 Law of Kyrgyz Republic on State Language *(N54);* Amended in December 8, 2008 *(N307)* and January 21, 2010 *(N8).*

The 1989 Law on State Language of Tajikistan, No. 150.

The 2009 Law on State Language of Tajikistan, No. 9-10.

The 1997 Law on Languages in the Kazakhstan, No. 151-I.

The 1989 Languages law, Supreme Soviet of Kazakhstan.

Minorities at Risk Project, Chronology for Russians in Kazakhstan, 2004, available at: http://www.refworld.org/docid/469f38ab1e.html. Accessed 8 January 2014.

Postanovlenie Konstitutsionnogo Soveta RK, N 10/2, May 1997.

Part IV
East and West: History, Liberalism, Culture and Political Change

14

The Horrors of Exclusion: Zygmunt Bauman's Sociological Journey

Raymond Taras

Bauman: A Chronicle of Our Age

The works of Zygmunt Bauman provide a chronicle of our age. In particular, the period that led from the dismantling of European communism in 1989 to the European crisis of migration in 2015 was one in which the Polish sociologist was at his most ingenious, productive, and impactful. He died in Leeds in 2017 at the age of 91.

The era in which he lived extends from the introduction of the People's Republic of Poland when he was already in his mid-20s to the collapse of the Soviet bloc in eastern Europe which began in Warsaw in spring 1989. Roundtable talks brought together incumbent communists and the Solidarity opposition. The fall of the Berlin Wall later that year was symbolic more than substantive.

Like many other Jewish intellectuals living in Poland in 1968, Bauman resigned from the Polish United Workers' Party in January 1968.

R. Taras (✉)
Australian National University, Canberra, ACT, Australia
e-mail: taras@tulane.edu

Following turbulent events in Warsaw in March of that year, attributed to an anti-Semitic faction in the communist leadership engaged in a power struggle with party head Władysław Gomułka, Bauman lost his post at the University of Warsaw, moved first to Israel, then a few years later took a position at Leeds University. His career soared from then on and the university became the premier home of sociology in the UK.

Observing from afar what had happened in Poland during the *Solidarność* social movement in 1980–1981 which, ten years later, had managed to overthrow the monolithic communist party-state, Bauman focused on what it was in Europe that divided a society rather than what united it. He critiqued communities seeking to exclude others, for example, Mont Saint Michel in France: it was simultaneously a hermetic cloister and an inaccessible, closely guarded fortress. In elaborating on the contingency of hospitality, the imagery of an exclusionary Mont Saint Michel loomed menacingly. It represented a community based on emotional urges that wished to exclude everything considered undesirable, threatening, and dangerous.

Exclusion—what had happened to Bauman in 1968—became a lifelong concern of his in the last books he published in the mid-2010s. He became almost single-mindedly fixated on migrants and the cynical use they were put to by governments, the labor market, people smugglers, and the divisions affecting migrant and refugee applicants—where they were from, what qualifications they had, and whether they were destined to live 'wasted lives' or not—a trope in his analysis.

As rarely before, fear was on the minds of politicians and the public in the first decades of the twenty-first century: terror attacks, economic fears such as job security or the 'precariate' (Žižek, 2015), fear of establishment parties, fear of populism, anxiety about rapidly-changing national and personal identities (Taras, 2012). Contrary to other observers, Bauman claimed that attachment to human company was a catalyst for fear rather than an antidote for it: 'the perception of human company as a source of existential insecurity and as a territory strewn with traps and ambushes tends to become endemic' (2000, p. 91).

Human company as a source of existential insecurity may have been what Bauman had discovered living under the communist system.

But when he moved to Leeds he became confounded by the fundamental illiberalism of Prime Minister Margaret Thatcher's mantra 'There is No Alternative' (TINA) that was launched not many years later. The race to the bottom that it produced was exacerbated by the polarizing arrival of refugees and migrants who often could not be distinguished (Angenendt, Kipp, & Meier, 2017), bringing what he considered to be a surplus of unskilled labor to the continent.

In a volume he published as early as 2004 he labeled this reserve army of labor as leading wasted lives. It was in keeping with the popular, simplistic sociological thesis of the time that one-third of society was indispensable and vital to its functioning, another third was insecure and vulnerable, and the last third was unneeded and superfluous.

Bauman's journey takes us from the era of unadulterated communism to that of unbridled globalization. It is a chronicle that also passes by way of the notion of liquid modernity that he made famous. Simply put, liquid modernity signifies a society that is transitioning from solid modern structures to the relativism, fragmentation, and uncertainty of postmodern life.

As Bauman put it, liquid modernity signified the danger of skating on thin ice: only more speed stops us from falling through into the ice. In Europe the era of free education, secure jobs, and peaceful home life was coming to an end and uncertainty and unpredictability were replacing them.

This sociologist also understood liquid modernity as entailing a shift in society toward more avaricious patterns of consumption. This had a deleterious effect on the poorer classes. In the past they suffered together and stood in solidarity. But in a mass consumer society they were unneeded, even suffered humiliation. The fortunate now confronted increasing poverty and, later, the addition of migrants and refugees joined the stratum of the poor, providing a warning that all of us were a breath away from joining the ranks of the undeserving poor. Fragility and fluidity make everything seem temporal and uncertain. Emotions—like fear, anxiety, envy, and shame—fanned the flames further, exacerbating the sense of insecurity, loneliness, and identity loss.

In many respects Bauman depicted a gloomy vision of societies, confined previously to developing states but now encroaching on Western countries too. It parallels unimaginable socioeconomic inequalities that for many people comprise a shift from plenty to empty.

In this Chapter, I wish to examine not liquid modernity—an area of considerable research over the years—but expendable lives that Bauman assayed in his later years. It is the first appraisal of Bauman in his role as migration politics specialist. Key to examining migration is the resurrected importance of emotions-based research.

Emotions and Hospitality

Among many different emotions, my objective is to consider the infrequently identified emotion of hospitality.[1] While reason in politics no longer holds a dominating position, its stand-in can involve noble human emotions like hospitality and welcome. French philosopher Emmanuel Levinas insisted that hospitality had by definition to be unconditional, but this was a view that Bauman incessantly wrestled with. Was he able to resolve the virtue of hospitality with the experience of wasted lives?

Hospitality and conviviality are among the virtues now being revitalized in emotions-related research—not to mention value-laden advocacy positions or social networks. Dominique Moïsi (2008) has noted how in place of the clash of civilizations it is more apt to speak of the globalization of emotions. These now dominate some of the social sciences where once reflexive sociology was a criterion (Gouldner, 1970).

Emotion today has, by and large, displaced interest as the critical factor shaping political action. In a letter to his son Johan written in 1648, Count Axel Oxiensterna cautioned: 'Do you not know, my son, with how little wisdom the world is governed?' The original Latin is: *An nescis, mi fili, quantilla prudentia mundus regatur*? Sometimes attributed

---

[1]The list of emotions that can be identified as affecting politics seems limitless. Here is my tentative vocabulary of applicable state-level emotions: Anxiety; Belonging; Compassion; Conviviality; Dependency; Disgust; Distrust; Envy; Fear; Glory; Grievances; Hate; Honor; Hope; Hopelessness; Hospitality; Hostility; Hubris; Humiliation; Loneliness; Melancholy; Narcissism; Paranoia; Passion; Prestige; Rage; Revenge; Rootedness; Shame; Submission; Suspicion.

to Cardinal Richelieu, the exhortation was intended to encourage his son, a delegate to negotiations preparing the draft of the Peace of Westphalia, to hold his own among experienced and eminent statesmen (Roberts, 1991).

In turn, Napoleon Bonaparte was more cynical, convinced that fear *and* self-interest were the main drivers of human emotions. Fear as an existential state is connected to a wide gamut of human emotions, some constructive, others destructive. As a case in point, the administration of Donald Trump appears more vested in emotions than, say, the Russian state is with its old-school calculations of national interest.

Hospitality is different from conviviality, another less-remarked upon emotion. In place of spontaneity, generosity, and emotion-laden expressions, hospitality is more demanding than conviviality and is offered at the owner's residence where the proprietor is regarded as dominant and controlling. In extreme cases it may even approach *droit de seigneur*—a feudal lord's right to have sexual relations with the bride of a vassal on her first night of marriage. Far removed from Levinas' understanding of the term (discussed next), hospitality establishes the limits of a place, retains authority over it, and regulates the gift that is being offered to the stranger.

For moral philosopher Martha Nussbaum, 'all societies are replete with emotions: anger, fear, sympathy, disgust, envy, guilt, grief, forms of love. Some have little to do with politics but public emotions take as their object the nation, the nation's goals, its institutions and leaders, its geography, and one's fellow citizens seen as fellow inhabitants of a common public space' (Nussbaum, 2013, pp. 1–2). They can have grave consequences for the advancement of the nation toward its end goals.

Promoting well-meant benign passions in place of hardheaded, cynical interests justifies adopting an emotional approach. Hospitality toward strangers forms part of the process of bringing the study of emotions back onto the research agenda leading to a more inclusive analytic framework.

Reason in politics appears indeed to be downgraded. If it is replaced with the 'noble' qualities in the gamut of human emotions, such as hospitality and welcome, then it may even have normative advantages. Nevertheless the appeal of demagoguery and xenophobia is precisely in its emotional rather than rational, charge. As noted by F.G. Bailey in *Treasons, Stratagems, and Spoils*.

> Ordinary Jane and Ordinary Joe are quicker to feel than they are to think; they respond more readily to a message that touches their emotions than to one that requires them to attend to a carefully reasoned argument. Reason does not mobilize support; slogans do. Reasoning is demanding; slogans are comfortably compelling. (Bailey, 2001, p. 8)

The permutations of emotions can be dissimilar depending on whose perspective is considered. In his theory of natural emotions that highlight their motivational effects, Justin D'Arms offers a shorter compendium: amusement; anger; contempt; disgust; envy; fear; guilt; jealousy; pity; pride; regret; shame (D'Arms, 2017).

Frequently the lists of emotions are skewed toward negative ones. Nussbaum (2013) emphasizes that in politics it is these that dominate:

> All societies are full of emotion. Liberal democracies are no exception.... The life of even a relatively stable democracy would include a host of emotions—anger, fear, sympathy, disgust, envy, guilt, grief, many forms of love. Some of these episodes of emotion have little to do with political principles or the public culture, but others are different: they take as their object the nation, the nation's goals, its institutions and leaders, its geography, and one's fellow citizens seen as fellow inhabitants of a common public space.

For Nussbaum, 'Such public emotions, frequently intense, have large-scale consequences for the nation's progress towards its goals' (2013, pp. 1–2).

I have singled out a benign passion—hospitality—to evaluate Bauman's perspective on the treatment of refugees and migrants in Europe today. But it is with Emmanuel Levinas, a standard setter who raised the bar high on the treatment of the stranger, with whom we must begin.

Point of Departure: Levinas' *L'inquiétante étrangeté*

Inclusion of citizens is the prevailing imperative in the moral philosophy of Levinas. Beginning in the 1960s, he developed a code of ethics on hospitality extended toward strangers. Its importance followed from people's inability to approach the other, the source of many episodes of horror and violence in human history. For Levinas (1961: IX–XII) violence was paradoxically the result of a striving for unity because unity can be achieved only by *excluding* anyone regarded as disruptive. A totality is possible only through exclusion of the other.

Almost tautologically, Levinas explained how 'the other is precisely that which cannot be included in a totality; the other is other, incomprehensibly and unreasonably so'. He insisted on assigning unconditional priority to ethics over ontology, that is, to welcoming strangers over harsh reality. The significance of *l'accueuil*—welcoming of the stranger—overrode everything else.

The unconditional nature of hospitality is disputed by many writers concerned with migration. Sociologist Meyda Yegenoglu (2005, pp. 141–142) stipulated its contingent nature this way: 'conditional hospitality is offered at the owner's place, home, nation, state, or city - that is, at a place where one is defined as the master and where unconditional hospitality or unconditional trespassing of the door is not possible.... the foreigner is allowed to enter the host's space under conditions determined by the host'.

It was not nationalism, as many writers had pinpointed, that for Bauman was responsible for the exclusion of migrants. Before the 2015 crisis hit, he had praised nationalism as 'an uplifting and ennobling idea, as well as a humanizing and civilizing practice of solidarity in action'. Indeed, a national home represented a site removed from 'cutthroat competition and bloody conflicts – a workshop inside which to develop and learn the skills of mutual understanding and assistance, and in which to practice humanity and amiable, warm-hearted togetherness' (Bauman & Donskis, 2013, p. 120). He regarded Europe as a force for integration and, in hyperbolic terms he may have regretted later on, 'a banquet of sisterly nations'.

It is a puzzle, then, how the same author could label refugees and migrants as leading wasted lives, unless nationalism had shut the door tight on 'warmhearted togetherness' in the interim. But viewing the arrival of a new influx of non-Western refugees into Europe—and that primarily bound for a prospering Germany rather than what were regarded as second rate countries—generated more critical assertions from the Polish sociologist. His critical Marxist thinking on display in Warsaw up to 1968 had been converted into critical postmodern thought.

Indeed in 2013 he refused to accept an honorary doctorate at the University of Lower Silesia because of a combination of right-wing and anti-Semitic attacks on him. Bauman's disillusionment with the inclusionary power of nationalism, even his disavowal with the politics of migration, had multiple sources. It may have produced harsher invectives against migrants.

A dystopian world was emerging propelled above all by shocking inequalities—a subject that jarred Bauman particularly since he had carried out research in his Polish years on, in retrospect, the miniscule income gaps that existed under communism. The 2019 report at Davos by Oxfam (2019) claims that the world's 26 richest people now own as much as the world's poorest 50%. Even if the report is out by 100% so that the 52 richest individuals own half what the rest of people owns, the inequality rates and the Gini coefficients around the world are stupendous.

Levinas' ethical reflections on hospitality remained constant in Bauman's analyses. However he was more persuaded by realist, empirical explanations than by ideal types. In *Wasted Lives: Modernity and Its Outcasts* (2004), he deplored the plight meted out to most migrants. He first sketched out how the 'images of economic migrants and asylum seekers stand for wasted humans—the waste of globalization'. It seemed perfectly natural and realistic that 'refugees and immigrants, coming from "far away" yet making a bid to settle in the neighborhood, are uniquely suitable for the role of the effigy to be burnt as the specter of "global forces"' (2004, p. 66). Was there a scornful tone to stigmatizing refugees as outsiders, or was it merely a descriptive phrase?

> Refugees, the human waste of the global frontier-land, are 'the outsiders incarnate', the absolute outsiders, outsiders everywhere and out of place everywhere except in places that are themselves out of place—the 'nowhere places' that appear on no maps used by ordinary humans on their travels. (2004, p. 80)

Well before the European migration crisis of 2015, Bauman rendered a harsh verdict on the reception of immigrants. They constituted 'large and growing agglomerations of "wasted humans", likely to become durable or permanent' (2004, p. 85). Indeed, 'Perhaps the sole thriving industry in the lands of the latecomers (deviously and deceitfully dubbed "developing countries") is the mass production of refugees' (2004, p. 73).

Bauman blamed the horrors of exclusion primarily on the forces of globalization.

> They reshuffle people and play havoc with their social identities, They may transform us, from one day to another, into refugees or 'economic migrants'... dump at our doorsteps those people who have already been rejected, forced to run for their lives, or scramble away from home for the means to stay alive, robbed of their identities and self-esteem. We hate those people because we feel that what they are going through in front of our eyes may well prove to be, and soon, a dress rehearsal of our own fate. Trying hard to remove them from our sight—round them up, lock them in camps, deport them—we wish to exorcise them. (2004, p. 128)

This was written a decade before Merkel's decision to allow 1.1 million migrants into Germany while insisting that many others would have to be admitted into other EU states; though farfetched, Merkel perhaps subconsciously had incorporated Levinas' conception of *accueuil*.

Liberal and Illiberal Dilemmas

As mentioned, social inequality had been a major research interest of Bauman's. In his book *Liquid Evil: Living with TINA*, he outlined the avaricious side of globalization that has had as profound an effect on migrants—maybe even more so—as it has had on settled communities. 'Steady dismantling of the increasingly deregulated greed-driven economy, growing public insensitivity to rampant social inequality coupled with the incapacity of rising numbers of citizens – now abandoned (since no longer viewed as a potential danger to capitalist order and a seed of social revolution)' (Bauman & Donskis, 2016, p. 14).

Bauman elaborated on the othering pattern that took place in the migration policies of affluent European countries. They are based on economic rather than country-specific criteria; so much, then, for humanitarian concerns that Merkel claimed she was embracing. Fortress Europe is a ghetto with acceptance criteria that are no longer country specific. This is because, for Bauman, state borders in a liquid Europe are unclear. Instead it is the economic standing of people that has become pivotal.

It is unlikely that at the end of his life Bauman had been made aware that 40% of Syrian refugees had graduate degrees and they could potentially become well-off through fast-tracking their skills in Germany. As he put it, while the affluent are welcome, the penniless—who will cost us—are not. The EU fortress is discriminatory in its *accueuil*.

In one of his last, most bitter books, *Strangers at Our Door,* Bauman described the reactions of many Europeans to the migration crisis. They exhibited 'carnivalesque explosions of solidarity and care' which accompanied 'images of successive spectacular tragedies in the migrants' unending saga'. He observed how 'Currently, the EU offers Syrians the prospect of heaven (life in Germany), but only if they first pay a crook and risk their lives' (2016, p. 97). There was no need to refer to terrorist threats posed by migrants. Possessing no entrepreneurial skills, their status was, for Bauman, hopeless: unskilled, unprepared, yet paying off crooks with the last of their savings.

The dystopian world Bauman saw around him, above all for migrants, revealed how far he had travelled from Levinas' idea of unconditional hospitality. European fears about migrants fed on the perception that strangers had overstayed their welcome. He put it this way: 'what we fear, is evil; what is evil, we fear' (2006, p. 54).

Arguably for Bauman hospitality was not a natural law and it was circumscribed. For as long as human history, processes of othering, marginalization, and exclusion have been in existence. Limits on welcoming strangers are much the same as in fifteenth-century Iceland where contingent relations between host and strangers followed the seasons.

The world's oldest parliament, the *Alþingi*, decided in 1431 that no foreigners (*útlenskir menn*) could remain in Iceland after 8 September, the feast of the Blessed Virgin when the last ships had to sail from the country. The 1490 *Píningsdómur* ('Pining's Verdict') provided some leeway: foreigners could overwinter in Iceland if sick, injured, or shipwrecked. But they were not allowed to engage in fishing or trade during this period (Parsons, 2011).

The point of this Verdict was to keep seasonal work seasonal. 'Outlanders' were expected to return to their native countries coinciding with the time set in the *Jónsbók* codebook, in other words, when Icelandic farmers took livestock from summer grazing lands to home pastures.

The parameters of hospitality to strangers were etched in stone, even in a remote periphery of Europe. Once again, contingency was valued more highly than unconditionality, except for the sick, the injured, or the shipwrecked.

Bauman was on the right track in underscoring the contingent nature of hospitality, even though he became susceptible to charges of abandoning the classic models of liberalism and tolerance. The laws of a country, the identity and provenance of strangers, state capacity to absorb greater numbers of foreigners, together with how welcome are social attitudes, all play a role in migration Realpolitik. These constraints are emotions-based, but they also reflect practical necessities as well.

Contemptuous Passions

Illiberal attitudes are often said to originate among the unneeded grassroots underclass; the *Shleppers*; Emile Zola's *Lumpen*; the drunkards and washerwomen. They cannot be permitted to partake in the gift of contingent, let alone unconditional, hospitality, or inclusion, or belonging. They are the doubly wretched of the earth, suffering the dehumanizing effects of being unwanted and unneeded. But are those who oppose the arrival of unskilled migrants and become equated with opponents of humanitarian principles themselves right-wing populists, riffraff themselves, in short, intolerant illiberals?

Just before the height of the migration crisis, in 2014, the unskilled made up 37% of working-age non-EU immigrants in the EU. Non-EU citizens' employment rates (aged 20–64) fell by six percentage points to 56%. Their risk of poverty or social exclusion increased four points to 49%, twice the level for EU citizens. The 2017 federal elections in which Merkel's CDU suffered the worst performance in its history showed that election results matter. Populist movements are to blame, it is said, but a series of regional elections since then confirmed the CDU's failure to elicit popular support. Similar outcomes have occurred in many other EU states.

Pouring contempt on illiberals also has a long history. A case in point may be Karl Marx's *The Eighteenth Brumaire of Louis Napoleon (1852)*. In it he gave this idiosyncratic definition of the *lumpenproletariat*. It is both far ranging and very specific.

> Alongside debased lecherers with dubious means of subsistence and of dubious origin, alongside ruined and adventurous offshoots of the bourgeoisie, were vagabonds, discharged soldiers, discharged jailbirds, escaped galley slaves, swindlers, charlatans, idlers, pickpockets, tricksters, gamblers, pimps, brothel keepers, porters, literati, organ grinders, rag pickers, knife grinders, tinkers, beggars—in short, the whole indefinite, disintegrated mass, thrown hither and thither.

In other places far from Europe, those stereotyped as illiberals have been classified as rednecks, welfare queens, conches, trailer trash, coon asses—the list goes on.

Xenophobia may reflect the desire on the part of affluent Western European societies to protect their 'islands of prosperity' against an outside world troubled by poverty, environmental degradation, interethnic violence, and widespread desperation. Or, absent islands of prosperity, they may just want to guard their societies against unskilled migration or even uncouth nations, Andrei Markovits' summation of how Europeans look down on Americans (2007).

Recent migration data from many parts of the globe—from Australia to the U.S., from Canada to Sweden—indicate that high-skilled workers are now preferred to unskilled ones. The latter often has no recourse but to seek asylum, framing themselves as refugees who fear for their lives when back in their sending countries. This is at least the sense of Bauman's criticisms of migration policies reported in his last books.

Work, as Marx insisted, should not alienate but liberate. Yet this has rarely been the case since he wrote 150 years ago. Radical income redistribution remains the way out of this quandary and it can apply to recent migrants as much as to ensconced nativists. In effect, it can incentivize work. On the other hand, Finland's universal basic income experiment has not worked other than making welfare recipients feel better (Nagesh, 2019).

Even then, however, 'wasted lives' remains a tragic blight on social life. It is fair to say that migration-skeptic attitudes have stuck in his hospitality repertoire.

Can We Tolerate the Intolerant Like Bauman?

Bauman's views described in this Chapter reflect his passage from communist authoritarianism to Western intolerance of political correctness. In both cases the backlash against each of the two has been forceful.

In *The Open Society and Its Enemies*, Karl Popper (2013) presented a spirited defense of the open society against its enemies. He unleashed a critique of historicism and a defense of liberal democracy and the open society.

While sharing some of Popper's anxieties, John Rawls theorized that liberty precedes social justice. But he was uncertain about the 'paradox of tolerance' posed by Popper in 1945. It claimed that if a society is tolerant without limits, its ability to be tolerant may eventually be destroyed by the intolerant. He arrived at the paradoxical conclusion that in order to maintain a tolerant society, society must be intolerant of intolerance.

Put differently, unlimited tolerance must lead to the disappearance of tolerance. If we are not prepared to defend a tolerant society against the onslaught of the intolerant, then the tolerant will be destroyed, and tolerance with it. An alternative exists: to counter them by use of rational argument, coupled with checks by public opinion. To be sure, some of the 'intolerant' may not be prepared to meet their opponents on the level of rational argument, but begin denouncing all argumentation. They may insist their followers not listen to rational argument because it is deceptive. For Popper, suppression of such intolerance would be needed, even if by force.

Rawls was nuanced about claiming—in the name of tolerance—the right not to tolerate the intolerant. In 1971, in *A Theory of Justice* (1999) he asserted that a just society must tolerate the intolerant for otherwise society would then itself be intolerant, and therefore unjust. To be sure, he, like Popper, believed that society has a reasonable right of self-preservation that supersedes the principle of tolerance: 'While an intolerant sect does not itself have title to complain of intolerance, its freedom should be restricted only when the tolerant sincerely and with reason believe that their own security and that of the institutions of liberty are in danger'.

In replying to the question 'Should we tolerate the intolerant?' Michael Walzer (1997) observed that most minority religions benefiting from tolerance are themselves intolerant. In a tolerant regime, such people may learn themselves to tolerate, or at least act as if they possessed this virtue. Another view is that intolerant speech—a signaling of exclusionary attitudes—should be subject to a different standard of justification than violent, repressive, direct action based on exclusionary attitudes.

As we see in Bauman's case, no such thing as virtuous liberalism exists, only a synthesis of different perspectives that need not be values-based. In the 1960s he had repudiated dogmatic communism and favored reflexive critical Marxism. In the last decade of his life he found unconditional hospitality to be unviable and preferred its pragmatic, conditional variant. To be sure, migration politics was not his forte and reflexivity had become a thing of the past. Exclusionary politics were what he had experienced rather than what he had rationalized. The politics of inequality and the nature of liquid modernity remain his two key legacies.

References

Angenendt, S., Kipp, D., & Meier, A. (2017). *Mixed migration*. Gütersloh: Bertelsmann Stiftung.
Bailey, F. G. (2001). *Treasons, stratagems, and spoils: How leaders make practical use of beliefs and values*. Boulder, CO: Westview Press.
Bauman, Z. (2000). *Liquid modernity*. Cambridge: Polity.
Bauman, Z. (2004). *Wasted lives: Modernity and its outcasts*. Cambridge: Polity.
Bauman, Z. (2006). *Liquid fear*. Cambridge: Polity.
Bauman, Z. (2016). *Strangers at our door*. Cambridge: Polity.
Bauman, Z., & Donskis, L. (2013). *Moral blindness: The loss of sensitivity in liquid modernity*. Cambridge: Polity.
Bauman, Z., & Donskis, L. (2016). *Liquid evil: Living with TINA*. Cambridge: Polity.
D'Arms, J. (2017, September 8). *Natural emotions as a psychological kind*. Paper presented at Tulane University's Murphy Institute.
Gouldner, A. (1970). Towards a reflexive sociology. In G. Delanty & P. Strydom (Eds.), *Philosophies of social science: The classic and contemporary readings*. Maidenhead and Philadelphia: Open University.
Levinas, E. (1961). *Totalité et infini: essai sur l'extériorité*. The Hague: Martinus Nijhoff.
Markovits, A. S. (2007). *Uncouth nation: Why Europe dislikes America*. Princeton, NJ: Princeton University Press.
Marx, K. (1852). *The eighteenth brumaire of Louis Napoleon (1852)*. Retrieved from https://www.marxists.org/archive/marx/works/1852/18th-brumaire/.
Moïsi, D. (2008). *La géopolitique de l'émotion: comment les cultures de peur, d'humiliation et d'espoir façonnent le monde*. Paris: Flammarion.
Nagesh, A. (2019, February 8). Finland basic income trial left people "happier but jobless". *BBC*. Retrieved from https://www.bbc.com/news/world-europe-47169549.
Nussbaum, M. C. (2013). *Political emotions: Why love matters for justice*. Cambridge, MA: Belknap Press.
Oxfam International. (2019). *Public good or private wealth*. Oxfam Briefing Paper January 2019. Retrieved from https://oxfamilibrary.openrepository.com/bitstream/handle/10546/620599/bp-public-good-or-private-wealth-210119-summ-en.pdf?utm_source=indepth.

Parsons, K. M. (2011, November 15). *Integration in Iceland: What can we learn from the (distant) past?* Paper presented at the Conference on Integration and Immigrants' Participation, University of Iceland, Reykjavik.

Popper, K. R. (2013). *The open society and its enemies.* Princeton, NJ: Princeton University Press.

Rawls, J. (1999). *A theory of justice.* Cambridge, MA: Belknap Press.

Roberts, M. (1991). Oxenstierna in Germany, 1633–1636 (pp. 6–54). Cambridge: Cambridge University Press.

Taras, R. (2012). *Xenophobia and Islamophobia in Europe.* Edinburgh: Edinburgh University Press.

Walzer, M. (1997). *On Toleration* (pp. 80–81). New Haven, CT: Yale University Press.

Yegenoglu, M. (2005). From guest worker to hybrid immigrant: Changing themes of German-Turkish literature. In S. Ponzanesi & D. Merolla (Eds.), *Migrant cartographies: New cultural and literary spaces in post-colonial Europe.* Lanham, MD: Lexington Books.

Žižek, S. (2015). *Trouble in paradise: From the end of history to the end of capitalism.* London: Melville House.

15

Failures and Successes: Soviet and Chinese State-Socialist Reforms in the Face of Global Capitalism

Roger D. Markwick

Introduction

Any consideration of the reform of state socialism, based on the experiences of the Union of Soviet Socialist Republics (USSR) or the People's Republic of China (PRC) must situate them historically. Invoking abstract categories such as state, communist party and market, without situating them concretely, is meaningless. In this regard, we must confront the fact that, in terms of their origins and their subsequent history, neither the USSR nor the PRC conformed to the script for socialist revolution and construction envisaged by Marx, Engels or Lenin. Classical Marxism, including Bolshevism, had

---

This chapter is an expanded version of a paper presented at the AACaPS 14th Biennial Conference, Griffith University, 31 January–1 February 2019. An earlier version was first delivered to the International Workshop on 'Socialism in Power', Renmin University of China, Beijing, 23–24 September 2017.

R. D. Markwick (✉)
University of Newcastle, Callaghan, NSW, Australia
e-mail: roger.markwick@newcastle.edu.au

assumed that socialism would have to be established in the advanced capitalist countries: citadels of industrial productivity that would provide the prerequisite economic abundance for socialist egalitarianism rather than generalised scarcity, otherwise 'all the old filthy business would necessarily be reproduced', as Marx put it in *The German Ideology* (Marx, 1846, p. 11). Furthermore, classical Marxism assumed that the industrial working classes of the most developed economies would be the driving forces of socialist revolution that would be inherently internationalist, breaching national boundaries. History decided otherwise, in the case of both Russia and China. The October 1917 Revolution shattered the 'weakest link' in the imperialist chain, as Lenin famously conceived it: semi-capitalist, overwhelmingly agrarian, Tsarist Russia.

The Bolsheviks, however, saw October as but the opening salvo that would ignite the world revolution, first and foremost in highly industrialised Germany, with its powerful, politicised working class (Markwick, 2017, p. 604). Again, the script faltered: Nazism rather than socialism triumphed in the citadel of European capitalism. Instead, the next great socialist breakthrough came on the periphery of capitalism: semi-feudal, semi-colonial China in 1949, spearheaded by a peasant army, not an industrial proletariat (Anderson, 2010, especially pp. 60, 64, 66). In this sense, the Chinese revolution was a 'gigantic jacquerie', as Isaac Deutscher put it (1964, p. 25), which stamped its imprint on the Chinese Communist Party (CCP) and state, and still does.

Most importantly here, Lenin assumed that while during the transition from capitalism to communism the 'dictatorship of the proletariat' would be required to suppress the bourgeoisie, the flourishing of socialist democracy would mean that the 'need for a special machine of suppression will begin to disappear'. This 'withering away of the state' was a fundamental thesis of Lenin's 1917 essay 'The State and Revolution' (Lenin, 1917). In the classical Marxist conception, the 'demise of the state', in the course of being 'subordinated' to society, was integral to the 'eliminating of class', the sine qua non for socialism (Krausz, 2015, pp. 180, 310). 'Withering away of the state' was expunged from Stalin's lexicon, although he officially declared the Soviet Union socialist in 1936; it has yet to reappear in Chinese political thought where, on the contrary, in the last four decades party and state have played a pivotal role in driving economic transformation and development (Gregor, 2014, pp. 111, 125, 236, 238).

Socialism in One Country

In contrast to Lenin, Stalin asserted that the more socialism advanced the 'sharper' the class struggle and the more necessary the 'dictatorship of the proletariat' (Stalin, 1928, pp. 171–172). Indeed, Stalin embraced Soviet great power 'statehood' (*derzhavnost*') (Lewin, 2016, p. 149). Stalin's étatiste socialism was a necessary corollary to his espousal of 'socialism in one country', in violation of the original Bolshevik tenets that socialism could only be realised on an international scale; in the first place in the most advanced capitalist states (Krausz, 2015, pp. 281–286; for a counter view, that argues 'complete socialism in one country' was endorsed by Lenin in 1923, see Van Ree, 1998). Stalin's justifiable fear that those very same states, primarily Britain, France and Germany, would unleash war against the beleaguered, infant Soviet state, saw a Soviet retreat from internationalising socialism by political means through the Communist International (Comintern). Instead, in the 1930s, crash construction of a near autarkic Soviet fortress, by forced-march industrialisation and agricultural collectivisation, became the primary means of thwarting imperialist invasion (Stone, 2000, pp. 3, 7, 212–216). The result was a 'militarised socialism' (Von Hagen, 1990, p. 337); a more or less permanent war economy, which prioritised military-industrial production overconsumption. A war economy would characterise the Soviet Union almost to the very end (Bisley, 2001, pp. 110–111, 116–131; Harrison, 2017). Indeed, ultimately it would contribute to the Soviets' undoing. Stalin, however, made a virtue out of military necessity. But the militarised Soviet model of 'barracks socialism' was never part of the classical Marxist script for a socialist state or society (Butenko, 1990, pp. 46–47). A lesson, as we shall see, Stalin's Chinese comrades would eventually come to learn in the 1980s.

The 1949 Chinese Revolution was certainly the 'child' of the October Revolution, which by first rupturing the world capitalist system had eased the birth of the PRC (Anderson, 2010, p. 60; Deutscher, 1967, p. 79). Further, Mao Zedong's Communist Party that led the revolution was certainly the offspring of Stalin's Communist Party of the Soviet Union (CPSU, from 1952): militarised, autocratic and 'monolithic' (Anderson, 2010, p. 66). Nevertheless, the CCP was not a clone of Stalin's CPSU. Instead of a political vanguard party, prolonged peasant 'people's war' forged a distinctive party-army alliance rooted in peasant movements, motivated by a populist 'mass line' that elevated a classless category of 'the people' to the driving force of a 'staged revolution', in the first instance ousting imperial powers and overturning feudal relations in the countryside (Wang, 2016, pp. 288–291). Mao saw China's 'new democratic' revolution as 'part of the world revolution' (Mao, 1940), but his priority was forging an independent, unified, industrialised nation-state on the road to socialism, not internationalising the revolution. In that sense, Mao's revolution was motivated by Sun Yat Sen's vision for a modernised China (Gregor, 2014, pp. 111, 125) and conceptually confined within Stalin's 'socialism in one country' paradigm (Deutscher, 1967, pp. 92–93). A partial break with this paradigm came post-Mao in the 1980s. CCP paramount leader Deng Xiaoping lamented 30 years of 'disastrous', 'closed door policy' for obstructing China's development (Deng, 1984b, p. 38). Development, not world socialism, was the essence of what Deng would proclaim as 'socialism with Chinese characteristics'.

Notwithstanding Stalin's belated support for the CCP-led revolution, an Alliance and Friendship Treaty signed in February 1950 between the USSR and the PRC forged a close bond up to the mid-1950s, laying the basis for 'the largest ever socialist development project' in the guise of Soviet economic aid, advice and expertise (Lüthi, 2010, p. 34). 'The Soviet Union's today will be our tomorrow', was a popular saying in China in the 1950s (Marsh, 2003, p. 264). In its first decade, the PRC assumed a socialist character in the Soviet political and economic mould, adopting its first Five Year Plan in 1952. However, relations went into freefall after Nikita Khrushchev's denunciation of Stain's 'cult of the personality' at the March 1956 Twentieth Congress of the CPSU. In this context, Mao viewed Khrushchev's espousal of 'peaceful coexistence' with the capitalist West as a betrayal of world revolution. He also condemned Soviet 'weakening' of its command economy model in the post-Stalin period. The CCP equated the Stalin economic model with 'the very definition of socialism'; any departure from it was tantamount to 'revisionism' of Marxism and the 'restoration' of capitalism (Kong, 2010, p. 161). Accordingly, Mao threw down the gauntlet to the Soviet leadership with his adoption of the catastrophic Great Leap Forward (1958–1962). Moscow and Beijing's paths abruptly parted in the summer of 1960 after the withdrawal of Soviet aid specialists, who had been subject to a Chinese campaign against the CPSU (Lüthi, 2010, p. 47). It was clear that the CCP leadership would not simply defer to the Soviet approach to world affairs.

For another two decades, however, the PRC cleaved as tightly as ever to the Stalinist command economy model while pursuing a distinctive campaign politics, climaxing with the Cultural Revolution which, despite considerable economic progress, brought 'disarray' to China's industrial sector (Bernstein, 2009, p. 6). By the late 1970s, breaking with the erroneous concepts that planning equals socialism and that markets equal capitalism were crucial ideological prerequisites for China to diverge from the developmental path bequeathed by the Soviet Union in favour of 'socialism with Chinese characteristics' (Kong, 2010, p. 163).

State Socialism Under Siege

Despite their shared origins in the October 1917 Revolution, it is obvious that distinct historical legacies, circumstances and challenges faced CPSU General Secretary Mikhail Gorbachev's USSR in 1985 and Deng Xiaoping's PRC in 1979 when they embarked on their reforms. Indeed, one could go so far as to say that despite their common political heritage, and their similar non-capitalist economies, the differences in development made reform in the two states almost incomparable. The Soviet Union, and even more so its allied Council for Mutual Economic Assistance (Comecon) socialist states in East-Central Europe, by the 1980s had passed through the fires of extensive industrial and agricultural development and urbanisation, not to mention the most destructive war in history. Although in this decade, the USSR still lagged far behind the core capitalist states in terms of productivity, per capita income, and consumption, the Soviet Union eclipsed China by these measures, especially the latter two, which in 1979 was only just embarking on its second wave of agricultural reform and mass industrialisation.

For this reason, while both party leaders rightly or wrongly made policy choices that ultimately reinvigorated or destroyed their respective socialist reform projects, they did so in circumstances not of their own choosing, to paraphrase Marx from *The Eighteenth Brumaire*. Briefly put, diverging from the path and degree of development the USSR had followed in the latter part of the twentieth century, the PRC possessed 'structural advantages' for reform, especially 'decentralization', that the rigidly centralised USSR lacked (Bernstein, 2009, p. 2). In many respects, Soviet institutional rigidity was the penalty the USSR paid for first breaking with international capitalism in 1917 and then, standing alone under threat of invasion, pursuing crash industrialisation from its own resources under the aegis of Stalin's 'military-mobilisational' state (Cherepanov, 2006, p. 424).

Until the advent of Gorbachev's *perestroika* [reconstruction], the Soviet state was caught in an exhausting military-industrial competition primarily with the USA, which waged a Cold War of attrition with the express purpose of breaking the Soviet Union if not directly confronting it. The Soviet civilian economy was encumbered by an onerous military-industrial apparatus which in 1985 consumed a staggering 15% of its Gross National Product, dwarfing the 6% expenditure of the USA (Davis, 2002, p. 156). This proved to be systemically fatal when the advanced capitalist states in the 1970s began transitioning to so-called post-industrialism and neoliberalism. In the Brezhnev era of 'stagnation' (*zastoi*), the Soviet economic of model of mass production serving primarily to sustain mass armies, which had served it so effectively since the 1930s, was being eclipsed in the West by service industries, flexible production and high-tech battlefield weaponry (Harrison, 2017, p. 205). Bearing the brunt of Western anti-communist enmity, with some respite during the 1970s decade of *détente*, the Soviet state had limited political and economic instruments with which to counter the growing technological edge of the advanced capitalist states. The militarisation of the Soviet state and its foreign policy proved its undoing; its ten-year war in Afghanistan (1979–1989) was the final straw.

Gorbachev's 'new thinking' determination to end the Cold War was in good part driven by the urgent need to shed this massive military burden in order to divert resources to the civilian sector. Despite Gorbachev's attempts to ameliorate Cold War competition through his 'new thinking' peace and disarmament initiatives (Gill & Markwick, 2000, pp. 35–36), ultimately the Soviet *étatiste* political and economic system foundered, not only under the weight of a cumbersome *nomenklatura* apparatus that defied reform but also entrenched economic structures and popular expectations of social security they engendered, not least in the collectivised farm sector.

Collectivised farming, which Gorbachev as late as 1988 regarded as the backbone of socialist agriculture, was the Achille's heel of the Soviet system, consuming resources that could have been mobilised to regenerate the non-agricultural sector. Despite huge investment in agriculture in the Brezhnev era, growing from 16% of total Soviet investment in 1965 to 28% in 1985, productivity stalled (Rozelle & Swinnen, 2009, p. 279). Massively subsidised, the state guaranteed incomes of farmworkers nearly equalled those of their urban counterparts. Accordingly, attempts under Gorbachev in the 1980s to reform collective agriculture by replacing wages with labour contract and leasing systems that reflected farm output, were resisted by farmers and farm administrators alike. Consequently, such initiatives did little to improve poor agricultural performance, in contrast to similar reforms in China which strengthened rural support for the CCP.

It would take the wholesale overturn of the Soviet economic and political system under the banner of 'shock therapy' by neoliberal capitalist politicians and their advisors, notably Russian President Boris Yeltsin, US economist Geoffrey Sachs and the International Monetary Fund, to decollectivise agriculture and privatise industry (Gill & Markwick, 2000, pp. 138–140). The economic and social consequences of the breaking of the Soviet state were disastrous (Rozelle & Swinnen, 2009, pp. 276, 278–279, 282, 284). Moreover, despite the expectations of both Gorbachev and Yeltsin that dismantling Soviet state socialism would open the way for it to rejoin the prosperous European 'home', post-Soviet Russia and its allied successor states remain on the 'periphery' of the world capitalist system, to invoke Wallerstein's world system's theory (Lane, 2009, pp. 101–102). Only Russia's powerful nuclear military apparatus has prevented it from being subordinated to expansionary global capitalism, spearheaded by NATO (Markwick, 2016).

For the first two decades of its existence, the PRC too was under fire from the West but unlike the infant Soviet state it was not alone. Economic and technical aid from the USSR meant that the PRC's industrialisation 'take-off' was not as traumatic as that of the USSR, which in the context of ferocious civil war and threatened invasion had completely expropriated the Russian industrial, financial and landed elites and forcibly collectivised agriculture to fuel its crash industrialisation. The PRC, however, allowed private capital to survive and retained the allegiance of the class that brought the CCP to power: the peasantry (Amin, 2013, p. 16). Mao's 1972 modus vivendi with US President Richard Nixon and the subsequent normalisation of relations with the USA in 1978, largely shielded the PRC from economically draining confrontation or even invasion. Coupled with improved relations with the USSR towards the end of the Brezhnev era (Bernstein, 2009, p. 10), China was much better positioned to drastically reduce the burden of its defence and military expenditure than its Soviet counterpart. Indeed, despite the resistance of a relatively backward military-industrial sector, between 1978 and 1997 China achieved an extraordinary reversal of military to civilian production within its defence sector. Whereas in 1978 military production was 92% of the annual output of the defence sector, by 1997 84.5% its production was civilian. Chinese conversion of defence expenditure to the civilian economy, 'one of the largest ever transfers of industrial capacity from the military to the civilian spheres', freed up enormous resources for modernisation (Tai, 2008, pp. 74–76, Table 3.2). Of course, this drastic conversion came at a price for millions of defence industry workers. As employment in the defence industries nearly halved from three million workers, the secure 'iron rice bowl' employment and welfare benefits of the Mao era were eroded (Tai, 2008, pp. 75, 92).

The PRC faced serious challenges in 1978 when Deng Xiaoping embarked on reform to bring what he called 'order out of the chaos' (cited in Bernstein, 2009, p. 3) after the ten-year turmoil of the Cultural Revolution (1966–1976). China was still an underdeveloped nation, even compared to Gorbachev's sclerotic USSR: 70% of China's workforce was engaged in agriculture, compared to 14% in the USSR; China's average income per capita was 14 times lower than the USSR's; and almost one-third of China's citizens were illiterate (Anderson, 2010, p. 75). By these measures, as argued above, China in 1978 was much more like Stalin's Soviet Union in 1929 than Gorbachev's Soviet Union in 1985. However, the PRC had made major industrial and agricultural progress, notwithstanding the upheavals of the Great Leap Forward (1958–1961) and the Cultural Revolution (1966–1976), but towards the end of the Mao period the economy was beginning to run out of steam as productivity slowed despite ever higher investment. In short, China's Stalinist model of 'extensive growth' needed to shift radically to 'intensive growth' (Blank, 2015, pp. 47–49). In this respect, in 1978 the PRC faced a similar developmental crisis as its much more industrialised Soviet cousin, but in a vastly different social environment, particularly in the countryside. It was in this context that CCP abruptly turned to market measures in 1978 and subsequently embraced a 'socialist market economy' in 1992.

More than a few Western commentators have variously concluded that this signalled China embracing wholehearted state, neoliberal, and even imperialist, capitalism (Hart-Landsberg & Burkett, 2005; Ho-Fung, 2015; Minqi, 2008); conclusions which seem premature. Others have explored the seeming similarities between the CCP's market socialism and the CPSU's New Economic Policy (NEP) pursued in 1921–1928 (Hooper, 2017; Kenny, 2007). Although in the 1980s opinions about NEP varied among Chinese scholars there was no ambiguity on the part of CCP leaders, who saw it as legitimising their turn to the market; indeed Nikolai Bukharin, praised for his patient, non-violent approach to the peasantry unlike Stalin, was partially rehabilitated as Lenin's 'heir' (Rozman, 2014, pp. 158–160). The leading theoretician of NEP was fully rehabilitated in the Soviet Union in

February 1988 at the height of *perestroika*, lending further legitimacy to economic and political liberalisation, in particular the introduction of market mechanisms (Gill & Markwick, 2000, p. 48).

NEP with Chinese Characteristics

Parallels between Deng's reforms and Lenin's NEP can be illuminating, particularly in relation to the role of the state utilising capitalist measures to manage a transition to socialism, although of course such parallels are limited. The specific historical circumstances that the USSR faced in 1921 and the PRC in 1978 were vastly different. The Bolsheviks were seeking to save the world's first socialist revolution which was threatened with defeat after seven years of war had ravaged the economy and society. True, China turned towards market mechanisms after the ten-year turmoil of the Cultural Revolution, but the PRC was facing nothing like the life or death choice that confronted the Bolsheviks. The challenge for China was more muted, but ultimately no less threatening: economic competition from Japan, South Korea and Taiwan. As Deng observed during the 1989 Tiananmen crisis:

> There was no way the economy could develop, no way living standards could rise, and no way the country could get stronger … The world is galloping forward these days, a mile a minute, especially in science and technology. We can hardly keep up. (Cited in Anderson, 2010, p. 79)

For the Bolsheviks, the NEP was not merely a matter of keeping up; it was a question of survival. NEP was a 'transitional', crisis strategy for socialism; a 'retreat' to state capitalism (Krausz, 2015, pp. 335–337) which combined centralised, Soviet controlled planning through Gosplan, with market mechanisms between and within town and country. The NEP entailed, as Lenin put it in brief notes:

(α) Retention of the commanding heights in the sphere of *means* of production (*transport*, etc.);
(β) Retention of the land in the hands of the state;

(γ) freedom of trade in the sphere of petty production;
(δ) state capitalism in the sense of attracting *private capital* (both concessions and *mixed companies*) (Lenin, 1922).

In the first instance, the NEP was a concession to the peasantry, who had security of land tenure and could sell their surplus grain; private, retail trade was legalised; and agricultural and commercial cooperatives could be formed. The NEP also entailed utilising Tsarist-era 'bourgeois' technical specialists and administrators and encouraging foreign, capitalist trade and investment (Suny, 1998, pp. 138–139). In short, Lenin's NEP entailed 'building socialism with capitalist hands' while the Soviet state retained the 'commanding heights' of the economy (Husband, 1997, pp. 274–275). The same metaphors could certainly be applied to China's turn towards the market under Deng from 1978 onwards. Like Lenin's NEP, the CCP has kept a firm hand on the tiller of state and key state assets, unlike Gorbachev's diluted version of it.

China's economic volte-face from 1978 to 1992 entailed, inter alia, the following measures:

1. A second land reform, in which a 'household responsibility system' replaced communes. In many respects it was analogous to the NEP: private agricultural production for the market was encouraged; farmers would be rewarded by becoming 'rich' and 'prosperous' for their own 'hard work' (Deng, 1983a, p. 12).
2. Very high peasant savings were achieved by increasing incomes, and by limiting welfare payments by implementing the 'one child' family policy. The resultant savings were channelled by banks into modernising state enterprises. This was certainly capital accumulation, pumping surplus income from the countryside into industry but it was not the harsh 'primitive socialist accumulation' Soviet economist Yevgenyi Preobrazhensky famously advocated in the latter years of NEP (Allen, 2003, pp. 57–58; Erlich, 1960, pp. 42–44).
3. Decentralisation of economic decision-making. This was the opposite of the Soviet Gosplan, which continued throughout the Soviet NEP and would become the hall-mark of Stalinist industrialist development.

4. State enterprises were effectively leased to managers who were able to sell products outside the plan at market prices; in so doing, there was no analogy with the NEP.
5. The establishment of Township and Village Enterprises (TVE) in the countryside: Again, there was no analogy with the NEP. The TVE entailed light industry based on abundant cheap labour; as a result, rural-industrial output and rural incomes dramatically increased.
6. Special Economic Zones (SEZ) had no counterpart with Lenin's NEP, although Soviet reformers toyed with the concept during *perestroika*. Taking advantage of the Chinese diaspora, the SEZ provided low-cost labour for the assembly of electronics and white goods. In 1984, Deng hailed SEZ as conduits for foreign 'technology, management, and knowledge' and for China to open up to the world. In the SEZ, workers employed under the 'contracted responsibility system' were to be rewarded 'according to their performance'. Deng made no apologies for the fact that people in the coastal SEZ could 'become rich first. Egalitarianism will not work (Deng, 1984a, pp. 26–27)'.

In Deng's unabashed advocacy of hard work being rewarded by 'prosperity' and 'wealth', there was an echo of Bukharin's call 65 years earlier to Soviet peasants to 'enrich yourselves'. However, not only was the Soviet NEP begun in far more threatening economic and military circumstances but in the 1920s NEP was a transitional measure during what the Bolsheviks assumed to be a lull before the next international revolutionary storm, which they were actively stoking through the Comintern, while the Soviet Union built diplomatic and economic state-to-state relations with the core capitalist powers. China has no such political instrument separate from the PRC and its priority is not international socialism but developing socialism within China's national boundaries.

Socialism in One China

Although in many respects, Deng adhered to the Marxist–Leninist heritage bequeathed by Stalin and paid homage to Chairman Mao, a major shift in Marxist analysis underlay the 'Four Modernisations' reform programme that the CCP pursued from 1978 onwards. At the CCP's 12th National Congress in September 1982, Deng emphasised that 'socialism with Chinese characteristics' meant that the CCP should recognise 'Chinese realities' and not 'mechanically copy' other models of development, by which he clearly meant the well worn Soviet path: 'We must integrate the universal truth of Marxism with the concrete realities of China (Deng, 1982, p. 3)'. Where Mao in the 1950s and 1960s had emphasised changing the social relations of production, irrespective of the underdevelopment of China's productive forces, manifest in disastrous experiments such as the Great Leap Forward and the Cultural Revolution, Deng effectively repudiated Mao's perspective: 'We ignored the development of the productive forces for a long time', he lamented in April 1983:

> In a socialist country a genuinely Marxist ruling party must devote itself to developing the productive forces and, with this as the foundation, gradually raise the people's living standards… So we are paying special attention to the building of a high standard of material civilization. At the same time, we are building a socialist civilization with high cultural and ideological standards. (Deng, 1983b, p. 16)

In stressing the development of 'material civilization', Deng was reviving the classical Marxist conception that the development of full-fledged socialism required the highest development of the productive forces: 'Pauperism is not socialism, still less communism', he insisted (Deng, 1984b, p. 37); a fundamental Marxist principle stressed again and again in the late 1920s by Stalin's Left opponents within the Soviet Communist Party against his conception of 'socialism in one country'.

The question, of course, was how socialism was to be achieved in an impoverished, pre-industrial, predominantly agrarian society? In this regard, in contrast to Stalin's semi-autarkic 'socialism in one country', China set itself on a path of opening itself up to the 'outside world', expanding international trade to secure 'foreign investment capital and technology', to catch up with the developed countries, a prolonged process that could take possibly '50 or 70 years (Deng, 1984c, p. 52)'. The assumption here, in integrating itself into the global capitalist economy, was a prolonged era of 'peaceful coexistence' with the Western powers. There was nothing like the urgency of Stalin's prescient warning in 1931 that 'we have ten years to catch up, or we shall go under (Stalin, 1931)'. Nazi Germany invaded the USSR on 22 June 1941.

China was certainly not facing immediate war in 1978 but economic liberalisation was far from smooth sailing. Precipitous reductions in state expenditure and abolition of centralised pricing that threatened 'iron rice bowl' social security, fanned popular discontent. In the wake of the 1989 Tiananmen crisis, China's decade-long march towards the market stalled. However, soon after Deng's famous 1992 'southern tour', in October 1993 the PRC defined itself as a 'socialist market economy'. What followed was the accelerated expansion of market measures: First, privatising State-Owned Enterprises (SOEs) and even more so provincial TVEs, so that by 2004 private sector employment was twice that of the public sector. Second, an extraordinary rise in foreign trade and exports boosted by foreign investment and cheap labour, making China the so-called new 'sweatshop of the world'. The net result of China's hypertrophied NEP in the four decades since 1978 has been an average annual GDP growth of 9.5%; a rate of growth 'unprecedented in human history'. In those forty years, 700 million people have been lifted out of poverty. Given its massive population, China thereby has contributed in its own right to global poverty reduction (Yifu & Shen, 2018, p. 117). This undeniable social progress has been achieved by the unleashing of market forces on an extraordinary scale. By the turn of the century, non-state, market production accounted for 75% of China's GDP (Chow, 2018, pp. 109, 113). The result, however, has been the spawning of a financial and industrial class that had no counterpart in the Soviet system, until the Soviet state collapsed.

Learning from Failure

The CCP leadership learned crucial lessons from the failure of Gorbachev's reforms, which they watched with 'urgency' (Meisels, 2013, p. 3). Notwithstanding the unravelling of state socialism in East-Central Europe in 1989 and the catastrophic collapse of the Soviet

Union itself in 1991, Beijing affirmed publicly that the PRC would draw strength from the lessons learned: 'Don't panic', declared Deng in early 1992, 'don't think that Marxism has disappeared, that it's not useful anymore and that it has been defeated. Nothing of the sort!' (Deng, 1992). In the aftermath of the Soviet collapse, the CCP established its own research groups dedicated to analysis of the causes and lessons of the Soviet demise and reoriented Chinese academic institutions to do same. Thus, for example, on this basis in 1992 at the Chinese Academy of Social Sciences, the former Institute for Soviet and East European Studies was rebadged as the East European, Russian and Central Asian Studies. Likewise, in 1994 the China Reform Forum at the Central Party School was established, with a particular focus at that time on Soviet transformation and downfall (Marsh, 2003, pp. 264–265).

One of the first systematic attempts to draw lessons from the fate of the Soviet Union was produced by the Ideology and Theory Department of *China Youth Daily* in the immediate aftermath of the failed attempt to overthrow Gorbachev on 21 August 1991, the final salvo in the USSR's demise. Pointedly titled, 'Realistic Responses and Strategic Choices for China after the Soviet Coup', among its recommendations were:

1. China should not move towards capitalism, as had occurred in the USSR.
2. The CCP needed to transform itself from a 'revolutionary' into a 'ruling' party.
3. CCP Marxist–Leninist ideology needed to become 'relaxed', democratic and liberal to broaden popular support, but invoking Chinese traditions such as Confucianism rather than Western ones.
4. Chinese nationalism should become the bedrock of CCP legitimacy to avoid the ethnic nationalism that had afflicted the USSR (Marsh, 2003, p. 266).

The failures of the CPSU and its leadership were at the heart of the lessons this document and the CCP drew from the Soviet collapse. Above all, the need to maintain the CCP's monopoly of power, on the one hand; on the other, to reinforce the ruling party's legitimacy by raising living standards by continued economic reform (Marsh, 2003, p. 266).

Clearly, unlike Gorbachev, for whom in his own words 'economic progress and social renewal were ultimately dependent on political democratization' (cited in Bernstein, 2009, p. 8), Deng did not prioritise political liberalisation over economic reform; nor have Deng's successors. Quite the opposite: where Gorbachev from January 1987 onwards increasingly turned to political liberalisation, especially as *perestroika* and the Soviet economy stalled, from the start of its reforms the CCP rejected any loosening of its grip on the apparatus of state as China's 'socialist market economy' surged.

Where the largely unified CCP leadership has reaffirmed its pivotal role at the helm of state, Gorbachev, unable to forge a unified party leadership, had made the fatal error of repudiating the leading role of the CPSU. Specifically, in October 1988 he effectively abolished the Party's central apparatus: The Secretariat. At a stroke, in Second Secretary Yegor Ligachev's words, 'The Party was deprived of an operating staff'. Gorbachev thereby surrendered his crucial weapon for directing economic reform and upholding the multinational USSR (Gill & Markwick, 2000, pp. 55, 75, 86).

Gorbachev's neutering of the CPSU and his embrace of liberal democratic institutions was no accident. Despite his continual invoking of Lenin, in elevating 'universal values' above class struggle, his conceptions of 'new thinking' and *perestroika* had much more in common with late nineteenth-century social democratic reformism that Lenin had condemned (Brown, 2007). From 1988, an increasingly desperate Gorbachev leadership abandoned its commitment to socialist reform in favour of parliamentarist liberalisation, compounding a dire situation and opening the way to capitalist transformation by the *nomenklatura* in the guise of 'privatisation of the state by the state' (Gill & Markwick, 2000, pp. 97, 208–209).

More than a few Chinese analysts have held Gorbachev and the CPSU's abandonment of Marxism–Leninism as the primary cause of the failure of perestroika and the Soviet Union's collapse (Li, 2011); still others blame the stagnation of the Soviet system or the influence of US 'bourgeois liberalization' peacefully undermining the Soviet Union (Meisels, 2013). Whatever explanations for the Soviet demise have been adopted by CCP leaders, academics and analysts, the CCP has reaffirmed time and again its determination to be at the helm of state and to be guided by Marxism–Leninism. In relation to the unabashed dominance of the Chinese party state, the CCP is true to the Stalinist maxim that the closer socialism the greater the necessity for state power. At the same time, however, there was no Soviet precedent for China's extravagant embrace of market economics and its unleashing of an opulent domestic bourgeoisie. Here is the contradictory essence of 'socialism with Chinese characteristics'.

Classes and the State

Classes are alive and well within China, a product of the liberalised economic policies the CCP has deployed over four decades. The resultant divisive class relations require a skilful balancing act on the part of the PRC party-state. On the one hand, it has fostered an extraordinarily rich financial and industrial class which has a growing international reach (although Chinese corporations are still dwarfed by US and European transnational corporations: Lane, 2009, p. 106) and which even has a presence in the CCP itself. China's wealthiest 1% control 30% of household wealth, equivalent to that in the USA, while wealth disparity in China, measured by its Gini coefficient, now exceeds that of the USA (Cheng & Ding, 2017, p. 51). But such inequality, particularly in a state that boasts it is 'socialist' is fraught; citizens demanding radical reforms in Czechoslovakia and Poland in the 1960s and 1980s did so in the name of socialism. In 2016, China had a Gini coefficient of 0.465, exceeding the 'international warning line of 0.45' (Yifu & Shen, 2018, p. 119), threatening 'dangerous' social instability (Jin, Qingxia, & Mengnan, 2015, p. 25), particularly in a society with a growing but disenfranchised working class.

Industrialisation always comes at a price. It certainly did for workers once employed in China's SOEs which in 1995–2003 shrank from 11,800 to 34,000 units. As a result, 44 million SOE workers lost their jobs (Ligang, 2018, p. 352), hitherto guaranteed under Mao's soviet-style 'iron rice bowl' life-time employment and social security benefits. This has been accompanied by massive migration from the countryside to the coastal cities, creating an impoverished, highly exploited, industrial working class. Yet despite the growth of an urbanised working class, the upshot has been

> a major decline of labour's share of GDP from about 53 per cent in 1990 to 42 per cent in 2007. The growing 'reserve army of labor,' the segregation of the labor market, and massive privatizations of state-owned enterprises have significantly depressed the power and weakened the solidarity of the working class. (Cheng & Ding, 2017, p. 51)

Witnessing the emergence of Poland's *Solidarność* (Solidarity) mass trade-union movement in 1980–1981, the precursor to the 1989 fall of state socialism in East-Central Europe, the CCP has been alert to any so-called civil society movements, including workers' movements, which might threaten its hegemony (Bernstein, 2009, pp. 3–4). Testimony to this came with the lethal repression of mass student Tiananmen Square protests in June 1989, which began to attract workers (Boswell & Peters, 1990, pp. 21–22). The willingness of the CCP under Deng to utilise the PLA to repress mass demonstrations, unlike Gorbachev who was manifestly opposed to the use of state violence even to maintain the Soviet Union, is suggestive of two different traditions in party-army relations: the Soviet Red Army was always unequivocally subordinate to the CPSU, whereas the PLA had been co-leader with the CCP of the vast peasant insurgency that drove the Chinese revolution. With its roots and mass support in the peasantry, the CPP has not been reluctant to wield its 'labour repressive system' against the very class that for Marxism is the driving force of socialism (Bernstein, 2009, p. 5). To date, despite mass protests, the state has proven very effective at thwarting sustained, organised, labour resistance.

Transitional, Contender State

The demise of the Soviet Union confirms the ultimate incompatibility between isolated, developmental, state socialism and militaristic, highly productive, hegemonic capitalism. Despite inserting China into the world capitalist economy (signalled by its admission to the World Trade Organisation in 2001: Panitch & Gindin, 2013, pp. 147–149), admitting wealthy businesspeople into the CCP, and the codification of private property rights, the Party insists that this model of development is 'socialism with Chinese characteristics', albeit still in the 'initial stage'. In reality, the Chinese model is a hybrid of a predominantly capitalist economy, including state-dependent capitalists, supervised by a powerful 'contender state' controlled by a CCP that maintains its grip on the 'commanding heights' of banking and strategic industries and resists subordination to the global capitalist system (Panitch & Gindin, 2013, p. 151; Van der Pijl, 2012). In this respect, the Chinese model remains a 'sovereign project' (Amin, 2013, p. 22), unlike Russia, which, while politically independent due to its powerful military state, economically has been reduced to a 'raw-materials supplying appendage' to international capitalism (Kotz, 2001; 2002, p. 391). And unlike, even more so, the former Comecon-Warsaw Pact states which have been completely subsumed within the European capitalist EU-NATO heartland. Nevertheless, as a hybrid, 'transitional' society (Blank, 2015, p. 4), with the CCP-led state riding the tiger of contending class forces externally and internally, China could yet go either way: to full-fledged capitalism or towards state or even democratic socialism.

Serious internal and external challenges confront China's hybrid, transitional state system. Internally, the class gulf between peasants, workers and capitalists threatens social stability. More to the point, the existence of classes, and a level of productivity which is still far from being able to abolish classes does not accord with the highly advanced, egalitarian socialism envisaged in classical Marxism. In the twenty-first century, China has generated a massive, largely urbanised, working class which will have to become an active agent of socialism if it is to become a genuine ruling class. As Marta Harnecker has argued, 'one of the essential elements of socialism is social ownership of the means of production', indeed, 'without participatory planning there can be no socialism (Harnecker, 2012, p. 243)'. By this measure, China is still a long way from being a socialist state, strictly defined.

Externally, the integration of China's economy into a global capitalist system, dominated by the USA (Panitch & Gindin, 2013, pp. 154–155), makes China vulnerable to the systemic crises and limits of international capitalism (Minqi, 2008, pp. 176–177) or to dispossession by overwhelming military power (Long, Herrera, & Andréani, 2018, p. 12; Van der Pijl, 2012, p. 504). Clearly, as the PRC demonstrates, the state apparatus can be not only a bulwark against Western hegemony but also tilt the relationship of nation-state forces favourably against the core capitalist states as China's 'One Belt, One Road' initiative suggests (Sit, Erebus, Lau, & Wen, 2017). But ultimately, the survival and flourishing of 'socialism with Chinese characteristics' depends on the course of progressive politics within the citadels of modern capitalism, especially fraught in Donald Trump's USA.

References

Allen, R. C. (2003). *Farm to factory: A reinterpretation of the Soviet industrial revolution*. Princeton and Oxford: Princeton University Press.
Amin, S. (2013). China 2013. *Monthly Review, 64*(10), 14–33.
Anderson, P. (2010). Two revolutions. *New Left Review, 61*, 59–96.
Bernstein, T. (2009). *Economic and political reform in China and the former Soviet Union* (CSD Working Papers: 1–21). Retrieved from http://escholarship.org/uc/item/8mf8f3kt.
Bisley, N. L. (2000). *Historical sociology and great power vulnerability: The end of the cold war and the collapse of the Soviet Union*. PhD thesis, London School of Economics and Political Science, University of London.
Blank, G. (2015). *Is the east still red? Socialism and the market in China*. Winchester, UK and Washington, USA: Zero Books.
Boswell, T., & Peters, R. (1990). State socialism and the industrial divide in the world-economy: A comparative essay on the rebellions in Poland and China. *Critical Sociology, 17*(1), 3–34. Retrieved from https://doi.org/10.1177/089692059001700101.
Brown, A. (2007). Gorbachev, Lenin and the Break with Leninism. *Demokratizatsiya, 15*(2), 230–244.
Butenko, A. P. (1990). Is Karl Marx to Blame for "barracks socialism"? *Russian Studies in Philosophy, 29*(2), 32–47.

Cheng, E., & Ding, X. (2017). A theory of China's "miracle": Eight principles of contemporary Chinese political economy. *Monthly Review, 68*(8), 46–57. Retrieved from http://dx.doi.org/10.14452/MR-068-08-2017-01_5.

Cherepanov, V. (2006). *Vlast' i voina. Stalinskii mekhanizm gosudarstvennogo upravleniia v Velikoi Otechestvennoi voine.* Izvestiia: Moscow.

Chow, G. C. (2018). China's economic transformation. In R. Garnaut, S. Ligang, & F. Cai (Eds.), *China's 40 years of reform and development: 1978–2018* (pp. 93–115). Canberra: ANU Press.

Davis, C. (2002). Country survey XVI the defence sector in the economy of a declining superpower: Soviet Union and Russia, 1965–2001. *Defence and Peace Economics, 13*(3), 145–177.

Deng, X. (1982, September 1). Opening speech at the twelfth national congress of the Communist Party of China. In X. Deng (Ed.), *Build socialism with Chinese characteristics* (pp. 1–5). Beijing: Foreign Languages Press, 1985.

Deng, X. (1983a, January 12). Our work in all fields should contribute to the building of socialism with Chinese characteristics. In X. Deng (Ed.), *Build socialism with Chinese characteristics* (pp. 10–13). Beijing: Foreign Languages Press.

Deng, X. (1983b, April 29). Build a socialist civilization with both high material and high cultural and ideological standards. In X. Deng (Ed.), *Build socialism with Chinese characteristics* (p. 16). Beijing: Foreign Languages Press.

Deng, X. (1984a, February 24). On special economic zones and opening more cities to the outside world. In X. Deng (Ed.), *Build socialism with Chinese characteristics* (pp. 25–27). Beijing: Foreign Languages Press.

Deng, X. (1984b, June 30). Build socialism with Chinese characteristics. In X. Deng (Ed.), *Build socialism with Chinese characteristics* (pp. 35–40). Beijing: Foreign Languages Press.

Deng, X. (1984c, October 6). Achieve the magnificent goal of our four modernizations, and our basic policies. In X. Deng (Ed.), *Build socialism with Chinese characteristics* (pp. 49–53). Beijing: Foreign Languages Press.

Deng, X. (1992, January 18–February 21). *Excerpts from talks given in Wuchang, Shenzhen, Zhuhai and Shanghai.* Retrieved from https://dengxiaopingworks.wordpress.com/2013/03/18/excerpts-from-talks-given-in-wuchang-shenzhen-zhuhai-and-shanghai/.

Deutscher, I. (1964). Maoism. Its origins, background and outlook. *The Socialist Register, 1*, 11–37.
Deutscher, I. (1967). *The unfinished revolution, 1917–1967*. Oxford, UK: Oxford University Press.
Erlich, A. (1960). *The Soviet industrialization debate, 1924–1928*. Cambridge, MA: Harvard University Press.
Gill, G., & Markwick, R. D. (2000). *Russia's stillborn democracy? From Gorbachev to Yeltsin*. Oxford: Oxford University Press.
Gregor, A. J. (2014). *Marxism and the making of China: A doctrinal history*. Houndmills, Basingstoke, UK: Palgrave Macmillan.
Harnecker, M. (2012). Social and long-term planning. *Science & Society, 76*(2), 243–266.
Harrison, M. (2017). The Soviet economy, 1917–1991: Its life and afterlife. *The Independent Review, 22*(2), 199–206.
Hart-Landsberg, M., & Burkett, P. (2005). *China and socialism: Market reforms and class struggle*. New York: Monthly Review Press.
Ho-Fung, H. (2015). China fantasies. *Jacobin*. Retrieved from https://www.jacobinmag.com/2015/12/china-new-global-order-imperialism-communist-party-globalization.
Hooper, M. (2017). Opposite directions: The NEP and China's opening and reform. *Australian Marxist Review, 64*, 14–22.
Husband, W. B. (1997). The new economic policy (NEP) and the revolutionary experiment 1921–1929. In G. L. Freeze (Ed.), *Russia a history* (pp. 263–290). Oxford: Oxford University Press.
Jin, H., Qingxia, Z., & Mengnan, Z. (2015). China's income inequality in the global context. *Perspectives in Science, 7*, 24–29. Retrieved from https://doi.org/10.1016/j.pisc.2015.11.006.
Kenny, T. (2007). Lessons for the "socialist market economy" of people's China from the Soviet "new economic policy". *Nature, Society, and Thought, 20*(1), 80–90.
Kong, H. (2010). The transplantation and entrenchment of the Soviet economic model in China. In T. P. Bernstein & L. Hua-Yu (Eds.), *China learns from the Soviet Union, 1949–Present* (pp. 154–167). Lanham, MD: Lexington.
Kotz, D. M. (2001). Is Russia becoming capitalist? *Science & Society, 65*(2), 157–181.
Kotz, D. M. (2002). Is Russia becoming capitalist? Reply. *Science & Society, 66*(3), 388–393.

Krausz, T. (2015). *Reconstructing Lenin: An intellectual biography* (B. Bethlenfalvy, Trans.). New York: Monthly Review Press.
Lane, D. (2009). Global capitalism and the transformation of state socialism. *Studies in Comparative International Development, 44*(2), 97–117. https://doi.org/10.1007/s12116-008-9039-3.
Lenin, V. (1917). The economic basis of the withering away of the state. In *The state and revolution*. Retrieved from https://www.marxists.org/archive/lenin/works/1917/staterev/ch05.htm.
Lenin, V. (1922). Notes for a report 'five years of the Russian revolution and the prospects of the world revolution' at the fourth congress of the Comintern. Retrieved from https://www.marxists.org/archive/lenin/works/1922/nov/13b.htm.
Lewin, M. (2016). *The Soviet century*. London and New York: Verso.
Li, S. (2011). The degeneration of the Soviet Communist Party as the fundamental cause of the disintegration of the Soviet Union. *International Critical Thought, 1*(2), 171–185.
Ligang, S. (2018). State-owned enterprise reform in China: Past, present and prospects. In R. Garnaut, S. Ligang, & F. Cai (Eds.), *China's 40 years of reform and development: 1978–2018* (pp. 345–373). Canberra: ANU Press.
Long, Z., Herrera, R., & Andréani, T. (2018). On the nature of the Chinese economic system. *Monthly Review, 70*(5). Retrieved from https://monthlyreview.org/2018/10/01/on-the-nature-of-the-chinese-economic-system/.
Lüthi, L. M. (2010). Sino-Soviet relations during the Mao years, 1949–1969. In T. P. Bernstein & L. Hua-Yu (Eds.), *China learns from the Soviet Union, 1949–Present* (pp. 33–67). Lanham, MD: Lexington.
Mao, Z. (1940). On new democracy. *Selected works of Mao Tse-tung* (Vol. 2). Retrieved from https://www.marxists.org/reference/archive/mao/selected-works/volume-2/mswv2_26.htm.
Markwick, R. (2016). A new cold war? *Arena Magazine*. Retrieved from https://arena.org.au/a-new-cold-war-by-roger-markwick/.
Markwick, R. D. (2017). Violence to Velvet: Revolutions—1917 to 2017. *Slavic Review, 76*(3), 1917–2017. The Russian Revolution a Hundred Years Later: 600–609.
Marsh, C. (2003). Learning from your comrade's mistakes: The impact of the Soviet past on China's future. *Communist and Post-communist Studies, 36*, 259–272.
Marx, K. (1846). *A critique of the German ideology*. Retrieved from https://www.marxists.org/archive/marx/works/download/Marx_The_German_Ideology.pdf.

Meisels, A. G. (2013). *Lessons learned in China from the collapse of the Soviet Union* (Policy Paper Series, No. 3, pp. 1–29). China Studies Centre, The University of Sydney.

Minqi, L. (2008). *The rise of China and the Demise of the capitalist world-economy*. New York: Monthly Review Press.

Panitch, L., & Gindin, S. (2013). The integration of China into global capitalism. *International Critical Thought, 3*(2), 146–158. https://doi.org/10.1080/21598282.2013.787248.

Rozelle, S., & Swinnen, J. F. M. (2009). Why did the communist party reform in China, but not in the Soviet Union? The political economy of agricultural transition. *China Economic Review, 20*, 275–287.

Rozman, G. (2014). *The Chinese debate about Soviet Socialism, 1978–1985*. Princeton, NJ: Princeton University Press.

Sit, T., Erebus, W., Lau, K. C., & Wen, T. (2017). One belt, one road: China's strategy for a new global order. *Monthly Review, 68*(8), 36–45. https://doi.org/10.14452/mr-068-08-2017-01_4.

Stalin, I. V. (1928). Ob industrializatsii i khlebnoi probleme: Rech' na plenume TsK VKP (b) 9 iulia 1928 g. *Sochineniia*. T. 11. Moscow: OGIZ, 1949.

Stalin, I. V. (1931). O zadachakh khozaistvennikov: Rech' na Pervoi Vsesoiuznoi konferentsii rabotnikov sotsialisticheskoi promyshlennosti, 4 fevraliia 1931 g. *Sochineniia*, T. 13. Moscow: Gipl, 1951.

Stone, D. R. (2000). *Hammer and rifle: The militarization of the Soviet Union, 1926–1933*. Lawrence, KS: University Press of Kansas.

Suny, R. G. (1998). *Soviet experiment: Russia, USSR and the successor states*. New York: Oxford University Press.

Tai, M. C. (2008). *Fortifying China: The struggle to build a modern defense economy*. Ithaca and London: Cornell University Press.

Van der Pijl, K. (2012). Is the east still red? The contender state and class struggles in China. *Globalizations, 9*(4), 503–516.

Van Ree, E. (1998). Socialism in one country: A reassessment. *Studies in East European Thought, 50*, 77–117.

Von Hagen, M. (1990). *Soldiers in the proletarian dictatorship: The Red Army and the Soviet socialist state, 1917–1930*. Ithaca and London: Cornell University Press.

Wang, H. (2016). The 'people's war' and the legacy of the Chinese revolution. In L. Panitch & G. Albo (Eds.), *Socialist register 2017: Rethinking revolution* (pp. 286–298). London: The Merlin Press.

Yifu, J., & Shen, Z. (2018). Reform and development strategy. In R. Garnaut, S. Ligang, & F. Cai (Eds.), *China's 40 years of reform and development: 1978–2018* (pp. 117–134). Canberra: ANU Press.

16

Legal Continuity and Change: Two Russian Revolutions and Perestroika Through the Prism of Kelsen's Grundnorm and Hart's Secondary Rules

Anna Taitslin

Introduction

The chapter focuses on legal change by way of *revolutionary* transformations that result in the shift from one legal order to another. The objective is to compare the three instances of such legal change: the February Revolution (that led to the collapse of the Russian Empire), the October Revolution and the *Perestroika* phase (that led to the dissolution of the Soviet Union).

The parallels between the post-revolutionary period and the collapse of the Russian Empire, on one side, and *Perstroika* and the collapse of the Soviet Union, on another side, have been a stock of common discourse, at least, since V. Pelevin's *Chapaev and Void* [Чапаев и Пустота] (1996) [part 2]:

A. Taitslin (✉)
University of New England, Armidale, NSW, Australia

Тимур Тимурович:

И, как мне кажется, ваш случай очень прозрачный. Вы просто не принимаете нового...
Вы как раз принадлежите к тому поколению, которое было запрограммировано на жизнь в одной социально-культурной парадигме, а оказалось в совершенно другой...
...Но вопрос тем не менее остается - почему одни устремляются, так сказать, к новому, а другие так и остаются выяснять несуществующие отношения с тенями угасшего мира... Да, Китай.... Для них абсолютный эталон остался в прошлом и любые новшества являются злом - в силу того, что уводят от этого эталона еще дальше.
- Простите, - сказал я, - это вообще свойственно человеческой культуре. Это присутствует даже в языке. Например, в английском. Мы, что называется, descendants of the past. Это слово обозначает движение вниз, а не подъем. Мы не ascendants.
- ... речь у нас шла о том, что для классической китайской ментальности любое движение вперед будет деградацией. А есть другой путь - тот, по которому всю свою историю идет Европа, что бы вы там не говорили о языке. Тот путь, на который уже столько лет пытается встать Россия, вновь и вновь совершая свой несчастный алхимический брак с Западом.
- Замечательно.
- Спасибо. Здесь идеал мыслится не как оставшийся в прошлом, а как потенциально существующий в будущем. И это сразу же наполняет существование смыслом. Понимаете? Это идея развития, прогресса, движения от менее совершенного к более совершенному.... Вы презираете те позы, которые время повелевает нам принять. И именно в этом причина вашей трагедии.

Timur Timurovich:

- Your case is quite transparent. You just cannot take change. **You belong to the generation that was programmed for life in one**

social-cultural paradigm but happened to inhabit a completely different one....But there remains a question why some people set their sights on future while others linger to sort out inexistent connexions with the shades of the extinct world?... Yes. China... For them the absolute yardstick remained in the past, and any novation is evil, owing to the move further away from this yardstick.
- Excuse me, - I says, - but it is an attribute of the human culture generally. It exists even in language, for example in English. We are so called 'descendants' of the past. This word denotes the descent, not ascend. We are not 'ascendants'.
- ...We talked that in the classical Chinese mentality any movement forward is degradation. But there is another path – that one taken by Europe through all its history, whatever you may say about the language. That path Russia attempts futilely to enter on for so many years, again and again performing its doomed alchemistic marriage with the West.
- Well said.
- Thank you. Here the ideal is conceived not as remaining in the past but as potentially existing in the future. Thus, it immediately gives meaning to the [people's] existence. Do you understand? It is the idea of development, progress, move from the less perfect to the more perfect.... You are contemptuous of the poses that the time dictate us to take. This is the reason for your tragedy... [tr. AT]

In the quote the reference is made to the 'social-cultural paradigm' that had been transformed in the post-revolutionary period, just as in the post-perestroika one. May Pelevin also imply that the ideal of 'progress' provided the justification for the revolutionary break with the past that accompanied a paradigm shift (such as from capitalism to socialism and back)?

The overall objective of the *Perestroika* 'paradigm transformation' (as originated by M. Gorbachev in 1985) was to modernise of a stagnant Soviet Union, rather than destroy it. Modernisation, no doubt, was something that the Russian Empire, marred by severe socio-economic inequality, direly needed as well. But modernisation may not necessarily mean revolution, as the Great Reforms of 1860s had shown in the reign of Alexander II. While the failed 'revolution' of 1905 might hasten further 'progressive' reforms, the latter originated from the top. Nikolai II's Manifest of 17 October 1905 (26803) led to establishment of a parliament (Государственная Дума) of 1906–1916, i.e. the limited popular representation, felling short of 'direct and equal' representation. The evolutionary transformation of the Russian Empire into the full-blown constitutional monarchy was the political objective of the main centre-left party of the Constitutional Democrats (*K-D*), as well as the centre-right 'Party of the 17 October'. But the two and a half years of the First World War had stretched the empire to its limits, bringing about the revolutionary cataclysms of unprecedented magnitude.

There may be little doubt of the revolutionary nature of the February Revolution and the October Revolution in 1917. Yet the nature and scale of legal change had been very different. And what about *Perestroika*: did it result in legal change that would meet the test for 'revolutionary' break with the preceding legal order? The chapter answers the question in affirmative. The chapter extends to delineate the precise nature and scale of legal change in each two revolutions of 1917 and *Perestroika*.

First, we outline the definition of 'revolutionary' legal change and elucidate the overall thesis in terms of Kelsen's *basic norm* and Hart's *secondary rules*, then, we survey the legal change following the February Revolution, the October Revolution and *Perestroika*, in terms of 'basic norm' [test for the revolutionary change] as well as of the secondary rules [test for the scale of the change].

Revolutionary Legal Change: Definition

In his *Pure Theory of Law* [1934] Hans Kelsen defined *revolutionary* legal change as comprising *every non-legitimate change* (i.e. breach) of the 'constitution' (Kelsen, 1967, p. 209). In Kelsen's theory, the validity of the legal order is anchored to a certain *basic norm* (*Grundnorm*), which all other norms could be derived from (pp. 197–198, 212, 218). Thus, in monarchies where the monarch is the ultimate source of all powers (including the constitution) the norm that *one ought to obey the monarch's command* would be the basic norm.

In case of a revolutionary change, the old legal order dissolve and a new legal order be born.

A change of the sociocultural paradigm *may or may not* be accompanied by revolutionary legal change. For example, the reform of Peter the Great resulted in dismantling the old key institutions, such as the court system (Приказы) and the old legislature (Боярская Дума) and might well represent the 'paradigm change'. Still the radical paradigm change might not necessarily amount to a revolutionary break with the old legal order, for instance, if the perpetrator of the change was the *absolute* monarch himself. Even so, to implement *radical* reforms the executive might well acquire the power at expense of other branches (such as the courts or legislature, which could serve as 'checks and balances'), thus, undermining the constitutional principle of 'separation of powers', and, hence, the Rule of Law.

In his *Concept of Law* [1961], instead of the basic norm, H. L. A. Hart introduced the three secondary rules: the rule of recognition, the rule of change and the rule of adjudication. The rule of recognition is 'a rule for conclusive identification of the primary rules of obligation' (Hart, 1994, p. 95). The rule of recognition provides the test for validity of the ordinary legal rules—primary rules of obligations, such as rules of private law, criminal law or administrative law. Thus, the test for validity/rule of recognition of the criminal law rules might be the criminal law code. But what would make the code valid? The rule of change provides the answer. Approximating to Kelsen's basic norm, it defines the test for introducing/changing the primary rules. In Harts' words, 'the rules may, besides specifying the persons who are to legislate, define in more or less rigid terms the procedure to be followed in legislation' (p. 96). For example, an amendment or enactment of the code may require the relevant bill to be approved by the parliament and assented by the head of the state. The rules of adjudication define the test for validity regarding litigation (i.e. the court system) in a given legal system. 'Besides identifying the individuals who are to adjudicate, such rules will also define the procedure to be followed … [as well as] the concepts of judge or court, jurisdiction and judgment' (p. 97). While not aimed at identifying a revolutionary change, Hart's secondary rules may assist with evaluation of the *scale* of legal change.

Hence, the present study distinguishes the two aspects of legal change:

i a revolutionary break with the old legal order: as a breach of the [former] basic norm, and
ii the scale of the legal order change, such as retaining/abolishing/ transforming the [former] law and the court system, as well as the legislature or the executive (that *may* take over the legislative or adjudicative role): in terms of the secondary rules of adjudication, recognition and change.

The chapter's overall thesis is that the February Revolution and the October Revolution as well as the dissolution of the Soviet Union were all the instances of revolutionary legal change. However, the new and the old legal orders may still have a degree of continuity. In this sense, the better parallel (than one, drawn by Pelevin, between the post October Revolution period and *Perestroika*) might be between the collapse of the Russian Empire (as a result of the February Revolution) and the dissolution of the Soviet Union (following *Perestroika* and the 1991 Putsch). In fact, in the both cases there was the reluctance to break completely with the preceding legal order. In contrast, the October Bolshevik Revolution aimed at dismantling the ancient regime in toto.

February Revolution of 1917

The disturbances in the capital (Petrograd, formerly St. Petersburg) started on 23.02.1917. On Sunday 26.02.1917 the sessions of the both houses of the parliament—Государственная Дума [*GD*] and the State Council (Государственный Совѣтъ [*GS*])—were suspended by the tsar's decrees till April 1917 (Shchegolev, 1926, pp. 168–169).[1]

---

[1]The decision was taken after the heated discussion at the meeting of the ministers' council. Nikolay Dm. Golitsyn (1850–1925), head since December 1916, had in his possession the 'ready-to-use' [signed by the tsar] *ukazy* (decrees) without a specific date to be inserted later. See (Shchegolev, 1926, pp. 168–169).

On 27.02.1917 the Provisional Committee of the *GD* members (Временный Комитетъ [*VK*]) was formed 'to restore the state and public order' ((SUVP 1, p. 4) I-2,). *VK*, at once, appointed the special 'commissars' the *GD* members to supervise over the ministers ((SUVP 1, p. 5) I-3). In effect, the former government—the council of ministers (Совѣтъ Министровъ)—became dissolved ((SUVP 1, p. 3) I-1).

On 1.03.1917 the first Provisional Government (Временное Правительство [*VP*]) was formed (formally by *VK*, but in consultation with the [Petrograd] Council of Workers' Deputies [Совѣтъ Рабочихъ Депутатовъ]) ((SUVP 1, p. 7) I-5). A new government started its own official newspaper [*Bulletin of Provisional Government* (*Вѣстникъ Временнаго Правительства* [*VVP*])], with the first issue (1/46) appearing on 05.03.1917. Still the Digest of Laws [*Собраніе Узаконеній* (*SU*)]—the official periodic publication by the supreme court of the Russian Empire [Правительствующій Сенатъ] from 1863—continued as well.[2]

On 02.03.1917 Nikolai II (1868–1918) had abdicated in favour his younger brother Michael (1878–1918) ((SUVP 1, pp. v–vi), *SU* 344).

The tsar's decrees on Suspension of *GD* & *GS* contributed to the power vacuum on the ground. The formation of *VK* by the *GD* members (while *GD* was suspended) as well as the creation of *VP* by *VK* were, strictly speaking, beyond their powers (*ultra vires*), as not envisioned by the Main State Laws [Основные Государственные Законы] of the Russian Empire of 23.04.1906 (*ПСЗ* III 27805). Crucially, the Main State Laws had not provided for the tsar's abdication (as there was no precedent of abdication by the monarch). The succession rules were settled by the laws of 5.04.1797 (*ПСЗ* I 17910) & 12.12.1825 (*ПСЗ* II 1): only an heir to the throne could abdicate. The succession laws, which had been part of the Full Digest of Law, were affirmed the

---

[2]Normative acts (published in the first part of *SU*) also appeared into the Full Digest of Laws of the Russian Empire [Полное Собраніе Законовъ Россійской Имперіи (*ПСЗ*)]. A law from the Digest is cited by its place in the Digest: [the collection number (either I (1649–1825), II (1825–1881) or III (1881–1913))] & [the law number]. The text of the digest laws [by the law date or/and the law number (in the collection)] are available at http://nlr.ru/e-res/law_r/search.php.

Main State Laws (art. 24).[3] The succession laws could only be changed by the tsar with sanction of *GS* & *GD* (art. 44).[4] These constitutional requirements were not met. Besides, Nikolai II could not abdicate on behalf of his heir (his underage son). In opinion of V. D. Nabokov, *even if* the tsar's 'abdication' *were* legally possible, it would be deem to amount to 'death' (Nabokov, p. 18).

In any case, on 3.03.1917 Michael declined to take over the throne, deferring the decision on the constitutional order to the future Constituent Assembly, as well as expressing support to the Provisional Government (*VP*) ((SUVP 1, p. vii), *SU* 345).[5] The Act of Refusal by Michael of 3.03.1917 was drafted by V. D. Nabokov, V. V. Shul'gin and B. E. Nol'de on the basis of the early sketch by N. V. Nekrasov (Nabokov, p. 20). The drafters presumed that Michael declined the grant of ultimate power (rather than himself abdicated) (p. 21). Nonetheless, they intended to bestow some legitimacy upon the new abode of power (*VP*) by inserting the statement that *VP* was created by the determination of the lower house of the parliament (*GD*) and became endowed with the 'whole and complete power'. According to Nabokov, this power encompassed the legislative (as well as the executive) power, even though in its first directive *VP* referred to itself as a 'cabinet', i.e. as the executive power (p. 21). If this view is accepted, then, alongside the executive power, the Act of Refusal 'sanctioned' the transfer of the legislative power from *GD* to *VP*, disempowering the former legislature. Notably, *VP* discharged the formerly

---

[3] Ст. 24. «Постановленія Свода Законовъ (т. I. ч. I, изд. 1892 г.) о порядкѣ наслѣдія Престола (ст. 3–17) … сохраняютъ силу Законовъ Основныхъ».

[4] Ст. 44. «Никакой новый законъ не можетъ послѣдовать безъ одобренія Государственнаго Совѣта и Государственной Думы и воспріять силу безъ утвержденія Государя Императора». See also (Korkunov, 1909).

[5] «…призывая благословеніе Божіе, прошу всѣхъ гражданъ Державы Россійской подчиниться Временному Правительству, по почину Государственной Думы возникшему и облеченному всею полнотою власти, впредь до того, какъ созванное въ возможно кратчайшій срокъ, на основѣ всеобщаго, прямого, равнаго и тайнаго голосованія, Учредительное Собраніе своими рѣшеніемъ объ образѣ правленія выразитъ волю народа».

'appointed' members of *GS* (the upper house) on 1.05.1917 ((SUVP 1, p. 239), II-102).[6]

The *GD* majority, as well as *VK* created by the *GD* members, was in favour of the constitutional monarchy. The initial *VK* 'objective' was not the tsar's abdication but a formation of the 'progressive' (responsible to *GD*) government under the tsar's auspices. The events on the ground might predetermine the revolutionary outcome in a practical sense. Still, in a legal sense, the abdication of the tsar (in breach of the Main State Laws), together with the suspension of *GD* & *GS*, made the dissolution of the former legal order inevitable. As a result, there was a revolutionary overthrow of the existing constitution (the Main State Laws), together with the monarch—the pinnacle of the legal order and the source of the 'basic norm'. Due to the revolutionary break with the former legal order there was, inevitably, an issue of the *VP* legitimacy (insofar as Michael's Act of Refusal was null in legal terms). In formal terms, *VP* was created by *VK* of the *GD* members, *as if* partaking in the old regime legitimacy. In contrast to the Council of the Workers & Soldiers Deputies of October 1917, *VP* did not claim a revolutionary legitimacy per se, but rather emphasised the provisional character of its jurisdiction—till the convocation of the Constituent Assembly (Учредительное Собраніе [*US*]) that *were* to provide for the proper 'basic norm' ['commands of *US* are to be obeyed']. The premise of *US* as a source of the ultimate democratic legitimacy by virtue of uninhibited popular will *as if* supplied the decisive justification for the revolutionary dismantling of the former legal order. This view (that might still be in vogue) may overlook the costs of a break with the previous legal order. These costs became apparent aftermath of the February Revolution.

The most notable change happened in relation to the executive branch of the government. The composition of *VP* and its program became public on 3.03.1917 ((SUVP 1, pp. 7–8) I-5).[7] The program envisioned the general amnesty, declaration of freedoms of press, meetings, etc. and the preparation for the summon of the Constituent

---

[6] *VVP* № 56/102 (05.05.1917); (1917) *SU* 602.
[7] *VVP* №№ 1/45 & 2/47.

Assembly, etc., as well as the *replacement of the police by the people militia under control of local self-government* (SUVP 1, p. 8). The dissolution of the police force furthered the collapse of 'law and order' on the ground. By 27 February the police, unable to control the protests and violently attacked by the protesters, largely disappeared from the streets. Meanwhile 'the workers militia' was formed, largely, under the Bolshevik control and in opposition to the emerging 'city militia' under the *VP* auspices (Gutman, 2007). The Department of Police was abolished, replaced by the Provisional Office 'for affairs of public police and for provision of security of citizens and their property' [Временное Управленіе по дѣламъ общественной полиціи и по обеспеченію личной и имущественной безопасности гражданъ] ((SUVP 1, p. 27) II-8 (10.03.1917)).[8] The inability to create a functioning militia under the *VP* control demonstrated the general impotence of the executive power under *VP*. As Nabokov noted, the perception [by the population] of the government incapacity to preserve the civil order ultimately led to the success of the October coup (Nabokov, p. 39).[9]

VP also dismantled the former executive 'vertical'—the gubernia governors (with their functions taken over by the head of local zemstvo)

---

[8]*VVP* № 24/70; (1917) *SU* 453. The Provisional Office of affairs of public police was later renamed into the Main Office of affairs of militia (*VVP* № 129/175; *SU* 1135; (SUVP 2, p. 58) II-8 (15.06.1917)). The Militia was formally established on 17.03.1917 (*VVP* № 35/81; (1917) *SU* 537; (SUVP 1, pp. 183–192) II-80). Available at http://elib.shpl.ru/ru/nodes/10721-vyp-1-27-fevralya-5-maya-1917-1917, http://elib.shpl.ru/ru/nodes/10722-vyp-2-5-maya-24-iyulya-1917-g-ch-1-otd-i-viii-1918. The Main Office was abolished on 14.12.1917 by the order of People's Commissariat of Internal Affairs (Приказ № 2 Народного комиссариата внутреннихъ дел. Государственный Архивъ Россійской Федераціи (ГАРФ) ф. 393, оп. 1, д. 22, л. 3). On history of the militia see also (Nekrasov, pp. 13–15).

[9]«Имѣли, напр., наивность думать, что огромная столица, со своими подонками, со всегда готовыми къ выступленію порочными и преступными элементами, можетъ существовать безъ полиціи, или же съ такими безобразными и нелѣпыми суррогатами, какъ импровизированная, щедро оплачиваемая милиція, въ которую записывались профессіональные воры и бѣглые арестанты. Всероссійскій походъ противъ городовыхъ и жандармовъ очень быстро привелъ къ своему естественному послѣдствію. Аппаратъ, хоть кое-какъ, хоть слабо, но все же работавшій, былъ разбитъ вдребезги. Городовые и жандармы во множествѣ пошли на пополненіе большевистскихъ рядовъ. И постепенно въ Петербургѣ и в Москвѣ начала развиваться анархія. Ростъ ея сразу страшно увеличился послѣ большевистскаго переворота. Но самъ **переворотъ сталъ возможнымъ и такимъ удобоисполнимымъ только потому, что исчезло сознаніе существованія власти, готовой рѣшительно отстаивать и охранять гражданскій порядокъ...**»

((SUVP 1, pp. 8–9) I-6).[10] There were also two extraordinary investigation committees regarding the former upper officials.[11] The tsar and his spouse were declared 'deprived of liberty' on 7 March.[12] Besides, *VP* assumed not only the executive but also some [provisional] legislative power.[13] At the same time, the body of law and the judicial system (with the Senate at the top) remained largely intact.[14]

The immediate effect of the February Revolution, hence, was an overnight delegitimating of the executive power. The break with the old order resulted not only in street lawlessness but also crucially, in the delegitimisation of state power itself. As V. Rosanov put it in *Apocalypse of Our Time*, 'Russia disappeared in two days, no more than three'.[15] Nonetheless, neither the court system nor the Digest of Laws of the Russian Empire was abolished. Hence, there was no immediate change in the rules of recognition with respect to the primary rules of private and [the bulk of] criminal laws, as well as the relevant rules of

---

[10] *VVP* № 2/47.

[11] *VVP* № 1/46; (1917) *SU* 351 & 362; (SUVP 1, pp. 265–266) III-2&3 (4.03.1917); *VVP* № 7/53; (1917) *SU* 363; (SUVP 1, pp. 272–273) III-11 (11.03.1917).

[12] *VVP* № 3/49. (SUVP 1, p. 365) V-5.

[13] There was a body [Юридическое Совѣщаніе] attached to *VP*, created for 'consideration of the public law issues in relation to the foundation of the new state order'. *VVP* № 18/64; (1917) *SU* 404; (SUVP 1, pp. 10–11) I-9 (23.03.1917). It was to prepare technical legislation (outside of principal or contentious issues) for the *US* election. *VVP* 52/98; (SUVP 2, p. 21) II-1 (10.05.1917).

[14] There were some changes, mostly in criminal law: abolition of capital punishment (*VVP* № 12/58; (1917) *SU* 375; (SUVP 1, p. 37) II-16 (16.03.1917)) and exile (*VVP* № 50/96; (1917) *SU* 556; (SUVP 1, pp. 207–210) II-89 (26.03.1917)) as well as some special courts, including the supreme criminal court (*VVP* № 1/16; (1917) *SU* 361; (SUVP 1, p. 21) II-2 (4.03.1917)); these measures were suspended in part (*VVP* № 15/61; (1917) *SU* 389; (SUVP 1, p. 44) II-28 (20.03.17); also (1917) *SU* 456; *VVP* № 21/67; (SUVP 1, pp. 137–138) II-54 (30.03.1917)). *VP* also abolished legal discrimination based on religion or ethnicity (*VVP* № 15/61; (1917) *SU* 400; (SUVP 1, pp. 46–49) II-32 (20.03.1917)) etc. Notably, *VP* established the commission for 'restoration' of the main provisions of the Court Statutes of 20 Nov 1864 (*VVP* № 18/64; (1917) *SU* 438; (SUVP 1, pp. 109–112) II-43 (23.03.1917)). On another hand, *VP* created provisional courts to deal with soldiers' misconduct towards civilians, first, in Petrograd (*VVP* № 7/53; (1917) *SU* 354; (SUVP 1, pp. 364–365) V-3 (3.03.1917), 364–365; *VVP* № 19/65 (22.03.1917); (SUVP 1, pp. 376–378) V-16) and, later, in several other towns ((SUVP 1, 1917) V-8, 13, 18, 19, 25, 26, 27, 31, 32, 40, 44). These courts were abolished on 19.07.1917 ((1917) *SU* 911).

[15] Розанов, В. В. *Апокалипсис нашего времени*: «Русь слиняла в два дня. Самое большое - в три». Retrieved from http://www.vehi.net/rozanov/apokal.html.

adjudication. The case of the rule of change might be different, as there was no 'regular' legislative process in the period, with the main legislative activity vested with the special body (Особое Совѣщаніе) that was to draft the legislation in relation to summon of US.[16] Non-existence of a clear rule of change was a sign of the disintegration of the legal order, alongside the collapse of the power on the ground (that might make a formal existence of the rules of adjudication of mostly academic importance).

To conclude, while the *VP* reign was of a 'reluctant revolution' (with the old secondary rules of recognition and change remaining in place), the basic norm of this period was nonetheless a new one. The new regime came into being by the will of members of the Provisional Committee (*VK*), formed at a private meeting of some *GD* members, after *GD* became suspended. Hence, the basic norm *might* be traced back to the *VK* formation of *VP* ['the *VK* commands were to be observed']. The deficiency of an unremitting legal legitimacy led *VP* to rely on a supervening legitimacy of being an engine to summon the Constituent Assembly (*US*) that *were* at last to supply the ultimate democratic basic norm. The partaking in the revolutionary discourse might not necessarily strengthen *VK*. The lack of its *own* legal legitimacy, together with the lack of control 'on the ground', fatally undermined *VP*, opening the way for the more radical legal revolutionaries, who may fully exploit the revolutionary appeal of starting anew.

October Bolshevik Revolution

Overview

Bolsheviks legitimated their new order precisely by their appeal for a complete break with the tsarist regime, assisted by their messianic

---

[16]The Special Council [Особое Совѣщаніе] was an independent body, responsible for the legislation regarding the forthcoming elections to the Constituent Assembly. *VVP* № 18/64; (1917) *SU* 406; (SUVP 1, pp. 11–12) I-10 (25.03.1917).

ideology of destruction of the unjust class-based society. In retrospect, the extra-judicial 'justice' unleashed by Bolsheviks, culminating in the Great Terror of 1937, dwarfed in comparison any injustices ever committed by the ancient regime.

Thus, in contrast to *VP*, Bolsheviks drew their legitimacy entirely from the revolution itself. They radically broke with the past dislodging the bulk of the pre-revolutionary institutions, together with the court system and the whole body of the pre-revolutionary law (i.e. dissolving the old secondary rules, alongside the old basic norm). Lenin explicitly pointed out the objective of the October revolution to demolish the entire old court system (Lenin v. 36, pp. 162–163).[17]

What was the basic norm of the new regime? On 25.10.1917 the Petrograd Martial-Revolutionary Committee [Петроградскій Военно-Революціонный Комитетъ (*PVRK*)] (formed by the Petrograd Council Workers & Soldiers' Deputies [Петроградскій совѣтъ рабочихъ и солдатскихъ депутатовъ] on 16.10.1917)[18] issued the *Declaration to the Citizens of Russia*, announcing the fall of the Provisional Government and the transfer of power to itself on behalf of the Council (Soviet Decrees, p. 2). Was then the new basic norm that the commands of *PVRK* were to be obeyed? The better view might be that in accord with the basic norm decrees [commands] of the All-Russia Congress of Councils of Workers and Soldiers' Deputies were to be obeyed. These decrees formed the foundations of the new regime.

By its 1st Decree of 26.10.1917 the II All-Russia Congress of the Councils of Workers and Soldiers' Deputies [Всероссійскій Съѣздъ Совѣтовъ Рабочихъ и Солдатскихъ Депутатовъ (*VSSRSD*)][19] formed

---

[17]«...безусловной обязанностью пролетарской революции было не реформировать судебные учреждения (этой задачей ограничивались кадеты и их подголоски меньшевики и правые эсеры), — а **совершенно уничтожить, смести до основания весь старый суд и его аппарат.** Эту необходимую задачу Октябрьская революция выполнила, и выполнила успешно».

[18]*PVRK* had dissolved itself on 5.1.2.1917. Available at https://w.histrf.ru/articles/article/show/pietrogradskii_voienno_rievoliutsionnyi_komitiet.

[19]739 delegates took part in the opening session: 338 Bolsheviks, 211 Social-Revolutionaries (S-Rs) & 69 Mensheviks. After the first session, when some delegates (including Mensheviks & Right S-Rs) left and some just arrived, there were present 625 representatives from 402 (of 974) Councils of Workers & Soldiers' Deputies, including 390 Bolsheviks (counting those moved from other factions) and 179 Left S-Rs. Available at https://history.wikireading.ru/305811.

the Council of People's Commissars [Совет Народных Комиссаров (*SNK*)]. This Decree on *SNK* provided its functioning *till the summoning of the Constituent Assembly (US)*, vesting the Congress and its [All-Russia] Central Executive Committee [(Всероссийский) Центральный Исполнительный Комитет ([*V*]*CIK*)] with control over *SNK* ((SU 1917–1918, pp. 1–2) 1-1 (1.12.1917)).[20] *SNK* started to issue the decrees straight away. The legislative power thus was de facto vested in *SNK*, with *CIK* having supervision over it. Hence, there was a fusion of the executive and the legislative powers in *SNK*. The Congress might be looked at as a final repository of the legislative power; since it was a periodically summoned body, in between some of its legislative power was vested in *VCIK*.

By its 5th Decree on 28.10.1917 the Congress declared all the power being transferred to the *Soviets* [Советы] ((SU 1917–1918, p. 6) 1-5 (1.12.1917)),[21] somewhat inconsistently with its first Decree that envisioned *US* as the ultimate seat of power. Still, notably, Bolsheviks did not immediately discard the *VP* mantra about *US* as an ideal (most legitimate) way to constitute a new legal order. On 27.10.1917 *SNK* fixed the date of election for *US* on 12.11.1917 ((SU 1917–1918, pp. 7–8) 1-8 (1.12.1917)).[22]

Just as *VP* before it, of *SNK* started its own official newspaper, initially called the Newspaper of the **Provisional** Workers & Peasants' Government [*Газета **Временнаго** Рабочего и Крестьянского Правительства* (*GRKP*)], with all above-mentioned decrees published in its first issue on 28.10.1917. According to the *SNK* decree on the procedure of approval and publication of laws (till the summoning of *US*), laws came in force from the date of the publication in *GRKP*

---

[20]Декрет № 1 II Всероссийского Съезда Советов Рабочих, Солдатских и Крестьянских Депутатов «Об учреждении Совета Народных Комиссаров». Retrieved from http://istmat.info/node/27645.

[21]Декрет II Всероссийского Съезда Советов Рабочих, Солдатских и Крестьянских Депутатов «О полноте власти Советов» («Вся власть отныне принадлежит Советам»). *GVRKP* № 1 (28.10.1917). Retrieved from http://istmat.info/node/27655.

[22]Постановление Совета Народных Комиссаров «О созыве Учредительного Собрания в назначенный срок». *GVRKP* № 1 (28.10.1917). Retrieved from http://istmat.info/node/27753.

16 Legal Continuity and Change: Two Russian Revolutions ...

(unless provided otherwise) (SU 1917–1918, pp. 13–14).[23] The same decree also provided for the Digest of Laws [Собрание Узаконений (*SU*)], now without auspices of the Senate and with new numeration.

The Constituent Assembly, elected by universal, equal, direct and secret vote, opened on 5 January. From 715 elected deputies (with Socialist-Revolutionaries (S-Rs), Mensheviks and other socialists receiving 59%, Bolsheviks—24%, K-Ds and other non-socialist parties—17%) there were present 410 delegates, including 155 Bolsheviks and Left S-Rs.[24] The Assembly declined to endorse the *Decrees on Land and on Peace*, proclaimed at the II All-Russia Congress of Soviets on 25–27.10.1917 (7–9.11.1917), as well as the *Declaration of Rights of Toiling and Exploited People* (drafted by Lenin and approved by *CIK*).[25] Bolsheviks then left and shut the Assembly down the early morning of 6.01.1918. On 6.01.1918 *CIK* issued the Decree On dissolution of *US*, published in № 5 *GRKP* on 09.01.18 (SU 1917–1918, pp. 235–236).[26] The III Congress of Soviets opened on 10.01.18, endorsing the *Declaration* on 12.01.18 (3 VSSRSD, pp. 43–44).[27] On 18.01.1918 the Congress voted in favour of erasing any references to the Constituent Assembly from all-new editions of Soviet decrees and laws, as well as deleting the adjective 'provisional' from the name of the Workers & Peasants' Government (3 VSSRSD, p. 85).[28] Henceforth, the Congresses of the Soviets (under the Bolshevik control) formed the only basis of Soviet legal order.

---

[23]*GRKP* № 2 (30.11.1917); *SU* 1-12 (1.12.1917). Retrieved from http://istmat.info/node/27655. *GRKP* continued as the official government newspaper at least till № 48 (15 (2).03.1918). Retrieved from http://istmat.info/node/29133. Following the move of the government to Moscow on 12.03.1918, the official newspaper became «Извѣстія Всероссійскаго Центральнаго Исполнительнаго Комитета Совѣтовъ Крестьянскихъ, Рабочихъ, Солдатскихъ и Казачьихъ Депутатовъ и Московскаго Совѣта Рабочихъ и Красноармейскихъ Депутатовъ» [*Izvestiia VCIK*], at least since № 54 (22(9).03.1918). Retrieved from http://istmat.info/node/29134.

[24]Available at http://www.hrono.ru/biograf/bio_u/uchredit.php.

[25]The original text of the Declaration (with references to *US*) is available at http://www.hist.msu.ru/ER/Etext/DEKRET/declarat.htm.

[26]*SU* 15-216 (13.01.1918). Retrieved from http://istmat.info/node/28337.

[27]For the approved text of declaration see (3 VSSRSD, pp. 90–92).

[28]For the draft decree [«проект декрета об устранении в советском законодательстве ссылок на учредительное собрание»] by Lenin see (Lenin v. 35, p. 285). Notably, on 20.01.1918 the 'Newspaper of the **Provisional** Workers & Peasants' Government' [№ 13] was renamed in the 'Newspaper of the Workers & Peasants' Government'. Available at http://istmat.info/node/28381, http://istmat.info/node/28382.

Courts, Revolutionary Tribunals and Extraordinary Commissions (ChKs)

Demolition of the Old Legal System

The *SNK* **Decree № 1 on Courts** of 24.11.1917 abolished pre-revolutionary courts [including the Senate] (art. 1), as well as all the laws of the Russian Empire *insofar as they were against the decrees* of *CIK* and the government (*SNK*) as well as the programs-minimum of the Russian Social Democratic Labour Party (Bolsheviks) and the party of the Social-Revolutionaries (S-Rs), to be guided [instead] by 'revolutionary conscience' and 'revolutionary sense of justice' (art. 5) (SU 1917–1918, pp. 41–43).[29]

The decree established new **local courts** for the civil claims of less than 3000 Rub and criminal charges with max sentence of 2 years; judges were to be elected [in future] directly by population, but till the election, [they were to be appointed] by the local Council of Workers, Soldiers and Peasants' Deputies; a judge was to adjudicate with two jurymen (art. 2). There was a possibility of cassation by the congress of local judges. The decree also **established the Revolutionary Tribunals** (*RT*) **to fight counter-revolution,** sabotage, etc. (comprised of the chair and 6 rotated jurymen elected by the Councils of Workers, Soldiers and Peasants' Deputies), as well as investigation commissions, attached to the Council (art. 5). The decree not only abolished the old courts but also legal representation (адвокатура), procurators and the court investigators (art. 3).

In response the Senate (as the supreme court) directed the lower courts to ignore the decree (Stuchka, 1922). The liquidation of the old

---

[29]Декрет СНК «О суде». *GVRKP* № 17 (24.11.1917); *SU* 4-50 (12.12.1917). Retrieved from http://istmat.info/node/27996. The decree was not approved by *VCIK* (to Left S-Rs' dismay). There was the *VCIK* direction [Резолюция ВЦИК «по поводу запроса левых эсеров о праве СНК издавать декреты»] on 4.11.1917 (§2) granting *SNK* the right to issue its own decrees in line with the Congress program in case of necessity (VCIK Minutes, 1920, pp. 31–32); (Soviet Decrees, p. 44). Also available at http://docs.historyrussia.org/ru/nodes/9628-4-17-noyabrya-rezolyutsiya-vtsik-po-povodu-zaprosa-levyh-eserov-o-prave-snk-izdavat-dekrety.

courts (including the Senate) had started in Petrograd on 29 November, completing by 5 December 1917 (Antonova, 1969).[30]

On 10 December Left Social-Revolutionaries entered in coalition with Bolsheviks (Kiselev, 1996, p. 149). Their representative I. Z. Shteinberg (Штейнберг) became a minister of Justice. He took the view that the old laws that were not expressly annulled ought to be applied by the courts (Antonova, 1969).[31] The **Decree № 2 on Courts** had been influenced by this S-R court reform vision. *CIK* issued the decree [after introduction the Gregorian calendar (SU 1917–1918, pp. 300–301)],[32] on 18 February and published it on 2.03.1918 (SU 1917–1918, pp. 363–368).[33] Councils (Soviets) of Workers, Soldiers and Peasants' Deputies were to form District Courts (art. 1) to deal with matters beyond the local court jurisdiction. District Courts were to have criminal and civil divisions (art. 2). There were also to be District Cassation Courts elected by general meeting of the district judges (art. 4). There was the supreme judiciary control over District Courts as well (art. 6). Art. 8 provided for the court procedures to comply with the Court Statutes of 1864, unless expressly annulled by Soviet decrees. However, there was no law of evidence (art. 14). Art. 36 provided that the **old law continued to be in force unless abolished** by the degrees of *VCIK* or *SNK* or were against the socialist legal conscience, with formal requirements (such as limitation time, etc.) disregarded for sake of justice. Preliminary investigation was to be done by Investigative

---

[30] The Senate was forcefully closed by the *PVRK* representative G. O. Damberg.

[31] According to Shteinberg, unless they were expressly annulled by the relevant decrees, all the old laws were in force, at par with the new laws [«все старые законы до тех пор, пока они не отменены соответствующими декретами, признаются в полной их силе и действуют наравне со всеми новыми…»]. He was speaking at the meeting of the All-Russia Central Executive Committee (*VCIK*) of 16.02.1918 (ГАРФ ф. 1235, оп. 18, д. 6, л. 45). The S-R plan was to codify the revolutionary laws (based upon the existed (but amended) Digest of Laws), as well to reform courts (ф. 353, оп. 2, д. 164, лл. 8-9, 10 и сл). On the S-R participation in *VCIK* & *SNK*. See also (Popova, 1998).

[32] Декрет Совета Народных Комиссаров «О введении западноевропейского календаря». *GRKP* № 18 (26.01.1918); *SU* 19-289 (30.01.1918). Retrieved from http://istmat.info/node/28617.

[33] Декрет Всероссийского Центрального Исполнительного Комитета Советов Рабочих, Солдатских, Крестьянских и Казачьих Депутатов «О суде» (Декрет № 2). *SU* 26-347 (7.03.1918). Retrieved from http://istmat.info/node/28915.

Commissions elected (till the popular election) by the Soviets (art. 21). There were to be the *collegia* of public accusers and defenders, elected by the Soviets (art. 24–28).

The S-Rs left *SNK* on 16.03.1918, aftermath of the IV Extraordinary Congress of Soviets (Leont'ev, 2000, p. 182), allowing Bolsheviks to pursue their own agenda.

The *SNK* Decree on Revolutionary Tribunals of 4.05.1918 enlarged *RT*, retaining the tribunals in large cities, administrative towns and key rail-ways localities (art. 1) (SU 1917–1918, pp. 494–495).[34] **The decree envisioned the transfer of ordinary criminal cases to the courts** (art. 3), the tribunal remaining jurisdiction ranged from pogroms, bribery, forgery, misuse of Soviet documents, hooliganism and espionage (art. 2) to profiteering[35] and counter-revolution (art. 4) (SU 1917–1918, pp. 560–561).[36] Decree of *VCIK* & *SNK* of 11.06.1918 established Cassation Department, under the *VCIK* auspices, for the *RT*s decisions, except ones by [the upper] *RT*, attached to *VCIK* (SU 1917–1918, pp. 611–612).[37]

The **Decree № 3 on Courts** of 20.07.1918 extended the jurisdiction of local [people's] courts (to civil claims up to 10000 Rub: art. 4), as well as any crimes except murder/attempt to murder, rape, robbery, banditry, corruption, speculation and counterfeit of money that were under jurisdiction of district courts (art. 1) (SU 1917–1918, pp. 687–688).[38] Local courts could sentence [offenders] up to 5 years of

---

[34] Декрет СНК «О Революционных Трибуналах». *Izvestiia VCIK* № 97 (4.05.1918); *SU* 35-471 (18.05.1918). Retrieved from http://istmat.info/node/29504.

[35] The *SNK* Decree *on Profiteering* transferred ordinary profiteering cases to local and regional courts (art. 13): Декрет СНК «О спекуляции» (22.07.1918). *Izvestiia VCIK* № 156 (25.07.1918); *SU* 54-604 (26.07.1918) (SU 1917–1918, pp. 725–726). Retrieved from http://istmat.info/node/30706.

[36] The decree expanded on the role of the *collegium* of prosecutors (обвинители): art. 5–9: Декрет ВЦИК «О Революционном Трибунале при Всероссийском Центральном Исполнительном Комитете Советов». *Izvestiia VCIK* № 117 (9.06.1918); *SU* 41-520 (14.06.1918). Retrieved from http://istmat.info/node/30040.

[37] Декрет ВЦИК «Об учреждении Кассационного Отдела при ВЦИК Советов и порядке кассации приговоров Революционных Трибуналов». *Izvestiia VCIK* № 127 (22.06.1918); *SU* (1917–1918) 45-545 (23.06.1918). Retrieved from http://istmat.info/node/30429.

[38] Декрет СНК «О суде» (Декрет № 3). *Izvestiia VCIK* № 152 (20.07.1918); *SU* 52-589 (23.07.18). Retrieved from http://istmat.info/node/30649. The decree was elaborated by the instruction of the Commissariat of Justice from 23.07.18 [Постановление Народного Комиссариата Юстиции «Об организации и действии местных народных судов

depravation of liberty, **guided by the decrees and 'revolutionary legal conscience'** (art. 3). The judiciary control over the district court decisions was replaced by a Cassation Court, consisted of civil and criminal divisions, set up in Moscow (art. 8). Drafted after the S-R exodus from *SNK*, with Stuchka's return to the Commissariat of Justice, the decree made no reference to laws/statutes of the preceding legal order. Hence, the S-R vision of the legal continuity was no part of it.

Finally, art. 22 of the *VCIK* Decree on People's Court (30.11.1918) directed local judges to be guided by Soviet Decrees, and, in the absence of those, by *'revolutionary legal conscience'*, expressly **prohibiting references to the preceding laws** (SU 1917–1918, pp. 1195–1204).[39]

Thus, by 1918 the Bolshevik regime largely succeeded in obliterating the Digest of Laws of the Russian Empire (Сводъ Законовъ Россійской Имперіи).

Regarding courts, the Bolshevik radical vision going back to the Decree № 1 on Courts (and somewhat revived by the Decree № 3 on Courts and the decree of 30.11.1918) ruled out a hierarchical court system (at least, at regional level). Hence, the *VCIK* Decree of 21.10.1920—Statute on People's Court of the RSFSR set out the unitary system of local people's courts with jurisdiction over all civil and criminal matters, with more serious matters dealing by a judge with 6 jurymen (instead of a judge with two jurymen) (SU 1920, pp. 599–608).[40]

The *VCIK* Statute on Courts and Court Procedure of 31.10.1922 had drawn a line under the revolutionary period

---

(Инструкция)»]. (SU 1917–1918, pp. 699–708); СУ 53-597 (25.07.1918). Retrieved from http://istmat.info/node/30669.

[39]«Ст. 22. При рассмотрении всех дел Народный Суд применяет декреты Рабоче-Крестьянского Правительства, а в случае отсутствия соответствующего декрета или неполноты такового, руководствуется социалистическим правосознанием. Примечание. Ссылки в приговорах и решениях на законы свергнутых правительств воспрещаются.» Декрет ВЦИК «О Народном Суде РСФСР (Положение)» (1918.11.30). *Izvestiia VCIK* №№ 269 & 270 (8&10.10.1918); *SU* 85-889 (6.12.1918). Retrieved from http://istmat.info/node/31884.

[40]Декрет ВЦИК «Положение о Народном Суде РСФСР» (21.10.1920). *SU* 83-407 (27.10.1920). Retrieved from http://istmat.info/node/42576.

(SU 1922, pp. 1531–1546).[41] In contrast to the 1920 decree, it returned to the court system of the earlier Decree № 2, envisioning two kinds of courts of the first instance: local & regional (district) ones (the latter dealt with more serious matter and acted as a cassation court). The statute also established the Supreme Court of the RSFSR (art. 1), chosen by the *VCIK*'s presidium (art. 56).

Thus, by the end of 1922, there was in place a not unconventional hierarchical court system. By 1923 the revolutionary period with its reliance upon 'revolutionary legal conscience' was over. There were enacted the criminal code (SU 1922, pp. 272–304),[42] the criminal procedure code (SU 1922, pp. 393–458),[43] the civil code (SU 1922, pp. 1573–1656)[44] and the civil procedure code.[45] Procurators were back as well as advocates (barristers) (SU 1922, pp. 810–814).[46]

Hence, it might be an over-exaggeration to say that the Bolsheviks succeeded in building a judicial system completely anew, insofar as by 1923 there was a hierarchical system of courts that were to adjudicate according to the codified civil, criminal and procedural law. Nonetheless, in terms of either Kelsen's basic norm or Hart's secondary rules, there had been the thorough replacement of the basic norm and the secondary rules of recognition (with new codes in place), change (with a new system of legislature) and adjudication (with a new court system).

---

[41] Положение о судопроизводстве РСФСР (Пост. ВЦИК 11.11.1922 о введении в действие). *SU* 69-902 (17.11.1922). Available at http://www.libussr.ru/doc_ussr/ussr_1438.htm.

[42] Уголовный Кодекс РСФСР (Пост. ВЦИК). *SU* 15-153 (1.06.1922). Available at http://xn--80abnlydpf.xn--80akegfdvbg0c.xn--p1ai/1922-1950.pdf.

[43] Уголовно-процессуальный Кодекс РСФСР (Пост. ВЦИК 25.05.1922). *SU* 20/21-230 (24.06.1922); (Пост. ВЦИК 15.02.1923). *Izvestiia VCIK* № 37 (18.02.1923); *SU* 7-106 (1.03.1923). Available at http://xn--80aagr1bl7a.net/static/upload/books/images/3622//3622.jpg.

[44] Гражданский кодекс (Пост. ВЦИК 11.11.1922). *Izvestiia VCIK* № 256 (12.11.1922); *SU* 71-904 (25.11.1922).

[45] Гражданский Процессуальный кодекс (Пост. ВЦИК 10.07.1923). *SU* 46/47-478 (23.07.1923). Available at http://xn--80aagr1bl7a.net/index.php?md=books&to=art&id=4586.

[46] Положение о прокурорском надзоре (Пост. ВЦИК 28.05.1922). *Izvestiia VCIK* № 132 (16.06.1922); *SU* 36-424 (18.06.1922). Положение об адвокатуре (Пост. ВЦИК 26.05.1922). *Izvestiia VCIK* № 132 (16.06.1922); *SU* 36-425 (18.06.1922).

Extra-Judicial Bodies

The abnormality the early post-revolutionary Bolshevik period was not only in the courts adjudicating in accordance with 'revolutionary conscience', but also in the presence of extra-judicial bodies that took over judicial functions. Not only was there an overlap between Rev. Tribunals and courts (with the former having jurisdiction over the 'regime-threatening' crimes) but also between the tribunals and the so called 'extraordinary commission' (чрезвычайная комиссия [*ChK*]). The latter was formed to fight counter-revolution on 7.12.1917 (Lenin&VChK, p. 17).[47] The *ChK* initial function was one of preliminary investigation,[48] that did not prevent *ChK* becoming the major perpetrator of 'the red terror' in 1918–1919. The infamous *SNK* decree of 21.02.1918, 'The Socialist Fatherland in Danger', re-introduced capital punishment,[49] without adjudication [i.e. on the spot] (§8) (Soviet Decrees, pp. 490–491).[50] The *SNK* 'Red Terror' decree of 5.09.1918

---

[47]Point 9 of the minutes of the 21st meeting of *SNK* on 7.12.1917 (ГАРФ, ф. 130, оп. 1, д. 1, л. 31 об.). On 10.12.1917 the official *VCIK* newspaper «Известия ВЦИК» (*Izvestiia VCIK*) published the following statement: 'by the decree of the Council of People's Commissars of 7.12.1918, to fight counter-revolution and sabotage, there had been created the All-Russia extraordinary commission, attached to the Council of People's Commissars. The commission is located at 2 *Gorokhovaia* [St]. It opens [to public] from noon to 5 pm' [«По постановлению Совета Народных Комиссаров от 7 декабря 1917 г. образована Всероссийская чрезвычайная комиссия при Совете Народных Комиссаров по борьбе с контрреволюцией и саботажем. Комиссия помещается: Гороховая, 2. Прием от 12 до 5 часов дня»]. Retrieved from http://royallib.com/read/lenin_vladimir/v_i_lenin_i_vchk_sbornik_dokumentov_19171922.html#122880.

[48]Point 9 of the minutes of the 21st meeting of *SNK* expressly referred to adjudication in relation to sabotage and counter-revolution by the revolutionary tribunals (§2), and to the *ChK* dealing only with the preliminary investigation (§3).

[49]Capital punishment was abolished by the Decree № 4 of the II All-Russia Congress of Councils of Workers and Soldiers' Deputies on 28.10.1917: Декрет № 4. II Всероссийского Съезда Советов Рабочих, Солдатских и Крестьянских Депутатов «Об отмене смертной казни». *GRKP* № 1 (30.11.1917); *SU* 1-4 (1.12.1917). Retrieved from http://istmat.info/node/27654.

[50]*GRKP* № 31 (23.02.1918); *Izvestiia VCIK* № 31 (22.02.1918): «8. Неприятельские агенты, спекулянты, громилы, хулиганы, контрреволюционные агитаторы, германские шпионы расстреливаются на месте преступления». Retrieved from http://www.hist.msu.ru/ER/Etext/DEKRET/opasnost.htm; Also (Lenin&VChK, p. 38). http://royallib.com/read/lenin_vladimir/v_i_lenin_i_vchk_sbornik_dokumentov_19171922.html#204800. According to *Izvestiia VCIK* № 32 (23.02.1918), relying on the *SNK* direction, VChK did not envision any other means besides merciless elimination at a place of the crime in fight with counter-revolutionaries, spies, speculators, raiders, hooligans, ones involved in sabotage and other parasites:

gave to *ChKs* the powers of incarceration of 'class enemies' in concentration camps and their execution by firing squads (SU 1917–1918, p. 883).[51] According to the *VCIK* Statute on All-Russia extraordinary commission [*VChK*] of 28.10.1918, the commission was to directly fight counter-revolution, profiteering and misuse of official position (art. 1), being an apex of the local commissions (art. 10–14), with the commissions operating the armed squads (art. 7) (SU 1917–1918, pp. 1110–1111).[52] The *ChKs* powers to arrest and detain with respect to certain 'responsible public servants' were somewhat mitigated by the Defence Council Decree of 14.12.1918 (SU 1917–1918, p. 1341).[53]

In the early 1919 the jurisdictional overlapping of *ChKs* and *RTs* led to the public exchange between their respective heads. At the all-Moscow *RKP(b)* conference on 19.01.1919,[54] the *RT* head Krylenko pointed out

---

[51] …Всероссийская чрезвычайная комиссия, основываясь на постановлении Совета Народных Комиссаров, не видит других мер борьбы с контрреволюционерами, шпионами, спекулянтами, громилами, хулиганами, саботажниками и прочими паразитами, кроме беспощадного уничтожения на месте преступления.

[51]*Izvestiia VCIK* № 195 (10.09.1918); *SU* (1917–1918) 65-710 (12.09.1918). Retrieved from http://istmat.info/node/31100. There was the *VChK* regulation on the *uezd* and *gubernia ChK* of 14.09.1918, that divided the gubernia's commissions into the departments by 'subject-matter: counter revolution, speculation, misuse of official position'. *Izvestiia VCIK* № 199 (14.09.1918); *SU* (1917–1918) 66-728 (SU 1917–1918, pp. 906–908). Retrieved from http://istmat.info/node/31486.

[52]Декрет ВЦИК «О Всероссийской и местных Чрезвычайных Комиссиях по борьбе с контрреволюцией, спекуляцией и преступлениями по должности». *Izvestiia VCIK* № 240 (2.11.1918); *SU* 80-842 (3.11.1918). Retrieved from http://istmat.info/node/31742. The legal chaos led to the Direction on Strict Observance of Laws by the VI All-Russia Extraordinary Congress of Councils of Workers & Peasants' Deputies [Постановление VI Всероссийского Чрезвычайного Съезда Советов Рабочих и Крестьянских Депутатов «О точном соблюдении законов» (8.11.1918)]. *Izvestiia VCIK* № 267 (6.12.1918); *SU* 90-908 (20.12.1918) (SU 1917–1918, p. 1262). Retrieved from http://istmat.info/node/31948. The congress also issued the Direction on Amnesty, aimed at release of hostages taken after the S-R revolt in July 1918 [Постановление VI Всероссийского Съезда Советов «Об освобождении некоторых категорий заключенных» (6.11.1918)]. *SU* 100-1033 (31.12.1918) (SU 1917–1918, p. 1445). Retrieved from http://istmat.info/node/32149.

[53]Постановление Совета Обороны «О производимых Всероссийской Чрезвычайной Комиссией арестах ответственных служащих и специалистов». *Izvestiia VCIK* № 274 (14.12.1918); *SU* 94-941 (24.12.1918). Retrieved from http://istmat.info/node/32010.

[54]Minutes of Moscow All-City Conference of RKP(b) of 30.01.1919: Стенограмма Московской общегородской конференции РКП(б) от 30.01.1919. Центральный архив научно-технической документации Москвы (ЦАНТДМ) [архив Института истории партии МГК и МК КПСС]

that when *ChK* and *RT* dealt with the same cases, *RT* may call witnesses, and its decisions were made by several tribunes, while the *ChK* decisions were based exclusively on investigation (следствие), with a preliminary search (розыск), moreover, not being separated from investigation.[55] Notably, Krylenko implied that *RT* were more like courts than *ChK*. The *ChK* head Dzerzhinskii defended *ChK* on [rather dubious] account of its speedy procedure.[56]

By the *VCIK* Directive of 24.01.1919 local [уездные] *ChK*s were abolished (SU 1919, p. 16).[57] The *VCIK* Directive of 17.02.1919 on *VChK*, reaffirmed that the right of sentencing belonged to *RT*s, with *VChK* retaining the **power of direct reprisal** in case of the armed rebellion or the martial law (§§2–3) as well as the power of incarceration in concentration camps (§8) (SU 1919, pp. 184–185).[58] The *VCIK*

ф. 3, оп. 1, д. 99, лл. 30-40. Available at http://libmonster.ru/m/articles/view/ИЗ-ИСТОРИИ-ВЗАИМООТНОШЕНИИ-ЧРЕЗВЫЧАЙНЫХ-КОМИССИИ-И-РЕВОЛЮЦИОННЫХ-ТРИБУНАЛОВ.

[55]N. G. Krylenko was a member of the collegium of the People's Commissariat of Justice of the RSFSR [an analogue of the Justice Ministry board] from March1918 and the chair of *RT* set by the All-Russia Executive Council [*VCIK*] (that became the Supreme *RT* in 1919).

[56]Available at http://libmonster.ru/m/articles/view/ИЗ-ИСТОРИИ-ВЗАИМООТНОШЕНИИ-ЧРЕЗВЫЧАЙНЫХ-КОМИССИИ-И-РЕВОЛЮЦИОННЫХ-ТРИБУНАЛОВ.

[57]Постановление ВЦИК «Об упразднении Уездных Чрезвычайных Комиссий по борьбе с контрреволюцией, спекуляцией и преступлениями по должности». *Izvestiia VCIK* № 16 (24.01.1919); *SU* 1-14 (26.01.1919). Retrieved from http://istmat.info/node/35469.

[58]Постановление ВЦИК «О Всероссийской Чрезвычайной Комиссии» (17.02.1919). *Izvestiia VCIK* № 40 (21.02.1919); *SU* 12-130 (24.04.1919). Retrieved from http://istmat.info/node/35829. Revolutionary Tribunal consisted of three members elected per month by the gubernia IK (art. 4). The sentencing sessions were to be public (art. 4). Art. 2–3 [on the martial law] of the decree of 21.02.1919 that granted to *VChK* the [extrajudicial] right of direct reprisal was elaborated by the *VCIK* Decree of 20.06.1919, listing nine 'criminal acts': membership in a counter-revolutionary organization and taking part in an anti-Soviet plot, state treason & espionage, hiding of weapons for a counter-revolutionary purpose, forgery, setting up fire or explosions for a counter-revolutionary purpose, sabotage, banditry, robbery, breaking into storages and stores for purpose of theft, trade in cocaine [Декрет ВЦИК «Об изъятиях из общей подсудности в местностях, объявленных на военном положении» (20.06.1919)]. *Izvestiia VCIK* № 134 (22.06.1919); *SU* 27-301 (30.06.1919) (SU 1919, pp. 435–436). Retrieved from http://istmat.info/node/38094. SNK's Decree of 21.10.1919 further expanded the *VChK* power with respect to theft in state stores, forgery and other misuse of official position in economic and distributary organs by creating a special revolutionary tribunal (of three members), attached to *VChK*, its decisions (reached purely on basis of interests of revolution without any judicial formality) were final and had no cassation [Декрет СНК «О борьбе со спекуляцией» (21.10.1919)].

Decree of 12.04.1919 defined the *RT* jurisdiction as encompassing counter-revolutionary and other acts directed against the attainments [завоевания] of the October Revolution (SU 1919, pp. 190–193).[59] Under the *VCIK* Decree of 15.04.1919 on Compulsory Work Camps, the regional *ChK* were to manage the camps where persons were placed by *ChK*, *RT* or the People's Courts (SU 1919, p. 180).[60]

The *VCIK* Decree of 18.03.1920 on *RT*s (SU 1920, pp. 161–170),[61] also abolished an adjudication jurisdiction of the extraordinary commissions (*ChKs*) and other extraordinary organs (such as the extraordinary martial courts) as well as of the special tribunal attached to *VChK* (art. 5). The IX All-Russian Congress of Soviets (23–28.12.1921) called for the transfer of the *VChK* judicial jurisdiction to the courts (SU 1922, pp. 55–56).[62] The *VCIK* decree of 6.02.1922 (SU 1922, pp. 313–315),[63] formally dissolved *VChK*, turning into a state political department (государственное политическое управление [*GPU*]) in the People's Commissariat of Internal Affairs [*NKVD*].

The *VCIK* Decree of 23.06.1921 centralised the tribunal system by effectively amalgamated the Supreme *RT* with the Cassation *RT* (besides, the military and transport *RT*s were merged with the 'civil' *RT*s) (SU 1921, pp. 544–549).[64] The *RT* trials continued

---

Izvestiia VCIK № 237 (23.10.1919); *SU* 53-504 (3.11.1919); (SU 1919, pp. 727–728). Retrieved from http://istmat.info/node/38619.

[59]Декрет ВЦИК «О революционных трибуналах» (Положение). *Izvestiia VCIK* № 79 (12.04.1919); *SU* 13-132 (30.04.1919). Retrieved from http://istmat.info/node/35837. Tribunals were set in all gubernia (art. 2). There were also the Supreme *RT* and the Cassation *RT* attached to *VCIK* (Ch VIII & IX).

[60]Декрет ВЦИК «О лагерях принудительных работ». *Izvestiia VCIK* № 81 (15.04.1919); *SU* 12-124 (24.04.1919). Retrieved from http://istmat.info/node/35823.

[61]Декрет ВЦИК «О революционных трибуналах» (Положение) (18.03.1920). *Izvestiia VCIK* № 67 (27.03.1920); *SU* 22-23 – 115 (5.04.1920). Retrieved from http://istmat.info/node/41441.

[62]Резолюция Съезда Советов о ВЧК. *Izvestiia VCIK* № 255 (30.12.1921); *SU* 4-42 (20.02.1922).

[63]Декрет ВЦИК «Об упразднении Всероссийской чрезвычайной комиссии». *Izvestiia VCIK* № 30 (8.02.1922); *СУ* 16-160 (6.02.1922).

[64]*Izvestiia VCIK* № 138 (28.06.1921); *SU* 51-294 (5.09.1921). Retrieved from http://istmat.info/node/46275.

as late as 1922, such as an infamous trail against the 'right' Social Revolutionaries.[65] Finally, the formation of the USSR court system spelled the end to the 'civil' *RTs*.[66]

In sum, the Revolutionary Tribunals, alongside the extraordinary commissions, were created to suppress 'counter-revolutionary' resistance and became the key tools of the Red Terror. The extra-judicial bodies were offshoots of the revolutionary destruction of the preceding legal order. Still *RTs* were more like 'courts' than *ChKs*. Unsurprisingly, the latter became the most notorious and ruthless institutions of 'direct reprisal'. In terms of Hart's secondary norms, *ChKs* could hardly be under a rule of adjudication, as there was no adjudication per se. After Bolsheviks obtained the upper hand in the civil war, there was a trend towards 'gentrification' of the tribunals, as well as abating of the extraordinary commissions power of 'direct reprisal'. The conflation of jurisdiction of the courts and *RTs* created the ambiguity as to the rules of recognition and adjudication. Notably, the 'civil' tribunals faded away with the court reform of 1922. In comparison, the formally abolished extraordinary commission had survived in a new disguise (as *GPU*), becoming part of *NKVD* and for the time shedding off its [extra]judicial functions. This metamorphosis exemplified a hibernation rather than an eradication of the extra-judicial body. In just two years the USSR *CIK* Decree of 24.03.1924 granted the Joint State Political Department [Объединенное Государственное Политическое Управление (*OGPU*)][67] power of sentencing of 'socially dangerous' persons to exile to inner [USSR] regions or abroad, or incarceration in concentration camps for up to three years (VChK-OGPU-NKVD,

---

[65] Available at https://topos.memo.ru/revolyucionnyy-tribunal-pri-vcik-verhsud-rsfsr.

[66] Постановление Президиума ЦИК СССР «Положение о Верховном Суде СССР» (23.11.1923). Утверждено 2-ой Сессией ЦИК СССР II созыва 24.10.1924. (1924) *Собрание Законов СССР* [*SZ*] 19-183. Ch. V provided for Martial Collegium [Военная Коллегия] of the Supreme Court of the USSR, with jurisdiction about particular persons, as determined by the *CIK* Presidium (or the Supreme Court plenum session) or the special list [of persons], approved by the *CIK* Presidium. Available at http://lawru.info/dok/1923/11/23/n1204513.htm.

[67] Art. 12 of the Treaty on Formation of the USSR of 30.12.1922 (approved by the I Congress of the USSR Soviets) established *OGPU* attached to *SNK* of the USSR. (USSR Doc., p. 217). Also available at https://lawru.info/dok/1922/12/30/n1204920.htm.

pp. 179–181).⁶⁸ This inability to function without extra-judicial bodies showed the depth of damage to the integrity of legal order (and, specifically, to the secondary rules of adjudication and recognition) done by the revolution.⁶⁹

Soviet Basic Norm Through Soviet Constitutions

Constitution 1918 (RSFSR): *The Same Basic Norm—'Commands' of the Congress of Soviets*

The first Constitution of the Russian Socialist Federative Soviet Republic [*RSFSR*] was approved by the V All-Russia Congress [Съезд] of [the representatives of] the Soviets of Workers, Peasants, Red Army Soldiers and Cossacks' Deputies on 10.07.1918, under the complete Bolshevik control (after expulsion of the Left S-R deputies) (SU 1917–1918, pp. 671–682).⁷⁰ A supreme power was vested in the Congress of the *Soviets* (art. 24), summoned by *VCIK* at least twice a year (art. 26). Only the Congress could amend the Constitution (art. 49 (а) & 51) or legislate regarding courts or civil and criminal laws (art. 49(о)). It had the executive power, having general supervision over all external and internal policy of the RSFSR (art. 49 (б)), appointing the *SNK* (art. 49 (п)) entering in the custom or trade treaties (art. 49 (и)), etc. In between the Congresses, the supreme power belonged to *VCIK* (art. 30), elected by the Congress (art. 29). *VCIK* was also a supreme executive, legislative and supervising body (art. 31). *VCIK* approved decrees, drafted by *SNK*, and other authorities, and issued its own decries (art. 33). *SNK* had a power to issue decries for 'correct and smooth flow of the state life' (art. 38),

---

⁶⁸«Положение о правах объединенного государственного политического управления в части административных высылок, ссылок и заключения в концентрационный лагерь». http://istmat.info/node/39055.

⁶⁹For an account of the Great Terror of 1937 see the Appendix to this chapter below.

⁷⁰Конституция (Основной Закон) Российской Социалистической Федеративной Советской Республики [РСФСР], принятая V Всероссийским Съездом Советов 10.07.1918. *Izvestiia VCIK* № 151 (19.07.1918); *SU* 51-582 (20.07.1918). Retrieved from http://istmat.info/node/30604.

informing *VCIK* about its decisions (art. 39), with *VCIK* retaining the right to overrule any *SNK* decision (art. 41).

The *Constitution 1918* did not envision a separation between executive and legislative powers. This became a feature of the whole Soviet system. The Marxist–Leninist aversion to the representative 'parliamentary' democracy (together with their alternative concept of the 'direct' (but restricted)[71] democracy) resulted in the 'pyramid' Soviet system. It consisted of four local/regional subsets of congresses of the Soviets and their executive committees (*IK*), as well as the town and village Soviets (Ch. 10-11), and, at central level, of the All-Russia Congress of the Soviets and its *CIK* (Ch. 6-7). At the top, the All-Russia Congress and its Executive Committee, fused together executive and legislative power. At local level, the Congresses of the Soviets, as well as the town and village Soviets, embodied the executive power.

The VII Congress of Soviets Decree *on Soviet Formation* [О Советском строительстве] established the *VCIK* Presidium, with powers to approve or suspend the *SNK* decrees between the *VCIK* sessions summoned every two months [I.8] (SU 1919, pp. 823–827).[72]

Formation of the USSR: The Same Basic Norm

On 30.12.1922 the I All-Soviet Congress of the representatives of the Soviets of Workers, Peasants and Red Army Soldiers Deputies (elected by the Congresses of Soviets of four Republics) approved the Declaration and the Treaty of Formation of the Union of the Soviet Socialists Republics (USSR Doc., pp. 213–218).[73] The II Congress approved the Constitution of the USSR on 31.01.1924 (USSR Doc., pp. 225–237).[74] According to art. 8 of the *Constitution 1924* (USSR), the Congress was the supreme

---

[71]The *Constitution 1918* expressly disenfranchised those who were: living on income from property, engaged in commerce or enterprise [with hired labour], formerly employed in police and other security services, members of the tsarist family, monks, priests (Ch. 13, art. 64–65).

[72]*Izvestiia VCIK* № 279 (12.12.1919); *SU* 64-578 (27.12.1919). Retrieved from http://istmat.info/node/38871.

[73]ГАРФ ф. Р-3316. оп. 1. д. 5. л. 1.

[74]Available at http://constitution.garant.ru/history/ussr-rsfsr/1924/.

organ of power, with the Central Executive Committee (*CIK*) (consisting from the Union Council & the Council of Nationalities) becoming the supreme organ in between the Congresses. The *CIK* Presidium was a supreme executive, legislative and supervising organ of the USSR in between the *CIK* sessions (art. 29). In 1924 the Council of People's Commissars [Совет Народных Комиссаров] of the USSR (together with the Council of Labour and Defence [Совет Труда и Обороны]) began to issue the *Digest of Laws and Directives of Workers & Peasants' Government of the USSR* [*Собрание законов и распоряжений Рабоче-Крестьянского правительства Союза Советских Социалистических Республик СССР (SZ USSR)*].[75]

The 'Stalin' *Constitution 1936* (USSR) (USSR Doc., pp. 345–359),[76] as well as the *Constitution 1977* (USSR) that replaced it, represented continuation of the legal order established by the October Revolution. Through the whole Soviet period the basic norm remained the same— one presupposing the Soviet Congress 'command'. Thus, while the *Constitution 1936* did not envision summoning the Congresses of Soviets anymore, it itself was enacted on 5.12.1936 by the VIII All-Soviet Congress of the Soviets. Ch. III (art. 30) defined the Supreme Council [Верховный Совет (*VS*)] of the USSR [СССР] as the [new] supreme organ of power of the USSR. Following the Supreme Council

---

[75] Постановление ЦИК и СНК Союза ССР «О порядке опубликования законов и распоряжений Союза ССР» (22.08.1924). [unpublished in *Izvestiia CIK & VCIK* № 192 (24.08.1924) (AT)?]; *SZ* № 7-71 (1.10.1924). According to art. 6 the most important decrees were to be published in *Izvestiia CIK*. The decrees could be left unpublished [even in *SZ*], in case of the direction of *CIK, SNK* & *STO* (art. 2 (a) & 4), though some information could be published in periodicals with express sanction of the *CIK* secretary etc. (art. 10). Retrieved from https://naukaprava.ru/catalog/1/129/179/275/55247?view=1. From 1938 to 1946 the bulletin (*SZ*) was called «Собрание распоряжений Правительства СССР», from 1946 to 1949—«Собрание постановлений и распоряжений Совета министров СССР», from 1957 to 1991—«Собрание постановлений Правительства СССР».

[76] *Izvestiia CIK & VCIK* № 283 (6.12.1936). The texts of the different editions of the *Constitution 1936* are available at http://constitution.garant.ru/history/ussr-rsfsr/1936/red_1936/. The *Constitution 1936* (USSR) was followed by the *Constitution 1937* (RSFSR), approved by the XVII All-Russia Congress of Soviets on 21.01.1937. *Izvestiia CIK & VCIK* № 20 (22.01.1937); *Собрание узаконений и распоряжений Рабоче-Крестьянского Правительства РСФСР (SU RSFSR)* № 2-11 (31.03.1937). According to Ch. 3 of the *Constitution 1937* (RSFSR), the Supreme Council of the RSFSR became a supreme organ of power in the RSFSR (art. 22) and the only legislative organ in the RSFSR (art. 24). Retrieved from https://naukaprava.ru/catalog/1/119/121/657/13390?view=1.

decree of 24.01.1938, *Vedomosti VS USSR* [*Ведомости Верховного Совета СССР*] became the official newspaper of *VS* of the USSR, with the first issue appearing on 7.04.1938.[77]

The last major USSR constitutional change happened in 1977 with the passing of the last Constitution of the USSR, approved by the USSR Supreme Council on 7.10.1977.[78] Art. 6 of the *Constitution 1977* codified the one-party system. The codification of the one-party system at least did away with a breath-taking hypocrisy of the Stalin constitution that made no mentioning of the communist party. The *Constitution 1977* (Ch. 12) renamed the councils of workers' deputies into councils of people's deputies, perhaps, implying the move towards the less class divided society.

With respect to the constitutional separation of legislative and executive powers, no radical change had been taken place between the Constitutions of 1936 and 1977. The *Constitution 1936* (USSR) [indirectly] addressed the subordinate legislative power of the government (*SNK*) (art. 66–67), with the Supreme Council Presidium having power to annul the *SNK* decisions (art. 49). The *Constitution 1977* (USSR) also recognised the subordinate legislation powers of the cabinet of ministers (art. 133). Notably, the Supreme Council Presidium had power to interpret the law (art. 49(ii) of the *Constitution 1936* and art. 121(5) the *Constitution 1977*). Under the *Constitution 1977* the Presidium had

---

[77] The last issue of *Vedomosti VS USSR* was № 2 on 31.05.1989, replaced by *Vedomosti of Congress of People's Deputies & VS USSR* [*Ведомости Съезда народных депутатов СССР и Верховного Совета СССР* (*Vedomosti SND & VS USSR*)] on 14.06.1989, briefly resuming its former title since 9.11.1991 to 25.12.1991. Retrieved from http://vedomosti.vs.sssr.su/.

[78] *Vedomosti VS USSR* № 41 (1907)—616, 617 [text of the Constitution] & 619 [Закон СССР № 6367-IX«О порядке введения в действие Конституции (Основного Закона) СССР»(7.10.1977)]. Retrieved from https://naukaprava.ru/catalog/1/127/138/51726?view=1. Texts of all five editions of the *Constitution 1977* (USSR) are available at http://constitution.garant.ru/history/ussr-rsfsr/1977/red_1977/. The *Constitution 1978* (RSFSR) was approved by the Supreme Council of the RSFSR on 12.04.1978. Ведомости ВС РСФСР № 15 (1017) (13.04.1978)—406, 407 [text], 408. https://naukaprava.ru/catalog/1/113/62/42498?view=1. The *Constitution 1978* (RSFSR) followed the outline of the *Constitution 1977* (USSR). Texts of all ten editions of the *Constitution 1977* (USSR) are available at http://constitution.garant.ru/history/ussr-rsfsr/1978/red_1978/.

express legislative powers: to issue decrees and by-laws (art. 123) and amend laws (art. 122 (1)).[79]

The conflation of executive and legislative powers was not the only ambiguity regarding the secondary rules of change and recognition. There was also a glaring issue of separation of judiciary power (i.e. the secondary rule of adjudication). While the Constitutions of 1936 and 1977, on the surface, envisioned a separate court system, in practice the courts were not independent, due to the pervasive party influence, even outside the periods of Terror (perpetrated by the extra-judicial bodies). The *Constitution 1977*, though, entrenched a five-year term [in place of formerly three-year one] for the lower court judges, as well as their [nominal] elections by local population. Through the whole Soviet period the lower courts mainly consisted of judges and several (mostly two) jurymen, with formally the same judicial power. There were besides the constitutional shortcomings in separation of powers due to the procurator office and the ministry of justice (formally belonging to the executive) supervising over the judiciary application of laws.[80]

In sum, through the whole Soviet period there remained a residual ambiguity with respect to the secondary rules of adjudication and change, if not the rules of recognition (which had been codified in relation to civil and criminal law and procedure).

---

[79]Similarly, under the *Constitution 1978* (RSFSR): art. 116 (1) & 117.

[80]The office was created by the decrees of 12.01.1722 & 27.04.1722 (& 2.04.1731). See the USSR law on the USSR Procurator's office of 30.11.1979 (art. 1) that envisioned the overall control over application of law. Available at http://www.lawrussia.ru/texts/legal_861/doc861a197x357.htm. The procurator's role in the post-Soviet period was defined by the Federal Law № 2202-1-ФЗ (17.01.1992). Available at http://www.consultant.ru/document/cons_doc_LAW_262/. By this law the procurator seemed to receive something a semi legislative power to request amendments of laws: art. 9.1. Available at http://www.consultant.ru/document/cons_doc_LAW_262/623e1f34405e338a3cb6649faaafe4a99ec1d887/. There is still a power to supervise the application of law: art. 21 [partly unconstitutional, according to the RF Constitutional Court decision № 13-П (18.07.2003)]. Available at http://www.consultant.ru/document/cons_doc_LAW_262/84a54a8d20de6522b1b1c60e5f5d537330ffed83/.

Perestroika: From Evolutionary to Revolutionary Transformation

Dissolution of Soviet Legal Order in the USSR

The *Perestroika* end result was a dissolution of the Soviet Union. Still, in contrast to the February Revolution and October Revolution, the reforms had commenced without a break with the preceding legal order, as defined by the *Constitution 1977* (USSR).

According to the original edition of the *Constitution 1977*,[81] the highest organ of the state power was the Supreme Council [Верховный Совет (*VS*)] of the USSR, with power to amend the Constitution (art. 108), as well as to enact laws (art. 13 (20)).

On 1.12.1988 the *VS* approved the amendments to the Constitution, including one to the art. 108, making the highest organ the Congress of the People's Deputies of the USSR, as well as providing for the election of the deputies (Ch.13).[82]

During 1989 there were two Congresses of the People's Deputies of the USSR on 25.05–9.06.1989 & on 12–24.12.1989. On 20.12.1989 the II Congress enacted some other [technical] amendments to the Constitution, such as to approval of laws (by the two-third majority of the Congress members),[83] as well as to the deputies' election.[84]

---

[81] Закон СССР № 6367-IX «О порядке введения в действие Конституции (Основного Закона) СССР» (7.10.1977). Available at http://constitution.garant.ru/history/ussr-rsfsr/1977/red_1977/5478732/.

[82] Закон СССР № 9853-XI «Об изменениях и дополнениях Конституции (Основного Закона) СССР» (1.12.1988). *Vedomosti VS USSR* № 49 (2487) (7.12.1988)—727. Retrieved from https://naukaprava.ru/catalog/1/127/149/45645?view=1, http://constitution.garant.ru/history/ussr-rsfsr/1977/zakony/185466/.

[83] Закон СССР № 961-I «Об уточнении некоторых положений Конституции (Основного Закона) СССР по вопросам порядка деятельности Съезда народных депутатов СССР, Верховного Совета СССР и их органов» (20.12.1989). *Vedomosti SND & VS USSR* (*Ведомости СНД и ВС СССР*) № 29 (27.12.989)—538. Retrieved from https://naukaprava.ru/catalog/1/127/152/46411?view=1, http://constitution.garant.ru/history/ussr-rsfsr/1977/zakony/185462/.

[84] Закон СССР № 963-I «Об изменениях и дополнениях Конституции (Основного Закона) СССР по вопросам избирательной системы» (20.12.1989). *Vedomosti SND & VS USSR* № 29 (27.12.1989)—540. Available at http://constitution.garant.ru/history/ussr-rsfsr/1977/zakony/185460/.

On 15.03.1990 the III Congress enacted further constitutional amendments, introducing the post of 'president' of the USSR and changing art. 6 (dismantling one-party system),[85] as well as modernising art. 10 (allowing for equal recognition of different forms of ownership: citizens, collective and state ownership).

Art. 72 of the *Constitution 1977* stated that the republics retained the right to leave the USSR (similarly to art. 17 of the *Constitution 1936*). On 3.04.1990 the *VS* enacted the law elaborating on the procedure of exit from the USSR by its member republic.[86] This law provided for the independence referendum, requiring the two-third of the permanent residents of the Republic to vote to exit the Union for the referendum to succeed (art. 6). The autonomous republics and regions were to have separate referenda, retaining the right to remain in the USSR (art. 3).[87]

The last amendments to the *Constitution 1977* were approved by the IV Congress of the USSR People's Deputies (14–27.12.1990), introducing the Council of Federation, renaming the Council of Ministers into the 'Cabinet' of Ministers, as well as allowing the Supreme Council to call a referendum between the Congresses.[88] On 27.12.1990 the

---

[85]Закон СССР № 1360-I «Об учреждении поста Президента СССР и внесении изменений и дополнений в Конституцию (Основной Закон) СССР» (14.03.1990). *Vedomosti SND & VS USSR* № 12 (21.03.1990)—189. Retrieved from https://naukaprava.ru/catalog/1/127/153/45504?view=1, http://constitution.garant.ru/history/ussr-rsfsr/1977/zakony/185465/chapter/49599213504d6956cf5503c571d6cc11/#block_200.

[86]Закон СССР № 1409-I «О порядке решения вопросов, связанных с выходом союзной республики из СССР» (3.04.1990). *Vedomosti SND & VS USSR* № 15 (11.04.1990)—252. Retrieved from https://naukaprava.ru/catalog/1/127/153/45507?view=1.

[87]While, there was no 'separate' referendum in Crimea, by a notable coincidence, in the Ukrainian independence referendum of 1.12.1991 only Crimea had not met the 2/3 of the permanent residents requirement (Crimean autonomous republic [Крымская АССР]: 67.50% (vote) 54.19% (participants); the city of Sevastopol [Севастополь]: 63.74 & 57.07%). Відомість про результати Всеукраїнського референдуму, 1 грудня 1991 р. (ЦДАВО України. ф. 1. оп. 28. спр. 144. арк. 6). Retrieved from https://archives.gov.ua/Sections/15r-V_Ref/index.php?11. Crimean autonomous district (область) became an autonomous republic owing to laws of the Ukrainian SSR of 12.02.1991 & 19.06.1991 (Закон Украинской ССР «О восстановлении Крымской Автономной Советской Социалистической Республики» (12.02.1991) & Закон УССР № 1213-XII «О внесении поправок в Конституцию УССР» (19.06.1991)). There was no corresponding amendment of the USSR Constitution.

[88]Закон СССР № 1861-I «Об изменениях и дополнениях Конституции (Основного Закона) СССР в связи с совершенствованием системы государственного управления» (26.12.1990). Available at http://constitution.garant.ru/history/ussr-rsfsr/1977/zakony/185464/.

law about the all-Soviet referendum was signed by the President of the USSR (M. Gorbachev).[89] According to the law, a successful referendum required more than half of the votes from more than a half of the registered voters (art. 23). The Congress called for organisation of the all-Soviet referenda, including one on the USSR itself,[90] as well as envisioning its renewal.[91]

On 16.01.1991 the USSR VS decided to hold the all-Soviet referendum about continuation of the USSR on 17.03.1991.[92]

Estonia, Latvia, Lithuania, Moldavia, Armenia and Georgia did not set central electoral committees to conduct referendum as required by law. The remaining nine Republics had conducted the referendum, with a 'yes' result in all of them (within Azerbaijan, there was no referendum in the mountainous Karabakh autonomic region in

---

[89] Закон СССР № 1869-1 «О всенародном голосовании (референдуме СССР)» (27.12.1990). (1991) *Vedomosti SND & VS USSR* № 1 (2.01.1991)—10. Retrieved from https://naukaprava.ru/catalog/1/127/154/46102?view=1, http://base.garant.ru/6336203/. Постановление СНД СССР № 1870-1 «О введении в действие Закона СССР „О всенародном голосовании (референдуме СССР)"» (27.12.1990). (1991) *Vedomosti SND & VS USSR* № 1—11.

[90] Постановление СНД СССР № 1856-I «О проведении референдума СССР по вопросу о Союзе Советских Социалистических Республик» (24.12.1990). (1990) *Vedomosti SND & VS USSR* № 52 (26.12.1990)—1161. Retrieved from https://naukaprava.ru/catalog/1/127/153/45544?view=1.

[91] Постановление СНД СССР № 1853-1 «О сохранении Союза ССР как обновлённой федерации равноправных суверенных республик» (24.12.1990). (1990) *Vedomosti SND & VS USSR* № 52—1158.

[92] Постановление ВС СССР № 1910-1 «Об организации и мерах по обеспечению проведения референдума СССР по вопросу о сохранении Союза Советских Социалистических Республик» (16.01.1991). (1991) *Vedomosti SND & VS USSR* № 4 (23.01.1991)—87. Retrieved from https://naukaprava.ru/catalog/1/127/154/46105?view=1. "1. Провести на всей территории СССР в воскресенье, 17 марта 1991 года, референдум СССР по вопросу о сохранении Союза ССР как федерации равноправных республик. 2. Включить в бюллетень для тайного голосования следующую формулировку вопроса, выносимого на референдум, и варианты ответов голосующих:
«Считаете ли Вы необходимым сохранение Союза Советских Социалистических Республик как обновлённой федерации равноправных суверенных республик, в которой будут в полной мере гарантироваться права и свободы человека любой национальности».
«Да» или «Нет». 3. Определить результаты голосования по Союзу ССР в целом с учётом итогов голосования по каждой республике в отдельности".

the Nakhichevan autonomous republic the participation was below the required one by law).[93]

The six 'absentees' republics, thus, decided on a revolutionary break with the Soviet legal order (with unilateral referenda to exit the USSR), starting anew. In the Baltic republics, perhaps, the new legal orders were intended to be in continuance with the pre-Soviet ones. But, in terms of Kelsen's basic norm, when a legal order had been overturned it had gone 'for good'. Perhaps, a once existing basic norm might be restored as a *new* basic norm. Though, it might not always be feasible to restore the old basic norm, for example, the monarchic one, if no old dynasty was left in existence and so on. Still, as the October Revolution (and the numerous other revolutions) had demonstrated, the revolutionary legitimacy (the revolutionary basic norm) might be just as good as any other. There, however, might be an issue of the lack of de facto control on the 'ground': of the six former Soviet republic, Georgia and Moldovia had not established such control over the parts of their 'nominal' territory.

Despite the successful 1991 referendum in nine republics, the Soviet Union was not 'renewed' on the basis on a new treaty, as envisioned by the IV Congress.[94] The last V Congress of the People's Deputies took

---

[93]«Об итогах референдума СССР, состоявшегося 17 марта 1991 года (Из сообщения Центральной комиссии референдума СССР)». *Izvestiia SND [Известия СНД СССР]* (27.03.1991). Постановление ВС СССР № 2041-1 «Об итогах референдума СССР 17 марта 1991 года» (21.03.1991). (1991) *Vedomosti SND & VS USSR* № 13 (27.03.1991)—350. Retrieved from https://naukaprava.ru/catalog/1/127/154/46114?view=1.

[94]The draft of a new Treaty on the Union of the Soviet Sovereign Republics (Договор о Союзе Советских Суверенных Республик. Проект) was published in the newspaper *Pravda* («Правда») on 15.08.1991. Available at http://doc.histrf.ru/20/dogovor-o-soyuze-sovetskikh-suverennykh-respublik/, https://sites.google.com/view/oldlaws/%D0%BF%D0%BE%D1%81%D0%B-B%D0%B5-1964/%D0%B4%D0%BE%D0%B3%D0%BE%D0%B2%D0%BE%D1%80-%D0%BE-%D1%81%D0%BE%D1%8E%D0%B7%D0%B5-%D1%81%D0%BE%D0%B2%D0%B5%D1%82%D1%81%D0%BA%D0%B8%D1%85-%D1%81%D1%83%D0%B2%D0%B5%D1%80%D0%B5%D0%BD%D0%BD%D1%8B%D1%85-%D1%80%D0%B5%D1%81%D0%BF%D1%83%D0%B1%D0%BB%D0%B8%D0%BA. Art. 23 of the Draft envisioned the dissolution of the 1922 Treaty [approved by the 1st Congress of the Soviets of the USSR on 30.12.1922]. The 1922 Treaty became incorporated into the 1924 Constitution of the USSR. The only way to dissolve the USSR in accordance with its basic norm would be by the constitutional transformation on the Congress of the USSR People's Deputies. In any case, The Putsch of 18–21.08.1991 made impossible the signing of the Treaty (as the events on the ground 'moved on').

place on 2–5.09.1991. The Congress enacted the law on the Organs of the State Powers in the Transitional Period.[95] According to this law, in the transitional period the supreme power was vested in the Supreme Council [Верховный Совет (*VS*)], now divided into the Council of the Republics [Совет Республик (*SR*)] (with representation according to the set quotas from the republics, including the autonomous republics and other autonomies) and the Council of the Union [Совет Союза (*SS*)] (in accord with the exited quotas) (art. 1). Besides, *SR* & *SS* jointly received power to amend the Constitution (art. 2). However, no amendment to the USSR Constitution had taken place (at the Congress) to give these changes a constitutional legitimacy (art.108 of the Constitution 1977 (USSR) [ed. 26.12.1990] granted power to amend the constitution exclusively to the Congress). Hence, in the constitutional sense, both new organs (*SR* & *SS*) had only 'shadowy' legal existence. As a result, the *SR* Declaration of 26.12.1991 (on the USSR ceasing to exist as a subject of the international law) had itself been in breach of the existing basic norm.[96]

The USSR became de facto dissolved in December 1991. As a result of the failed coup in August 1991, the power on the ground shifted away from the USSR authorities. In effect, the break with the Soviet legal order was a revolutionary one in each post-Soviet republic.

Dissolution of Soviet Legal Order: The RSFSR

The *Constitution 1978* (RSFSR) was amended on 27.10.1989 to introduce, among other changes, the Congress of the RSFSR People's

---

[95]Закон СССР № 2392-I «Об органах государственной власти и управления Союза ССР в переходный период» (5.09.1991) *Vedomosti SND & VS USSR* № 37 (11.09.1991)—1082. Retrieved from http://vedomosti.sssr.su/1991/37/. The archive copy: ГАРФ ф. Р-9654. оп. 1. д. 184. л. 45-47. Retrieved from http://portal.rusarchives.ru/statehood/09-42-postanovlenie-organy-gosvlasti.shtml.

[96]Декларация Совета Республик Верховного Совета СССР в связи с созданием Содружества Независимых Государств [№ 142—Н от 26.12.1991]. (1991) *Vedomosti VS RSFSR* [*Ведомости ВС РСФСР*] № 52 (2.12.1991). Retrieved from http://vedomosti.sssr.su/1991/52/#1493.

Deputies as the supreme organ of power and the Constitutional Court (elected by the Congress).[97] The I Congress (16.05–22/06.1990) approved the Declaration of the State Sovereignty of the RSFSR.[98] On 16.06.1990 the Congress made further amendments to the 1978 Constitution, discarding the one-party political system (art. 6 & 7).[99] The RSFSR VS enacted the law of all-Russia referendum on 16.10.1990.[100]

The II Congress took place 27.11–15.12 1990, amending the Constitution to allow for different form of ownership (art. 10), to discard the exclusive state ownership (art. 11 &11.1), apart of a number of technical constitutional amendments (as well as deciding on drafting a new federal agreement).[101] On 7.02.1991 the RSFSR VS decided to hold a separate RSFSR referendum together with the USSR referendum on 17.03.1991.[102] While, the VS direction did not explicitly mention it, the

---

[97]Закон РСФСР«Об изменениях и дополнениях Конституции (Основного Закона) РСФСР» (принят одиннадцатой сессией Верховного Совета РСФСР одиннадцатого созыва) (27.101989). (1989) *Vedomosti VS RSFSR* № 44 (2.11.1989)—1303. Retrieved from http://vedomosti.rsfsr.su/1989/44/#1303, http://constitution.garant.ru/history/ussr-rsfsr/1978/zakony/183129/, http://constitution.garant.ru/history/ussr-rsfsr/1978/zakony/183129/chapter/5633a92d35b966c2ba2f1e859e7bdd69/. Закон РСФСР № 14-1«О внесении изменений в статью 104 Конституции (Основного Закона) РСФСР» (31.05.1990). (1990) *Vedomosti SND & VS RSFSR* [Ведомости СНД и ВС РСФСР] № 2 (14.06.1990)—14. Retrieved from http://vedomosti.rsfsr-rf.ru/1990/2/#14.

[98]Декларация о государственном суверенитете Российской Советской Федеративной Социалистической Республики (12.06.1990). (1990) *Vedomosti SND & VS RSFSR* № 2 (12.06.1990)—22. Retrieved from http://vedomosti.rsfsr-rf.ru/1990/2/#22.

[99]Закон РСФСР № 38-I«Об изменениях и дополнениях Конституции (Основного Закона) РСФСР» (16.06.1990). (1990) *Vedomosti SND & VS RSFSR* № 3—25. Retrieved from http://vedomosti.rsfsr-rf.ru/1990/3/#25, https://base.garant.ru/183133/1cafb24d049dcd1e7707a22d98e9858f/.

[100]Закон РСФСР № 241-I«О референдуме РСФСР»(16.10.1990). (1990) *Vedomosti SND & VS RSFSR* № 21 (25.10.1990)—230. Retrieved from http://naukaprava.ru/catalog/1/113/117/40386?view=1, http://www.consultant.ru/cons/cgi/online.cgi?req=doc&base=LAW&n=7595&fld=134&dst=100006,0&rnd=0.2172381701968158#07618577039464973.

[101]Закон РСФСР «Об изменениях и дополнениях Конституции (Основного Закона) РСФСР» (15.12.1990). *Vedomosti SND & VS RSFSR* (1990) № 29 (20.12.1990)—395. Retrieved from https://naukaprava.ru/catalog/1/113/117/40395?view=1, http://constitution.garant.ru/history/ussr-rsfsr/1978/zakony/183128/.

[102]Постановление Верховного Совета РСФСР«О мерах по обеспечению проведения референдума СССР и референдума РСФСР от 17.03.1991» (7.02.1991). *Vedomosti SND & VS RSFSR* № 7 (14.02.1991)—104. Retrieved from https://naukaprava.ru/catalog/1/113/75/40404?view=1. On the organisation of the referenda see also the decrees

RSFSR referendum was to be on introducing the post of president of the RSFSR. The results of the RSFSR referendum were published in *Izvestiia* on 26.03.1991, with majority of the electorate voting 'yes'.

The III Congress (28.03–5.04.1991) decided to hold the president election on 12.06.1991, summoning another Congress just before the election (art.3 of the Congress decree on redistribution of power between the supreme government organs of 5.04.1991).[103] On 24.05.1991 the IV Congress (21–25.05.1991) amended the *Constitution 1978* (RSFSR), introducing the post of president of the RSFSR.[104]

On 8.12.1991 the RSFSR President B. Yeltsin signed the *Beloveshsk (Bialowieza)* agreements with the Republics of Ukraine and Belorussia to leave the USSR and create a new union of the independent countries.[105] The agreement was ratified by the RSFSR Supreme Council on 12.12.1991, together with the denunciation of the Treaty of Formation of the USSR of 30.12.1922.[106] Notably (in reminiscence of the early Soviet

---

[постановления] of the Presidium of the RSFSR Supreme Council [Президиум Верховного Совета РСФСР] of 1.03.1991 & 4.03.1991 ((1991) *Vedomosti SND & VS RSFSR* № 10 (7.03.1991)—271, 275. Retrieved from https://naukaprava.ru/catalog/1/113/75/40407?view=1), as well as the decree of 13.03.1991 ((1991) *Vedomosti SND & VS RSFSR* № 11 (14.03.1991)—358. Retrieved from https://naukaprava.ru/catalog/1/113/75/40408?view=1) & the decree of 18.03.1991 ((1991) *Vedomosti SND & VS RSFSR* № 12 (21.03.1991)—429. Retrieved from https://naukaprava.ru/catalog/1/113/75/40409?view=1).

[103]Постановление Съезда народных депутатов РСФСР «О перераспределении полномочий между высшими государственными органами РСФСР для осуществления антикризисных мер и выполнения решений Съездов народных депутатов РСФСР» (5.04.1991). *Vedomosti SND & VS RSFSR* № 15 (11.04.1991)—495. Retrieved from https://naukaprava.ru/catalog/1/113/75/40412?view=1.

[104]Закон РСФСР «Об изменениях и дополнениях Конституции (Основного Закона) РСФСР» (24.05.1991). *Vedomosti SND & VS RSFSR* № 22 (30.05.1991)—775. Retrieved from https://naukaprava.ru/catalog/1/113/75/40419?view=1, http://constitution.garant.ru/history/ussr-rsfsr/1978/zakony/183124/.

[105]ГАРФ ф. 10026. оп. 4. д. 1303. л. 1-5. Retrieved from http://portal.rusarchives.ru/statehood/10-12-soglashenie-sng.shtml.

[106]Постановление Верховного Совета РСФСР от 12.12.1991 «О ратификации Соглашения о создании Содружества Независимых Государств»; Постановление Верховного Совета РСФСР «О денонсации Договора об образовании СССР» (12.12.1991). *Vedomosti SND & VS RSFSR* № 51 (19.12.1991)—1798 & 1799. Retrieved from https://naukaprava.ru/catalog/1/113/75/40448?view=1. The archive copies: ГАРФ ф. 10026. оп. 1. д. 576. л. 175. Retrieved from http://portal.rusarchives.ru/statehood/10-03-postanovlenie-ratifikaciya-sng.

decrees), according to the *VS* ratification decision, a USSR law continued to be in force only if it was not contradicting the RSFSR Constitution, the RSFSR laws and the [*Beloveshsk*] agreement. The RSFSR *VS* denunciation decision of 12.12.1991 implied that within the Soviet legal order there was an option of the unilateral return to pre-1922 Union formation. But this was not the case. The Treaty itself became incorporated into the *Constitution 1924* (USSR), i.e. subsumed by the Constitution. Henceforth, the USSR legal existence was defined by the USSR Constitution. Besides, since the constitutional amendment of 27.10.1989, the RSFSR highest seat of power (with the exclusive power to amend the constitution and decide on the state issues 'in competence of the RSFSR') was the Congress, not the Supreme Council (*VS*) (art. 104 of the *Constitution 1978* (RSFSR) [ed. 1.11.1991]). As a result, the RSFSR basic norm going back to the October Revolution became overturned on 12.12. 1991.

The violent events of 1993, preceding the approval of a new Constitution of the Russian Federation on the referendum on 12.12.1993, might just be the last agony of the Soviet regime that outlived itself. But these events had showed again the dangers and pitfall of a revolutionary development.

On 12.12.1993 a new basic norm came into being, tied up to the popular will. The *Constitution 1993* (RF), on the face of it, has the prerequisites for separation of the judiciary power. The judges of the Constitutional and Supreme Courts are appointed by the Soviet of Federation (on presentation by the President of the RF) (art. 128).[107] Only a head of the Constitutional Court and his/her deputies are appointed for unlimited term, all other federal courts heads and their

---

shtml; ГАРФ ф. 10026. оп. 1. д. 576. л. 176. Retrieved from http://portal.rusarchives.ru/statehood/10-02-denonsaciya-dogovor-sssr.shtml.

[107]Available at http://ivo.garant.ru/#/document/10103000/paragraph/727:0. Art. 9 of Federal Constitutional Law on the Constitutional Court of the RF [Федеральный конституционный закон № 1-ФКЗ «О Конституционном суде Российской Федерации»] (21.07.1994). Available at http://base.garant.ru/10101207/. Art. 6 of Federal Law on the Status of Judges in the RF [Федеральный закон № 3132-I «О статусе судей в Российской Федерации»] (26.06.1992). Available at http://base.garant.ru/10103670/. Federal Constitutional Law on the Supreme Court of the RF [Федеральный конституционный закон № 3-ФКЗ «О Верховном суде Российской Федерации»] (5.02.2014). Available at http://base.garant.ru/70583616/.

deputies are appointed for 6 years.[108] With respect to the status of a federal judge generally, the tenure is of unlimited duration.[109] One notable change in comparison with the Soviet period is no emphasis on popular election of judges (even of the first instance courts),[110] another is discarding of regular jurymen's participation in trials [at par with judges] as well as introduction of the justices of peace (dealing with minor issues and appointed for a fixed term no more than 5 years).[111]

Still, the post-Soviet courts do not have a de facto entrenched standing as an independent power. This had been the most notable failing of the post-Soviet period and, perhaps, another sign of the damage done to the integrity of legal order by revolutionary or radical transformation. The latter is necessarily perpetrated by the new executive, at expense of competing branches of powers. The Soviet period had demonstrated too well that there could not be such thing as 'revolutionary legality'. Notably, the pre-Soviet system of separation of power had been a product of 150 years of the evolutionary development.

Conspicuously, the *Constitution 1993* (RF) provided for the extensive executive and legislation presidential powers. One power (that even the tsar did not quite have since 1906)[112] is to legislate without

---

[108]Art. 6.1 of the Federal Law on the Status of Judges in the RF [Федеральный закон № 3132-I «О статусе судей в Российской Федерации»] (26.06.1992). Available at http://base.garant.ru/10103670/.

[109]Art. 11 of the Federal Law № 3132-I on the Status of Judges (26.06.1992).

[110]The popular elections of the people's court judges were codified in art. 109 of the *Constitution 1936* (USSR) and in art. 113 of the *Constitution 1937* (RSFSR)—for three years (similarly, art. 152 of the *Constitution 1977* (USSR) & art. 164 of the *Constitution 1978* (RSFSR), but for five year). The judges of respective Supreme Court were elected by the Supreme Council: art. 105–107 of the *Constitution 1936* (USSR) & art. 110–111 of the *Constitution 1937* (RSFSR), similarly, art. 152–153 of the *Constitution 1977* (USSR) & art. 164–165 of the *Constitution 1978* (RSFSR).

[111]Federal Constitutional Law on the Court System of the RF [Федеральный конституционный закон № 1-ФКЗ «О судебной системе Российской Федерации»] (31.12.1996). Available at http://base.garant.ru/10135300/. Federal Constitutional Law on the Courts of General Jurisdiction in the RF [Федеральный конституционный закон № 1-ФКЗ «О судах общей юрисдикции в Российской Федерации»] (7.02.2011). Available at http://base.garant.ru/12182692/.

[112]In accordance with the Main State Laws of 1906 (*ПСЗ* III 27807), the tsar had the legislative power in conjunction (in accord [в единеніи]) with the State Council [Государственный Совѣтъ] and the State *Duma* [Государственная Дума] (art.7), as well as the power, in accord with laws, to issue decrees [указы] to commence operations [для устройства и приведенія в дѣйствіе] of various parts of the state government, as well as directives [повеленія], necessary for implementation of laws (art. 11). The legislative power under art. 11 might be more like a subordinate legislative power.

the approval of the *Duma* [the lower house of the parliament]. Art. 90 of the *Constitution 1993* grants presidential powers to issue decrees (указы) and by-laws (постановления) that do not contradict to federal laws [enacted by the parliament] and the Constitution.

Aside from the post-Soviet Constitution, there are also in place new *Civil Code* (Гражданский Кодекс),[113] *Criminal Code*,[114] as well as several other codes.[115] Hence, not only there had been change in the basic norm, but also in the secondary rules of recognition, change and adjudication.

To conclude, in case of the twentieth-century Russia there had been at least three revolutionary breaks with the preceding order: in February 1917, in October 1917 and in December 1991. While the most recent break had not resulted in the loss of human lives comparable to one following the Bolshevik Revolution (that ended in the civil war, as well as starvation and epidemics), nonetheless in legal terms the change was revolutionary (in terms of the basic norm as well as of the secondary rules), as it was in the people's minds. At the start of Perestroika there was nothing like the Bolshevik agenda of abolition of the ancient regime in toto. Moreover, in contrast to the February Revolution, there was no even recognition of revolutionary rapture with the preceding order. Notably, the Soviet legal order had been reformed in relation to the one-party system and the privileged legal status of state ownership prior to the revolutionary break with the Soviet legal order on 12.12.1991. Hence, there could well be further changes in the secondary rules without any revolutionary dissolution of the preceding legal order. Non-revolutionary way of dismantling the Soviet system would be the best closure to the whole Russian revolutionary century. Perhaps, the rule-breaking way of the USSR dismantling made it also harder for many to reconcile with its dissolution. There might well be unforeseen deferred effects of the revolutionary dissolution of legal order.

In legal theory terms, this study shows not only that Kelsen's basic norm has the descriptive capacity to pinpoint the break down in the

---

[113]Гражданский Кодекс Российской Федерации № 51-ФЗ (21.10.1994). Available at http://base.garant.ru/10164072/.

[114]Уголовный кодекс Российской Федерации № 63-ФЗ (13.06.1996). Available at http://base.garant.ru/10108000/.

[115]Available at http://www.garant.ru/doc/main/.

legal order, but also that a rupture of the basic norm has far-reaching consequences for the integrity of legal order as such. This observation may affect Natural Law—Legal Positivism debates (such as, between Gustav Radbruch and Hans Kelsen and between H. L. A. Hart and Lon Fuller on the Nazi law). A violation of Kelsen's basic norm might itself signify the collapse of 'formal legality' ('thin' Rule of Law). The fall of the basic norm is just a legal sign of the old regime's downfall. The revolutionary power struggle itself might be conducive to the emergence of extra-legal bodies to fight the enemies and the corresponding weakening of [conventional] judicial power. Accordingly, there would be breakdown in Hart's secondary rules of adjudication and recognition, as well as Fuller's desiderata of generality, publicity and prospectivity of the law. On more general level, Kelsen's basic norm and Hart's secondary rules complement each other. The former denotes the rupture of legal order, the latter—the scale of legal transformation.

Appendix: The Great Terror—Revival of Extra-Judicial 'Justice'

The Great Terror of 1937

On the face of it, the *Constitution 1936* (USSR) delineated the courts as a separate branch of the state power. At level of local courts, the constitution even envisioned the popular election of judges (but this did not happen in practice till after the war).

Insofar as the actual sentences were pre-determined by the party authorities prior to any trial, the difference in choice of trial might look as being of merely academic significance. However, the choice of trial was a very practical question: it is not by chance that the main instrument of the terror became the [novel species of] extra-judicial bodies.[116] The ordinary courts were rarely used.

---

[116]Multiple documents of the Great Terror period are available at http://www.alexanderyakovlev.org. See the revealing letter by Beria to Stalin of 30.11.1937, asking on behalf of the *CK* of Georgian KP(b) for more trials by the *NKVD* troika in Georgia, with special *collegia* being

The only institution within the court system that became actively engaged in the Great Terror was the martial collegium (division) [военная коллегия] of the Supreme Court [Верховный суд].[117] Its sphere of activity was infamous 'open' trials of 1936–1937, which rubber-stamped the sentences approved the politburo of the central committee of the all-Russia Communist Party (*VKP(b)*).[118] Still, while the martial collegium of the Supreme Court could sentence to death, there was an expediency of open trials.

The USSR *CIK* decree of 10.07.1934 established the All-Soviet People's Commissariat of Internal Affairs (Общесоюзный Народный Комиссариат Внутренних Дел [*NKVD*]).[119] The former OGPU[120] became the *NKVD* department, now renamed as the main department of the state security [Главное управление государственной безопасности (*GUGB*)] (art. 3(a)).

The USSR *CIK* decree of 10.07.1934 provided that the state crimes of treason, espionage, terror, etc. (art. 6, 8 and 9 of the *Criminal Code* (RSFSR)), investigated by *NKVD*, were to be in jurisdiction of *VK* and the district martial tribunals [attached to the army units].[121]

---

his second preferred method of trial (since the martial *collegium* of the USSR Supreme Court was overstretched). According to the letter, of 12 000 arrested persons (at that point in time in Georgia) 7374 persons were convicted: of those about 1%—by local people*'*s courts, about 1.3%—by the martial tribunals, 6.3%—by the special *collegium* of the Supreme Court of Georgian republic, about 8%—by *OS* [within *NKVD*], 16.3%—by the martial *collegium* of the USSR Supreme Court, 71%—by the *NKVD* troikas. Available at http://www.alexanderyakovlev.org/fond/issues-doc/61223.

[117]There were also special *collegia* of Supreme Court of the USSR republics. The system of the *collegia* was linked to the system of the martial tribunals that had the common pedigree with the Revolutionary Tribunals of the revolutionary period.

[118]For example, see the politburo's directions regarding the trial of Piatakov, Radek, Sokol'nikov, Serebriakov and others of 22.01.1937. http://www.alexanderyakovlev.org/fond/issues-doc/60980.

[119]Постановление ЦИК СССР «Об образовании общесоюзного Народного комиссариата внутренних дел» (10.07.1934). Available at https://lawru.info/dok/1934/07/10/n1196544.htm.

[120]See above n. 68.

[121]Постановление ЦИК СССР «О рассмотрении дел о преступлениях, расследуемых Народным комиссариатом внутренних дел Союза ССР и его местными органами» (10.07.1934). Available at https://lawru.info/dok/1934/07/10/n1196543.htm. Постановление ЦИК СССР «О дополнении Положения о преступлениях государственных (контрреволюционных и особо для Союза ССР опасных преступлениях против порядка управления) статьями об измене родине» (08.06.1934). (1934) *Собрание законов и распоряжений Рабоче-Крестьянского Правительства СССР* (*SZ USSR*) № 33-255. Ст. 2 Постановления ВЦИК «О порядке изменения кодексов» (7.07.1923). (1923) *SU RSFSR* № 54—530.

The RSFSR *CIK* decree of 20.07.1934, enlarging art. 58 of the *Criminal Code* (RSFSR) by a new crime of treason.[122]

The USSR *CIK & SNK* decree of 05.11.1934 established an special body [особое совещание (*OS*)], attached to *NKVD*, with the sentencing powers to exile or sent to 'reforming' labour camps for five years (art. 1), in presence of the USSR procurator or his deputy (art. 3).[123] *OS* was, perhaps, the only repression organ having the pre-revolutionary pedigree.[124]

Aftermath of the assassination of Sergey Kirov (the secretary of VKP(b) and the politburo member), the USSR *CIK & SNK* decree of 1.12.1934 ((1934) *SZ* 64—459) introduced the speedy proceeding regarding the 'terrorist' acts (art. 58.8 & 58.11 of the *Criminal Code* (RSFSR) [allowing for capital punishment]).[125] The decree that became

---

[122] Постановление ВЦИК, СНК РСФСР от 20.07.1934 «О дополнении Уголовного кодекса РСФСР ст. ст. 58-1а, 58-1б, 58-1в, 58-1г». Available at https://lawru.info/dok/1934/07/20/n1196527.htm. The decree of 20.07.1934 was in conjunction with the *CIK* Decree of 8.06.1934 that enlarged the statute on State Crime, with the new crime of treason (currying a death penalty or 10 years imprisonment) as well as criminalizing non-informing by the family members (with penalty up to 10 years loss of freedom). *Izvestiia CIK* № 433 (9.06.1934); (1934) *SZ USSR* № 33—255. Retrieved from http://istmat.info/node/41012.

[123] Постановление ЦИК СССР, СНК СССР № 22 «Об Особом Совещании при НКВД СССР» (05.11.1934). Available at https://lawru.info/dok/1934/11/05/n1196387.htm. On 8.04.1937 the politburo of *CK* VKP(B) decided to amend the 1934 the *OS* directive [Положение об Особом Совещании] to allow *NKVD* to incarcerate persons in prison for 5 to 8 years for espionage, terrorism etc. РГАСПИ. ф. 17. оп. 3. д. 986. л. 4, 24. Available at http://www.alexanderyakovlev.org/fond/issues-doc/61031.

[124] *OS* was established by the tsarist government in 1880s to exile of the suspected revolutionary without trial for five years, following the acquittals of the revolutionary terrorists by the juries in the ordinary court trials. The VCIK Presidium directive of 10.08.1922 established a special commission [особая комиссия] with power to exile up to 3 years. *Izvestiia VCIK* № 185 (18.08.1922); (1922) *SU* № 51—646, pp. 813–814. Available at http://www.hrono.ru/dokum/192_dok/19220810vcik.html, http://www.ihst.ru/projects/sohist/document/deport/dekret.htm.

[125] Постановление ЦИК СССР «О внесении изменений в действующие уголовно-процессуальные кодексы союзных республик» (1.12.1934): "Центральный Исполнительный Комитет Союза ССР постановляет: Внести следующие изменения в действующие уголовно-процессуальные кодексы союзных республик по расследованию и рассмотрению дел о террористических организациях и террористических актах против работников советской власти:

part of Chapter XXXIII of the *Criminal Procedure Code* (RSFSR) did not expressly provide for the court adjudication.
The Great Terror stated in earnest in the middle of 1937. The infamous secret order of *NKVD* of 30.07.1937,[126] approved the creation of 64 local troikas, attached to *NKVD*, and consisting of local officials. The order was aimed at 'anti-Soviet elements', that were divided into two categories: the first encompassed 'the most hostile elements' that were to be arrested and, after investigation by the troikas, to be executed by the firing squads; the second included 'hostile, but less active elements', to be sentenced by the troikas to [at least] 8–10 years of incarceration in camps. There were the set local quotas for the both categories. The troikas, thus, had powers to condemn to capital

---

1. Следствие по этим делам заканчивать в срок не более десяти дней.
2. Обвинительное заключение вручать обвиняемым за одни сутки до рассмотрения дела в суде.
3. Дела слушать без участия сторон.
4. Кассационного обжалования приговоров, как и подачи ходатайств о помиловании, не допускать.
5. Приговор к высшей мере наказания приводить в исполнение немедленно по вынесении приговора."
Available at https://lawru.info/dok/1934/12/01/n1196371.htm, http://doc.histrf.ru/20/postanovlenie-prezidiuma-tsik-sssr-ot-1-dekabrya-1934-goda/. This *CIK* USSR decree was implemented at the RSFSR level by the VCIK RSFSR decree: Постановление ВЦИК, СНК РСФСР «О дополнении Уголовно-процессуального кодекса РСФСР главой XXXIII» (10.12.1934). Available at https://lawru.info/dok/1934/12/10/n1196344.htm. The *CIK* Decree of 8.06.1937 enlarged the statute on State Crime, with the new crime of treason (currying a death penalty or 10 years of incarceration) as well as criminalizing non-informing by the family members (with penalty up to 10 years of incarceration). *Izvestiia CIK* № 433 (9.06.1934); (1934) *Собрание законов и распоряжений Рабоче-Крестьянского Правительства* СССР (*SZ USSR*) № 33—255. Retrieved from http://istmat.info/node/41012. The USSR *CIK* decree [Постановление ЦИК СССР «О внесении изменений в действующие уголовно-процессуальные кодексы союзных республик»] of 14.09.1937 directed to amend s 58 (7) & (9) of the *Criminal Code* (RSFSR) to abolish cassation rights for crime of sabotage [диверсия &.вредительство] (1937) *SZ USSR* № 61 (27.09.1937)—266. Retrieved from https://naukaprava.ru/catalog/1/129/187/208/61050?view=1, http://www.memorial.krsk.ru/DOKUMENT/USSR/370914.htm. The *Criminal Code 1922* (RSFSR) was substantially amended by the decree of *VCIK* of 20.11.1926. (1926) *SU RSFSR* [*Собрание узаконений РСФСР*] № 80–600.

[126]Оперативный приказ народного комиссара внутренних дел СССР Н. И. Ежова № 00447 «Об операции по репрессированию бывших кулаков, уголовников и других антисоветских элементов» (30.07.1937). Retrieved from http://istmat.info/node/32818. See also https://www.alexanderyakovlev.org/almanah/inside/almanah-intro/1005111. The politburo approved the order on 31.07.1937. Available at http://www.alexanderyakovlev.org/almanah/inside/almanah-doc/1006179.

16 Legal Continuity and Change: Two Russian Revolutions ... 397

punishment (by a firing squad), exile and incarceration in prison and labour camps. The troikas became the Terror key vehicle. They were like the organs of 'direct reprisal'—*ChKs*—during the revolutionary terror, but with larger 'industrial' scale of operation, and with difference that the choice of victims of the Terror was now in the hand of the party authorities.

The Great Terror was rolled back in by the end of 1938. Trials by the troikas, martial tribunals and *VK* were suspended by the order of 15.11.1938, signed by the USSR *SNK* head Molotov and the VKP(b) *CK* secretary Stalin.[127] *OS* became the main extra-judicial form of trial.[128] The war gave a new spell of life to *OS*.[129] The USSR *SNK* Decree of 2.06.1943 created a separate Commissariat of State Security,[130] with

---

[127] Директива СНК СССР и ЦК ВКП(б) «О приостановке рассмотрения дел, направленных на рассмотрение троек, военных трибуналов и ВК Верховного Суда СССР в порядке особых приказов» (15.11.1938). АП РФ. ф. 3. оп. 58. д. 212. л. 204-205; РГАСПИ. ф. 17. оп. 162. д. 24. л. 62. Retrieved from http://istmat.info/node/36067, http://www.1000dokumente.de/?c=dokument_ru&dokument=0010_trj&object=translation&l=ru.

[128] The *SNK* and VKP(B) *CK* [secret] directive (signed by Molotov and Stalin) № П 4387 of 17.11.1938 regulated arrest, investigation and procurator's supervision. РГАСПИ ф. 17. оп. 3, д. 1003, л. 85; ф. 17, оп. 3, д. 1003, л. 85об; ф. 17, оп. 3, д. 1003, л. 86.; РГАСПИ ф. 17. оп. 163. д. 1204. л. 108-117. Retrieved from http://istmat.info/node/36068. The *SNK* and VKP(B) *CK* secret directive (also signed by Molotov & Stalin) (№ 27) of 1.12.1938 amended the 1935 arrest procedure. РГАСПИ ф. 17. оп. 3. д. 1004. л. 6, 51. Retrieved from http://istmat.info/node/33222. The *SNK* & VKP(b) *CK* directives of 17.06.1935 on the arrest procedure. ГАРФ ф. 5446. оп. 1. д. 481. л. 478-479. Retrieved from http://istmat.info/node/40431. The directive of 17.11.1938 was followed by the *NKVD* directive of 26.11.1938 № 00762 that annulled some previous orders by *NKVD*. The latter directive instructed to proceed via procurator by ordinary court trial, and by *OS*, when the evidence could not be presented in court (art. 7). АП РФ ф. 3. оп. 58. д. 6. л. 92—96. Available at http://www.alexanderyakovlev.org/fond/issues-doc/61414.

[129] The Martial Collegium of the USSR Supreme Court also partook in a new wave of repression by sentencing to death 170 men on 8.08.1941, based upon the secret order № 634-сс of the Council of the State and Defence [Государственный Комитет Обороны] of 6.09.1941 signed by Stalin. АП РФ ф. 3. оп. 24. д. 378. л. 191. Available at https://www.alexanderyakovlev.org/fond/issues-doc/58836.

[130] Постановление СНК СССР № 621-191сс«Положением о Народном комиссариате государственной безопасности СССР» (2.06.1943). Available at http://shieldandsword.mozohin.ru/nkgb4353/index.htm. This secret statute (omitted from the official Digest of the USSR Laws) was based upon the directive by *CK* VKP(b) [Постановление ЦК ВКП(б) «Об организации народного комиссариата государственной безопасности»] of 14.04.1943 (Yakovlev, pp. 622–623). Available at https://www.alexanderyakovlev.org/fond/issues-doc/58872. The draft of the re-organisation of *NKVD* was prepared yet in January 1941 [«Проект постановления ЦК ВКП(б) о реорганизации наркомата внутренних дел СССР»]. РГАСПИ ф. 17. оп. 163. д. 1295. л. 103—106, 109. Available at http://hrono.ru/

OS attached to it. The State Committee of Defence secret decree of 17.11.1941 granted to *OS* powers of sentencing to death under ss 58 & 59 of the Criminal Code, without appeal or cassation.[131] By the *VCIK* Presidium Decree of 26.11.1948 *OS* could sentence up to twenty years of hard labour.[132]

---

dokum/194_dok/19410101ck.php. However, on 21.07.1941, the politburo decided to amalgamate the two commissariats back into one (*NKVD*) [Постановление политбюро ЦК ВКП(б) «Об утверждении указа Президиума Верховного Совета СССР об объединении НКВД в единый наркомат»]. Available at https://www.alexanderyakovlev.org/fond/issues-doc/58804. The Decree of the USSR Supreme Council Presidium of 13.03.1954 (№ 137/49) established the Committee of State Security (*KGB*), attached to the Council of Ministers. *SZ USSR* 1938–1956, стр. 93. Available at http://www.rusarchives.ru/evants/exhibitions/state_protection/334.shtml, http://istmat.info/node/38998, https://ru.wikisource.org/wiki/%D0%A1%D1%82%D1%80%D0%B0%D0%BD%D0%B8%D1%86%D0%B0:Sbornik_zakonov_1938-1956.djvu/128. KGB was abolished by art. 2 of the USSR Law on Reorganisation of the State Security Organs of 3.12.1991: Закон СССР № 124-Н «О реорганизации органов государственной безопасности» (03.12.1991). Available at https://base.garant.ru/1583807/. The Council of the Republics was a creature of the USSR Law of 5.06.1991 (№ 2392-I). ГАРФ. ф. Р-9654. оп. 1. д. 184. л. 45-47. Available at http://www.rusarchives.ru/projects/statehood/09-42-postanovlenie-organy-gosvlasti.shtml. The Council of the Republics was not mentioned in art. 111 the *Constitution 1977* (USSR) in force at that time (in the ed. of 26.12.1990 [the USSR law № 1861-1]).

[131] Государственный Комитет Обороны. Постановление № ГКО-903сс (17.11.1941). РГАСПИ ф. 644, оп. 1, д. 14, л.101. Available at http://www.soldat.ru/doc/gko/text/0903.html.

[132] Указ Президиума Верховного Совета СССР № 123/12 «Об уголовной ответственности за побеги из мест обязательного постоянного поселения лиц, выселенных в отдаленные районы Советского Союза в период Отечественной войны» от 26.11.1948. ГАРФ. ф. Р-7523. оп. 36. д. 450. л. 87. This unpublished decree aimed at members of the [small] nations exiled from their original place of settlement during the war [1941–1945] who escaped from the place of exile. Available at http://www.alexanderyakovlev.org/fond/issues-doc/1023242. This decree was abolished on the Supreme Council Presidium decree of 13.07.1954: http://www.memorial.krsk.ru/DOKUMENT/USSR/540713.htm. Theses escapees were sent to exile by the *VS* Presidium decree of 21.02.1946 on expiration of their sentences. There was also the related secret direction of the USSR Council of the Ministers № 416-159сс of 21.02.1948. These were elaborated by the joint order of the Ministers of Internal Affairs, State Security & General Prosecutor of 16.03.1948. ГАРФ ф. 9401. оп. 12. д. 318. лл. 2–5. Available at https://www.alexanderyakovlev.org/fond/issues-doc/1009135. The OS powers were extended (on 17.11.1951) to the escapees from the place of exile—originally convicted for serious state crimes. Available at http://www.memorial.krsk.ru/DOKUMENT/USSR/481126.htm. The Decree of 21.02.1948 was annulled on 10.03.1956. Available at http://www.memorial.krsk.ru/DOKUMENT/USSR/540713.htm. All the decrees/decisions sanctioning the repressions against these ethnic groups were finally annulled by the USSR Cabinet of the Ministers on 6.06.1991 [Постановление Кабинета Министров СССР № 336 «Об отмене постановлений бывшего Государственного Комитета Обороны СССР и решений Правительства СССР в отношении советских народов,

The USSR Supreme Council Presidium Decree of 4.02.1947 abolished the death penalty.[133] However, the USSR Supreme Council Presidium Decree of 12.01.1950 reinstated the death penalty with respect to treason, espionage, sabotage.[134] The both decrees were annulled by the USSR Supreme Council Presidium decree of 13.04.1959 due to coming into force of the Fundamentals of Criminal law.[135]

Post-Stalin Soviet Union

The post-Stalin liberalisation started with the amnesty of 27.03.1953.[136] The USSR Supreme Council Presidium of 1.09.1953 finally abolished *OS*.[137]

подвергшихся репрессиям и насильственному переселению»]. Available at http://www.alexanderyakovlev.org/fond/issues-doc/68261. This decree was based upon the USSR VS decree [Постановление ВС СССР] № 2013-1 on 7.03.1991. Available at https://www.alexanderyakovlev.org/fond/issues-doc/68240.

[133]Указ Президиума Верховного Совета СССР об отмене смертной казни от 26.05.1947. (1947) *Ведомости Верховного Совета СССР* № 17 (31.05.1947). Available at https://ru.wikisource.org/wiki/%D0%A1%D1%82%D1%80%D0%B0%D0%BD%D0%B8%D1%86%D0%B0:Sbornik_zakonov_1938-1956.djvu/430, http://www.libussr.ru/doc_ussr/ussr_4642.htm

[134]Указ Президиума Верховного Совета СССР«О применении смертной казни к изменникам родины, шпионам, подрывникам-диверсантам» (12.01.1950). (1950) *Ведомости Верховного Совета СССР* № 3 (20.01.1950). Available at http://www.libussr.ru/doc_ussr/ussr_4771.htm.

[135]Указ Президиума Верховного Совета СССР«О признании утратившими силу законодательных актов в связи с введением в действие Основ уголовного законодательства, Законов об уголовной ответственности за государственные и за воинские преступления, Основ законодательства о судоустройстве, Положения о военных трибуналах и Основ уголовного судопроизводства» (13.04.1959). Available at http://base.garant.ru/70785462/.

[136]Постановление Президиума ЦК КПСС«Об амнистии» (27.03.1953). РГАНИ ф. 3. оп. 8. д. 20. л. 2. Retrieved from http://istmat.info/node/57746. Указ Президиума Верховного Совета СССР«Об амнистии» (28.03.1953). Available at http://base.garant.ru/70805432/.

[137]Указ Президиума ВС СССР«Об упразднении Особого совещания при Министре внутренних дел СССР»(01.09.1953). Available at http://www.consultant.ru/cons/cgi/online.cgi?req=doc&base=ESU&n=9149#0674650645954343. Постановление Президиума ЦК КПСС«Об упразднении Особого Совещания при МВД СССР» (1.09.1953). АП РФ. ф. 3. оп. 58. д. 11. л. 60–61. Retrieved from http://istmat.info/node/57789. See also Ignat'ev's secret letter to Stalin on *OS* of 26.12.1951 with proposal to limit the *OS* jurisdiction to cases with the evidences that could not be disclosed in courts (№ 1760/и). АП РФ. ф. 3. оп. 58. д. 10. л. 56—62. Available at http://shieldandsword.mozohin.ru/documents/letter281251.htm. In a secret note of 15.06.1953 Beria proposed retaining *OS* but curtailing its powers. ГАРФ ф. 9401, оп. 2, д. 416, лл. 123-125. Retrieved from http://istmat.info/node/26485. See also (Medovnik, 2008).

The key long-term effect on the legal system of the post-Stalin thaw was a disavowal of non-judicial forms of trials (though new ways of punishing the dissenters emerged, such as involuntary incarceration in mental asylums). The dissident movement, since the famous 'Glasnost' demonstration of 5.12.1965 at the Pushkin squire in Moscow, organised by Esenin-Vol'skii (who held the poster 'Respect your own Constitution'), might be credited with the Soviet authorities' grudging acceptance of the constitutional requirement of open court trials: art. 11 of the *Constitution 1936* (USSR) as well as art. 115 of the *Constitution 1937* (RSFSR) declared that courts were to have open trials (similarly, art. 157 of the *Constitution 1977* (USSR) & art. 169 of the *Constitution 1978* (RSFSR)).[138]

Introduction of an alternative sentence (of maximum 15 years) to the death penalty was the key liberalisation of criminal law.[139]

Summing up, the Great Terror could only be perpetrated by means of the extra-judicial bodies (attached to the executive branch), such as the *NKVD* troikas. The existence of such bodies showed the breakdown of the secondary rules of adjudication. The Terror case study underlines the descriptive capacity of Hart's secondary rule of adjudication, particularly, to account for the extra-judicial repression.

---

[138]Art. 112 of the *Constitution 1936* (USSR) declared that judges were independent and governed by the law only as did art. 116 of the *Constitution 1937* (RSFSR) (similarly: art. 157 of the *Constitution 1977* (USSR) & art. 169 of the *Constitution 1978* (RSFSR)).

[139]Уголовный кодекс РСФСР от 27.10.1960. Available at http://base.garant.ru/10107062/. In the *Criminal Code 1960* (RSFSR), there remained several state crimes with the maximum penalty of death: treason (art. 64), espionage (art. 65) and terrorism (in case of death/s: art. 66–67), [aggravated] sabotage (art. 68), beside of multiple other (non-state) crimes that may result in the death penalty.

References

Antonova, L. I. (1969). The great October revolution & creation of people's courts, 1917–1918 [Великая Октябрьская революция и создание народных судов, 1917–1918 гг.]. *Pravovedenie [Правоведение]* (3). Retrieved from http://law.edu.ru/doc/document.asp?docID=1133185.

Collection of Decrees and Ordinances of the Provisional Government (in Russian) [Сборникъ Указовъ и Постановленiй Временнаго Правительства] (Vols. 1 (27.02.1917–5.05.1917)). (1917). Petrograd [Петроградъ]: Gosudarsvennaia Tipografia [Государственная Типографiя]. (SUVP 1). Retrieved from http://elib.shpl.ru/ru/nodes/10721-vyp-1-27-fevralya-5-maya-1917-1917#mode/inspect/page/5/zoom/4.

Collection of Decrees and Ordinances of the Provisional Government (in Russian) [Сборникъ Указовъ и Постановленiй Временнаго Правительства] (Vols. 2 (5.05.17–24.08.17)). (1918). Petrograd [Петроградъ]: Gosudarstvennaia Tipografia [Государственная типографiя]. (SUVP 2). Retrieved from http://elib.shpl.ru/ru/nodes/10722-vyp-2-5-maya-24-iyulya-1917-g-ch-1-otd-i-viii-1918#mode/inspect/page/5/zoom/4.

Collection of Laws and Directives of the Government (in Russian) [Собранiе Узаконенiй и распоряженiй правительства (1917)]. (1917). Pravitelstvuiushchii Senat [Правительствующiй Сенатъ].

Collection of Laws and Directives of the Government: 1917–1918 (in Russian) [Собрание узаконений и распоряжений правительства за 1917–1918 гг.]. (1942). Moscow [Москва]: Upravlenie delami Covnarkoma SSSR [Управление делами Совнаркома СССР]. (SU 1917–1918). Retrieved from http://xn--80abnlydpf.xn--80akegfdvbg0c.xn--p1ai/19171918-1942.pdf.

Collection of Laws and Directives of the Government: 1919 (in Russian) [Собрание узаконений и распоряжений правительства за 1919 г.]. (1943). Moscow [Москва]: Upravlenie delami Sovnarkoma SSSR [Управление делами Совнаркома]. (SU 1922). Retrieved from http://xn--80abnlydpf.xn--80akegfdvbg0c.xn--p1ai/1919-1943.pdf.

Collection of Laws and Directives of the Government: 1920 (in Russian) [Собрание узаконений и распоряжений правительства за 1920г.]. (1943). Moscow [Москва]: Upravlenie delami Sovnarkoma SSSR [Управление делами Совнаркома СССР]. (SU 1920). Retrieved from http://xn--80abnlydpf.xn--80akegfdvbg0c.xn--p1ai/1920-1943.pdf.

Collection of Laws and Directives of the Government: 1921 (in Russian) [Собрание узаконений и распоряжений правительства за 1921 г.]. (1944).

Moscow [Москва]: Upravlenie delami Sovnarkoma [Управление делами Совнаркома]. (SU 1921). Retrieved from http://xn--80abnlydpf.xn--80akegfdvbg0c.xn--p1ai/1921-1944.pdf.

Collection of Laws and Directives of the Government: 1922 (in Russian) [Собрание узаконений и распоряжений правительства за 1922]. (1950). Mosccw [Москва]: Upravlenie delami Sovnarkoma [Управление делами Совнаркома СССР]. (SU 1922). Retrieved from http://xn--c80abnlydpf.xn--80akegfdvbg0c.xn--p1ai/1922-1950.pdf.

Decrees of the Soviet Authorities (in Russian) [Декреты Советской Власти] (Vols. 1: 25.10.1917–16.03.1918). (1957). Moscow [Москва]: Politizdat [Политиздатъ]. (Soviet Decrees). Retrieved from http://www.hist.msu.ru/ER/Etext/DEKRET/.

Gaidukov, D. A. (Ed.). (1957). *History of Soviet constitution: Collection of documents (in Russian) [История Советской Конституции. Сборник документов: 1917–1957].* Moscow [Москва]: Izdatel'stvo AN SSSR [Издательство АН СССР]. (USSR Doc.). Retrieved from https://www.prlib.ru/item/416968.

Gutman, M. I. (2007). Legal bases of operation of the provisional government militia, workers' militia & Red Guards in Petrograd [Правовые основы организации и деятельности милиции временного правительства, рабочей милиции и красной гвардии Петрограда (март-октябрь 1917 г.)]. *Vestnik Sankt-Peterburgskogo universiteta MVD Rossii [Вестник Санкт-Петербургского университета МВД России]*, *36*(4), 32–44. Retrieved from https://cyberleninka.ru/article/n/pravovye-osnovy-organizatsii-i-deyatelnosti-militsii-vremennogo-pravitelstva-rabochey-militsii-i-krasnoy-gvardii-petrograda-mart.

Hart, H. L. (1994). *The concept of law* (2nd ed.). Oxford: Claredon Press.

III All-Russia Congress of Soviets of Workers' & Soldiers' Deputies (in Russian) [Третiй Всероссiйскiй Съѣздъ Совѣтовъ Рабочихъ и Солдатскихъ Депутатовъ]. (1918). Petersburg [Петербургъ]: Priboi [Прибой]. (3 VSSRSD). Retrieved from http://elib.shpl.ru/ru/nodes/10866-tretiy-vserossiyskiy-sezd-sovetov-rabochih-soldatskih-i-krestyanskih-deputatov-peterburg-1918#mode/inspect/page/5/zoom/4.

Kelsen, H. (1967). *Pure theory of law* (2nd ed., M. Knight, Trans.). Berkeley: University of California Press.

Kiselev, A. (Ed.). (1996). *Readings in Russian history (1914–1945) (in Russian) [Хрестоматия по Отечественной истории (1914–1945)].* Moscow [Москва]: Gumanitarnyi izdatel'skii centr VLADOS [Гуманитарный издательский центр ВЛАДОС]. Retrieved from http://illuminats.ru/component/content/article/29-new/299-2009-12-15-22-12-53?directory=29.

Korkunov, N. M. (1909). *Russian state law (in Russian) [Русское государственное право]* (Vol. 2). St. Petersburg [С.-Петербург]: Tipografia M. M. Stasiulevicha [Типография М. М. Стасюлевича]. Retrieved from http://istmat.info/node/25799.

Lenin, V. I. (1974a). *Complete collection of works (volume 35) (in Russian) [Полное собрание сочинений (том 35)]* (5 ed., Vol. 35). Moscow [Москва]: Politizdat [Политиздат]. (Lenin v. 35). Retrieved from http://uaio.ru/vil/35.htm.

Lenin, V. I. (1974b). *Complete collection of works (volume 36) (in Russian) [Полное собрание соч.инений (том 36)]* (4 ed., Vol. 36). Moscow [Москва]: Politizdat [Политиздат]. (Lenin v. 36). Retrieved from http://uaio.ru/vil/36.htm.

Leont'ev, Y. V. (Ed.). (2000). *Party of left social revolutionaries: Documents and materials (July 1917–May 1918) (in Russian) [Партия левых социалистов-революционеров. Документы и материалы. Июль 1917-май 1918 гг.]* (Vol. 1). Moscow [Москва]: Rossiiskaia polirticheskaia enciklopediia [Российская политическая энциклопедия].

Medovnik, A. A. (2008). Osoboe Soveshchanie in the USSR MGB of the postwar time: Unsuccessful attempts of its control (in Russian) [Особое Совещание при МГБ СССР в послевоенное время (1945–1953 гг.): полномочия и неудавшиеся попытки их ограничения]. *Obshchestvo i pravo [Общество и право]* (3). Retrieved from http://w.pc-forums.ru/m2635.html.

Minutes of Meetings of All-Russia Central Executive Committee of 4th Convocation (in Russian) [Протоколы заседаний Всероссийского Центрального Исполнительного Комитета 4-го созыва (Стенографический отчет)]. (1920). Moscow [Москва]. (VCIK Minutes, 1920).

Nabokov, V. D. (1921). Provisional government [Временное Правительство] (I. V. Gessen, Ed.) *Archiv russkoi revoliutsii [Архивъ русской революціи]*, 1, 9–96. Retrieved from http://istmat.info/files/uploads/33587/arhiv_russkoy_revolyucii_t._1_1921.pdf.

Nekrasov, V. F. (2002). *Ministry of interior affairs of Russia: Encyclopedia [МВД России. Энциклопедия]*. OLMA Media Group [ОЛМА Медиа Групп].

Popova, O. G. (1998). Left social revolutionaries (S-Rs) & formation of Soviet statehood (in Russian) [Левые эсеры и формирование советской государственности]. *Problemy istorii Rossii [Проблемы истории России]* (2: Опыт государственного строительства XV-XX вв), 124–146. Retrieved from http://elar.urfu.ru/bitstream/10995/2743/1/pris.

Shchegolev, P. E. (Ed.). (1926). *The fall of the Tsarist regime (in Russian) [Падение царского режима]* (Vol. 6). Leningrad [Ленинград]: Gocudarsvennoe izdatel'stvo [Государственное издательство]. Retrieved from http://elib.shpl.ru/ru/nodes/5017-т-6-1926.

Stuchka, P. I. (1922). Five years of revolution in law (in Russian) [Пять лет революции права]. *Ezhenedel'nik sovetskoi iustitsii [Еженедельник советской юстиции]* (44/45), 1–3. Retrieved from https://www.prlib.ru/item/331804.

V.I. Lenin & VCh. Collection of Documents (in Russian) [В. И. Ленин и ВЧК. Сборник документов (1917–1922)]. (1987). Moscow [Москва]: Politizdat [Политиздат]. (Lenin&VChK). Retrieved from https://royallib.com/read/lenin_vladimir/v_i_lenin_i_vchk_sbornik_dokumentov_19171922.html#0.

Yakovlev, A. N. (Ed.). (2003). *Liubianka. Organs of VChK-OGPU-NKVD-MGB-MVD-KGB: 1917–1991. Referencebook (in Russian) [ЛУБЯНКА: Органы ВЧК-ОГПУ-НКВД-НКГБ-МГБ-МВД-КГБ. 1917–1991. Справочник]*. Moscow [Москва]: MFD [МФД]. (VChK-OGPU-NKVD). Retrieved from http://history.org.ua/LiberUA/5-85646-109-6/5-85646-109-6.pdf.

17

'Fleeing Communism': Yugoslav and Vietnamese Post-war Migration to Australia and Changes to Immigration Policy

Nina Markovic Khaze and Adam Khaze

Introduction

'We will decide who comes to this country and circumstances under which they will come…' became a controversial federal election slogan in 2001 that has marked Australian migration politics ever since (Howard, 2001, pp. 8–9). Following the 'Tampa crisis', the Australian Government implemented the so-called 'Pacific solution' policy that has featured negatively in the international press and been heavily criticised by human rights advocates (ACSJC, 2002; Hamilton, 2017; Oxfam Australia, 2007). This policy was introduced by the Coalition Government under Prime Minister John Howard in September 2001 in response to the incident with the Norwegian freighter *MV Tampa*, which carried 438 rescued-at-sea asylum seekers from Afghanistan into

---

N. Markovic Khaze (✉)
Macquarie University, Sydney, NSW, Australia

A. Khaze
Law School of the Australian National University, Canberra, ACT, Australia

Australian territorial borders (Cue, 2002). The Australian Government refused to grant permission to the ship's captain, Arne Rinnan, to dock in the closest port to the rescue, the Australian territory of Christmas Island. Instead, the government sent a military unit to storm the ship in a dramatic fashion, triggering an unprecedented diplomatic rift between Australia and Norway (the 'Tampa affair'). The asylum seekers were eventually transferred to the islands of Nauru and Manus (part of Papua New Guinea). The majority only acquired refugee status after spending at least three years in detention (Foschia, 2004). While Captain Rinnan was later awarded the highest international human rights honour for his role in the Indian Ocean rescue, the Australian Government used the incident as an excuse to excise thousands of surrounding islands from Australian jurisdiction and implement a controversial policy of the Pacific solution from 2001 to 2007. Its remnants continue to this day, in the guise of mandatory exile of maritime asylum seekers on Naura and Manus, masking the historical precedent of 'unauthorised' maritime arrivals following the fall of South Vietnam in 1975 which radically changed Australia's migration program in relation to Asia.[1]

This chapter analyses Australia's migration policy in the context of its Cold War anti-communist stance. It argues that geopolitical transformation in the Communist and post-Communist countries have had a major impact on Australia's national policies, much more than previously recognised in the scholarly literature. We adopt a critical comparative approach to explain political and economic reforms in socialist Yugoslavia and Vietnam before the end of the Cold War. On this basis, we will describe, using data from the Australian Bureau of Statistics and other sources, the impact of migration from socialist Yugoslavia and Vietnam on Australia's migration policy and trends. Our comparative analysis seeks to show the transnational nature of developments in these socialist countries and the impact which their internal socio-political changes and transformation have had on international migration trends and more specifically, on Australia's migration program.

---

[1] The authors would like to particularly thank Professor Roger Markwick and Dr. Alexandr Akimov for their comments on earlier versions of their chapter.

In the decade following the Vietnam War, Australia accepted over 80,000 Vietnamese refugees (many of whom were the so-called 'boat people'). This was the most dramatic overhaul of Australia immigration policy, which hitherto had been focussed on European, especially British, immigration in accordance with Australia's tacit 'White Australia' policy. Yugoslavia's break-up caused another international wave of refugees, with Australia (together with many other Western countries) adopting a special visa category for Yugoslavs fleeing the conflict. The remaining Communist states in Southeast Asia, including Vietnam, have adopted economic reforms to adapt to the Post-Cold world. However, their political, social and intellectual isolation from global democratising trends could exacerbate pre-existing internal divisions, possibly causing another immigration explosion should their Communist regimes collapse. This would have profound and far-reaching consequences for countries like Australia, whose migration policies would once again need to alter to accommodate such upheaval. Therefore, this chapter concludes, it is important for Australia to keep abreast with developments in the post-communist world as well as to be well-informed of any changes in the remaining communist states in its region to prepare for all eventualities, including a new wave of refugees from those countries.

'Fleeing Communism' and Australia's Anti-communist Agenda

Herta Mueller, a Romanian novelist of German descent who left Romania in 1987 and later won a Nobel Prize for literature in 2009, wrote in her critique of Romania's totalitarian communist state in *The Land of Green Plums* that 'If only the right person would have to leave, everyone else would be able to stay in the country' (Mueller, 1996). Literature on 'fleeing communism' and, related to that, diaspora politics in the West is extensive but spread widely across many disciplines: political science and international relations, migration studies, sociology, history and economics, to name a few. This phenomenon of political flight specifically refers to the citizens of communist countries departing, often covertly or under pretence of an imminent return, overseas and mostly to the West. During the Cold War, protection visas were issued by many Western states, including Australia, to political emigres and defectors from the communist regimes. The dramatic Petrov affair in 1954, which involved defection by the Third Secretary of the Soviet embassy in Canberra and covert Soviet spy Vladimir Petrov and his wife, a KGB captain, has been a well-studied event in Australia's political history (Bialoguski, 1955; Manne, 2004; Whitlam & Stubbs, 1974). This chapter, however, goes beyond individual defections from communist states, focussing instead on mass migration from former Yugoslavia and Vietnam to Australia as part of the latter's national migration program, and the consequences this has had for Australian multiculturalism and its relations with the communist world, past and present.

The history of Australia's migration program is closely connected to its Britishness and anti-communist policies. The Communist Party of Australia (CPA) was banned by the War Cabinet from 15 June 1940 due to its links with Moscow at the time of the Soviet Union's war neutrality and deeply rooted fears among government officials about the spread of Soviet influence in Australia (Lovell & Windle, 2008, p. 339). The prohibition was reversed in December 1942, two months after Canberra and Moscow established official diplomatic relations and the Soviets entering the war as an ally (Lavrov, 2018). After the war, the CPA emerged with increased popularity. However, its members and meetings were placed under government surveillance, with new migrants being denied citizenship or marked for deportation if Australian authorities suspected they had links to the CPA (Kukolja & Arkley, 2016). There was an attempt to ban the party again in the post-war era through a national referendum in 1951, but it was unsuccessful, much to the Menzies Government's displeasure. Since then, the Australian Secret Intelligence Organisation (ASIO) and state police services were used to monitor CPA activities domestically (Curthoys & Damousi, 2013). Successive Australian post-war governments kept a close eye on developments within the communist world, although they pragmatically maintained both trading and political links, and in some cases migration ties, with such states, especially in East-Central Europe.

When Australia's first national migration program was launched in 1945 under the Labour Government, the notion of solely Australian citizenship did not yet exist. Australians were at that time British subjects, with federal legislation evolving throughout the late 1940s and 1950s to institute a separate Australian citizenship category (Klapdor, Coombs, & Bohm, 2009). Federal Minister for Immigration Arthur Calwell tried to persuade the Australian public that post-war Australia must 'populate or perish'. This was necessary, the Government deemed, for post-war reconstruction and development of the Australian federation, with many regions still in dire need people in order to rebuild, populate and prosper. Migration centres were established, the first one in Victoria's Bonegilla in 1947, to accept new arrivals.[2] However, the Cold War cast a shadow over post-war mass immigration. Australia's anti-communist agenda increased with the election of the Liberal Menzies Government, the longest Liberal government in Australian history (1949–1966). Under the leadership of Prime Minister Robert Menzies, Australia viewed the communist world and its adherents and sympathisers with suspicion (Kukolja & Arkley, 2016). In this environment, new migrants with anti-communist views were welcomed and their political activities often tolerated, including the military-style training of anti-communist groups in the Australian outback by members of individual ethnic communities including those from former Yugoslavia.

According to researcher Kristy Campion, militant individuals from the Australian wing of Ustashe organisation were in the 1960s regarded as those who belonged to a group of 'good anti-communists' (in the words of former ASIO Director General); Australian intelligence and police turned a blind eye to their activities until the Whitlam Government (Campion, 2018, p. 41). Tensions within and among different Yugoslav communities had put enormous pressure on Australia's melting-pot policy of integration, as many new migrants, especially anti-communist activists, did not conform to the expectation of that time that they would simply come to Australia and blend into the mainstream community

---

[2]The Bonegilla Migrant Reception and Training Centre received its first assisted migrants in 1951.

without any trouble. Migrants from former Yugoslavia formed social, political and religious institutions in Australia often in parallel to the official institutions that were supported by the communist regime (Jupp, 2001). Australian multiculturalism became a battle of hearts and minds between anti-communists and those who did not oppose communism but still choose to resettle in Australia, mostly for economic rather than ideological reasons.

While, the Menzies Government was staunchly anti-Communist, both domestically and internationally, it was also pragmatic in its conduct vis-à-vis the Communist states. It established embassies in the capitals of many Communist countries, entering into provisional agreements even with members of the Warsaw camp. In 1970, Yugoslavia and Australia signed the official migration agreement to bring temporary workers to Australia. This was the same historical period in which Vietnamese refugees' arrival would forever change Australia's migration policy. However, some important steps preceded this large-scale migration scheme, including historical changes to the official government's policy on migration which previously excluded people of non-white descent. The dismantling of the White Australia Policy in the post-war era had major consequences for Australian relations links with communist countries, especially regarding immigration.

The End of 'White Australia'

The Immigration Restriction Act 1901 notoriously became known as the 'White Australia Policy' as it restricted non-white people from migrating to Australia, with minor exemptions for several professions (such as pearl diving). It was designed to maintain racial and British cultural homogeneity in Australia; being 'as much a cultural as political phenomenon … it could not be simply extinguished with an act of Parliament' (Jones, 2017). A 50-word dictation test in any European language was administered to non-white migrants in order to exclude them. Only 2000 people ever took the test, mostly unsuccessfully. Undesirable migrants with supposedly communist sentiments were deliberately administered linguistic tests that they could not pass in order to justify their deportation (Kukolja & Arkley, 2016).

Post-war demographic priorities, however, eventually watered down if not extinguished the 'White Australia Policy'. Labour parliamentarian Arthur Caldwell, Australia's first immigration minister, argued that Australia needed new migrants as a matter of national survival, provided they were European; 'Two Wongs don't make a white', he declared in 1947 (Munro, 2017). A decade later The Migration Act (1958) eliminated the dictation test. In 1966 the Harold Holt Liberal Government legislated legal equality between British, European and non-European migrants to Australia. Despite the 1966 Act, the government was slow to implement practical changes in the migration program; British citizens were still prioritised. The '10 Pounds Pom' scheme (1945–1972) was Australia's best known migration campaign, with over one million British citizens arriving under that arrangement (Meaney, 1995).

Australian immigration policy conflicted with shifting international policies and instruments. On 28 July 1951 the United Nations adopted the Refugee Convention, designed to tackle the refugee crisis that was brought about by the Second World War. The convention obliged its signatories to accept refugees of European descent. On 4 October 1967 the protocol relating to the status of refugees abolished the limitations to European refugees and included refugees from all nations. Australia became one of the first to join the Refugee Convention on 22 January 1954, however it delayed accepting the Protocol at that time. Only in December 1973 did Australia become a party to the 1967 Protocol, six years after its introduction. This move demonstrated a political shift towards accepting Australia as multicultural where non-white immigrants were equally welcomed as those from European backgrounds. In 1973 the Whitlam Labour government definitively renounced the White Australia policy, replacing it with a policy of multiculturalism that has remained to this date (NMA, 2019). In the mid-1970s, after the fall of South Vietnam to the Viet Cong, the Australian Government decided to lift the lid on Asian migration who were refugees from communism. However, there were no migration offices in Asian countries as Asian migration outside conflict zones was not officially encouraged.

European migrants from communist countries, refugees and workers, started to arrive from former Yugoslavia and Poland in larger numbers in the 1960s. After changes to Yugoslav laws on emigration in that decade, Yugoslavia (an independent/non-aligned communist state) was in the top ten source countries for foreign workers in Australia, with economic migrants filling up spaces fast and later bringing their families too. People from the countries of the Warsaw Pact, like Poland, were also allowed to immigrate despite Australia's anti-Communist stance domestically and internationally. The first post-war wave of Polish refugees had arrived into Australia between 1947 and 1954, with the Poland-born population increasing almost eight-fold from 6573 to 56,594 people (Department of Social Services, 2014). After the Polish Government lifted some of its restrictions on immigration, a further wave of 15,000 Poland-born people migrated to Australia between 1957 and 1966. Between 1980 and 1991, with the advent of the Solidarity opposition movement and subsequent repression in Poland that followed the imposition of martial law in 1981–1983, Australia accepted more than 25,000 Poland-born settlers, many as refugees (ibid.). Clearly, upheavals in these communist states, including changes to their domestic migration laws, had a direct impact on Australia's migration intake and the make-up of the Australian population. Two factors were simultaneously in play: On the one hand, Australia's need for foreign workers to rebuild the nation and the gradual phasing out of the White Australia Policy; on the other, changes in policy of some of Europe's communist countries regarding migration of their citizens. The next section specifically discusses migration from former Yugoslavia into Australia, and the impact of that migration on both Australia's migration program and its increasingly multicultural society.

Yugoslav Migration During the Cold War

Australia accepted small numbers of migrants originating from Yugoslavia as part of its early post-war migration program, mainly through the International Organisation for Migration and after 1952, through assisted or sponsored migration. Yugoslavs worked on the

Snowy Mountains Hydroelectric Scheme which began in 1949, with some losing their lives there as part of 121 fatalities which are now recorded and displayed on the Snowy Mountains Scheme Workers Memorial. Yugoslavia's socialist flag with the red star can still be seen in the town centre of Cooma in New South Wales, which is where this memorial is located. There is no systematic study on Yugoslav migrants to Australia but there are several community-based studies which collectively can shed light on the phenomenon of post-war migration to Australia from different parts of socialist Yugoslavia. Ethnic-based representation of Yugoslav communities in Australia has been a permanent feature of their migration story.

Yugoslavia was the only socialist state from the Balkans to actively promote emigration based on economic motives, starting in the 1960s. In fact:

> Between the 1960s and 1970s, [Yugoslavia] became one of the major sources of labour force, thus contributing to the industrial development of North-Central Europe.
> …In the early 1990s the overall number of Yugoslavian labour migrants and their family members exceeded 1.3 million. (Bonifazi & Mamolo, 2004, p. 521)

High levels of unemployment in the 1960s due to economic slowdown in Yugoslavia was a key reason for the resultant policy on emigration. Evidently, national policies and internal developments in Communist countries, as in the case of Yugoslavia, directly contributed to mass emigration from the Balkans, mostly to richer, Western countries.

In the early stages of the program, temporary guest workers, or 'Gastarbeiter', were expected to return to Yugoslavia after a period of working overseas under bilateral agreements made between Yugoslavia and West European countries, such as Germany and Austria (Breznik, 1982, p. 234; Brunnbauer, 2017, p. 16). They were also sending money back home in remittances but the high cost of living in the West meant that only a fifth of their salary was returning to Yugoslavia (Vinski, 1972, cited in Brunnbauer, 2016). Social scientist Ulf Brunnbauer contends that Yugoslavia's emigration policy was an 'ambitious project' that became questionable as it did not generate the domestic revenue the Communist Party leadership was hoping for, with Yugoslav *Gastarbeiter* becoming, according to Marxist scholars, 'an industrial reserve army for the capitalist economy'. Brunnbauer also suggests that Yugoslavia's social scientists developed very sophisticated methods, 'on pair with their Western peers', to measure domestic impact of labour emigration (Brunnbauer, 2016). Interestingly, former Yugoslav migrants still send large remittances to the Balkan countries, comprising in 2018, 8.6% of Serbia's GDP, 10.7% of Bosnia-Herzegovina's GDP, 10.8% of Montenegro's GDP and 4.7% of Croatia's GDP, all from recorded personal remittances (World Bank data, 2019).

Australia, a migrant nation, was not immune to the impact of Yugoslavia's new migration policy from the 1960s. As a country which accepted many people from Yugoslavia through the Displaced Persons program between 1948 and 1955 (circa 25,000, many of whom were opposed to Communism), it also attracted job-seeking Yugoslav settlers during the 1960s and 1970s (DIAC Community Information Summary, 2014). In the state of Victoria, for instance, there was a threefold increase between 1961 and 1971 to nearly 50,000 persons of Yugoslavia-born migrants (Museum of Victoria, n.d.). On 12 February 1970, Tito's Yugoslavia set up an immigration agreement with Australia, under which unskilled and semi-skilled workers came to work in Australia's 'growing manufacturing industry' (Queensland Health, n.d.). Entitled the Agreement on the Residence and Employment of Yugoslav Citizens in Australia, it entered into force in May of that year (Lillich, 1980, p. 146). Australia's development needs found an unlikely partner in Yugoslavia's labour export emigration program, even though the Australian Government's outlook was openly anti-communist, geared towards fighting the Red Peril in Asia in particular. Yugoslavia was a peculiar communist country oscillating between the East and the West in its foreign policy. Apart from its export of workers overseas as a revenue mechanism, it attracted scholarly and parliamentary attention in Australia due to its limited openness and specific model of workers-led councils and economic self-management system (Australian Parliament, 1971).

For socialist Yugoslavia, unlike for Vietnam which was at that time involved in a protracted civil war and international conflict, the early 1970s period was one of the domestic reforms, such as the transformation of state powers into a looser federation under the 1971 Constitution. A few decades had passed since the Communist Party's post-war mass purges and centralised infrastructure development, resulting in workforce changes that altered the pattern of internal migration flows. The dire consequences of clumsy economic liberalisation in 1961 brought high levels of inflation and a recession the following year that could still be felt one decade later.

In 1970, Yugoslavia signed a long-awaited trade agreement with the European Economic Community (EEC) which opened new commercial opportunities that led to better economic ties to larger West European countries (many of which members of the EEC). Citizens of socialist Yugoslavia were already present in many EEC countries (particularly France, Germany and Italy) as temporary workers, with diaspora communities containing both pro- and anti-communist migrants. The latter consisted mainly of those who saw themselves belonging to an ethnic or religious group (such as Albanians, Croats, Serbs, Slovenes, Macedonians or Bosnian Muslims) rather than to a political identity of being 'Yugoslav' despite communist Yugoslavia's passport they were carrying. Expatriate religious communities were also divided, with parallel church institutions being formed as in the case of the schismatic Free Serbian Orthodox Church and non-ecumenical Macedonian church communities, including in Australia where the former was established in 1964 (Kazich, 1989).

As in the countries of the Mekong Delta in the 1970s and early 1980s when the communist regimes were consolidating, socialist Yugoslavia's state-building was also characterised by large-scale internal migration trends. From rural to urban, hundreds of thousands of Yugoslavs were needed to fill in the Yugoslav Communist Party vacancies, and many more undertook labouring jobs required for national reconstruction (voluntarily and by force). Breznik (1982) observes that 'according to the 1971 census, the share of the urban population of Yugoslavia was about 38%, while the share of the non-agricultural population was 62%', whereas only two decades earlier, 70% of people lived in agricultural areas (Breznik, 1982, p. 229). In terms of overseas migration trends, the data is incomplete, but the 1971 census showed that at least 800,000 Yugoslavs went abroad to work in temporary jobs (ibid.). This number excluded those who have permanently left the country during the two previous decades to countries such as the United States of America, Canada, New Zealand or Australia. Communist Yugoslavia also developed friendly relations with many newly independent Asian states, where it began to export its engineering know-how, with Yugoslav companies engaged on large-scale construction projects across Asia. Yugoslavia's brand of self-managed socialism became a subject of study internationally. Other Communist states regarded it as revisionist and dangerous because of Yugoslav President Tito's being open to Western influence and cooperation. An accusation of 'Titoism' became common in the Eastern bloc as justification for purging non-like-minded communists.[3] According to Charles P. McVicker, the Titoist system developed as a blend of Marxism–Leninism and carefully selected Western liberal democratic traditions and practices, such as limited pluralism (McVicker, 1958, p. 107). Dissent was still quashed heavily, however, with capital punishment its most extreme form.

Yugoslav migration was marred with public controversy in Australia. Anti- and pro-Yugoslav factions of the migrant communities were often at loggerheads, including violence such as bombings and shootings, and the distribution of defamatory material. At the community level, according to Dona Kolar-Panov:

> Soccer clubs based on or associated with various ethnic clubs became the first openly nationalist-oriented organisations at the time of 'ethnic revival' in the [Australian] Yugoslav community in the 1970s. (Kolar-Panov, 2003, pp. 66–67)

The Whitlam Government was at the centre of controversy regarding the issue of anti-Yugoslav nationalists and extremists. In 1973,

---

[3]Yugoslavia was expelled from Cominform in June 1948 because of Tito's opposition to Stalin.

the Australian Government strongly formally protested the execution by a firing squad of three dual Australian-Yugoslav nationals of Croatian ethnic origin. They were apparently survivors of a 9-member group which clashed with the Yugoslav police the previous year in an alleged attempt to overthrow the Yugoslav regime and who were allegedly trained in Australia as part of an Australian Ustashe organisation. The Yugoslav Government described their execution as a warning to all anti-Yugoslavia groups and individuals abroad (*The New York Times*, 1973, p. 5). According to ASIO files:

> The long-running conflict between the then Yugoslav Government and Croatian separatists translated into violence in Australia with the bombing of the Yugoslav Consulate in Sydney in June 1969. This violence continued through to the mid-1970s—including the bombing of the Yugoslav General Trade and Tourist Agency building in Sydney in 1972. (ASIO, 2019)

Furthermore, according to *The Canberra Times*, Yugoslav authorities purportedly planted a network of spies across Australia to conduct surveillance of the more extremist pockets of Yugoslav migrant communities and possibly even infiltrated some of radical groups, such as the Movement for the Liberation and Unification of Macedonia (which the Australian government in the 1970s regarded as of 'minor security interest'). The same source indicates that the Croatian-Yugoslav tensions, especially two weeks before the Yugoslav Prime Minister's official visit to Australia, were the primary reason behind the federal government's raid on ASIO in 1973 which was authorised by Attorney-General Lionel Murphy; an event which to this day attracts heated scholarly debate (Raggatt, 2014). These examples, which were only the most dramatic ones in ongoing community tensions in Australia, indicate that events in physically and culturally distant socialist lands such as Yugoslavia during the Cold War came to bear a direct impact on Australia, influencing the conduct of its governing elites.

The next section will contextualise Vietnamese migration to Australia during the conflict between the communist and anti-community forces in Indo-China during the Cold War.

Vietnamese Migration: The First 'Boat People'

Australia today hosts the world's fourth-largest Vietnamese community, primarily because of the federal government opening the door to Vietnamese refugees during the conflict in Indo-China. Australia was originally neutral when the First Indo-China War concluded with the Geneva Accords of 1954 which temporarily split Vietnam along the 17th parallel, with future elections in sight on the reunification of Vietnam. Under one of the international agreements as part of the 1954 Accords, Vietnamese borders were open for 300 days, during which up to one million anti-communist North Vietnamese (many of whom were Roman Catholic) were transferred by the French and the Americans to South Vietnam in an operation called *Passage to Freedom*. This exercise in large-scale intra-regional migration was a consequence of both great power rivalry in Asia during the Cold War as well as symptomatic of the developments in the communist world. While Yugoslavia embraced the idea of non-aligned status and economic self-management, the two Vietnamese states were preparing for war that erupted in late 1955 and lasted two decades. Vietnam's troubles were firstly felt by its immediate neighbours, but by the 1970s they would have a profound impact on Australia's migration policy.

Prior to 1975, the number of Vietnamese coming to Australia was low. The first Vietnamese refugees to reach Australia were the orphan infants evacuated by Operation 'Babylift' which took place after the fall of South Vietnam in 1975 (DVA, n.d.). On 26 April 1976 the first ship bringing Vietnamese refugees onto Australian shores sailed into Darwin Harbour, with more than fifty boats arriving over the next three years. Under the Whitlam and Fraser Governments, Australia changed its image from a state with discriminatory migration policy against Asian migrants to a country with humanitarian intake of all migrants, regardless of their skin colour.

After the Vietnam War ended, the Australian Government sent officials to the refugee camps in Southeast Asia to select those refugees that would be allowed to migrate to Australia. In 1982, Australia and Vietnam agreed on an orderly migration program, emphasising family reunion; two-thirds of arrivals over the next few years were women. Until 1983 Australia had accepted more than 15,000 Vietnamese refugees per year. In 2016, the Census showed that 219,355 people in Australia were born in Vietnam (ABS, 2018). Most of these people, almost 69,000, came between 1971 and 1980. In comparison, in 1970, only 700 Vietnamese-born people were registered in Australia. However, even after the Cold War's end, Vietnamese continued to migrate to Australia. For example, between 2011 and 2016, 34,000 Vietnamese came to Australia. Almost 294,000 people in Australia claimed Vietnamese ancestry, according to the 2016 Census (ID Community Profile). Therefore, events in communist Vietnam continue to influence migration flows into Australia, especially since many Vietnamese have family members here and continue to seek family reunion opportunities.

The Cold War's End and Yugoslavia's Dissolution

Civil war in Yugoslavia coincided with the end of the Cold War. Forces that have kept the unified state together no longer existed by 1991, as there was no clear successor to President Tito, who died in 1980. Separatism was fanned by Germany, Austria and the Vatican, particularly in the 'predominantly Roman Catholic republics of Slovenia and Croatia' (Cowell, 1992; McGreal & Willan, 1999). The decade of the 1980s in Yugoslavia was marked by increasing economic pressure, by a growing gap in wealth between and within regions. In such circumstances, citizens were receiving vouchers for necessities that were not to be found on supermarket shelves (even to the extent of baby goods, washing powder and even coffee). After pro-independence referendums in Slovenia and Croatia passed with overwhelming support (but with the boycott of the sizeable Serbian minority in Croatia), the Serbian Government mobilised the remaining Yugoslav resources and engaged in interstate conflict with Slovenia (a 10-day war), Croatia (1991–1995) and Bosnia-Herzegovina (1992–1995), and internally, in the disputed southern province of Kosovo (1997–1999). Because of the conflict, in which about 100,000 people from all sides lost their lives, millions of people crossed borders and hundreds of thousands sought asylum in Western European countries and further away, including Australia and New Zealand.

The Australian Government opened pathways for migration for persons who were deemed to be genuine refugees, with tens of thousands of former Yugoslav citizens arriving after 1991. The end of communism in former Yugoslavia, which brought with it state disintegration and the creation of new, smaller pro-democratic elites that were advocating for regime change (in Croatia and Serbia in particular) had far-reaching consequences. The Australian migration program was not immune from the effects of the Yugoslav conflict, which was the bloodiest one in Europe since the Second World War. This new wave of migration of refugees affirmed Australia's place as a welcoming nation for persons escaping conflict, which a role it proudly assumed in the 1970s towards the first 'boat people' from Vietnam.

In 1999, Australia reluctantly accepted (after repeated requests from the UNHCR and international partners) 4,000 refugees of Albanian origin fleeing conflict in former Yugoslavia. In yet another mass displacement, over 800,000 Kosovar refugees fled across borders into neighbouring countries, creating a humanitarian emergency. The government led by Liberal Prime Minister John Howard introduced a new strategy to the management of refugee intake through the introduction of the *Migration Legislation Amendment (Temporary Safe Haven Visas) Act 1999* (Cth) on 11 May 1999. These changes would set the scene for years to come by introducing controversial policies that would allow the future government to fulfil Australia's treaty obligations under the UN Convention while keeping those who fled conflict and persecution at bay. The changes in 1999 gave enormous powers to then immigration minister Peter Ruddock, to cancel, extend or refuse visa's with limited review rights or freedoms. In most instances refugees who had fled the Kosovar conflict were only given a three-month temporary visa and were restricted from integration into the community because of strict visa conditions placed upon them to ensure that they do not stay with relatives or members of their ethnic community. The Kosovo conflict, which was the last 'domino' to fall in the 1990s following Yugoslavia's violent post-Communist transformation, introduced the notion of a 'temporary refugee', implementing controversial policy that would be reintroduced a decade later after the Afghanistan war and drastically change conditions for subsequent irregular maritime arrivals (Carr, 2017). The policy that set the scene for Operations Sovereign Borders, which remains as one of the world's most internationally controversial policies of asylum-seeker management to this day.

Conclusion

Immigration from former Yugoslavia and Vietnam by individuals 'fleeing Communism' has had irreversible consequences for Australian policies of immigration and multiculturalism. Despite obvious regional (geographical), social and historical differences, migration waves from these two countries were similar in the fact that many people leaving their homelands in those waves were ideologically opposed to communism. Some even used Australian territory as a base to exercise anti-communist activities, as in the case of Ustashe organisation, the activities of which were somewhat curtailed with the election of the Whitlam Government. Vietnamese immigration to Australia symbolised the end of White Australia policy, with the government accepting asylum seekers coming by boat in what was to become the biggest overhaul of Australia's immigration policy. This was preceded by a wave of new post-war refugees and economic migrants from Southeast Europe, in which the Yugoslav migrants were one of the largest cohorts. Yugoslavs and their intraethnic differences changed the face of Australian multiculturalism by adding new complexities and reality cheque that successive Australian governments have had to deal with pragmatism ever since. Australia was not immune to developments in the communist world; its anti-Communist stance at home and in the region had to be carefully balanced with the domestic needs and changes to Australia's population.

This paper has thus demonstrated, using historical analysis, that developments in communist countries during the Cold War and after have had a profound impact on Australia. There is a further need to study links between overseas developments in communist and post-communist states and their impact on Australia. This limited study sought to contribute to this issue, highlighting the need for the Australian Government to maintain interest in and research into communist and post-communist countries, the fates of which can still have profound consequences for Australian multiculturalism, especially if Southeast Asian communist and other regimes, were to collapse in the foreseeable future, due to economic, military or environmental cries.

References

Australian Bureau of Statistics (ABS). (2018). *Quick stats census data: Vietnamese*. Retrieved June 2, 2019, from quickstats.censusdata.abs.gov.au/census_services/getproduct/census/2016/quickstat/5105_036.

Australian Catholic Social Justice Council (ACSJC). (2002). *Discussion guides: The pacific solution*. Retrieved June 2, 2019, from https://www.socialjustice.catholic.org.au/publications/discussion-guides/134-the-pacific-solution.

Australian Parliament. (1971). Official report of the Australian Parliamentary Mission to the Council of Europe, Turkey, France, Belgium, Britain and Yugoslavia: Led by the Hon. Sir William Aston, Speaker of the House of Representatives, and Senator the Hon. Sir Kenneth Anderson, Minister for Supply, 9 January–12 February 1971. Canberra: Australian Government Publishing Service.

Australian Security Intelligence Organisation (ASIO). (2019). *Terrorism emerges in Australia*. Retrieved June 2, 2019, from https://www.asio.gov.au/about/history/terrorism-emerges-australia.html.

Bialoguski, M. (1955). *The Petrov story*. Melbourne: Heinemann.

Bonifazi, C., & Mamolo, M. (2004). Past and current trends of Balkan migrations. *Espace, Populations, Societies, 3*, 519–531.

Breznik, D. (1982). The dynamics of population in Yugoslavia. *Eastern European Economics, 20*(3–4), 215–249.

Brunnbauer, U. (2016). *Migration and Economic Development in Socialist Yugoslavia, Ostblog*, 17 March 2017. Retrieved October 20, 2019, from https://ostblog.hypotheses.org/728.

Brunnbauer, U. (2017). *Globalizing Southeastern Europe: Emigrants, America, and the state since the late nineteenth century*. Maryland: Lexington Books.

Campion, K. (2018). The Ustaša in Australia: A review of right-wing Ustaša terrorism from 1963–1973, and factors that enabled their endurance. *Salus, 6*(2), 37–58.

Carr, R. (2017). The safe haven visa policy: A compassionate intervention with cruel intentions. *Australian Policy and History*. Retrieved June 2, 2019, from http://aph.org.au/the-safe-haven-visa-policy-a-compassionate-intervention-with-cruel-intentions/.

Cowell, A. (1992, January 14). Vatican formally recognizes independence of Croatia and Slovenia. *New York Times*, p. 3.

Cue, E. (2002). *Captain, crew and owner of "Tampa" win Nansen Award for rescue at sea*. Retrieved June 2, 2019, from https://www.unhcr.org/news/latest/2002/3/3c975a254/captain-crew-owner-tampa-win-nansen-award-rescue-sea.html.

Curthoys, A., & Damousi, J. (2013). Remembering the 1951 referendum on the banning of the Communist Party. *Australian Historical Studies, 44*(1), 1–3.

Department of Immigration and Citizenship. (2014). *Community information summary: Serbia-born*. Retrieved June 2, 2019, from https://www.dss.gov.au/sites/default/files/documents/02_2014/serbia.pdf.

Department of Social Services. (2014). *The Poland-born community*. Retrieved June 2, 2019, from https://www.dss.gov.au/our-responsibilities/settlement-services/programs-policy/a-multicultural-australia/programs-and-publications/community-information-summaries/the-poland-born-community.

Department of Veterans Affairs (DVA). (n.d.). *Australia and the Vietnam War*. Retrieved June 2, 2019, from https://anzacportal.dva.gov.au/history/conflicts/australia-and-vietnam-war/australia-and-vietnam-war/royal-australian-air-force-3.

Foschia, L. (2004). Many Tampa asylum seekers granted refugee status. *ABC PM*. Retrieved June 2, 2019, from https://www.abc.net.au/pm/content/2004/s1110098.htm.

Hamilton, R. (2017). Australia's refugee policy is a crime against humanity. *Foreign Policy*. Retrieved June 2, 2019, from https://foreignpolicy.com/2017/02/23/australias-refugee-policy-may-be-officially-a-crime-against-humanity/.

Howard, J. (2001). *Campaign launch speeches: Address at the Federal Liberal Party campaign launch*. Sydney. Retrieved June 2, 2019, from https://parlinfo.aph.gov.au/parlInfo/search/display/display.w3p;query=Id%3A%22library%2Fpartypol%2F1178395%22.

ID Community Profile. (n.d.). *Vietnamese in Australia*. Retrieved June 2, 2019, from https://profile.id.com.au/australia/ancestry?WebID=10.

Jones, B. T. (2017). Australian politics explainer: The White Australia policy. *SBS*. Retrieved June 2, 2019, from https://www.sbs.com.au/nitv/nitv-news/article/2017/04/10/what-was-white-australia-policy-and-how-does-it-still-affect-us-now.

Jupp, J. (2001). *The Australian People: An encyclopedia of the nation, its people and their origins*. Cambridge: Cambridge University Press.

Kazich, T. (Ed.). (1989). *Serbs in Australia: History and development of Free Serbian Orthodox Church Diocese for Australia and New Zealand*. Canberra: Monastery Press.

Klapdor, M., Coombs, M., & Bohm, C. (2009). Australian citizenship: A chronology of major developments in policy and law. *Australian Parliamentary Library*. Retrieved June 2, 2019, from https://www.aph.gov.au/About_Parliament/Parliamentary_Departments/Parliamentary_Library/pubs/BN/0910/AustCitizenship#_ftn26.

Kolar-Panov, D. (2003). *Video, war and the diasporic imagination*. London, UK: Routledge.

Kukolja, K., & Arkley, L. (2016). "Unwanted Australians" call for official acknowledgment. *SBS News*. Retrieved June 2, 2019, from https://www.sbs.com.au/news/unwanted-australians-call-for-official-acknowledgment.

Lavrov, S. (2018). *Russia and Australia: 75 years of cooperation*. Retrieved June 2, 2019, from https://www.internationalaffairs.org.au/australianoutlook/russia-australia/.

Lillich, R. B. (1980). The promotion of human rights through Bilateral treaties: The Australian experience with migration and settlement agreements. *Australian Year Book of International Law, 8*(5), 142–161.

Lovell, D., & Windle, K. (Eds.). (2008). *Our unswerving loyalty: A documentary survey of relations between the Communist Party of Australia and Moscow, 1920–1940*. Canberra: ANU Press.

Manne, R. (2004). *The Petrov affair*. Melbourne: Text Publishing.

McGreal, C., & Willan, P. (1999). Vatican secretly armed Croatia. *The Guardian*. Retrieved June 2, 2019, from https://www.theguardian.com/world/1999/nov/19/chrismcgreal.philipwillan.

McVicker, C. P. (1958, May). Titoism. *The Annals of the American Academy of Political and Social Science*. The Satellites in Eastern Europe, 317, 107–114.

Meaney, N. (1995). The end of 'White Australia' and Australia's changing perceptions of Asia, 1945–1990. *Australian Journal of International Affairs, 49*(2), 171–189.

Mueller, H. (1996). *The land of green plums*. Germany: Rowohlt Verlag.

Munro, K. (2017). A brief history of immigration to Australia. *SBS News*. Retrieved June 2, 2019, from https://www.sbs.com.au/news/a-brief-history-of-immigration-to-australia.

Museum of Victoria. (n.d.). *History of immigration from Serbia*. Retrieved June 2, 2019, from https://museumsvictoria.com.au/origins/history.aspx?pid=79.

National Museum of Australia. (2019). *End of White Australia policy 2019*. Retrieved June 2, 2019, from https://www.nma.gov.au/defining-moments/resources/end-of-the-white-australia-policy.

Oxfam Australia. (2007). *The pacific solution: A $1 billion "living hell"?* Retrieved June 2, 2019, from https://www.oxfam.org.au/media/2007/08/the-pacific-solution-a-1-billion-living-hell/.

Queensland Health. (n.d.). *Socialist Federal Republic of Yugoslavia, a guide for health professionals*. Retrieved June 2, 2019, from https://www.health.qld.gov.au/__data/assets/pdf_file/0023/154139/sfr_yugo.pdf.

Raggatt, M. (2014, April 6). Film lifts lid on Cold War-era spying activities in Australia. *The Canberra Times*.

The New York Times. (1973, April 14). *Australia protests Yugoslav execution*, p. 5.

Whitlam, N., & Stubbs, J. (1974). *Nest of traitors: The Petrov affair*. Milton (QLD): Jacaranda.

World Bank data. (2019). *Personal remittances, received (% of GDP)*. Retrieved June 2, 2019, from https://data.worldbank.org/indicator/BX.TRF.PWKR.DT.GD.ZS.

Index

A

accession (to the European Union) 57, 62, 64, 67, 69–72, 76, 77
  conditions 57, 61, 67, 77
  negotiation chapter(s) 64, 67, 70, 75
  negotiations 62, 64, 73
ACF. *See* Anti-Corruption Foundation
acquisition 296
administrative 5
affordability 252
Afghanistan 145
Africa 99
agriculture 333–335
Albania 59, 63, 64, 66, 67, 69, 77, 84–87, 100, 104
Anti-Ballistic Missile (ABM) Treaty 128
Anti-colonialism 223
Anti-Corruption Foundation 192, 196, 197
anti-corruption industry 203, 204, 208, 210
anti-Semitism 312, 318
anti-systemic opposition 191, 197, 210
Arab Spring 143
Arkan 91, 92
Armenia 4, 157–159, 164, 179
ASEANAPOL 105
Asian values 224
asymmetry of interests 163, 172
Australia 92, 94
Australian Communist Party 408
Australia's anti-Communist policies 408
Austria 75
authoritarian 2, 7

© The Editor(s) (if applicable) and The Author(s), under exclusive license to Springer Nature Singapore Pte Ltd. 2020
A. Akimov and G. Kazakevitch (eds.), *30 Years since the Fall of the Berlin Wall*, Palgrave Studies in Economic History, https://doi.org/10.1007/978-981-15-0317-7

leader 217, 219, 238
regime 217, 219
Azerbaijan 2, 4

B

Balkans 58, 64, 65
   states 57, 59, 62, 67
Baltic states/Baltics 58, 59, 61, 62
Bauman, Zygmunt 311–314, 316–321, 323, 324
Belarus 153, 155, 157, 158, 163–165, 178, 179, 181
Belgium 86
Belgrade-Pristina Dialogue 66, 70, 75
Belt and Road Initiative (BRI) 47, 48, 53
Berisha, Sali 86
Berlin Process 72, 73
Berlin Wall 1, 2, 5, 217
Bipolar world 117, 118
black societies 93
Bolashak 232, 233
borderless world 102
Bosnia and Herzegovina (B-H) 59, 64, 66, 67, 71, 72, 75, 92
   Reform Agenda 73
Bo Xilai 95
Bribery 231, 232
British Empire 220
Brussels talks 75, 76
Brzezinski, Zbigniew 119, 121, 133
Bulgaria 57, 59, 62, 63, 65, 67, 69, 76, 84, 87, 88, 102, 104
Bureaucracy 227
Bush, George H.W. 122
Bush, George W. 126–128
Business freedom 16, 23, 27

C

Cambodia 96
Camorra 90
capitalism 328, 331, 332, 334–337, 341, 344–346
Central and Eastern Europe 3
Central Asia 1, 4, 5, 7, 272
Central Provident Fund (CPF) 227
China 1, 3, 6, 84, 86, 93, 94, 96–100, 103–105, 217, 221, 222, 226
ChKs [extraordinary commissions] 368, 374–377, 397
Citizenship 289–299, 302–305
civil society 105
class 328, 329, 334, 340, 342–345
Clientelism 5
Clinton, Bill 123, 126
Clinton, Hillary 130, 131
cluster analysis 21, 24
Cold War 117, 118, 120–124, 126, 129, 130, 134, 332, 333
Collusion 92, 94, 97, 104
Colonial 223
Common Electric Power Market (CEPM) 160, 161, 163, 180, 181
common energy markets (CEMs) 151, 154, 160, 165, 177–180
Common Gas Market (CGM) 160, 161, 163, 180–183
Common Market for Oil and Petroleum Products (CMOPP) 160, 161, 180, 183, 184
Communism 311, 313, 318, 324
Communist party 3, 5
Communist revolution 220, 228

Communist systems 101
Confrontation 117, 118, 120, 130, 132, 134
Confucian values 220
Conspicuous consumption 271, 273, 277, 283
Constitution 1918 (RSFSR) 378, 379
Constitution 1924 (USSR) 379, 390
Constitution 1936 (USSR) 380, 381, 384, 391, 393, 400
Constitution 1937 (RSFSR) 380, 391, 400
Constitution 1977 (USSR) 380–384, 387, 391, 398, 400
Constitution 1978 (RSFSR) 381, 382, 387, 389–391, 400
Constitution 1993 (RF) 390, 391
Consumer behaviour 245
consumption 243–246, 248, 250, 254, 255, 258, 260, 262–264
Containment 118–121
contingent (contingency) 312, 317, 320, 321
contract killing 88, 89, 95
Cooperation and Verification Mechanism (CVM) 87
Copenhagen conditions 60, 76. *See also* accession (to the European Union)
Corruption 14, 16, 22, 27, 84, 87, 89, 94, 95, 101, 102, 224, 225, 230–233, 235, 238
Corruption Perception Index 231
Corrupt Practices Investigation Bureau (CPIB) 225
cotton 46
counterfeiting 88, 95, 99
crime, organised (OC) 83–105

gentrification of 94, 103
Croatia 57, 59, 63, 64, 66, 67, 69, 74, 77
Cronyism 231
Cultural Revolution 331, 335, 336, 339
Culture 273
cybercrime 90, 91, 101
Czechia 97
Czechoslovakia 58, 69

D

demand 244, 245, 260, 264
Democracy/democratisation 58, 59, 68, 69, 71, 74, 76
democracy score. *See* Freedom House
illiberal 59, 62
Democratic 1, 2, 5
Democratic People's Republic of Korea (DPRK). *See* Korea, North
Deng Xiaoping 95, 100, 222, 330, 331, 335
Détente 120
Deterrence 118, 120
Development Economics 272, 284
Dictatorship
benevolent 219
diet quality 245
digital media 191, 198, 210
Disintegration 221
Dissolution of Soviet Union 353, 358, 383
Djindjić, Zoran 92
Djukanović, Milo (President of Montenegro, 1998–2002, 2018–) 70

documentary films 196, 203
drugs, illicit 84, 85, 87. *See also* trafficking
dystopia 318, 320

E
economic assistance 62
Economic Development Board (EDB) 227
Economic Freedom data 15, 16
economic transition 61, 62
   indicators. *See* European Bank for Reconstruction and Development (EBRD)
emotions 313–316
energy integration 151–156, 159–161, 164, 165, 177–179
Energy Package 169, 170, 175
Energy Union 153, 156, 168–170, 172, 177, 178
Entrepôt 222
Estonia 84
Ethnical 221, 226, 235
ethnicity 291, 296, 297, 299, 303, 305
EU. *See* European Union (EU)
Eurasian Economic Union (EAEU) 151, 154–157, 159–161, 163–165, 172, 177–182
European Bank for Reconstruction and Development (EBRD) 61
   transition indicators 61
European Commission 65, 67, 70–75

European Council 61, 62, 65
Europeanisation/EUropeanisation 58–61, 64, 66, 68–72, 76, 77
European Union (EU) 84, 87, 153–157, 163, 166–172, 174, 176, 178, 179
   accession conditions. *See* accession
   (policy) incentives 71
   accession negotiations. *See* accession
   enlargement 57, 74, 76
   enlargement strategy 74
   EU Council 72
   three pillars (approach) 69
Europol 86, 90, 96, 103
Exceptionalism 120
Export-oriented strategy 227

F
fear 312, 313, 315, 316, 320, 323
February Revolution 353, 356, 358, 361, 363, 383
Financial freedom 17, 24
Financial sector 232, 234–236
First-world 219, 223, 236
food 243, 246, 248, 250, 252, 254–256, 259–265
Foreign direct investments 231, 234, 235, 238
Former Soviet Union 272
Former Yugoslav Republic of Macedonia (FYRM). *See* North Macedonia
frame mapping 199, 200
France 86, 88
Freedom House 63, 71

Index   431

democracy score (Nations in Transit) 61
fruit and vegetables 243–245, 250, 251, 254–256, 258–265

G

gas 33, 35, 38–40, 42–44, 46, 50
GDP 3, 232, 234–236
GDP per capita 15, 25
Georgia 128–130
Germany 75, 91
Global Competitiveness Report 99
globalisation 102, 313, 314, 318, 319
Goh Keng Swee 225
Gorbachev, Mikhail 90, 122–124, 134, 331–333, 335, 337, 340–342, 344
Gore, Al 125
Government integrity 22
Government spending 16, 23
Great Terror 365, 378, 393, 394, 396, 397, 400
Greece 57, 70, 71, 73, 75
guest workers 413

H

Hahn, Johannes (European Commissioner for European Neighbourhood Policy and Enlargement, 2014–2015) 73, 75
Haradinaj, Ramush (Prime Minister of Kosovo) 76
Hart's secondary rules 356, 357, 372, 393, 400
Hong Kong 93, 94

horticultural 243, 245, 246, 248, 262
hospitality 312, 314–318, 320, 321, 323, 324
Human rights 2, 61, 62
Hungary 2, 4, 58

I

Iceland 320, 321
ideas 152, 153, 156, 178
illiberalism 313
Import-substitution 234, 239
income 250, 252, 253, 255, 259–262, 264
Independence 217, 218, 220–222, 224, 228–230, 236, 238
industrialisation 329, 332, 334, 343
inequality 314, 318, 319, 324
institutional complementarity 178
institutional discrepancy 178
institutions 152, 153, 155, 156, 178
intake 243–245, 250, 255–260, 262–264
Integrity 224, 228
interests 152–156, 164, 178, 179, 182
Intermediate-Range Nuclear Forces (INF) Treaty 122, 134
International remittances 273, 276
International trade freedom 23
Interpol 90, 103
intolerant 322–324
Investment freedom 17, 23
Iran
    1979 Revolution 140

Iran–Iraq war 140
Islamic Revolutionary Guard Corps (IRGC) 146, 148
Khamenei, Ali 141, 145
Mosaddegh, Mohammad 140
Rouhani, Hassan 147, 148
Israel 91, 142, 146, 149
Italy 75, 86, 87, 91

J

Judiciary 228, 229
Junker, Jean-Claude (President of the European Commission, 2014-2019) 74

K

Karimov, Islam 217–221, 229, 230, 232, 234, 238, 239
Kazakhstan 31, 34, 35, 38–40, 42–44, 46–48, 50, 53, 151, 153, 156–158, 163–165, 174, 179, 180, 217–223, 228–236, 238, 239
Kazhegeldin, Akezhan 229, 232
Kelsen's basic norm 356, 357, 372, 386, 392, 393
Kennan, George 120, 125, 132
Khrushchev, Nikita 330
Kim Jong-un 98
knowledge 245, 250, 255, 256, 259, 262–264
Korea
    North 2, 84, 97–100, 103–105
    South 98, 99
Kosovo 59, 63, 66, 67, 69, 71, 75, 76, 86

Kyrgyz Republic 31, 34, 35, 38, 39, 42–44, 46, 48, 50, 52, 54, 55
Kyrgyzstan 34, 48, 52–55, 157, 159, 164. *See also* Kyrgyz Republic

L

Labour migration 274, 277, 278
La Cosa Nostra 86, 91
Landbridge 46, 47
language 290, 291, 293–297, 299–305
Laos 96, 99
Latinisation 233
Latvia 62, 69
law enforcement 84–86, 88, 90, 92, 93, 96, 104, 105
Lee Kuan Yew 218–220, 222–225, 230, 236, 238, 239
legally binding agreement (Serbia and Kosovo) 75, 76
Liberal 2, 3
liberalisation 336, 340, 342
liberal market systems 14
Life expectancy 237
liquid modernity 313, 314, 324
Lithuania 62, 69, 84
Lumpen 321

M

Mafia 89, 91
Malaysia 219–222, 226
Manchu Dynasty. *See* Qing Dynasty
Mao Zedong 330
Marchenko, Illya 232

Marxism 324
Max Weber 4
Media 2, 7
Medvedev, Dmitry 130, 131
Menzies Government 408–410
Meritocracy 224, 225, 232
Messianism 120
Middle East 86, 99
migrants 312, 313, 316–321, 323
migration 311, 314, 317–324
militarisation 333
Mirziyoyev, Shavkat 239
modernisation 334
Mogherini, Federica (EU High Representative for Foreign Affairs and Security Policy, 2014–2019) 71, 75
Monetary Authority of Singapore 228
Monetary freedom 17, 23
money-laundering 90, 96
Montenegro 59, 63, 66, 67, 69, 70, 74, 77, 92
multi-ethnic 297
Multinational corporation (MNC) 227
Munich speech 121, 129
Myanmar 96

N

naming issue (North Macedonia and Greece) 66, 71, 73
Nano, Fatos 86
Naša Stvar 91
National Bank of Kazakhstan 232
National Bank of Uzbekistan 234
National delimitation policy 220

nationalism 317, 318
nationality 291, 292, 295, 297, 300
National Trades Union Congress (NTUC) 228
National University of Singapore 226
Nation-building 218, 221
Nationhood 297
NATO 118, 124–126, 128, 129, 131
NATO expansion 117, 121, 124–126, 128
naturalization 293–296, 298, 299, 305
Navalny, Alexey 191–200, 202–208, 210
Navalny LIVE 192, 197
Nazarbayev, Nursultan 217–219, 221, 229, 231, 232, 238, 239
Nazarbayev University 233
negotiation process 64
neo-liberalism 102, 332
Nepotism 231, 232, 238
Netherlands 88, 96
New Economic Policy (NEP) 335–338, 340
New START 130
'new thinking' 333, 342
NGO. *See* non-governmental organisation
NKVD troikas 394, 400
nomenklatura 88
non-governmental organisation 192, 196
Nord Stream 2 174–176
North Macedonia 67, 70, 71, 74
Nuclear 141, 142
    Bushehr 142, 144

Joint Comprehensive Plan of Action (JCPOA) 145
Nuclear security 120, 134
nutrients 255, 260
nutrition 244, 255, 262, 264, 265

O

Obama, Barack 126, 130–132
October Revolution 353, 356, 358, 365, 376, 380, 383, 386, 390
oil 33, 35, 38–40, 42, 44, 46, 50
Ombudsmen 2
Oralman 294
organised crime 73
Othering 320

P

Pacific solution 405, 406
Passport 291, 292, 297
Pension 234, 235
People's Action Party (PAP) 220, 223–225, 229
perestroika 332, 336, 338, 342, 353, 355, 356, 358, 383
permanent residence 292
Poland 2, 8, 58, 69, 84
police. *See* law enforcement
political communication (PC) 191, 193–195, 198
Political stability 223, 224, 230, 238
populism 191, 193–195, 208–210, 312
populist style 191, 192, 195, 198, 208–210
Post-communist 2–6, 8

post-communist countries 13–15, 21, 26, 27, 29
post-communist transition/transformation 58, 61
political 58, 62, 64, 77
socio-economic. *See* economic transition
Prespes agreement 71
prices 245, 249, 250, 252–255, 260, 262–264
Primakov, Yevgeny 125
Privatisation 235
Property rights 16, 22
propiska 292
protection (criminal) 88, 94
Provisional Government 359, 360, 365
public and private ownership 14
Putin, Vladimir 121, 126–132, 217

Q

Qaddafi, Muammar 131
Qing Dynasty 93

R

Rajaratnam, Sinnathamby 225
Rapprochement 121, 123, 126
Reagan, Ronald 122, 134
Red Terror 373, 377
refugees 313, 316–320, 323, 406, 407, 410–412, 418–421
regime change 420
Reset 130, 131
resource boom 33, 39, 40, 42, 44, 50
restoration 290
Revolutionary Tribunals 368, 370, 373, 377, 394

Romania 57, 59, 62, 63, 65, 67, 69, 76, 84, 87, 88, 102
rule of law 58, 61, 62, 67, 69, 71, 74, 104, 228, 229, 235
Russia 84, 89–91, 99, 100, 103–105, 151, 153, 155–159, 163–165, 167–170, 172, 174–176, 178–180, 217, 221, 222, 235, 272, 273, 281
   Collapse of Soviet Union 140
   "Instrumentalism" 141
   Military intervention in Syria 143
   Putin, Vladimir 141, 144, 149
   Russian-Persian Treaty of Friendship 140
   S-300 missiles 142, 144
   Yeltsin, Boris 140, 141
Russian Empire 220, 228
Russo-Georgian war 121, 130

S

sanctions 88, 92, 98, 103
Saudi Arabia 140, 143, 149
Schengen 87, 88, 102
seasonality 245, 260, 262, 263
Seasonal migration 272
Security dilemma 118, 120
semi-authoritarian 196, 203, 205, 208
Serbia 59, 63, 66, 67, 69–71, 74–76, 84, 91, 92, 100, 103, 104
Sinaloa Cartel 90
Singapore 218–232, 234, 236, 238
Skills Development Fund (SDF) 226
Slovakia 62, 63, 69
Slovenia 2, 4, 84

smuggling
   cigarettes 88, 92
   nuclear materials 91
   oil 92
   people 95, 99
   wildlife 97, 99
Snowden, Edward 131
(social) exclusion 322
'socialism in one country' 329, 330, 339
'socialism with Chinese characteristics' 330, 331, 339, 343, 345, 346
'socialist market economy' 335, 340, 342
social media 193–195
Social status 271, 273, 284
socio-economic 259, 260
Solntsevskaya Bratva 90
Soviet Courts 391
Soviet republics 1, 4
Soviet Union (USSR) 90, 101, 217, 353, 355, 386
Spain 167
Stabilisation and Association Process (SAP) 64, 72
   conditions 65
Stalin, I.V. 328–332, 335, 338–340
START I 122
state 327–329, 331–338, 340, 342–346
state continuity 290, 293
statelessness 289, 298, 299
Status Oriented Expenditures 272, 273, 277
Strategic rivalry 118, 132
supply 243–245, 254, 262, 264
Survival ideology 224

436　Index

Syria 144, 146, 147, 149
　　Astana peace process 146
Syria campaign 117, 131, 132

T
Tajikistan 33, 35, 38, 39, 42–44, 48, 50, 53
Tampa affair 406
Technology 117, 141, 142, 144, 170, 178, 194, 226, 264, 336, 338, 339
Thachi, Hashim (President of Kosovo, 2016–) 75
Thailand 96, 99
Third World 219, 223, 236
Tiananmen crisis 336, 340
Timocracy 219
Toh Chin Chye 225
Tokayev, Kassym-Jomart 239
tolerance 321, 323, 324
Totalitarianism 219
Traditional ceremonies 273
trafficking
　　cars 87, 89
　　drug 94, 96–99, 104, 105
　　human 85, 87, 88, 91, 95, 96, 99, 104
　　weapons 87, 99
transition 13, 14
Triads 85, 93–95
Trump, Donald 126, 133, 134, 217
Turkey 143, 146, 149
Turkmenistan 35, 38–40, 42–44, 48, 50

U
Ukraine 84, 90, 117, 121, 128, 129, 132, 133

UK. *See* United Kingdom (UK)
Umid 233
UN. *See* United Nations (UN)
Unemployment 227
Union of Sovereign States 221
United Kingdom (UK) 75, 84–86, 96
United Nations (UN) 71, 75, 88, 92, 99
United States (US) 84, 86, 88, 89, 91, 96, 98, 99, 101
　　Obama, Barack 142, 148
　　sanctions 142
　　Trump, Donald 148, 149
　　twin pillars strategy 140
US. *See* United States (US)
US administration 75
USSR. *See* Soviet Union
U.S. presidential election 117, 121
U.S.–Russian relations 117, 118, 126, 127, 130, 133
U.S.–Soviet relations 120, 122
Ustashe 409, 417, 421
Ustashe organisation 409, 417, 421
Uzbekistan 31, 35, 38, 39, 42–44, 46, 48, 50, 52, 53, 55, 217–223, 228–236, 238, 239, 243, 244, 246–249, 252, 260, 262, 264, 272, 273, 277, 278, 280, 281, 283

V
video blog 192, 193, 204
Vietnam 1, 8, 84, 96, 97, 99, 100, 104, 105, 406–408, 411, 415, 418–421
vory v zakone 89, 90

Vucic, Aleksandar (President of
    Serbia, 2017–) 75, 76

W

War on terror 121, 127
Warsaw Pact 118
wasted lives 312–314, 317, 323
Western 2, 3
Western Balkans
    EU incentives. *See* European
        Union (EU)
    statehood disputes/status 66
    states 57, 58, 60, 64–68, 71, 72,
        74, 76, 77
Westminster International University
    in Tashkent (WIUT) 233
White Australia Policy 410–412, 421
Whitlam Government 409, 416, 421
Winsemius, Albert 227

X

xenophobia 315, 322
Xi Jinping 94

Y

Yakuza 90
Yeltsin, Boris 89, 123
YouTube 192–196, 198, 199, 208,
    210
Yugoslavia 88, 92, 103, 406–410,
    412–421

Z

zero-option 292, 293, 298, 299,
    303, 304

Printed in the United States
by Baker & Taylor Publisher Services